The Peggy Seeger Songbook

forty years of songmaking

Drawings by Jacky Fleming
Editing and Layout by Irene Scott

Oak Publications
New York/London/Sydney

Thanks to:

Ewan MacColl, my partner, lover and friend for more than thirty years, for widening my political and literary vistas and constantly encouraging me.

Irene Scott, who applied her patience and invaluable critical faculties during the whole of the writing of this book; who was my chief support after Ewan died; who took part in instigating and writing some of the songs. She also took charge of the final layout.

Peter Morgan and Trish Carn for preliminary organisation of the manuscripts; Clare Hanrahan for proof-reading and suggestions that were beyond the call of duty; my sons, Calum and Neill MacColl for cataloguing the discs and discography; Kitty MacColl (my daughter), Melissa Benn, Paul Gordon, Jennifer Stuart, and Liberty (previously known as the NCCL) for research; Simon Platz, Amanda Cockerton, and Lisa Walsh at Bucks (Harmony) Music for detective work on copyrights and permissions; Stormking Music, Tyler Music, and Pete Seeger for allowing me to use songs which are under their copyright; and Penny Smith, my administrator in England. To all those who provided sustenance, information, food, and patience—and those whom I interrupted during dinner, television, showers, and goodness knows what in order to ask about computer glitches, events, people, names of tunes, sources of information: Jay and Ricky Ball, Paul Beasley, Bob Blair, Sheila Douglas, Tony Engel, John Foreman, Vic Gammon, Frank Harte, Joe Mulheron, Sandra Kerr, Ralph Samuels, Irwin Silber, Rod Stradling, Norma Waterson… and many others.

Finally, best of thanks to all those whom I interviewed, whose lives and words provided me with the ideas and substance for songs; and to those othersÑthe artists, writers, singers, musicians, songwriters, storytellers, and so-called ordinary people who from whom I took inspiration, ideas, words, and tunes… and more.

About the Artist

Jacky Fleming went to a suffragette school in London, emerging awesomely uneducated due to the teacher's inexplicable preference for Latin as a first language. A year at Chelsea School of Art and a degree in fine art at Leeds University greatly improved her table football technique. Other qualifications include A- for posture and a silver medal in Latin-American dancing. She spent eleven years teaching art as a foreign language. She lives in Yorkshire (England) and hates cooking. Her cartoons have been published widely and appear in three popular Penguin books: *Falling in Love, Be a Bloody Train Driver,* and *Never Give Up*. Some of the images in this book have been taken from the latter two publications. *Hello Boys,* her most recent collection, is also published by Penguin.

Photo Credits
From the collection of the author: pages 7, 8, 9, 10, 42, 49, 83, 97, 127, 147, 148 (bottom), 168, 233, 235, 257, 281, 329 (left), 338, 341
Jesse Andrews: page 333
Pam Benjamin: page 329 (right)
John Logan: page 196
Brian Shuel: page 148 (top), 234
Norman Stockwell: page 197
Mike Taylor: page 13
Eddis Thomas: page 49

Cover illustration "Cupid On Wheels" by Judie Bomberger
Project editor: Peter Pickow

Order No. OK 65054
US International Standard Book Number: 0.8256.0344.7
UK International Standard Book Number: 0.7119.9140.5

Exclusive Distributors:
Music Sales Corporation
257 Park Avenue South, New York, NY 10010 USA
Music Sales Limited
8/9 Frith Street, London W1D 3JB England
Music Sales Pty. Limited
120 Rothschild Street, Rosebery, Sydney, NSW 2018, Australia

Printed in the United States of America by
Vicks Lithograph and Printing Corporation

Contents

Introduction

My mother, Ruth Crawford, was short and round in stature, a fiery, creative woman. We called her Dio. She was an *avant-garde* composer but her mind was open to music of any kind. I was fifteen when she revealed that she had written a few pop songs when she was in her twenties. I am filled with compassion at the memory of her face as she abashedly showed me "Lollipoppa Poppa" for my comments—and although I feel ashamed when I remember my noncommittal response, I too am a mother who has endured many a mute salvo from my children. My father, Charles Louis Seeger, was a music professor and already married with three sons (Charles, John, and Peter) when he fell in love with my mother (one of his pupils). As his new family increased in number (Mike, Peggy, Barbara, and Penny) he was obliged to take a job as a music administrator. We called him Charlie. He was a tall, thin, gentle, passive man who, unlike Dio, had endless patience. He made things with his hands, spoke softly, and played the piano gently. He was born in Mexico City and was partially deaf. He taught me guitar chords and we sang Spanish songs together an eighth of a tone apart.

Dio

During the 1930s, my parents became interested in folk music, and this interest had turned into an obsession by the time my memory was in full swing. In the 1940s, they acted as music editors for several seminal anthologies of American (see "Glossary") folksong. Dio transcribed songs from disc and notated them onto staff paper—we children couldn't help but listen and osmose the music. She and Charlie divided up the songs and made piano settings for them. Their styles were very different, taking the songs into other musical realms. We'd always sung as a family, but when Mike and I learned folk banjo and guitar, the singsongs became weekly events.

Dio and Charlie with Mike and me on harmonicas

Dio was a superb piano player and a full-time piano teacher. My "lessons" began before I even knew they were lessons—and they were very unorthodox. We sang songs and played the chords on the piano; we made up stories and poems in which the words began with the letter of whatever note she was playing; she would set the theme of the "Moonlight Sonata" to a sequence of folksong chords with a thumping bass, or play "Barbara Allan" in the style of a Bach Invention. She was intrigued by the connection between mathematics and music and transmitted her excitement to me. I remember spending several challenging weeks learning to play one tune right through the circle of fifths. Then I would take the tune through every mode in every key—and unless you've played "The Irish Washerwoman" in C♯ in the Lydian mode at the age of ten, you haven't lived. By the time I was eleven, she had taught me to listen to a melody and take it down on paper. I was very proud when some of my actual notations were sent off as top copies to the publishers of Ben Botkin's *Western Folklore.* This wasn't just child psychology in action—it was a relic of the old family work ethic. I didn't get paid for doing the work. It wasn't work. My folks did it—so I'd do it, too. And as I listened and struggled to get the right notes and correct meter, I learned the songs. I learned the forms. I learned the language and the styles of singing. I came into contact with ways of life that were light years away from our suburb in Washington, D.C.

Folksongs were not only entertaining, they were useful. Dio could adapt an old text instantly to a new situation. Barbara didn't want to put her galoshes on? Remake "Mary Wore Her Red Dress" and—hey, presto!—Barbara's galoshes were on before the verse was ended. We proved Pavlov's theory single-handedly. We'd start dancing up to bed the minute "Cindy," our goodnight song, was broached on the piano. In the end, Dio only had to play the *chord sequence* and up we'd go. Exciting people were always dropping in—Leadbelly, Woody Guthrie, John Jacob Niles, Bess Hawes, Henry and Sidney Cowell, John and Alan Lomax, Lee Hays, composers and writers, assorted refugees from Hitler's Germany . . . and, of course, beloved Pete, our tall exotic half-brother, with his long, long-necked banjo and his big, big feet stamping at the end of his long, long legs. Dio said Pete was better for us than our teachers, and she kept us home from school whenever he turned up. He'd sit and talk and sing and we'd stay up late and toast marshmallows and bawl out the choruses and try and lay our hands over the strings and detune the pegs while he played . . .

Pete and Charlie (1950s?)

I became a proficient pianist but I played better by ear than from sight. There were two pianos in the teaching room and Charlie would occasionally challenge me to a musical duel with Beethoven's First as weapons. I was good enough to play in public, but the presence of even one member of that public was enough to reduce me to a jelly. At fifteen, I entered the talent show at Leland Junior High School in Chevy Chase. I donned Grandfather Seeger's elegant top hat, my father's tuxedo and my mother's walking shoes and sang "My Mother-in-Law." I will never forget *that* attack of nerves. Fear flooded my entire being; my voice developed a brilliant but uncontrollable vibrato; my lungs shrank to half an inch in diameter; my knees knocked together so violently that my classmates congratulated me on my excellent portrayal of a drunk husband. I swore I would never sing for a living.

1953. McCarthyism was in full spate. Interesting people vanished from all sections of public life; at home there were long, hushed discussions. Pete was subpoenaed by the House Un-American Activities Committee; Charlie, anticipating HUAC's probing into his own political beliefs, resigned from his job as head of the Music Division of the Pan American Union before he could be dismissed. Dio got very ill that summer, but no one told me just how serious it was, so at the age of eighteen I went off to Radcliffe College in Cambridge, Massachusetts. Two months later, Charlie phoned. Dio was dying. A flight home had been arranged for me, a sad and terrifying first air journey. Dio's red cheeks and black hair had lost their glory and she was shrunken, wasted by cancer. Morphine injections were keeping the pain at bay and she drifted in and out of consciousness. She couldn't bear having the windows closed. The cold, damp Washington air flowed into every corner of the room and combined with the aura of death to make an atmosphere that was palpable to all the senses. Even now, remembering it, my body re-creates the numb hours of sitting by her bed waiting for her to need something. When pain brought her to the surface for her next injection, she would ask if I was cold, if I'd had dinner, if I had all I needed at Radcliffe, and would I please sing "Barbara Allan," "Johnson Jinkson," "The Nightingale." . . . I sang to her conscious and sang to her unconscious as dusk and dawn changed guard outside the windows. She died at noon on the 18th of November, 1953. Charlie asked the undertaker to go slow down West Kirke Street. He walked behind until they were out of sight.

It was the end of childhood. Children expect to leave home—they don't expect their parents to die. Mike had flown the coop a year earlier and was roaming the Washington environs in search of traditional musicians—but the house hadn't echoed then, as it did now with Dio's absence. Charlie insisted on my going back to college. The following autumn, the house was sold, and Charlie, Barbara, and Penny joined me in Cambridge. We rented a tiny fifth-floor apartment on the main road to Boston. Charlie had insisted on bringing Dio's huge grand piano with him, but it wouldn't fit into the elevator so it had to be winched up and manoeuvred through the window, to the amazement of the nuns in the convent next door. Once it was in place, we realised that it was either the piano or the sofa. The sofa went. I was in charge of the household and I did my best to care for Penny, who was ten years old at the time. I learned to play in the dark whilst singing her to sleep every night. I shopped, cooked, partied, courted, danced, and occasionally studied. I learned (the hard way) how *not* to drink. I cut my first record and began to sing professionally.

Charlie mid 1970s

Charlie began to fly off to musicological conferences and meetings with old friends. In the spring of 1955, he began to play Chopin, Debussy, and Schubert late into the night. He sat at the piano composing songs, crooning them tunelessly, hampered by the infidelity of his hearing aid. At the age of sixty-nine, Charlie was in love—with his childhood sweetheart, Margaret Taylor. (This was the Margaret for whom, incidentally, I had been named, much to Dio's amusement. Barbara had been named for another of Charlie's early flames. Penny was named after Ulysses' wife.) Mar (as she preferred to be called) had an independent income and was very fit for her sixty-five years. Charlie declared that she could "put her stockings on without sitting down" and assured Penny that there would be "no more children." A quiet marriage took place and we all drove west, to Mar's palatial home in southern California. It had been planned that I would take a year out from college to visit relatives in Leiden, which meant that I would need to learn Dutch. In Santa Barbara I located a grocer who hailed from Arnhem, a survivor whose horrific stories of the war in Holland took up most of our lessons. I learned the basics of the language . . . I needed it, for I was intending to continue my Russian studies—in the language of Dutch. I headed back east, bought a long-necked Vega banjo, boarded the SS *Maasdam* in Quebec in September 1955, and virtually never looked back—until now.

I traveled, sightsaw, and hitchhiked for a year. I was staying in a Danish youth hostel when the folklorist Alan Lomax put a call through from England. Granada Television needed a female singer-cum-banjo-player for a production of *Dark of the Moon*. So at the age of nearly twenty-one, on March 25, 1956, at 10:30 in the morning, I entered a basement room in Chelsea, London, and sealed my fate. Ewan MacColl was sitting on the other side of the room. Twenty years my senior, he was a singer and songwriter *par excellence* and it is to him that I owe the basis of my political education and commitment. He said that he fell hopelessly in love the first moment he saw me. Ewan was a married man with a child. I returned to America.

I came back in July 1957 to attend the World Festival of Democratic Youth in Moscow. From there I was invited, with 300 members of the U.S. contingent, to go to China. Forty of us went, to the consternation of our paranoiac government. I returned again to England in the spring of 1958 to work with Ewan, displacing the four-string-banjo player who had been accompanying him. Mrs. Banjo-Player reported my expired work-permit to the Home Office and I was given two days to leave. I went to France via Dover but made the mistake of trying to return too early. I was kept overnight in the marine police cells and put on the boat back to France. The French authorities shoved me over the border into Belgium. The Belgians bequeathed me forcibly to the Dutch who discreetly slipped me back into Belgium a week later. The Belgians made a deal with the French and there I was, back in France again. They must have made deals with each other for none of this traffic appeared on my passport. The Pentagon had made a deal with them all—but this time they all slipped up. I had a two-month respite in Lucienne Idoine's microscopic fifth-floor flat in the Rue Jacob, St-Germain-des-Prés. Idoine: Thank you with all my heart, for by that time I was in love—and seven months pregnant. Ewan thanked you too, for he had followed me by plane, train, boat, bus, and on foot to Boulogne, Antwerp, Rotterdam, Dieppe, Amsterdam and was glad to have a resting place in Paris. Alex Campbell, the Scots singer, broke the chain of events by marrying me in Paris on January 24, 1959. Thank you, Alex. It was a hilarious ceremony. The American priest, in surplice and sneakers, lectured Alex at length on his forthcoming lifetime commitment to the poor girl whom he had gotten into such trouble. The following day I arrived, unimpeded, in London, six weeks before the birth of my first son. In the flyblown office of a Commissioner of Oaths, I swore allegiance to Her Majesty the Queen (and all her issue thereof into perpetuity) and then settled down with Ewan, with great upheaval for everyone concerned.

We had three children: Neill (1959), Calum (1963), and Kitty (1972). I learned that you packed the pram into the boot (not the baby-carriage into the trunk) of the car and that labor, while still being work, was now labour. Neighbors were now neighbours and gar*age* was pronounced *gar*age. I began to be quite English. I lost whatever twangs I'd had in my speech and most of the glottals in my singing style. Americans would ask me if I was Irish and the Irish would mistake me for a Canadian. I still *felt* American but I gradually gained a European perspective on the U.S.A. I began to write songs regularly. I added the autoharp and the dulcimer to our touring burden and learned the English concertina the better to accompany some of Ewan's songs. We toured extensively, wrote books, composed film music, made programs for radio and television, ran a theatrical singing group . . . and other things. They were productive, creative years. We were together twenty-four hours a day for three decades, two people rolled compatibly into one.

In 1979, Ewan's heart trouble—and my stress problems—began. We toured less frequently and started to take on separate projects. The twenty years between our ages seemed to stretch. Tomorrow had arrived. We began to be familiar with medical establishments. We became old hands at intensive-care-ward procedures. Ewan went into hospital in Venice on holiday, in Corsica on holiday, in Italy on holiday. He was in Guys, Kings, Bromley, Farnborough hospitals . . . in Boston and San Francisco hospitals on tour. He kept going right up to the end, sometimes having to stop in the middle of a concert and step down. His short bouts of severe depression alternated with longer bouts of humour and cheer. His voice and his courage were superb—it was his heart that betrayed him, as it had in 1956. He died in hospital on October 22, 1989.

I first met Irene Scott on a concert stage in Belfast in 1964, at a benefit for Dave Kitson, a South African white activist. She is fond of saying that Ewan and I were the stars and she was the local talent. In actual fact, she is a politically involved traditional singer. She moved to London in 1966 and we saw each other sporadically until we cemented our friendship at Greenham Common in 1982. In 1983 she joined BANG (Beckenham Anti-Nuclear Group). We began to sing together. She would often step in whenever a last-minute attack prevented Ewan from taking his place onstage. I owe her an incalculable debt of gratitude for her support since Ewan's death and for shared love and companionship. She is full of ideas and inspirations (among which is the name we occasionally sing under: No Spring Chickens). She is also my new life partner.

It's taken me a long time to really get going again. I had to clear my mind and heart. I am wary of being a professional widow, so I swept through the house and sent more than sixty boxes of Seeger-MacColl work materials off to an archive at Ruskin College in Oxford where the Ruskin angels are cataloguing them. From 1989 onward I had chronic "give-away fever." My children joked about being in the house "at the right time" if you wanted this picture, that plate, this book, or that chair. I began to tidy up unfinished projects, all of which are finished now: proofreading and finalising Ewan's plays, assembling a book of Ewan's songs and, of course, this book of my own songs. I began to play the piano again and, at Irene's insistence, now incorporate it in stage performances.

Calum, Neill, and Peggy, 1992

The last ten years have been traumatic—years of change, insecurity, and adventure. I am rediscovering the pleasure of singing with Mike and Pete again. Penny was just beginning to sing professionally with us when she was struck down by cancer in 1993. I miss her. My children are all grown now and I have seven grandchildren. I have ploughed up the back garden in Beckenham and converted it into a wildlife sanctuary. I have rented out the house, whose every nook and cranny have witnessed my life with Ewan and our children, and moved to western North Carolina. I've bought a house and am getting it into shape, somewhat like the bowerbird, hoping to entice Irene to the U.S.A. I tour and sing for two weeks out of every month and for the other two weeks I try to become a part of Asheville. I am renewing contacts with friends and family, finding new spirits, and seeing new sunrises.

That's my life up to now in fifteen nutshells.

PEGGY SEEGER
Asheville, North Carolina
May 1998

In General

Which writer was it who complained of agonising for weeks over one sentence? Was it Brahms who wrote standing up for five hours every morning then spent the rest of the day pottering and the evening playing in a drinking joint? Some of my sons' best songs began in the studio with a drum track, followed by a pattern of guitar chords. (Brainstorming would produce an idea, then some lines and gradually a song would materialise while the record company shelled out hundreds of pounds an hour on studio costs!)

People have different ways of working. These two chapters, "In General" and "In Particular," are about the ways in which *I* write songs. They are not meant as a comment upon other writers' methods or their work. My songs tend to be rather formal, tight, and structured. The same applies to my writing and speaking styles when it comes to discussing work. I may adopt a *teaching tone,* a preaching manner. I think I began holding forth like this when I became a mother—I transferred the method to stagework when trying to give coherent introductions to songs. One had to sound purposeful and concise, with a minimum of pauses, *ums* and *ers* and *wells.* This stood me in good stead when I began lecturing on nuclear power for BANG but it may be disconcerting on paper.

Two traditions were ever-present and interlaced throughout my childhood: the formal and the traditional. They presented me with a vision of music that is wide and elastic.

Formal Music Training

I am glad to have had it. It lets me know in theory what I am doing in practice. It encourages me to see the relationships between the kinds of music that I enjoy. It got my hands and my stamina into shape with endless scales and arpeggios. Participation in Dio's projects gave me an invaluable skill which I have used ever since: the ability to hear a tune and write it down on paper.

In songwriting, my training was especially helpful in constructing (and I choose that word carefully!) Brechtian pieces like "The Plutonium Factor" and "R.S.I." Knowledge of harmonic progressions helped in songs like "Nine-Month Blues" and "Gonna Be an Engineer." My love affair with the Lydian mode has consciously led to songs like "Four-Minute Warning" and the cross-relations I often use. My classical training has helped me to seek out different modes, formats and meters: "Emily," for instance, has been cast into $\frac{5}{4}$ for unaccompanied singing because the subject cried out for an uneasy meter. (I recently re-recorded "Emily" accompanied and the song slipped into $\frac{6}{4}$.) Knowing how to read music helps me to grasp a tune quickly and makes it easier for me to pitch unaccompanied songs before opening my mouth to sing. Charlie used to say he could hear me thinking when I sang and played folksongs. He did not mean it as a compliment. He felt it deprived me of the ability to really let go and sing "from the heart." Maybe he was right. Is it really a blessing to close your eyes while you sing and, if you choose, see the notes skipping across the staff lines? On the other hand, when I hear a tune or get an idea and am nowhere near a tape recorder I can just write it down. This has made my tune-memory lazy—but what you gain on the Ferris wheels you sometimes lose on the merry-go-rounds. Instinct is of paramount importance in the arts: there are elements of instinct that—paradoxically—I may have to relearn—or that I may have lost forever.

Traditional Music

. . . gave me an approach to language and a knowledge of the tunes that had developed along with that language. It introduced me to a variety of forms and subjects. My mother learned from listening to traditional singers and musicians that music can be simultaneously skilled, informal, and improvisational. Above all, it is obvious that folk traditions have unique survival qualities. Like a beneficent virus, the folksongs I grew up with not only permeated the society of my time (a horizontal spread) but they had penetrated the generations before me (a vertical spread). Logic tells me that they will continue *ad infinitum.*

Words and Music

For four decades I have sung traditional songs in concerts, clubs, and pubs; schools, street fairs, meetings, festivals, telethons, conventions, trains, and planes . . . I even sang once in a circus tent. And it still intrigues me when, for instance, a group of teenage secretaries in Harlow (England) listen entranced to "Barbara Allen." Is this the kind of music they normally listen to? If not, what is it that holds their attention? As a child, I felt that the folksongs always seemed to fit in the mouth so easily. You didn't have to work to learn them the way you did the hymns at school. They kind of drifted in with the tide and fastened themselves to rocks on the shores of memory. Embedded in the form and content of the songs are codes that are the same as (or similar to) those buried in speech—and these codes, along with other linguistic factors, are highly particular to each language. Why is it that one language (Scots Gaelic) has more than two dozen words for "rain" and another language (English) has very few? Codes. How is it that two dissimilar languages can produce the same thought in very different words? (In "Union Woman II," Mrs. Desai used the phrase "born rich in the womb" . . . English-speakers usually refer to the privileged citizen as "born with a silver spoon in the mouth.") Codes.

So why did the Harlow office workers respond to forms of speech they themselves would probably not use, like "it was in the merry month of May," and "the rose hangs round the briar"? They are urban English people and the song is rural American (albeit from British roots). It is the 1990s and the songs were made, as far as they were concerned, in the Dark Ages. I am convinced that even if we believe we are "with it," "right on" and that "advertising lingo rules, O.K.?" there is, deep down in all of us, a wellspring of traditional words and usages that we all hold in common. "Once upon a time" and "they all lived happily every after" are more than just the top-and-tailing of fairy tales. Each society has a water-table, a race memory of experiences and expectations that we all recognise, so that "Barbara Allen" can seem *déjà vu* to English-speaking people of almost any musical persuasion. Thousands of years of speaking, singing and telling stories has given us a set of what might be termed "cultural genes" that help to set the parameters of our cultural identity. It sounds high-flown and is surely not an original theory, but it should be explored and employed more by artists, writers, and singers, to say nothing of architects, road-makers, and builders of societies.

I have therefore used traditional models as a jumping-off point many times in songmaking. You can jump off at several stages in this process:

1. I began in 1956 by making ersatz folksongs ("When I Was Young," "I'll Never Go Back to London Again"). These pieces seem gauche to me now, as they employed language that I did not use in my own everyday speech (like *lad* and *O, sorrow be to me)* and outdated concepts like "I knew no greater pleasure than to follow where he led," *etc.* But then I was rather gauche myself at the time, so the song was an honest representation of that point in my development.

2. I put new sets of words to folk tunes ("Better Things," "Sentimental Journey," *etc.*) It is an easy way to write songs—half of the job has already been done by someone else. It is also easy for people to learn your song if you put it to a tune they already know ("Votecatcher in the Rye," "My Old Man's a Dustman," *etc.*).

3. I graduated to making better songs in the folk idiom; that is, songs that *sound* like folksongs ("The Ballad of Springhill," "The Lifeboat *Mona*").

4. I have occasionally used the old tune *and* the old form and just changed the words (as in "N is for Nobody," "Housewife's Alphabet").

5. I have used a folk tune as a starting point only. You use the first line or phrase as a basis then take off into your own tune ("My Son," "Different Tunes," *etc.*). Only trouble with this is that often you don't really know if the tune is yours or not. But then, does it matter?

Not everyone needs to enter the songwriting process so gradually. Courageous songmakers just jump in the deep end. I copied and borrowed by default because I lacked confidence. Later on, I copied and borrowed confidently, but I had to write several dozen original songs before I regarded myself as a *real* songwriter.

Content

Folksongs cover so many subjects! The battle of the sexes, class, children, racism, incest, strikes, murder, love, war, history, religion, *etc.* And in so many ways! (They can also perpetrate unconstructive ways of thinking.) They can be humorous, tragic, trivial, and earth-shaking, ranging from songs about the loss of a goose to epic laments on the fate of Napoleon. Anglo-American folksongs tend to convey information as well as atmosphere and emotions. The words are of paramount importance. There was a time when songs were printed on broadsheets and sold by the yard in the city streets. The longer your song the more money you'd get for it—so broadsheet pieces were notoriously tautological. The seasoned traditional songs are more economical. They have been honed by generations of singers, who added to (but mostly subtracted from) the original text. The fewer words there are, the more important each word becomes, and these processed texts can be wonderfully sparse. Much of the background information is implicit. Because many of the folksongs were made at a time when a songmaker could count on listeners having a stock of community experience in common, there was much information that was left out because everyone already knew it. So you are often given a skeletal story and expected to flesh out the details from your own imagination.

This often allows the writer to operate outside of a strict chronological or literal framework. The old songmakers could skip years between verses or leave out several links in the chain of cause-and-effect. They would switch abruptly from dialogue to description, from the present tense to the past tense (see "Emily"). They'd begin the song right in the middle of the action (see "Song for Calum"). "The Judge's Chair" was consciously patterned after traditional ballad forms, which use a number of these features (see "In Particular" for an analysis). It is quite common for a song to be moving sensibly along when all of a sudden a seeming *non sequitur* is thrown in to provide a new insight into the situation, to turn the action in a new direction, or maybe to check if the listener is still awake. I used this technique in the first verse of "Woman on Wheels." In line 1, you are an able-bodied listener. By the end of line 3, you have a set of brakes. By the end of the verse you are directly included through the use of the pronoun 'we'. The real turning point is line 7, which is a total *non sequitur* but which assumes that you were present at a crucial time, pushing the wheelchair. So by the end of the first verse you, the listener, are totally involved.

The folksong traditions that I grew up with are largely narrative and rarely deal in generalisations. The detail that is given is important. The hero or heroine are recognisable figures—they are often named and they are not there just so that things may happen to them. They are working, doing something, or going somewhere. They have family connections. Their economic status is important, as is the time of year and the place. As the "folk" made music not for a commercial market but for their own pleasure and that of their communities, the local features of the song were vital and helped to reaffirm the community identity (see "Abbey Wood Roads"). The texts often contain time-honoured traditions and assumptions, instructions as to acceptable behaviour, pointers to social expectations. All of these things contribute to cultural continuity and can be powerful props for the status quo. On the other hand, oppressed groups can give voice to their feelings either subtly or blatantly through the songs. These are just a few of the messages carried in folksong. Decoding them and learning how to use the methods in which they have been musically and linguistically packaged can be of invaluable use to a songwriter who wants pers (see "Glossary") creations to stand the test of time.

Form

What a treasure-chest of types and formats the folk tradition holds: catalogue songs, riddle songs, narratives, lyric songs, historical, funny, solemn, short, long, philosophical, nonsense songs . . . patient Griselda, the biter bit, the surprise ending . . . parody, satire, joke songs, riddle songs . . . the ABCB quatrain, the rhyming couplet, the repeated burden . . . you could go on forever. The old songs have given me so many ideas for new songs! "Hey Ho, Cook and Rowe!" was originally entitled "The Landlord's Nine Questions" and was based on "The Devil's Nine Questions." The idea for "Bush Has Gone to Rio" came directly from a children's scatological piece. "Can't Pay, Won't Pay" is the same format and tune as "Pick a Bale of Cotton." "Enough Is Enough" was written after reading an Elizabethan catalogue song.

I try to write different *types* of songs. If I wrote totally out of feeling and in character with my own body-rhythms and emotional leanings, I would probably only make slow, lyrical songs. But three of those in a row and the audience (see "Glossary") is asleep. Also, there are subjects I wish to tackle that would be ludicrous in a slow, lyrical style. When I was evangelising on the subject of nuclear power, I needed songs that would appeal to different types of people. I wrote five contrasting pieces, each effective in its own way. Because they are so different, you can even sing several of them in a row.

Consider: A cat peeps round a corner at a mouse. Write about it in the first person singular, from the point of view of: (1) the mouse, (2) the cat, (3) yourself as spectator . . . and so on. From there you can go to a projected scenario and write in the first person singular from the point of view of (a) the dog that is about to chase the cat; (b) the driver who is about to swerve to avoid the chase when it starts; (c) the canary, watching from the safety of the cage in the kitchen window; (d) the hungry kitten awaiting its meal . . . and so on. Or you can approach it from the first or third person and write (a) a sad song about the cat's deprived kittenhood and the emotional importance of food; (b) a bawdy song about the cat's love life and why it is ravenous all the time; (c) a dialogue song between the cat and the mouse; (d) a catalogue song about all the things the cat would like to eat or catch, ending with the mouse; (e) a descriptive song about the cat's present home life; (f) an anti-advertisement for canned cat food; (g) a philosophical song about the theory and practice of hunting . . . and so on. The mind boggles at the possibilities.

A song can be any length. The Elizabethan song "Constance of Cleveland" lasts twenty minutes. The following gem from the U.S.A. can last from twenty to thirty seconds, depending on how you milk it:

Meet me tonight in the cowshed,
Until the cows come home.
O, I know it is only a cowshed
But to me it is home, sweet home.

I had a broadsheet mentality for several decades. Many of my songs were very, very long and included every single thing I wanted to say on the subject (see "Talking Matrimony Blues," "I'm Gonna Be an Engineer," "Different Tunes," *etc.*). I have recently been trying my hand at musical squibs and songs of no more than three or four verses. These require much more self-discipline as you cannot afford to waste a single preposition. They often take longer to write than a song with a plethoric, tautological overabundance of superfluous words, but they are wonderfully satisfying. I have starred these shorter pieces in the "Subject Index" so that they may be easily located.

Generally Speaking

I have put the songs in chronological order because I was interested in the *process* of songwriting. The notes benefited from this sequence, and as I wrote them the book began to be an historical as well as a personal document. A number of the songs are so particular to their time that they needed a long note to explain them. But even if a song is out of date, it can be interesting as an expression of its time and it can show how a particular writer tackled a particular subject. Such songs can also contribute to the huge ideas pool that I myself fished in. I couldn't cope with the idea of living in an ivory tower, smiting my brow for inspiration. I stole ideas from almost anywhere—cartoons, newspaper articles, people's conversations, books, advertisements, *etc.* As T.S. Eliot said, "Immature poets imitate. Mature poets steal." *(The Sacred Wood)* For twenty years, I ran a new song magazine, the *New City Songster,* and I am grateful to all the contributors who sent their work in. I stole from them as well—words, ideas, forms . . . I even stole from myself (see "Women's Union," "Old Friend"). Stole? No, I borrowed, changed, and gave back.

I have included songs that I now view as incompletely worked, politically outdated, or less than satisfactory. I can use these pieces in songwriting classes. It is important to know what to avoid and how writers feel about their own mistakes and development. I've left out early stinkers like "Song of the Forts," "Let My People Go," and others. I've omitted a quite clever song about Ireland because the changing political scene in that country rendered the piece not only obsolete but unconstructive in the long run—and the song could not be remade. I have resisted the temptation to modernise songs like "Come Fill Up Your Glasses" and "Jimmy Wilson" or to shorten epics like "Manner of the World Nowadays."

Criticism

A good criticism session has to be as controlled as a visit to a marriage counsellor. The writer has fallen in love with the song but things just aren't working out. Perhaps per's (see "Glossary") discussed it with friends and family . . . fatal. You cannot always depend totally on someone who loves you: They will usually come down automatically on your side in a conflict. Objective counselling is needed. Begin with the positive aspects. The chorus and the verses may have a lot in common, but they've gotten bored with each other and their union needs spicing up. Maybe they're too alike. Perhaps their domestic arrangements are working but one of the partners (tune or words) is carrying more than its fair share of the load. Or the style of language is effective *per se* but incompatible with the subject chosen. Maybe the song just needs to spend more quality time with itself and its writer . . .

In the beginning, Ewan was not a good critic. I didn't ask for his opinion and he didn't give it. He was so pleased that I had started to write at all that he accepted everything blindly. It took an acquaintance like Bert Lloyd to comment critically on the flaws in "Lifeboat *Mona*" and a coworker like Denis Turner to suggest that "Cambrian Colliery Disaster" needed more work. Unfortunately, I ignored such comments. Later on, Ewan and I developed a more healthy mutual criticism technique that made it possible for both of us to produce much better songs. I grew a thicker skin and began to criticise other people's songs mercilessly though fortunately not very often out loud. For years now, songwriters have been sending me songs and asking for my comments, but I feel that no headway can be made unless positive codes of conduct and constructive criteria of criticism are first laid down, followed by talking sessions—as with a marriage counsellor.

Nowadays I take my songs to Irene, who is not a good songwriter but an excellent critic and catalyst. She is already living in the twenty-first century and many of the ideas for the new songs—both mine and ours—come not only from our arguments and discussions but directly from her inspiration. Her participation has been so fundamental that I have included her in the authorship credits.

Opinions

A book such as this would be impossible to write without including the beliefs of the author. Such beliefs are often labeled *opinions* when someone else takes exception to them or when they are expressed strongly. This book has a lot of *opinionated* statements, many of them used with malice aforethought. I have tried to present them in a manner that will entertain and stimulate.

The Politically Correct (to use the jargon of the day) will take exception to some of the lines in the songs. (Those aspiring to be one hundred percent PC will not have bought this book at all as it could not have been printed without chopping down trees.) "Billy and George and Me" refer to Spring as 'him'. Over and over, I used the word 'men' when I really meant 'all humans'. A feminist song, "Different Therefore Equal," contains the word *prickless,* thus reinforcing Freud's theory of penis envy. Even my own life-story, "Song of Myself," ended originally with "When I sing of my *brothers*, I sing of myself"! Jimmy Wilson was originally termed Negro, acceptable at the time but unacceptable now. Thoughtless references to animals appear frequently throughout. My development has been as slow and as tunnel-visioned as the political scene that has unrolled during my lifetime.

In the early days, *politically correct* referred to working-class or Marxist politics, the bywords of which were the *struggle* and the *movement*. I graduated into feminism but, paradoxically, brought the old terminology with me. I now feel that many of the old terms, and much of what they represent, are destructive unless they are accompanied by an ecological awareness, without which they merely refer to the civil war of human versus human. I feel that PC should now embrace not only classism, nationalism, religionism, differently-abled-ism, sexism, ageism, sizeism, ruralism, and racism (all of which are human *isms)* but also animalism, plantism, speciesism, and earthism. Even the term *humanism,* so often used in a positive context, will have to undergo a quality check.

Signposts

In 1993, a new program graced the British national television network: *Nature Perfected*, in which we saw tortured topiary, orchestrated flower beds, idle acres of clipped grass, concrete paths, military rows of trees, and many varieties of contrived "wilderness." This program intimated that any plants and animals that do not contribute to the overall chocolate-box effect are not only discouraged but are killed off when they appear. Nature *PERFECTED?* The earth is four and a half billion years old. Think of her (to quote Greenpeace) as a forty-six-year-old. Modern humans have been here during the last four hours. The industrial revolution began just one minute ago. In those sixty seconds we have trashed our beautiful home. We have colonised it and enslaved it in an effort to bring it under *our* control. We are now "progressing" outward into space and inward into the most minute components of atomic structure.

> Civilization has itself been on a journey from its foundations in the world of nature to an ever more contrived, controlled, and manufactured world of our own imitative and sometimes arrogant design. . . . At some point during this journey we lost our feeling of connectedness to the rest of nature. We now dare to wonder: Are we so unique and powerful as to be *essentially separate from the earth?*
>
> Al Gore
> Vice President of the U.S.A.

Many of the old signposts seem to me to be pointing in the wrong direction. Scores of old values and assumptions are coming under scrutiny as the ecological apocalypse looms. This may sound overdramatic, but then the end of the world may be *very* dramatic. As a singer and songmaker, all this affects me very deeply, for these road signs and values were part and parcel of my working paraphernalia. Work songs, union songs, and songs agitating for full employment: How can I sing these with conviction in a society most of whose industry (in both senses of the word) is responsible for the devastation of the planet? Old love songs and ballads: So many of them advocate sexual and gender codes that I can no longer support. My responses and behaviour are changing as well. I am less patient in political arguments. Haunted by the spectre of overpopulation, I find it difficult to automatically congratulate every new mother on her baby, no matter how lovely and welcome it is . . . and that is saddening.

After World War II, the East German authorities held up a merciless mirror to their people. When I went to East Berlin in 1958, I saw them: enormous posters in every public building. These posters had one *visual* theme: the concentration camps. Mountains of skeletons and bony bodies, armies of hollow faces assaulted you in post offices, banks, concert halls, museums, schools, on buses and street hoardings. The posters had one *textual* theme: WE DID THIS—NEVER AGAIN. The posters had one *purpose:* to make the German people confront daily what they had done and what had been done in their name. *During* that war, only the very daring put up such posters, and many died for doing so. We have to put up our posters now, at the beginning of this new war. Songs can help to do that. The old songs point to where we have been. The new songs, whether they be love songs, political chants, or sitcom, can be signposts.

Songs entertain us; they influence our thinking and, often, our actions; they make us feel better (or worse); and at best they can help us to cope with modern life. Some of our songs may tell future generations what our time was like. Songmaking is one way of expressing individuality, even if what we are expressing is what one hundred million other individuals also feel and wish to express. We all want to make our mark, from the animal that sprays in order to designate the boundaries of its little patch to the misguided souls who built Canary Wharf. As a lover, mother, political being, American-cum-Englishwoman, I write about my time, my place, and my life. I can't paint, sculpt, pot, weave, write novels, or build. I'm also hopeless at mathematics, Mastermind, chess, closing cupboard doors, washing dishes, winning raffles, changing fuses, *etc.* I could write a whole series of books about the things I *can't* do. Instead, I wrote a book of songs.

In Particular

This section is for the people who read footnotes and check out bibliographical references. "There's many a slip 'twixt the cup and the lip," and there's many a hitch between the desire to write a song and the actual writing of it. This section doesn't deal with general problems like how to find a good rhyme or which-comes-first-the-tune-or-the-words. It is concerned rather with a few problems, processes, and techniques that I have found particularly interesting or useful.

Slogans, clichés, and well-worn phrases

. . . are scattered throughout my songs. Sometimes I wish they had been nipped in the bud. At other times, they seem to be well chosen and happily placed. Slogans represent viewpoints and are often associated with opinionated groupings. Clichés and truisms are self-evident enough to have entered our common speech and traditional music. The effective use of such forms often depends on the context in which each is found. For instance, the phrase "the poison, the bomb, the gun" in "The Dead Men" has a very different flavour from "the guns, the planes and the Bomb" in "March with Us Today." The stylised poetry of the former song somehow makes the phrase less identifiable as a slogan. "Reclaim the night," which opens the chorus of "Reclaim the Night," was not a worn phrase when I first employed it. It was a battle cry for a fresh stage in an old war. The song itself, stark and dignified, places the words where they were so effectively used: in the mouths of thousands of women as we marched through the streets of London at night reclaiming the right not to be under curfew.

So the choice and placement of such phrases is crucial. I should not have set the "Lifeboat *Mona*" "out on the main" with a "gallant crew." "A vision of hell, then death came a-raging" ("Cambrian Colliery Disaster") is just plain pompous. But the final line of the chorus of "Come Fill Up Your Glasses" consists of what must be the most popular of all the clichés in this book—and I think it works excellently.

Dogma

The *Shorter Oxford English Dictionary* defines 'dogma' as (among other things) "an arrogant declaration of opinion" or "the body of opinion formulated and authoritatively stated." I prefer the second definition but the first is commonly leveled at left-wing songwriters, who find themselves in a real dilemma: When does an authoritative opinion become an arrogant declaration? Is it only a matter of linguistics? Take these two statements:

1. Religion is the opium of the people.

2. A particular system of faith and worship is the narcotic of the populace.

The former would more likely be considered dogmatic because it is concise and coded—and because it was originally said by Karl Marx. The latter might be construed simply as a philosophical observation. Like 'politics', the word 'dogma' somehow takes on a pejorative meaning when applied to left-wing or revolutionary activities. Defenders of the status quo use status-quo language, status-quo assumptions, status-quo politics, and status-quo dogma (which is never called *status quo* and rarely called *dogma*). It's a wonderful camouflage because 'status quo' literally means "the unchanged position." Therefore, 'status quo' means "what we are accustomed to": the whole burden of the way we live, our laws, religions, custom-built social mores, entrenched economic systems, and so on. In a nutshell, we have changed ourselves to become comfortable with features that are really quite inconvenient, unjust, and *un*comfortable. Change is uncomfortable. Radical thinking implies change and therefore implies discomfort. But radical slogans comfort, reassure, and solidify the community of the left. Do songs with such conviction therefore preach to the converted? Of course they do. That's what they are meant to do. Who needs comfort more than those who have stuck their noses out into the frozen air of conservatism?

All this is to say that I have made a number of "dogmatic" songs which were very effective at meetings and on marches ("Follow Harold," "Crooked Cross," "March with Us," "The Ballad of Jimmy Wilson," "L.B.J.," "Forty-five, Eighty-five," *etc.*). On paper some of them look like political tracts set to music. Yes, indeed.

Alienation, humour, and hope

It was one of Brecht's theses that capitalist society alienates people on many levels: one religion against another, rich against poor, men against women, city against country, and so on, until we come down to the very basic premise that the individual is alienated from perself and per own feelings (see "Glossary"). Brecht encouraged theatregoers to confront their own personae by making them uncomfortable. He did this by contrasting one theatrical style with another, by juxtaposing form and content, by softening the audience up with nostalgia, then punching them in the belly with realism (see "Bread and Wine"). To a certain extent this can be done by marrying a heavy subject to a light style, a serious matter to a light treatment. Laughter relaxes the nervous system, lightens the heart, and has been known to open the mind. Makes you live longer, too.

It has taken me a long time to learn this and I still slip back into my natural tendency to see only the serious side of things, to wed serious texts to serious tunes, sad stories to sad styles. Of course, there are issues like torture, rape, incest, murder, *etc.* which are not to be treated lightly. Satire, sarcasm, irony, or humour of any sort must be used carefully in such cases—or maybe not at all. But most contemporary subjects can be dealt with from a variety of perspectives. "The Judge's Chair" and "Nine-Month Blues" are two very different songs about the right to choose. They are intended to produce entirely different reactions. This also applies to the six songs about violence against women and the five songs about nuclear power (two serious, two light, and one Wagnerian). Those which are light seem to automatically generate optimism. Those which are heavy need something else to make them more than just a catalogue of miseries.

Which brings us to the subject of hope. Only one of my songs ends in despair ("Lost")—but then it speaks of the permanent loss of a dearly beloved partner. In general, one is not spurred to action by hopelessness. When dealing with depressing, tragic, abysmal, or horrifying subjects, it is important not to leave the listener ready to jump in front of a bus. This first came to my attention when I wrote "I'm Gonna Be an Engineer." The first final draft condemned my heroine to eternal drudgery in the house, which might have been acceptable in a black-humour song like the traditional "Housewife's Lament." Ewan gave me a lecture on the importance of hope and I changed the last verse. I gave myself a lecture on trite endings and have tried ever since to incorporate optimism or promise subtly into such songs. There are any number of ways of ending a song hopefully ever after:

- Explain why the situation is as it is ("Turn Up the Music").
- Suggest group action ("Winnie and Sam").
- Investigate the social ingredients of a personal tragedy ("The Judge's Chair").
- End a personal story with a personal declaration of hope ("Emily").
- Intersperse the solution throughout the song (the choruses of "Sellafield Child" and "Reclaim the Night").
- Contrast hope directly with no hope ("Bread and Wine") ending with hope.
- Juxtapose a no-hope situation with a "hopeful" tune, a Brechtian alienation technique ("The Mother").
- Take the no-hope situation into an arena where it can be fought, as the last verse of "Good War" brings "the bastards" home where you can get your hands on them.
- Transform the situation into a fantasy ("Please, Mr. Reagan").
- Make the whole matter laughable ("Vital Statistics"), heroic ("We Remember"), exaggerated ("Enough Is Enough"), casual ("Use It Again") . . . and so on.

When I first sang "My Son" for some friends, one of them was pleased that I had not included something "trite and political" in the last verse. The combining of those two adjectives is a sad commentary on too many political songs. It *is* often tempting to sum up grandly in militant songs (see "Forty-five, Eighty-five," "When I Was Young," or "The Ballad of Jimmy Wilson") but it's too easy—and it's boring.

Models

This is a very long book. Some folk might say that in the interests of ecology I could have omitted some of the songs that may seem trivial, or others that refer to obscure events in the distant past—i.e., songs that may never get sung again. I have included many of these "Why-the-heck-did-she-include-these?" pieces because they are models. They are song types, idea formats that can be used by other songwriters (I probably stole many of them from other songmakers myself). Most of these models are in the folk idiom and they are in the book to use in songwriting seminars and for other people to use. One of my favourite models is the traditional ballad form, into which "The Judge's Chair" has been cast. It is a song about abortion, a subject (along with incest , menstruation, childbirth, etc.) that has hardly been touched in the traditional songs.

The traditional ballads have always fascinated me. As a singer, I never tire of them. Every one of the British field singers that we collected from felt that these pieces were special and very old. Caroline Hughes, a Gypsy queen of Dorset, referred to them as *relegends*, an interesting mixture of religion and legend, and declared, "Without them, what we got? We got nothing." Well sung, they produce in listeners a reaction quite unlike any other type of song. The Anglo-American traditional ballads have a number of unique stylistic features, many of which I have used in "The Judge's Chair." Among these features are:

- The use of short-line ACBC quatrains
- The absence of long words, complex adjectives and adverbs—the language is deceptively simple and economical.
- The form goes from dialogue to description to direct address without any qualifying or linking material.
- The perspective of the song is objective—there is no moralising, no sympathising, no histrionics.
- The song begins in the middle of the action—it jumps in without introducing the cast or the preceding action (verse 1).
- The dialogue has no named speaker (verses 1, 2, 3, 4).
- The use of days of the week, numbers of weeks, names of the months to indicate passage of time (verses 5, 6, 7).
- The use of incremental repetition—a phrase is repeated several times, each time with a small change to take the action further (verses 1, 2, and 11; also verses 5 and 6).
- The reiteration of a word or a phrase for emphasis, reminiscent of *Othello:* "Put out the light, and then put out the light" (verses 9, 10). This is one of the stock-in-trade arts of the traditional storyteller.
- The swift and often unheralded change of tense (verses 6, 7)—another of the storyteller's devices.

Many of us employ these features in our everyday speech: I use them constantly in the notes of this book. But when we come to make a song we go all formal, literal, and poetic, and work according to preconceived notions of what a "song" is or should be. I thought "Judge's Chair" should be a new "traditional ballad" but by the time I got to the end of the story it began to feel like a superior tearjerker and the form had kind of taken over. So I forsook the ballad form entirely and delivered a kick in the belly with verse 12. When I sent the song to one of the pro-choice pressure groups they were lukewarm about it. They felt it wasn't hard-hitting enough . . . not enough slogans? But in concert, "The Judge's Chair" is greeted by three or four seconds of shocked silence before applause begins. The assembled company has been jolted, and I can hear them thinking and carrying the story on from where I left it.

Sometimes the model doesn't do the whole job itself. Sometimes it benefits from mixing and matching with complementary forms. This is apparent in "Different Tunes," where several song styles are used. On disc, I interspersed the verses of "Lady, What Do You Do All Day?" with verses of "Twenty Years." In the *Festival of Fools,* we dovetailed "It's All Happening Now" with "The Children." "B-Side" takes on a different slant when you follow it immediately with "Turn Up the Music." Giving a song to two singers instead of one can often broaden the message by giving the listener a new auditory dimension.

Radio Ballads

From 1957 to 1964, the BBC commissioned a series of radio programmes that came to be known as radio ballads. They were the work of Ewan MacColl, Charles Parker, myself, and the dozens of singers, instrumentalists, informants (see "Glossary"), and technicians who worked on them. Each of the eight programmes was an hour long and dealt with a different group of people in Britain: railway workers, road builders, fisherfolk, miners, polio victims, teenagers, boxers, and nomadic peoples. One of them, *Singing the Fishing*, won an Italia prize in its field. They have been considered as seminal works in the development of radio documentary technique.

A radio ballad was a tapestry of *actuality* (material that we recorded from informants), sound effects, instrumental music, and songs. We felt that we didn't know enough about the subjects of each programme so we went to those who did know: the railway workers, road builders, fisherfolk, *etc.* These protracted encounters yielded information, terminology, experience, attitudes, mannerisms, speech patterns, breathing rhythms, vocal pitches, and a myriad of unspoken thoughts behind the spoken ones. The actuality formed the basis of the authenticity of the programmes. When the writing was finished, we always took the script and songs back to the people whom we had recorded (see "Union Woman II"). Their reactions and comments helped us to finalise the programme.

When the series was finished, Ewan and I continued to use the technique. I have used it on twelve of my songs (they are marked with the symbol † in the "Subject Index"). I wanted to write about a battered woman—I went to help with a women's refuge in South London where I recorded Emily and Winnie. I wanted to write about R.S.I.—Joy Mingard gave me new insights and new language. "Woman on Wheels" was written after I went to see Jennifer Jones—who actually used the phrase "woman on wheels"—and came away so infected with her spirit and courage that I skipped all the way to the underground station with the first verse of the song already in my head. In order to write "Missing," I spent a day with Murielita's mother and sister and went home emotionally drained. The interview was so painful that I couldn't start the song for six weeks. When I began to write the song I felt I had undergone a small part of the experience myself.

Using this method, you almost merge with the person you are interviewing. I begin the session by telling the person what I am going to do, that I am ignorant of what they have been through and would they please explain anything and everything to me. They cried and laughed and confided the most intimate details you can imagine. I am infinitely grateful to them for their trust and each time I finish writing a song in this manner I am looking forward to the next time.

"Guilty"

It is wonderful when a song just flies into your brain whole and finished—but that doesn't happen often. Sometimes I employ another technique, an offshoot of the radio ballad routine. Instead of interviewing someone else I interview myself. This song is an example. It was conceived between New York and Washington and recorded a year later. Irene and I toured a lot and we talked about anything and everything. We still talk about what we see—and when you're on a concert tour anywhere between Boston, Massachusetts, and Richmond, Virginia, much of what you see is very depressing. Those cities are the North-South borders of a megalopolis, a monstrous conurbation. At its worst, it consists of huge motorway junctions, horizons that resemble tangles of concrete spaghetti, strip development, high-rise towers, chain restaurants, petrol stations, traffic, and smog. At its best, subtract the smog. I would turn on the tape recorder and put long sections of our conversation into it. As soon as I could find a typewriter, I undammed a stream of consciousness. Fortunately I am a fast typist. When I brainstorm, everything goes down until there are pages of the stuff. This is what *part* of it, added to the recordings, looked like. Read it out loud. Then read each following draft of the song out loud.

(BEGIN AS A LOVE SONG SO IT ISN'T OBVIOUS THAT IT IS THE EARTH SINGING TO MAN/ MAYBE PEOPLE TWO OR THREE VERSES AS A LOVE SONG THEN SAY:)

I was here before you got here and I'll be here when you're gone
I will watch when you're dying, I was watching when you were born
I was here first, this is my scene
Without me you are nothing; without you I'm the same
I've been roving through these skies since earth and skies began

I allowed you on my rivers, I let you cut my trees
You cut them down for masts and ships to sail upon my seas
I'm accusing you of murder, I'm accusing you of rape
You've only been here a fraction of my time and already I'm dying
I nursed you at my breast, you were born out of the atoms that make me up
You're killing off my water, my air

Look at my waters, look at the leaves on my trees
My fish float dead on my lakes
Do you ask before you pour poisons into my rivers?
Listen to my rivers, listen to my trees
I have no choice and because of what you are doing I will kill you
And then I will spin on through the earth's death alone
This is a fight to the death between you and me
The forces that made me and made you are the same

You pour acid into my air and I will give it back to you into your lungs
You poison my rivers
My rivers will seep down through the earth and come back again into your food
You and I are inseparably bound
We will die together but I'll do my best to see that you die first
We began as friends - you roamed the earth and cared for me
But now it seems that you are out for what you can get.

When you love someone do you care,
Do you tenderly stroke their hair?
Hold their hand, look into their eyes?
Or are you out for what you can get
For your own satisfaction?

<u>first verse</u>
When you love someone or
I love you or I thought you loved me
IT SHOULD BE A SONG OF ANGER, OF DISAPPOINTMENT, OF THREAT.
Now I am going to kill you because you loved me and you left me.

All the things that I let you do
All the things that I gave you
Gifts that I gave you you threw them away

When you sit in your car and throw out your beer cans
When you go to see my mountains and drop your trash
When you sit by my rivers and pour your sewage in

There was a time when my rivers had life
There was a time when my water tasted good
There was a time when you could walk through my forest and not see tree stumps
If you go on the way you're going, you will die and I will sit and lick my wounds
No animal ever treated me as badly as you do.

I first met you in the morning when you opened up your eyes
You cut you, you cut me
And I sure was never thinking that you'd cut me down to size
And just what size you were thinking
Or any thoughts that you were thinking
When you started on your voyage, it was MY boat that was sinking

FORM—ACDCDCED ACDCDCE (A-MINOR)

Who are you to think that you can own me?
Who are you the way that you disown me?
You covered up my sunshine
I gave you hands to work with and I sharpened up your brain
I'm as good as any lover, I'm the mother of your child
I'm your father and your brother
I'm the future and the past
And if we're racing for the future it'll be me that's coming last
You're the viper in my bosom
I gave you everything I had

(A LIST OF ALL THE THINGS THAT PEOPLE HAVE DONE TO THE EARTH)
You've pulverised my mountains
You have (something to the effect of "rerouted the rivers")
There was a time when you were cautious, didn't want to make me mad
.... 'cause I was all you had.

You depended on my kindness
And I had you on the run
And the secrets that surrounded me

Were mine and mine alone.
I was mine when I was wealthy
And now that I'm poor/dying you don't want me

(TAKE A HIGHER PART WHEN THE HARMONY GOES IN THIRDS AND SLIDING UP WITH A DISAPPEARING VARNAL SOUND)

You've been dipping in my belly
You've been hauling out my coal
You lay roads across my country
You mortify my soul.

There's no place that I'm private
No place where I can dream
Do you ever watch my sunsets
Or listen to my streams?

VERSES ABOUT THE SENSES:
the trees have eyes
the rocks have ears
and the breezes touch you
my waters taste you and
now my senses tell me that it's time for you to go
and all my senses tell me that you're killing me

(A MINOR CHORD)
You didn't steal for passion
You didn't steal for need
You only stole for money
You only stole for greed

(MAJOR THIRD ON THE TOP - CADENCE AT END OF SECOND PART SHOULD ALSO BE A MAJOR THIRD - ALL IN THIRD ON SECOND HALF)

Verse about the elephants lying dead with no tusks in the African countryside
My fishes floating up on top of the lakes with their bellies to the sky

(verse about)
Your ancestors just took what they needed
Your ancestors hunted in the forest

(this verse should include)
Poison waters leaching into the watertable
Acid rain
50 species that die/disappear every day
rain forest
4 disasters: one for each line

etcetera

Words, ideas, phrases, odd rhymes, musical motifs, anything and everything. The next step was to underline poignant or well-expressed ideas and cross out the duff ones. By this time, I began to realise what I wanted the song to say. Its final form had started to emerge as well: fast, angry, and agitated, with short lines, in minor . . . and so on. Time to start in on verse organisation and uncertainty sets in. There is almost too much material from which to choose. It would help to decide on a form. Narrative . . . lyrical . . . epic . . . random . . . ? Maybe a mixture. It will be the story of the rape of the earth, a courtship gone wrong. Make each verse answer the question, "What do I want this verse to say?" Could the first verse have as its theme "the beginning" or "the origins of the relationship between humanity and earth"? Then the second verse could cover, perhaps, our teenage years as a species. The third verse will cover the crimes and desecrations, the disillusion and accusation. There's the title, "I Accuse." The fourth will have premonitions of the future and the fifth will wind it all up. My first draft looked like this:

FIRST DRAFT

1. The first time that I saw you, you were just another creature;
I raised you from a baby, 'cause we both belong to nature;
Yes, I gave you all my beauty and the treasures of my heart,
You know you can't live without me yet you're tearing me apart,
I AM YOUR MOTHER! YOU TREAT ME LIKE A WHORE,
NOW I'M TELLING YOU, DON'T DO THAT ANY MORE.

2. There was a time when you were cautious, didn't want to make me mad;
You sacrificed yourself to me 'cause I was all you had;
We didn't always pull together but somehow we got along,
Now you're too big for your britches, everything you do is wrong.
YOU WERE MY LOVER! NOW YOU'RE DECLARING WAR,
I GAVE YOU EVERYTHING AND STILL YOU'RE WANTING MORE.

3. You been ripping out my belly, you been poisoning my blood,
You been trying to control me since you crawled out of the mud;
No, you didn't kill for passion, you didn't steal for need,
You ravaged me for profit, you devoured me for greed.
I AM YOUR HEAVEN. I AM YOUR OCEAN FLOOR,
BUT NOW YOU THINK YOU'RE GOD, YOU DON'T NEED ME ANY MORE.

4. You put acid in my rainfall, cut down my precious trees,
You dissolve my ozone layer and you know you're killing me,
And when you fear the sunshine, when you dread the morning dew,
When you're scared to eat and drink and breathe, you'll know I'm killing you,
I AM ETERNITY, BUT YOU BREAK MY LAW;
SOMETIMES IT SEEMS TO ME THAT YOU GOT NO BRAIN AT ALL.

5. I'm accusing you of murder, I'm accusing you of theft;
You'll rape and waste and plunder till we both got nothing left;
In your human race for progress, it is me that's coming last,
It's a game without a winner and the end is coming fast.
YOU WANT THE WHOLE WORLD, THE SEA AND THE SKY,
AND IF YOU DON'T STOP TAKING, I'LL KILL YOU - WHEN I DIE.

It's an odd mixture of idioms. Some of the poetry is classic and some is colloquial. Some of the ideas stop midstream, some are stated twice. A lot of the lines are in the wrong order. The song doesn't build to a climax. At this point, I showed the song to Irene. Out came the red pencil. She felt the song needed to be more economical. So I took out some of the fifth and sixth lines and shifted and added and subtracted. This made the song more to the point, but it wasn't much shorter.

SECOND DRAFT

1. (first four lines of verse 1 above)

2. (first four lines of verse 2 above followed by:
YOU WERE MY LOVER - YOU TREAT ME LIKE A WHORE,
I GAVE YOU EVERYTHING AND STILL YOU'RE WANTING MORE.

3. (first four lines of verse 3 above)

4. You kill my other creatures, you put poison on the breeze;
Blow bombs up in my deserts and pour oil on my seas;
You breed too many babies, you cut down my precious trees,
You dissolve my ozone layer and you know you're killing me,
I GAVE YOU HEAVEN - I GAVE YOU PARADISE -
BUT WHEN THE DEVIL RULES, THE ANGELS PAY THE PRICE.

5. When you can't walk on your beaches, when all the birds are gone,
When your cities turn the night to day and darkness comes at dawn,
When you fear the summer sunshine, when you dread the morning dew,
When you're scared to eat and drink and breathe, you'll know I'm killing you,
IT'S JUDGEMENT DAY -

6. (first four lines of verse 5 above, followed by:
YOU WANT THE WHOLE WORLD, THE SEA AND THE SKY,
AND IF YOU DON'T STOP, I'LL KILL YOU - WHEN I DIE.

It was still too long to be punchy, and the image of the earth as a vengeful killer did not please either of us. Although it was clear that she was killing in self-defence her personality had lost its grandeur. So we changed the speaker, got out another red pencil and got vicious.

THIRD DRAFT

1. (sung) IT'S JUDGEMENT DAY -

(spoken) I'M ACCUSING YOU OF PLUNDER, I'M ACCUSING YOU OF WASTE,
I'M ACCUSING YOU OF MURDER, I'M ACCUSING YOU OF RAPE!

2. We been ripping out her belly, we been sickening her blood,
We been trying to control her since we crawled out of the mud,
No we didn't kill for passion, no we didn't steal for need,
We ravaged her for profit, we devoured her for greed.

3. We kill the other creatures, we put poison on the breeze,
Blow bombs up in the deserts and pour oil on her seas,
We put acid in the rainfall, cut down her precious trees,
We dissolve the ozone layer - and you know you're killing me.
SHE GAVE US HEAVEN, SHE GAVE US PARADISE,
BUT WHEN THE DEVIL RULES, THE ANGELS PAY THE PRICE.

4. When you can't walk on the beaches, when all the birds are gone,
When the cities turn the night to day and darkness comes at dawn,
When you fear the summer sunshine, dread the morning dew,
When you're scared to eat and drink and breathe - you'll know she's killing you

That was the draft we went into the studio with. We knew it wasn't totally right but our patience resembled the red pencil, which was by now down to a stub. We knew from experience that as you sing the song in, you may sing parts of it out—but the song had not yet been sung in public. In the studio, we laid down a track of accompaniment and improvised over it, testing the text out as we went along. We kept expanding and contracting it until it finalised (see "Guilty").

At the time it often seemed as if too many wonderful lines were being casually discarded, as if carefully built structures were being dismantled prematurely. Each time a suggestion was made I had to force myself to adopt immediate optimism rather than take a defensive stance. Writing "Guilty" was almost like a chemical process in which the mixture had to be exposed to searing heat before the liquids would evaporate and expose the precious crystals. Unifying the mode of utterance meant that some very strong lines simply had to go because they unbalanced the whole text. When I look at the brainstorm material now, I feel there are several more songs hidden in it. If anyone wants to use it, we'd love to see the result.

* *

Starting out

. . . can be daunting: that very first moment of putting pen to paper (or fingers to computer) can instigate the most awful silences in the brain. A song can be anything from a rhymed couplet to "The Song of Solomon." If you've never made a song before, try making a verse. Just a verse. Then make another one—about anything (preferably a subject you know something about). Have fun, be silly. Make words without a tune or a tune without words. Don't expect Immediate Undying Art. Pile a few stones satisfactorily together before you attempt a pyramid. Once the muscles of creativity are loosened you'll be ready for longer runs.

Continuing.

A good thesaurus is a staunch ally. I also find a rhyming dictionary invaluable in a pinch. I prefer the one by Clement Wood where the words are listed vertically rather than in long horizontal lines. If I'm well and truly stuck, I sometimes try a different format and brainstorm within another poetic form. Or I spend days singing any other type of song than the one that is refusing to mature. I treat it like a sulking child and pretend not to notice it at all for a while. I know it's there in my head, along with all the other incomplete detritus of my life: the names I cannot remember, the half-faded memories, the things I forgot to do, the shopping list. Sooner or later the song will return in one form or another. If it doesn't, forget it.

Owner's Manual

These are your operator's instructions. If you've skipped cursorily through the chapters up to now some of the items in this section may be confusing—in which case, you might as well skip this one as well and go straight to the songs. Some notes on troubleshooting are at the end of this manual.

Date of composition is to be found just below the title of each song.

The notes: I got very involved while writing these, hence the fact that some of the notes are longer than the songs they preface.

Information about the songs is to be found just above the top right-hand corner of the notation.

- *Alternative titles:* just in case you know the song by another title.
- *Words and music:* who wrote them. As I work quite closely with folksong, it is possible that I have inadvertently claimed a folk tune as my own. *C'est la vie.* Where I consciously employed a folk tune, I have given the name that *I* know it by. Some songs have no music notation at all. This may be because the music is improvised or too complicated—or simply because the tune is very well known.
- *Disc* refers you to the "Discography" in the back of the book.
- © refers you to "Copyrights and Recording Companies" in the back. The notations looked too crowded with full copyright details sitting on their shoulders. It is interesting to observe that if you write a new set of words to someone else's melody, the copyright belongs to the writer of the tune. You can claim *credit* for your new words but you cannot *copyright* them. The tune-writer or per (see "Glossary") publisher can do so and can refuse permission for you to print or even refer to their tune. I had to leave out one song entirely because the owners of the tune would not allow me to print it or hint that it was involved. I couldn't even give you the words because they make it obvious what the tune is. What is interesting, however, is that, as far as the music business is concerned, the chief ingredient of a song is its melody, not its words.

The music is laid out visually. This was one of Dio's predilections. She felt that song music is easier to read if it corresponds to the poetic form of the text. Four lines in the verse = four lines in the music = ease in comprehending the song at first glance. Where the lines are too long or where the song is too irregular, I have forsaken this format, but for the most part the notations are *displayed* like a map. Some of the layouts are therefore not space-savers. "Different Therefore Equal," for instance, could have been laid out as longer lines with internal rhymes. I have put it into short lines because I sing it in short lines, with irregular pauses in between each little phrase. *Seeing* it in short lines is helpful. We can then fill up the space to the right with other visual images or leave a blank for doodling. There were several format options for call-and-response songs ("Can't Pay, Won't Pay," "We Remember," "Hey Ho, Cook and Rowe!," "It's a Natural Thing"). I tried as many as possible.

Music notations always appear severe to me. They *are* severe! They are skeletons which the singer must flesh out with imagination and vocal technique. If a song were to be notated *exactly* as sung it would be extremely difficult to sight-read. Béla Bartók and Percy Grainger—and sometimes Dio—were famed for their ability to write down *everything* the singer sang. They found it pleasing and satisfying to fill the staff lines with forests of little semiquavers, melismas, grace notes, and irregular meters. But if you want to just open the book and sight-read, it is neither pleasing nor satisfying to wade through a welter of big notes, little notes, flags, and dotted rests, counting as you go. So my notations are just guides. Singing them exactly as written may sound wooden and mechanical until you've sung the song in.

I have mentioned *melodic* variations. I am assuming that you will make your own *rhythmic* variations to adapt to the verses as they roll by. Remember that all text from verse 2 onward will have to adapt to a notation that has been determined by the text of verse 1. You will generally want to sing words with their spoken inflections and accents. If a song is marked down as a blues, you will bend the rhythm and jump the beat, as in bars 3 and 5 of "A Good War." You should add and subtract rests as needed. Clothe the skeleton and make it dance.

During my childhood, Dio's hints were known in the family as "things you had to do." I have given some hints as to musical treatment in the upper left-hand corner of each notation. Most of my songs are written in the folk idiom, the byword of which is *consistency.* You pick a pace, a volume, a style—and you stick to it. Increase in the decibels, exaggerated changes in pace, and the use of histrionics are not generally part of the style of these songs.

"Free" songs are hard to deal with only if you don't know how. I have written them out in a meter that reflects or is dictated by the footage of the poetry. This gives you a starting point. Begin by reciting the text in rhythm, as a poem. This is the meter into which I have cast the song. Then sing the song, in rhythm, in that meter. Then let conversational phrasing dictate the rise of a phrase and the fall of a cadence. Add a little vocalising. A *little.* Give a slight emphasis to significant words and minimalise the accent on less important ones. Sing the song line by line, thinking about what you are singing, pausing at the fermatas. By now you should be singing *freely*, with pulse instead of rhythm. I am probably telling granny how to suck eggs—but even experienced singers have been known to freeze at the sight of staff lines with flocks of note-heads fluttering all over them.

The keys were chosen for easy reading. I tried not to fly above the upper limit of the staff. Sometimes I chose quite low keys because I reckon a lot of guitar players may use this book and they can always capo up and use my chord patterns. Where the songs are best sung high in the singer's register, I have placed them high on the staff—visual association strikes again! Please believe the signatures. If a sharp or a flat is not there, don't sing it. The key of F doesn't necessary need a B-flat; the song could be in the Lydian mode (as in "Four-Minute Warning").

Chords: If chords are not given, it means that I feel that the song is best left unaccompanied. Where chords are given, those are the ones I prefer. Optional chords are enclosed in parentheses. When there is a vertical snake next to the chord symbol, that just means that you hit the chord once, either straight or with a quick arpeggio, rather than continue a rhythmical vamp.

The texts: Scattered throughout the texts are asterisks which refer you to some particular feature of the song. Actual melodic variations have been marked with the symbols Δ, †, «, and ∞. These refer you to (a) the place in the music where the variation occurs and/or (b) to the variation itself, which lies below the main notation. I usually give bar numbers to help you take off and land. You may want to invent your own melodic flights—fine, but why not try mine first? Brackets enclose words that were appropriate at the time the song was written but which would need changing to suit contemporary issues. I am sure you could have worked this out for yourself, but then there are always people who take the printed word as gospel.

Music notes at the end of the text contain pertinent information about the song. They occasionally refer you to original recordings, the majority of which are unfortunately no longer available. Even if they were, many of the songs were recorded so close to their dates of composition that they were not sung in and occasionally sit uncomfortably with their accompaniments. They may be stilted, they are sometimes sung too fast or too slow, or I may have chosen the wrong instruments. Also, subsequent years of singing often changed the texts and tunes, so that the disc version may differ considerably from the one in this book. In case of doubt, use the one printed here and listen with compassion to the recorded ones.

Production pieces: These are pieces made up of more than just the repetition of a simple verse form. They are lengthy and somewhat theatrical. They can consist of a variety of melodic forms ("Different Tunes"), they can be made up predominantly of music with interpolated speech ("R.S.I.," "Plutonium Factor"), or they can have a great deal of speech with interpolated music ("Items of News"). Instrumentation is an integral part of these songs, especially in "Plutonium Factor," where the whole tone of the piece is set and sustained by a bowed psaltery and two guitars, dissonant and stark. In "Items of News," motifs from the song were expanded and used as backing for the speech. The whispering was done in total silence, close to the microphone. Such techniques are the stock-in-trade of radio, television, and theatre. In a songbook, it is difficult to describe and impossible to notate properly.

Subject Index: This section will help you find songs about women, politics, ecology, love, and so on. Some songs span several categories.

Glossary: Many of the terms in the songs are in the accepted English of Great Britain. So is most of the spelling. The English language varies greatly from one English-speaking country to another. So if there are unfamiliar words, spellings, personalities, places, *etc.*—look in the "Glossary."

Troubleshooting: Check out the "Glossary" or the opening chapters. I have tried to cover all possibilities and hope that any mistakes I have made will be funny ones.

The Songs

There's Better Things to Do

like SINGING
and DANCING

I arrived in London in 1956, an American in England during the height of the Cold War. It was the skiffle era, when it seemed that practically every male between the ages of fifteen and twenty-five had a guitar—preferably twelve-string (like Leadbelly's), without a case (like Woody Guthrie's), and battered (because this was folk music). You learned three chords in the key of G and off you went! The skifflers mostly sang North American folksongs, but some new songs were being made up as well, in much the same way as this one was: out of the stuff of the old songs. What could be easier than to take the idea, the tune and part of the opening line from a traditional song: "There's better things for you, no one on earth can do." Yes, it was a religious song, from a culture of chorus-singing and handclapping . . . just the thing, as it proved, for the first Aldermaston march in 1958.

tune: traditional U.S.A. ("Better Things")
new words and trad. arr.: Peggy Seeger
disc 17
© 1963 Stormking Music, Inc. (2)

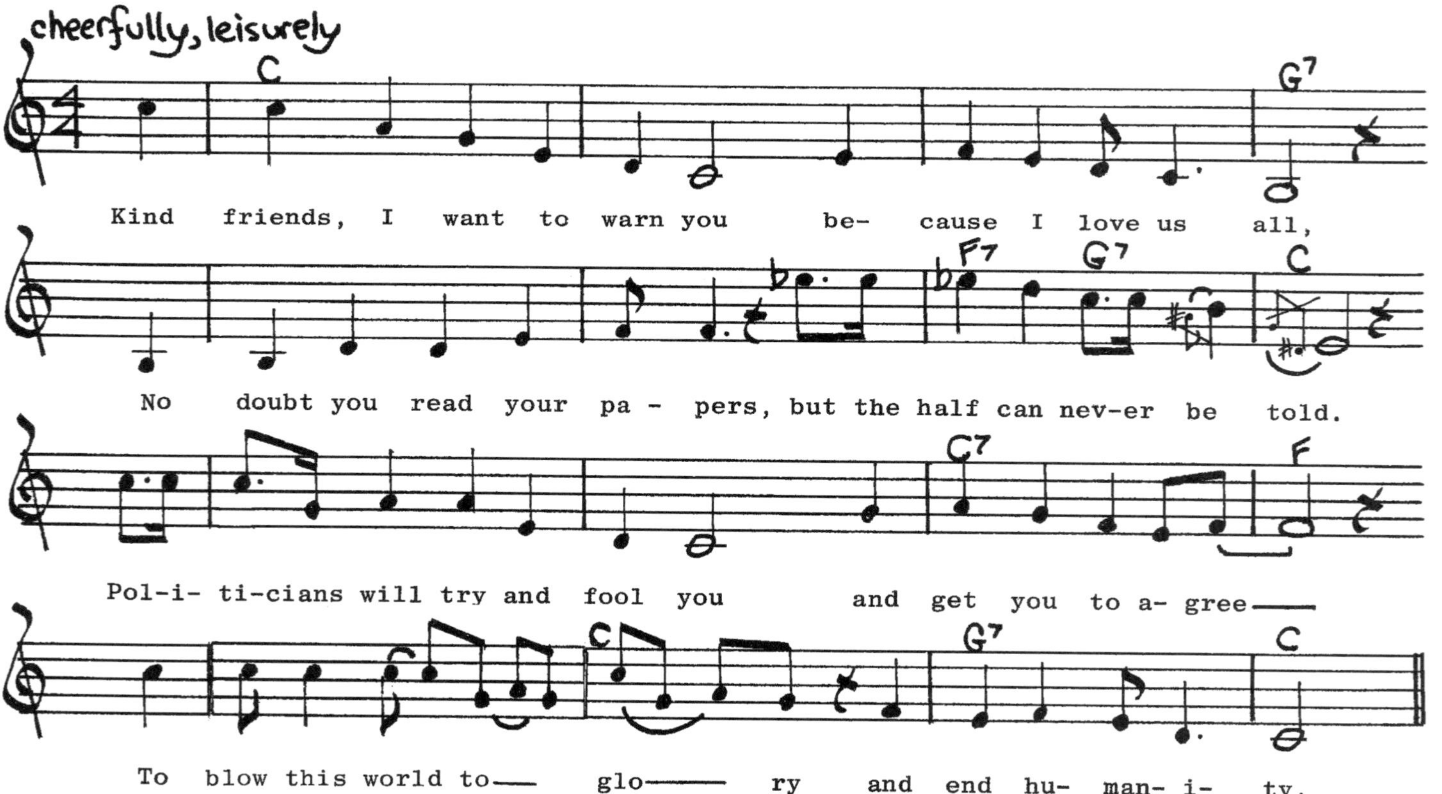
cheerfully, leisurely
C
G7
Kind friends, I want to warn you be- cause I love us all,
F7
G7
C
No doubt you read your pa - pers, but the half can nev-er be told.
C7
F
Pol-i- ti-cians will try and fool you and get you to a- gree
C
G7
C
To blow this world to glo ry and end hu- man- i- ty.

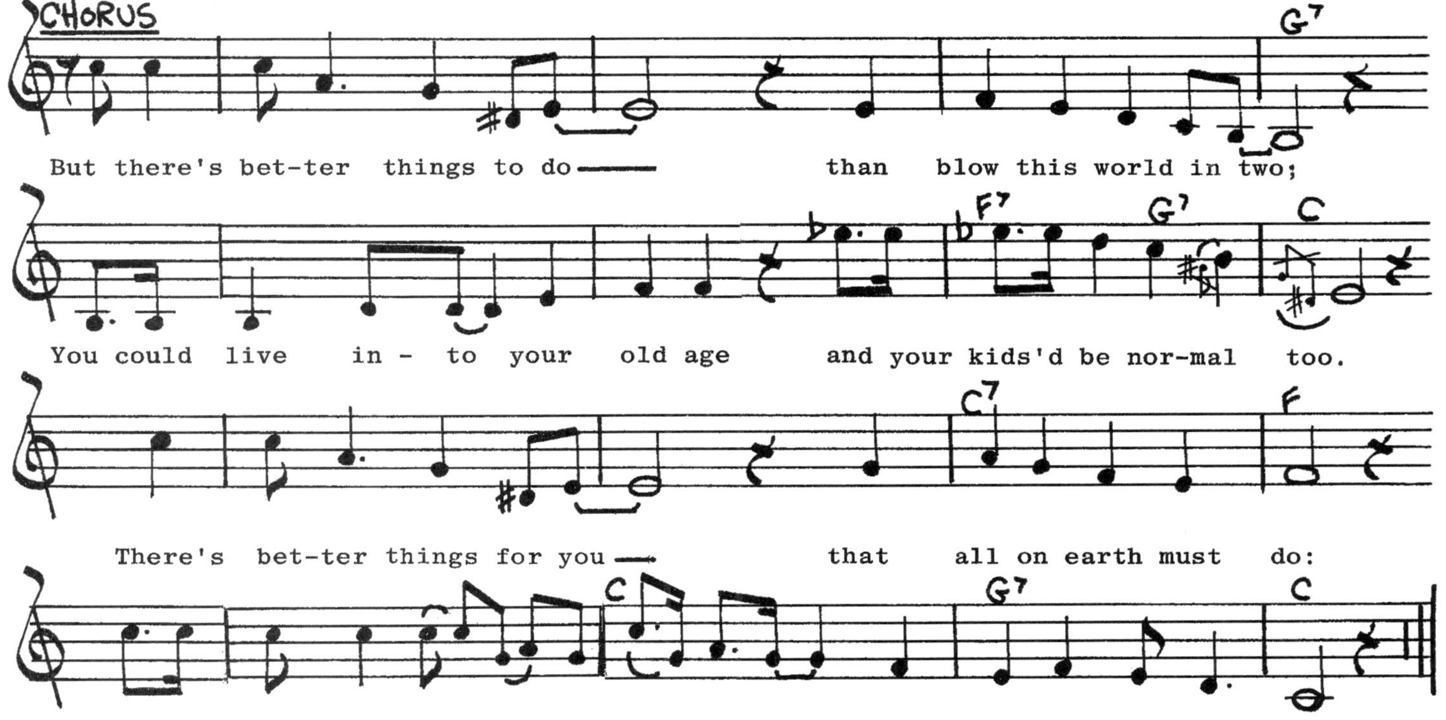

Got- ta pledge your feet on the road to peace and see your jour-ney through.

Kind friends, I want to warn you because I love us all,
No doubt you read your papers, but the half can never be told.
Politicians will try and fool you and get you to agree
To blow this world to glory and end humanity.

Chorus: But there's better things to do than blow this world in two;
You could live into your old age and your kids'd be normal too.
There's better things for you that all on earth must do:
Gotta pledge your feet on the road to peace and see your journey through.

Now some folks think that danger can't reach this peaceful shore,
They must see planes and soldiers before they call it war.
Kind friends, I will remind you: the atom's very small,
It can blow us all to glory and you can't see it at all. *(chorus)*

Now some folks they are holy—in the Bible it is told
That judgment comes tomorrow so today pray for your soul.
Friends, that is not sufficient. Tomorrow is today—
They'll blow us all to glory while we just sit and pray. *(chorus)*

When I Was Young

I am including this song for one reason only: to remind myself of how far I have come in both politics and songwriting. Many twenty-two-year-olds have written far better songs than this, so I cannot use my age as an excuse. It was a direct copy of Ewan's "Trafford Road Ballad" but without the teeth and claws of that tender song. In "There's Better Things," I used someone else's tune and form. In this song, the tune and words are mine. My next attempt, "I'll Never Go Back to London Again," has tune, words, *and* form all out of my own head. In all three songs I am still fighting the need to employ clichés. In the four verses below, we have cardboard-cutout characters who seem to have stepped straight out of a Hollywood B-movie: helpless, tragic figures who abdicate any responsibility for what happens to them and who still depend on those amorphous "politicians" to save them. It sings well enough, but I hope you don't like it.

words and music: Peggy Seeger
disc 18

very free
When I was young I loved a lad and gai- ly we were wed;
I knew no great-er plea - sure than to fol-low where he led;
But when he went a- way to war, O sor-row be to me,
For you can-not fol-low sol- diers bear-ing guns a-cross the sea.

When I was young I loved a lad and gaily we were wed;
I knew no greater pleasure than to follow where he led;
But when he went away to war, O sorrow be to me,
For you cannot follow soldiers bearing guns across the sea.

They made him leave his wife and child to march in foreign lands,
Can they make him stalk a stranger with a bayonet in his hands?
What kind of men can force a man who's married to agree
To take the lives of men with wives in lands across the sea?

I know no field more barren than this life I walk alone,
I know no sorrow greater than to see our growing son;
Will he, too, become a lively man till other men decree
That he lie still, as his father does, in a grave across the sea?

Were I the wind, I'd bring the clouds to lands that need the rain,
Were I a bird I'd sing of things that comfort those in pain;
Were I a statesman leading men in near or distant lands,
I'd pass a law that only tools of peace be in our hands.

Peggy, this bit where it says 'I knew no greater pleasure than to follow where he led'. .

The Ballad of Springhill

The pit disaster at Springhill, Nova Scotia, October 23, 1958, was the first of its kind to be televised. More than 150 miners were trapped, some of them a mile below the ground. Eighty-one miners were rescued but 90 died. Attempts to rescue the entombed men, and interviews with those rescued, were seen by millions of people. I was living on the north coast of France at the time. I have since been down many mines, but back then I had never been down a pit, knew no miners and no mining terms, so when Ewan came to visit he supplied several lines for verse 4. The Canadians have adopted the song—it is occasionally mistaken for a folksong.

July 1997. Whilst travelling to the Stan Rogers Festival in Canso, Nova Scotia, I decided to visit Springhill, a community of some 5,000 people. I went to the library and asked if Caleb Rushton still lived there. "Caleb? Sure," said the librarian with a big smile. Everyone knew Caleb. I asked if she knew where he lived. She gave me his address without looking around for it. I explained that in 1958 I had written a song about the disaster and would like to meet Caleb. She knew the song. She'd sung it in school. She phoned Caleb but he wasn't home. "Come back in a half an hour. I'll find him by then." I went down to the mining museum, which is not very big but very local and very moving. There I learned that the Cumberland Mine was not two miles down but (a) one mile, if you delved directly down from the earth's surface to pit-bottom, or (b) three miles down, if you went via the long sloping drift-mine entrance. I learned that the rescuers were not barefaced at all—they wore the Draeger apparatus, complete with oxygen tanks, masks, and protective suit. Stan Pashkoski was one of the Draegermen heroes who saved the lives of Caleb Rushton and many of his comrades. He took a group of us around on a guided tour chatting and lecturing casually as we went. He reminded me of the extraordinarily articulate miners I had met while recording the radio ballad *The Big Hewer.* A photocopy of the hand-written text and note that I had sent to Caleb in 1958 was on exhibit. Apparently lots of people ask for a copy of that photocopy. "Mostly New Yorkers," said the attendant with a wry smile. My half hour had stretched to over an hour so it was now back to the librarian, who had tracked Caleb down in Amherst, twenty miles away. He'd meet me at Tim Horton's doughnut joint down the road in fifteen minutes. It was an emotional meeting, made more so by the presence of Caleb's wife, Pat. We sat talking for an hour while a constant flow of customers moved in and out of the restaurant. The Rushtons knew and greeted so many of them . . . Caleb told me about the schoolchildren singing the song at an assembly, a performance in which he stood up and spoke his part in verse 6. A wonderful day in July 1997—the three of us brought together by an event and a song from nearly forty years before . . .

alternative titles: "Springhill Mine (Mining) Disaster"
words and music: Peggy Seeger
disc 1, 7, 17, 28

In the town of Springhill, Nova Scotia,
Down in the dark of the Cumberland Mine;
There's blood on the coal and the miners lie
In the roads that never saw sun nor sky,
  Roads that never saw sun nor sky.

In the town of Springhill you don't sleep easy,
Often the earth will tremble and roll;
When the earth is restless miners die,
Bone and blood is the price of coal,
  Bone and blood is the price of coal.

In the town of Springhill, Nova Scotia,
Late in the year of '58;
Day still comes and the sun still shines
But it's dark as the grave in the Cumberland Mine,
  Dark as the grave in the Cumberland Mine.

Down at the coal face miners working,
Rattle of the belt and the cutter's blade;
Rumble of rock and the walls close round
The living and the dead men two miles down,
  The living and the dead men two miles down.

Twelve men lay two miles from the pitshaft,
Twelve men lay in the dark and sang;
Long hot days in a miner's tomb,
It was three feet high and a hundred long,
  Three feet high and a hundred long.

Three days passed and the lamps gave out
And Caleb Rushton he up and said,
"There's no more water nor light nor bread
"So we'll live on songs and hope instead,
  "Live on songs and hope instead."

Listen for the shouts of the bareface miners,
Listen through the rubble for a rescue team;
Six hundred feet of coal and slag,
Hope imprisoned in a three-foot seam,
  Hope imprisoned in a three-foot seam.

Eight days passed and some were rescued,
Leaving the dead to lie alone;
Through all their lives they dug a grave,
Two miles of earth for a marking stone,
  Two miles of earth for a marking stone.

I'll Never Go Back to London Again

Was it Wordsworth who said he would give anything to be able to write a folksong? I was still trying with this one. It sings nicely, although it has some linguistic inconsistencies. Its subject had nothing whatsoever to do with my life at the time.

words and music: Peggy Seeger

Chorus: I'll never go back to London again,
I'll never go back any more;
Not even if I must live and die
Upon some foreign shore.

When I first came down to London Town
The young men followed me;
They'd whistle and cry when I passed by,
Δ "There goes a girl from the North Country."
(chorus)

But there was one among them all
And he was the one for me;
His face so fair, his beauty rare,
Δ There's none like him in the North Country.
(chorus)

He might have chosen another one,
He might have chosen three;
But he vowed and he swore none pleased him more
Δ Than the handsome girl from the North Country.
(chorus)

Why didn't he watch the stars in the skies,
Or the moonlight on the sea?
That would take more art than to win the heart
Δ Of a lonely girl from the North Country.
(chorus)

His hand did rest upon my breast,
And then upon my knee.
And then he found and there he crowned
Δ The love of the girl of the North Country.
(chorus)

Before I knew his love was true,
I'd a baby on my knee;
Now everyone knows where my love goes
Δ On the days and the nights he's away from me.

Final chorus: I'll never go back to London again,
I'll stay in my own country.
I'll never have another true love
Though there's many that would have me.

March with Us Today

This song falls into a format that many early left-wing songwriters used:

> I have a brother in Tokyo,
> A sister in Paree
> A cousin in Valparaiso,
> All family to me . . .

or something like that. Easy to sing and join in on. Many of us (Earl Robinson, Phil Ochs, Tom Paxton, Pete Seeger, the Weavers, Ewan MacColl, *etc.*) produced something of that ilk in the forties, fifties, and sixties. We wanted to reach out to everyone of whatever age, country, profession, sex, *etc.*, during a time when the world seemed to be fragmenting into little bits. It was a commendable instinct but it produced a lot of songs that now feel like musical Esperanto: I feel that they lack character and colour, but they communicate a deep yearning for solidarity and peace within the human race. You didn't have to specify *what* war (just in case you were wondering about line 3 of the chorus). It was the time of the Cold War, when you felt as if conflict was all around and the Bomb could drop any day. We needed to reassert the idea that the human race was one group of people, not many hostile nationalities. This song was made for the first Aldermaston march. The later marches were bigger but the first one sticks in my memory. On Good Friday, 1958, 1,000 people left Trafalgar Square in London and walked for four days to the Atomic Weapons Research Establishment at Aldermaston, Berkshire. The countryside rolls gently away to the west—men, women, and children mingle, stop, eat, sing, and talk as we move along. As you topped the rises, you could see the procession snaking ahead, hyphenated by jazz bands, folk music groups, and companies of dancers. The flags and banners would have put a medieval jousting tournament to shame. We ate and slept in school halls, town halls, and gymnasiums, gathering ranks as we marched along. Ten thousand peacemongers walked past the barbed-wire fence of Aldermaston in total silence.

tune: traditional English ("Galopede")
new words and trad. arr.: Peggy Seeger
disc 18

cheerfully
C G7 C
O, I heard a man in the street
F G7
Com- plain-ing of the tax-es he must pay
C G7 C
For the guns, the planes and the Bomb.
F G7 C
And he's march-ing here a-long with us to- day.
CHORUS
F C G
Then fol- low the march and join us in the cho- rus
C F G
And sing so that ev-ry one will know;
C F C G7
Ban the Bomb! End the war! That's what this march is for,
C G7 C
To the base at Al-der-mas- ton we will go.

O, I heard a man in the street
Complaining of the taxes he must pay
For the guns, the planes and the Bomb.
And he's marching here along with us today.

Chorus: Then follow the march and join us in the chorus
And sing so that everyone will know;
Ban the bomb! End the war!
That's what this march is for,
To the base at Aldermaston we will go.

O, I heard a woman in her home
Singing as she worked the time away;
She sang of happiness and peace.
And she's singing here along with us today. *(chorus)*

O, I heard the children at the school
Learning to recite the Golden Rule;
First it said, "Thou shalt not slay."
So the children came and marched with us today. *(chorus)*

O, I heard the lawyer at the bar
And he said, "What we must have without delay
Is a law against the Bomb."
And he's marching here along with us today. *(chorus)*

O, I saw a preacher in the church
As he opened up the Bible for to pray;
He declared that the good Jesus Christ
Would have walked along the Aldermaston way. *(chorus)*

O, I asked the singers why they sing,
I asked the musicians why they play.
O, we work for harmony
That's why we're marching here with you today. *(chorus)*

Fitzroy Coleman

On the day I arrived in England, I joined a group called the Ramblers, assembled by Alan Lomax, the American folklorist, in an attempt to create a British answer to the Weavers. It consisted of two women and eight men: Shirley Collins (a Sussex country singer); myself; Alan Lomax; Jim Bray (an English double-bass player); Bruce Turner (an English clarinet and sax jazzman); Brian Daly (an English session guitarist); Bert Lloyd and Ewan MacColl (two English revival folksingers); Nat (a Nigerian percussionist and singer whose last name I never knew); and the man himself, Fitzroy Coleman, a West Indian musician and singer. The group never took off—its goal was the Top Ten but it had no artistic destination. Every week we went to Manchester to do a television program. They would invariably dress me in jeans and plaid shirt and sit me on the country gate with my banjo; then they'd send out for medicine to deal with my allergy to the bales of hay that, of course, accompany American folksingers wherever they go. Shirley was dressed in ginghams with her lovely yellow hair always in view. Alan stamped his big Texan feet—his speciality was cowboy songs and chain-gang shanties. Nat would try and teach the viewers (and us) a song from his country . . . and so on. It was a stew made of good ingredients but impossible to cook. We didn't deserve to succeed—and we didn't.

Fitzroy sailed through everything with charm and a beguiling sense of humour. Soon he was joining us onstage at the Sunday night "Ballads and Blues" sessions, held in the Princess Louise on High Holborn. We encouraged anyone with a guitar to sit in the front row and help with accompaniments. We hadn't yet realised that democracy and art have a hard time mixing: the first forty minutes of every evening was always *devoted* to *trying* to tune several dozen instruments. It was *devotion* on the part of the seasoned musicians and *trying* to all. Before you sang your song, you called out the key and the chords. The whole front row would glaze with concentration and left hands would search finger by finger for the correct string and fret.

Now Fitzroy was a brilliant calypso guitarist. He never let on, but I believe it secretly irked him to have us all tagging along. So with gestures that included everyone, he would reel off the number of bars to be covered by each chord and then launch into something impossible to follow. One by one we'd drop out of the race and Fitzroy would get happier and happier. He always ended the song by himself. What was the tune of this tribute of mine? One bar of A, one bar of D6, one bar of E9, one bar of A7 . . . and happy landings. Sing as you go. Almost any calypso melody will do.

words: Peggy Seeger
© 1992 Peggy Seeger (1)

I went to the hootenanny last night,
I take my guitar for my delight;
Now it has six strings and a capo and natch-
Urally majors and minors and the Carter Scratch;
But all these features do not mean a thing
When Fitzroy Coleman get up to sing.
When he call out the chords I think he meant
That I should help with the accompaniment,

Chorus: "But Fitzroy," I say,
"What are all those things you play?
"H-demented and a pye-R-square
"Chords that make Segovia despair,
"And that formula you explain in a hurry,
"Make Einstein worry."

Now it all begin with a bar of D
Then a half of A and a quarter of G,
Now I tell you the truth that the trouble start
With the E-13th in the seventh bar,
Well, I find the E and I count 13
And try and fit the other strings in between.
I conclude only one of these chords exist,
And that one is on the guitar of Fitz. *(chorus)*

Now I tell you the truth that it got much worse
When he take the break in between each verse,
But it's me that breaks with the worry and strain
When Fitz takes off like a rocket plane.
I try to keep up but I fall behind
And Fitz plays ten notes to one of mine.
My heart is sad and my fingers sore,
But Fitz he grin and he shout, "Once more!" *(chorus)*

Fitzroy in full flight, 1959

The Ballad of Jimmy Wilson

This song should have been entitled "The Ballad of $1.95." In August 1958, James Wilson, a black janitor, was sentenced to death in Alabama, having been convicted of robbing an eighty-year-old white woman of a nickel less than two dollars. The National Association for the Advancement of Colored People was barred from helping Wilson because it was not allowed to operate in Alabama. Petitions of protest flooded in from all over the world. These may have had some effect in getting the sentence reduced . . . to life imprisonment.

alternative titles: "Alabama 1958," "Jimmy Wilson"
words and music: Peggy Seeger
disc 18, 21A, 27, 31A

energetically
Dm C Dm G Dm
In A-la-ba-ma, nine-teen fif-ty- eight, The cost of hu- man life is ver-y low;
G Dm C Am Dm
A man that's black is tram-pled down Just like men were a thou-sand years a-go.
CHORUS
C Dm Gm Dm
But these are more en- light-ened days, The cru-el men and sa- vage ways
Gm C Dm
We left long a- go.
G Dm C Dm A7 Dm
Now eve- ry man may walk his road in peace For all are free.

In Alabama, 1958,
The cost of human life is very low;
A man that's black is trampled down
Just like men were a thousand years ago.

Chorus: But these are more enlightened days,
The cruel men and savage ways
We left long ago.
Now every man may walk his road in peace
For all are free.

Five thousand years ago a million men
Were gathered into royal Egypt's hands,
Were bound together, forced to build
Pyramids of stone in desert sands. *(chorus)*

Mary's son walked through a land of woe
Dreaming of the world as it could be;
The good and lawful men of Rome
Nailed him like a robber to the tree. *(chorus)*

In Britain just a hundred years ago,
The jails were full of poor and hungry men;
Diggers, Chartists, many more,
Fought and died and rose to fight again. *(chorus)*

Last year a Negro stole a dollar bill.
The judge he said, "We mustn't be severe.
Instead of death we'll give him life
Imprisonment to show there's justice here." *(chorus)*

And so throughout the ages we have seen
How progress marches ever on its way;
No rack, no wheel, no Spanish boot
For Alabama's prisoners today. *(chorus)*

The plague still runs throughout the world today,
Johannesburg to Little Rock and back;
A plague of ignorance and hate,
Men walk in fear because their skin is black.

Final chorus: In these more enlightened days
No room for all these savage ways,
Leave them, let them go!
Now every man should walk his road in peace,
Let ~~men~~ be free.

Lifeboat *Mona*

My memory of writing this song is absolutely clear. We were living in a tiny first-floor flat (we always had to walk up a flight of stairs to reach our digs) on Godstone Road, Purley. It was teatime and the radio was on. Neill (nine months old) was in his highchair just learning to feed himself—kind of. He had chocolate pudding all over his face and was very happy. The radio was on and the announcer listed the names of the men who had perished on the lifeboat *Mona* in the early hours of the morning: Donald Anderson, James Ferrier, Alexander Gall, Ronald Grant, John Grieve, John D. Grieve, George Smith, and George Watson. I had been along that wild east coast of Scotland several years before on my Lambretta scooter. I immediately pictured their homes, their families, maybe a kitchen like mine with a baby being fed, and I received a keen sensation of personal loss and sorrow—like being hit by something that has been thrown from afar. We always kept a shopping list pad with a pencil nearby and the first draft of the song went down on that. I didn't realise then, as I do now, just how small lifeboats really are. Forty to fifty feet in length, they look very fragile when you see them perched along the coast. They are crewed by volunteers who, like their boats, are always at the ready.

words and music: Peggy Seeger
disc 17

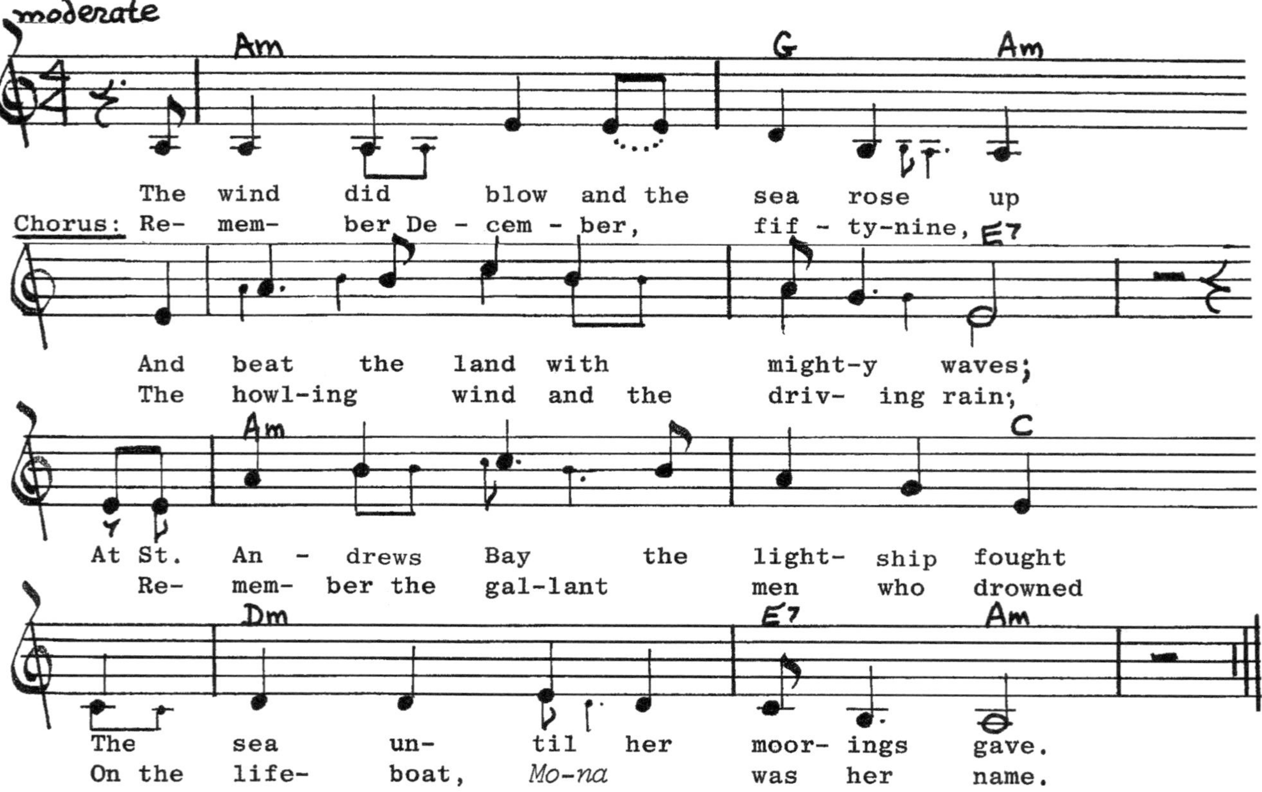
moderate
Am G Am
The wind did blow and the sea rose up
Chorus: Re- mem- ber De - cem - ber, fif - ty-nine, E7
And beat the land with might-y waves;
The howl-ing wind and the driv- ing rain;
Am C
At St. An - drews Bay the light- ship fought
Re- mem- ber the gal-lant men who drowned
Dm E7 Am
The sea un- til her moor- ings gave.
On the life- boat, Mo-na was her name.

The wind did blow and the sea rose up
And beat the land with mighty waves;
At St. Andrew's Bay the lightship fought
The sea until her moorings gave.

Chorus: Remember December, '59,
The howling wind and the driving rain;
Remember the gallant men who drowned
On the lifeboat, *Mona* was her name.

The captain signalled to the shore:
"We must have help or we'll go down."
From Broughty Ferry, at 2 A.M.,
They sent the lifeboat *Mona* out. *(chorus)*

Eight men formed that gallant crew,
They set their boat out on the main;
The wind's so high and the sea's so rough
We'll never see land or home again. *(chorus)*

Three hours went by and the *Mona* called
"The wind blows hard and the seas run high."
In the morning on Carnoustie beach
The *Mona* and her crew did lie. *(chorus)*

Five lay drowned in the cabin there,
Two were washed up on the shore;
Eight men died when the boat capsized
And the eighth is lost forevermore. *(chorus)*

Remember December '59,
The howling wind and the driving rain;
Remember the men who leave the land
And the men who'll never come home again. *(chorus)*

Hey Ho, Cook and Rowe!

The local council of the London Borough of St. Pancras raised the rents of its municipal flats. Two World War II veterans, Don Cook and Arthur Rowe, organised a rent strike which immediately became a focus of national interest. When the bailiffs were sent in, it took on the character of a military siege. The tenants barricaded the buildings with barbed-wire, old pianos, and junk of all kinds. From all over the country, sympathisers sent a constant supply of tinned food. Actors, dancers, singers and comedians would turn up unexpectedly at the house to entertain the strikers and their supporters. Television coverage provided Britain with one of its most popular daily shows. Finally, an army of police and bailiffs batonned their way through a sea of demonstrators and entered the house at its only vulnerable point: the roof. Cook, Rowe, and Co. greeted them with the offer of a cup of tea.

alternative title: "The Landlord's Nine Questions"
words and music: Peggy Seeger
disc 18

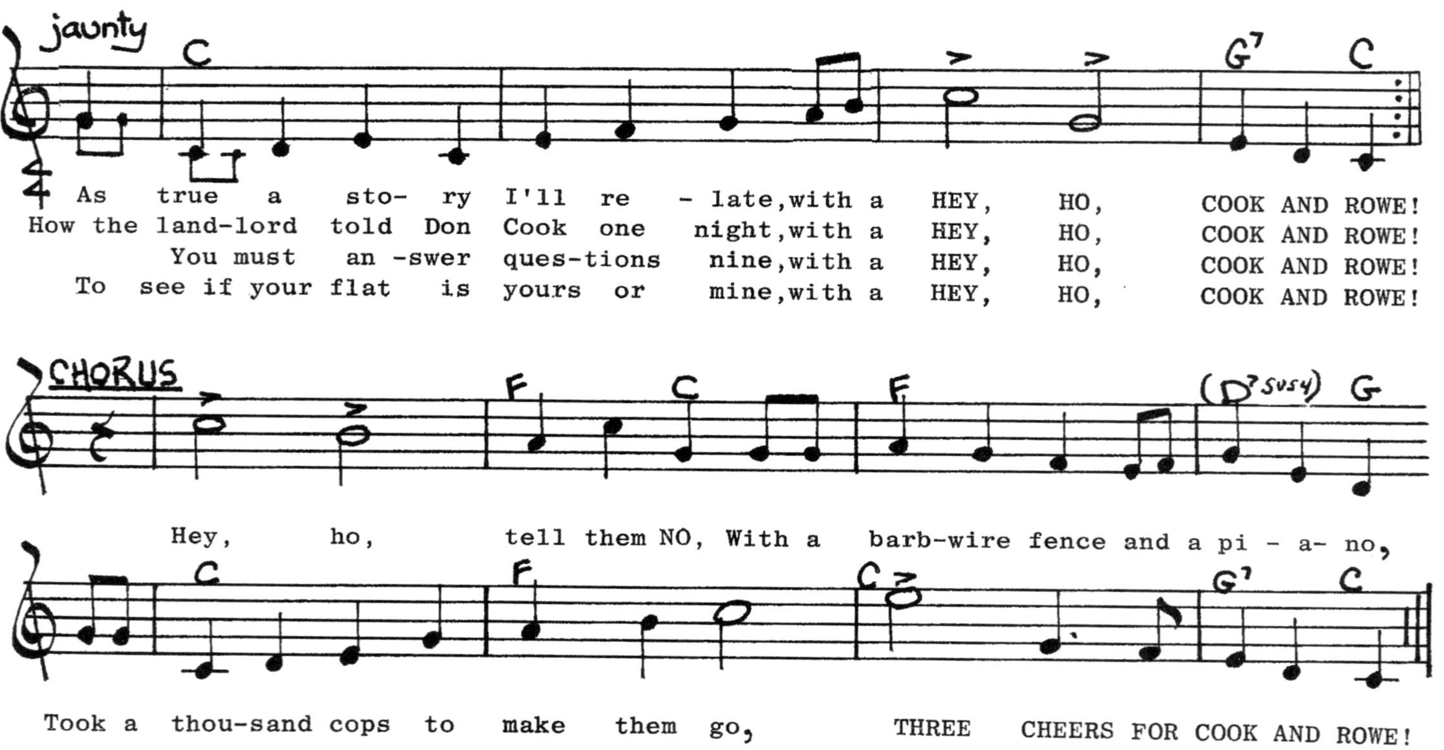
jaunty
C G7 C
As true a sto- ry I'll re - late, with a HEY, HO, COOK AND ROWE!
How the land-lord told Don Cook one night, with a HEY, HO, COOK AND ROWE!
You must an -swer ques-tions nine, with a HEY, HO, COOK AND ROWE!
To see if your flat is yours or mine, with a HEY, HO, COOK AND ROWE!
CHORUS
F C F (D7sus4) G
Hey, ho, tell them NO, With a barb-wire fence and a pi - a- no,
C F C G7 C
Took a thou-sand cops to make them go, THREE CHEERS FOR COOK AND ROWE!

As true a story I'll relate, with a
HEY, HO, COOK AND ROWE!
How the landlord told Don Cook one night, with a
HEY, HO, COOK AND ROWE!

You must answer questions nine, with a
HEY, HO *(etc.)*
To see if your flat is yours or mine, with a
HEY, HO *(etc.)*

Chorus: Hey, ho, tell them NO,
With a barbed-wire fence and a piano,
Took a thousand cops to make them go,
THREE CHEERS FOR COOK AND ROWE!

What is higher than a tree? *(etc.)*
And what is lower than a flea? *(etc.)*

My rent is higher than a tree,
And the landlord's lower than a flea. *(chorus).*

What goes on and never stops?
And what is kinder than the cops?

The tenant's fight will never stop,
And the devil's kinder than the cops. *(chorus).*

What is stronger than a door?
And tell me what a roof is for?

Barbed-wire is stronger, we have proof,
That's why you came in through the roof. *(chorus).*

Will you get off my property?
Or will you pay the rent to me?

I've settled in, as you can see,
Now won't you stop for a cup of tea? *(chorus).*

Well, since I've lost my board and bed,
I'll barricade the streets instead.

So all you tenants, settle in,
Keep up the fight, you're bound to win. *(chorus).*

Music note: This is, of course, based on the old folksong "The Devil's Nine Questions" and was originally entitled "The Landlord's Nine Questions." The verses are call-and-response between a soloist (the lowercase lines) and a GROUP (THOSE LINES THAT ARE IN CAPITALS)*. Everyone sings the chorus.*

Crooked Cross

In 1918, he was a conservative MP. In 1924, he went over to Labour. In 1932, he founded the British Union of Fascists. He was Sir Oswald Mosley, Britain's answer to Hitler. In 1959, he stood for election in the Notting Hill constituency of North Kensington, London. Commentators dubbed it "the ugly election," so vitriolic was the level of political debate. Mosley set up the campaign headquarters of his Union Movement directly opposite a synagogue and systematically leafletted the area, calling for the repatriation of Jews and black people. London was plastered with swastikas. He lost the election. Nine years later he was to say, "I am not, and never have been, a man of the right. My position was on the left and is now in the centre of politics." He died in 1980, leaving the boys to carry on. At the time of writing, swastikas are still appearing in London and large fascist rallies in Germany are becoming commonplace.

words and music: Peggy Seeger
disc 17, 30

Have you seen (Have you seen?)
The butcher's sign, (Have you seen?)
The killer's medal, (Have you seen?)
The crooked cross? (Have you seen?)
On that cross (Have you seen?)
Millions died (Have you seen?)
When the world (Have you seen?)
Was crucified. (Have you seen?)

Did you hear (Did you hear?)
Hitler yelling, *(etc.)*
Hitler ranting,
Hitler screaming?
"Don't want no Jews,
"In our land,
"Strike them down,
"On every hand."

I remember (I remember)
Paris conquered,
London blazing,
Warsaw shattered,
Children dying,
Smoke and flames,
Bombs exploding,
Fascist planes.

Did you see (Did you see?)
On the walls
Of your city,
Crooked crosses?
Millions suffered,
Millions starved,
On their graves,
That cross is carved.

Were you there (Were you there?)
In the camps?
Ten million
Were murdered there.
Did you question,
Did you agree
When they set,
The killers free?

I remember (I remember)
Nazis marching,
Nazis bragging,
Nazis killing,
Nazis running,
In retreat,
Nazis crawling
On their knees.

They are free: (They are free)
Nazi judges,
Nazi statesmen,
In Germany.
Δ Free to walk among us still,
Free to poison, lie and kill,
Free to finish Hitler's plan,
Stop them now while you can,
WHILE YOU CAN.

Come Fill Up Your Glasses

What with overfishing, overpopulation, and new concepts of how humanity should organise itself, this song feels outdated. From time to time I have brought the original version up to date but it still doesn't seem one hundred percent to me. I change it nearly every time I sing it. I am printing it here in its latest version, remade with gender and ecology considerations in mind. The final line of the chorus should, in my opinion, remain the same. Wars are set in motion and largely conducted by men. Women may support them, but the impetus, technology, management (etc.) are all in the hands of men. The song still needs sharpening and focus, localising and globalising, personalising and any other -isings you can think of. I'd be pleased if you would send me your version of it.

alternative title: "Fill Up Your Glasses"
tune: traditional English ("Pretty Polly Perkins of Paddington Green")
new words and trad. arr.: Peggy Seeger
disc 17

with a swing
A E7 A
Come fill up your glas-ses with whis-key and beer,
E B7 E7
And drink a full glass to a hap-py New Year,
A D E7
To our sis - ters and broth-ers and may they live long,
A D E7 A
So lift up your voi- ces and join in this song.
E7 CHORUS
A D E7
So we'll fill up our glass - es and drink once a- gain
A D E7 A
To peace on this earth and good will a-mong men.

Come fill up your glasses with whisky and beer,
And drink a full glass to a happy New Year,
To our sisters and brothers and may they live long,
So lift up your voices and join in this song.

Chorus: So we'll fill up our glasses and drink once again
To peace on this earth and good will among men.

Long life to the miners who work underground,
And also to the farmers the whole world around;
To the builders and nurses and bold engineers,
May your wages keep rising, friends, over the years, (chorus)

A toast to the casual labouring hands,
Who live where their work is, who work where they can;
To the writers and artists, whose work is our wealth,
And to those on the dole, a good job and good health. (chorus)

To our sisters who spend their whole workday at home,
To the parents who're raising their children alone;
Also to our comrades, our jobs never cease
As we spend our lives fighting for freedom and peace.

Let the men drink a health to their partners and friends,
And the women likewise, to their partners and friends.
May your pleasures be many, your troubles be few,
May you treasure the day you made one out of two. (chorus)

Let's drink to the children and let us prepare
A world where they'll live free from sorrow and care,
A world where good will among men is the law,
A world with a future, a world without war. (chorus)

My Love and I Are One

In the autumn of 1961, a huge tour of North America was planned for us. Ewan and I had only been living together since January 1959 and we were inseparable. We had been to the Newport Festival the year before so it was odd that this time Ewan's visa application was turned down. McCarthyism still had the U.S.A. by the throat—and we could not afford to cancel the tour. So I went alone and gave concerts from New York to San Francisco, via Canada. Three months . . . three long, long, long months. This is the first love song I ever wrote. I feel that it is unfinished, a little awkward and artificial. It does not really express what I was feeling at the time.

alternative title: "Parted"
tune: Ewan MacColl
new words: Peggy Seeger
disc 23

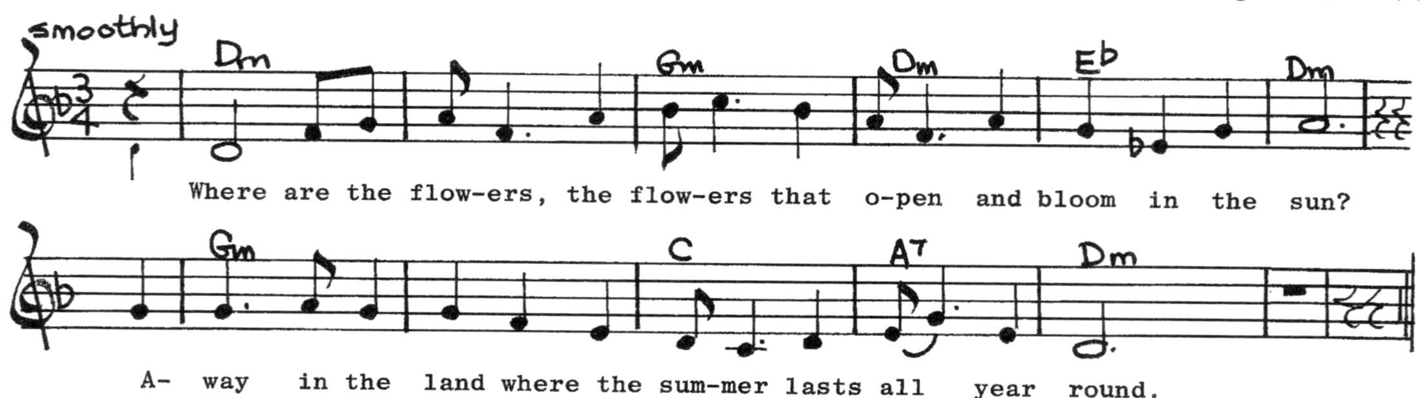

Where are the flowers, the flowers that open and bloom in the sun?
Away in the land where the summer lasts all year round.

Where are the days and the nights we have spent, the years that are gone?
Away in the land where my love and I are one.

Over the mountains, the valleys and plains and over the sea,
Thousands of miles lie between my love and me.

I'll walk through the field and the forest, the mountain, the valley and plain,
Across the wide ocean to be with my love again.

I'll bring him the flowers, the flowers that open and bloom in the sun;
I'll bring him the flower that's blooming the whole year round.

I'll bring him the days and the nights we have lost, the years yet to come;
I'll pray for the day when my love and I will be one.

you're going to be OLD
SINGLE and LONELY

and only YOU could make
it sound SO ATTRACTIVE

Affair of State

Everyone knew who did the deed: John Profumo, Minister of War in Harold MacMillan's cabinet. He resigned after admitting that he had lied to the House of Commons about the nature of his relationship with a certain Christine Keeler. The real action followed when Perry Mason was trying to find out who *else* knew he did it. MacMillan resigned soon after the Denning Report, commenting that the government (like Profumo?) had mishandled the affair. This song is very clever with its use of rhymes to suggest the cast, but it only lasted while listeners were *au fait* with that cast, whose names are used or suggested in puns and rhymes:

Stephen Ward — the West End osteopath whose flat was used by Keeler and Profumo. He was later prosecuted for living off immoral earnings and committed suicide during the trial.

Mandy Rice-Davies — Ward's mistress and Keeler's flatmate, also mistress of slum landlord Peter Rachman. She appears in the news every so often when the media is in a "Where are they now?" mood.

Lord Astor — It was rumoured that . . . and quickly suppressed.

"Lucky" (Aloysius) Gordon — Keeler's boyfriend, who was convicted of assaulting her. He opened up the whole can of worms by informing in the first place.

Christine Keeler was also involved with Eugene Ivanov, a Russian naval attaché. She was jailed for perjury over the case and now leads a fairly conventional life. Like Mandy Rice-Davies she surfaces every few years.

Profumo has since been held up as a kind of role model for Important Figures in Our Government whose marital wanderings lead them, and their grim-lipped loyal wives, onto *Newsnight* and Page One. Sometimes, like Tim Yeo, they lose their jobs. Sometimes, like Cecil Parkinson, they don't. If you're in the Labour Party, nobody cares. If you're Clinton, voters seem to take it for granted.

tune: traditional Scots ("Hiram Ho for Donald Don")
new words and trad. arr.: Peggy Seeger

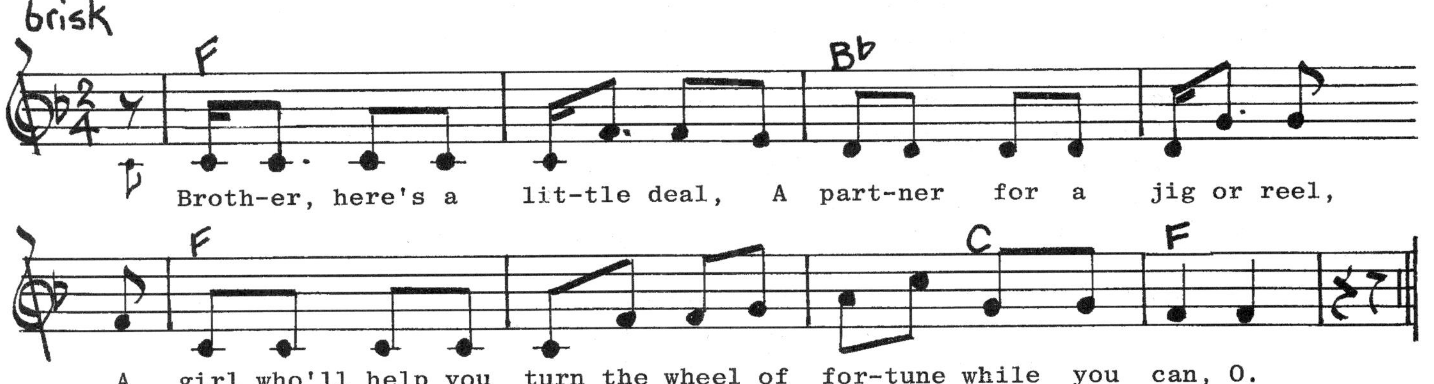

Brother, here's a little deal,
A partner for a jig or reel,
A girl who'll help you turn the wheel
Of fortune while you can, O.

Many a lusty duke and lord,
Have come to me when they were bored,
I put them in my private Ward
And there they also ran, O.

Pristine though she looks to you,
The old guard knows her through and through,
Enlisting in her books assures you
Many a valiant stand, O.

Darling, if I may presume, O
That you'll let me in your room, O
I will put a rare Perfumo
In your pretty hand, O.

I will be your sugar candy,
I will be at your comMandy,
Till I find someone more handy,
Catch me if you can, O.

And then up spoke the Lord and MAstor,
He said, "All I did was ask her!
She replied so well that I passed her
To another man, O."

The affairs of state were so rewarding,
Till a lad who couldn't afford 'em
Went and fell into the Cordon,
Now we're in demand, O.

To be discreet he is MacWilling,
When they come in for the kill
In case he makes a double billing
In the frying-pan, O.

The morals cannot be concealed,
There's no disguising how you feel,
A ship that rests on such a Keeler
Founders on the land, O.

I Support the Boycott

September 19, 1880: Charles Parnell, president of the Irish National Land League, is addressing a meeting of land reformers:

> When a man takes a farm from which another has been evicted, you must show him in the roadside when you meet him. You must show him in the streets of the town. You must show him in the fair and the market place and even in the house of worship, by leaving him severely alone, by putting him into a moral Coventry, by isolating him from his kind as if he were a leper of old. You must show him your detestation of the crimes he has committed.

The *leper* to which Parnell referred was Captain Boycott, a County Mayo landowner. Thus began the use of the term 'boycott' and the practice of boycotting. The action against South African goods in Britain lasted from early in 1960 to late in 1993—a third of a century. It was so effective that the producers of "Cape" fruit had to change their brand name to "Outspan." As the South African presidents were assassinated or replaced, the new leader's name was slotted into the chorus. This song may seem out of date, but it has been remade for subsequent boycotts.

alternative title: "The Boycott Song"
words and music: Peggy Seeger
disc 9, 13, 26A
© 1992 Peggy Seeger (1)

cheerfully
D
A7
I am a bus-y house-wife, I cook and wash and clean,
D
And eve- ry day I go to shop down at Gol-ders Green;
10
A7
Now the shop-keepers they trem-ble when I walk in- side the door,
14
D
If I see the la- bel Cape, then they know I'm bound to roar: No!
10
A7
to 14
On ap-ples, wine, tins of meat, eve- ry-thing they sell,

I am a busy housewife, I cook and wash and clean,
And every day I go to shop down at Golders Green;
Now the shopkeepers they tremble when I walk inside the door,
If I see the label "Cape," then they know I'm bound to roar: No!

Chorus: I support the boycott, and here's the reason why:
I can smell apartheid in an Outspan lemon pie;
And it suits old de Klerk fine if you drink his sherry wine,
So I support the boycott all along the line.

I went down to the grocery and bought a tin of fish,
And I looked at the label when I poured it in the dish (too late!)
I saw it was South African, so I gave it to the cat instead,
But she turned pale and walked away, and this is what she said: Meow! *(chorus)*

I went up on the mountain top to take the pleasant air,
An avalanche came rolling down and left me lying there.
A great big dog came lolloping up, with brandy in a cask,
I says, "Friend, if that's South African, just you lollop past!" Yes! *(chorus)*

Last week the Prime Minister asked me out to dine.
She said, "Now, an aperitif! How 'bout some sherry wine?"
I took a sip; "What brand?" says I. "South African," says she.
I says, "Stuff it up your cabinet and tell them this for me: No!" *(chorus)*

I look on all the bottles, the boxes and the tins,
And I look under orange peels and under fishes' fins;
Δ On apples, wine, tins of meat, everything they sell,
And if you don't agree with me, I boycott you as well. YES! *(chorus)*

Music note: Chorus is sung to the same tune as the verse.

Harold the Bootblack

The *Times*, March 2, 1965: "At a press conference yesterday, Mr. Harold Wilson told assembled pressmen: 'I am probably the only Prime Minister who cleans his own shoes.'" (See also "Follow Harold round the Bend.")

tune: traditional English ("The Female Frolic")
new words and trad. arr.: Peggy Seeger

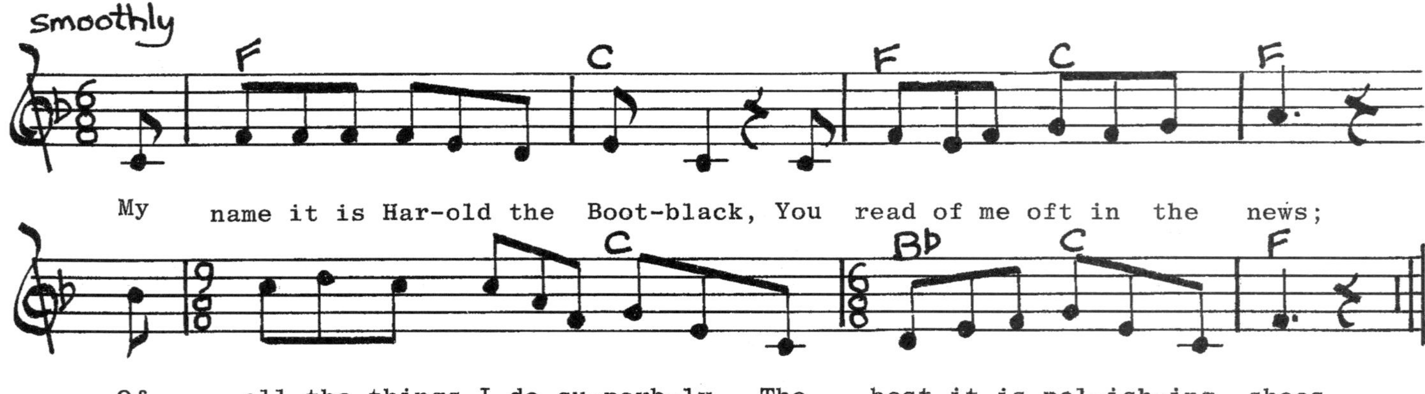

My name it is Harold the Bootblack,
You read of me oft in the news;
Of all the things I do superbly
The best it is polishing shoes.

When I was a boy I was clever,
I learned the correct way to kneel.
I first learned to polish up leather
And now I will polish off steel.

I've polished up court shoes and slippers
And jackboots that reach to the knee;
Not one of the leaders of Europe
But brings dirty footwear to me.

I clean off the mud with the water
I clean off the dirt and the sludge;
I clean off more blood than I oughta
And all for my Rover Scout badge.

First I undo all the laces,
Then I loosen the tongue;
But I only polish the uppers,
The lowers are covered with dung.

And as for those union vandals,
The wreckers and beatniks as well;
I'll very soon buff up their sandals
And send them barefooted to hell.

We'll very soon brush up the nation,
We'll lace 'em tight under control;
We teach 'em to use moderation
And find peace and rest for their soles.

Where Have All the Felons Gone?

All over the country, police forces were arresting their own members for activities that covered an astounding variety of crimes. At the same time, the *Daily Worker* (February 11, 1965) commented that "thousands quit the police each year and one of the main reasons for their going is because it is too undemocratic." Is there a connection here?

tune: Pete Seeger ("Where Have All the Flowers Gone?")
new words: Peggy Seeger

Where have all the felons gone?
Long time passing—
Where have all the sinners gone?
Long time ago—
Where have all the sadists gone?
They're all in uniform.
O, when will we ever learn?
When will we ever learn?

When the superintendent leaves,
Long time passing—
When police-inspectors leave,
All have to go—
When detective sergeants leave,
What's in your pocket was up their sleeve.
O, when will we ever learn?
When will we ever learn?

Some lack influential kin,
Long time passing—
Some don't like the discipline,
All have to go—
Some have left to save their skin,
And some are in the loony bin.
O, when will we ever learn?
When will we ever learn?

Music note: Pete says that he based his tune on the first two lines of an Adirondack lumberjack song.

Sentimental Journey

Queen Victoria was part German and she spoke English with a German accent. Britain's present royal family comes from a coalition of the Houses of Hanover and Saxe-Coburg. In 1917, responding to popular anti-German feeling, George V changed the family name to the House of Windsor. On May 23, 1965, the *Daily Mirror* howled THE ROYAL FAMILY FOR GERMANY! and an ensuing article reminded everyone that the public may be fooled but the press *never* forgets.

tune: traditional English ("Fourpence a Day")
new words and trad. arr.: Peggy Seeger

simply
C
G7
C
O, when I was a lit-tle girl my moth-er used to say,
Am
D7
G
You have a lov- ing fam-i-ly not man-y miles a- way.
F
C
G7
There's un-cles, aunts, and gran-nies and there's sec-ond cou-sins too,
C
G7
C
And when you go to vis-it them they're sure to wel-come you.

O, when I was a little girl my mother used to say,
"You have a loving family not many miles away.
"There's uncles, aunts, and grannies and there's second cousins too,
"And when you go to visit them they're sure to welcome you."

My granny came from Stuttgart, a fine Teutonic town,
My relatives all are royal and they're scattered all around
In Holland, Greece and Germany, four hundred souls or more—
They call me "Sister Lizzie" since we've finished with the war.

One morning Philip said to me, "I really think you should
Go and see the family." Mr. Wilson said I could.
So I quickly packed up fifty bags and headed for the road,
On a sentimental journey to the family abode.

When I got to the border there was sauerkraut and beer,
And a German army band played "The British Grenadier."
Three thousand handsome bobbies and a fifteen-wagon train,
When I stepped aboard I knew I was really home again.

At Bonn I took up residence in the Petersberg Hotel,
Where thirty years ago Mr. Chamberlain came to dwell;
There's police with dogs to guard me wherever I may go,
Such an openhearted welcome do the German people show.

The family gave a banquet on the twentieth of May;
Ex-royals came from miles around their titles to display.
Four hours or more of Let's Pretend and gobbling up cuisine,
And then we pushed the tables back and played at Kings and Queens.

Then I met some generals, pinned medals on their chests
(Apart from christening ships it's the work that I do best).
They may have once been beastly but the darlings didn't win,
So I gave them decorations and they'll never do it again.

I think we should respect them, I think we should be friends;
We need them for our allies so it's time to make amends.
Let's treat them just like other folks; we really should, you know,
For they treated *us* like other folks just twenty years ago.

When I get back to London, I'll let my subjects know
How the welcome of the German folk has set my heart aglow.
Good-natured and kindhearted and of well-bred family,
They're well-intentioned, simple folk—the same as you and me.

Cambrian Colliery Disaster

May 17, 1965: Thirty-one miners were killed and thirteen injured in an underground explosion 800 feet below the surface in the Cambrian Colliery, Clydach Vale, Wales. July 7, 1965: The public inquiry opens and reveals that there were a series of significant mishaps on the fatal morning. This song was written for the *1965 Festival of Fools*. It was felt at the time to be a little portentous and too studied, but it was used nonetheless and never remade. Unfortunately, it sings beautifully.

words and music: Peggy Seeger

Thirty-one voices cried out in the darkness,
Thirty-one lamps blew out in the gale;
Thirty-one check discs are left in the lamp-room,
Thirty-one miners lie low in the Vale.

Never did gas ever come to Cambrian,
Never was gas ever known to prevail.
But one Monday morning it came without warning,
Took thirty-one miners away from the Vale.

No warning to men below at the coalface,
No warning to women above in the town;
No warning, no warning but weeping and mourning
For thirty-one miners laid low underground.

Fathers and sons, husbands and brothers
Swept from the face in a fiery wave;
A vision of hell, then death came a-raging
And thirty-one miners lie low in one grave.

Silent the seam, the dust and the darkness—
Silent the women and children above—
Silence in Clydach, for hope is abandoned
And thirty-one comrades will never come up.

L.B.J., What Do You Say?

Written for The 1965 *Festival of Fools*. I didn't write any satisfactory songs about Vietnam—the horror was too great. The U.S.A. stepped in as the French stepped out after Dien Bien Phu in 1954. More tonnage of bombs was dropped on Vietnam than had been dropped during the whole of World War II. Seventy percent of the northern villages were destroyed and ten million hectares of productive land were left barren, to say nothing of the human casualties. The U.S.A. spent $150 billion on a war they never declared—and changed forever America's image, in the eyes of herself and of the world. Lyndon Johnson presided over the war but Kennedy had been involved in the unofficial escalation, a fact often overlooked in accounts of recent history. On being asked why he had not presented his intentions and decisions vis-à-vis Vietnam to the public more openly, L.B.J. replied, "If you have a mother-in-law with only one eye and she has it in the centre of her forehead, you don't keep her in the living room."

words and music: Peggy Seeger
© 1994 Peggy Seeger (1)

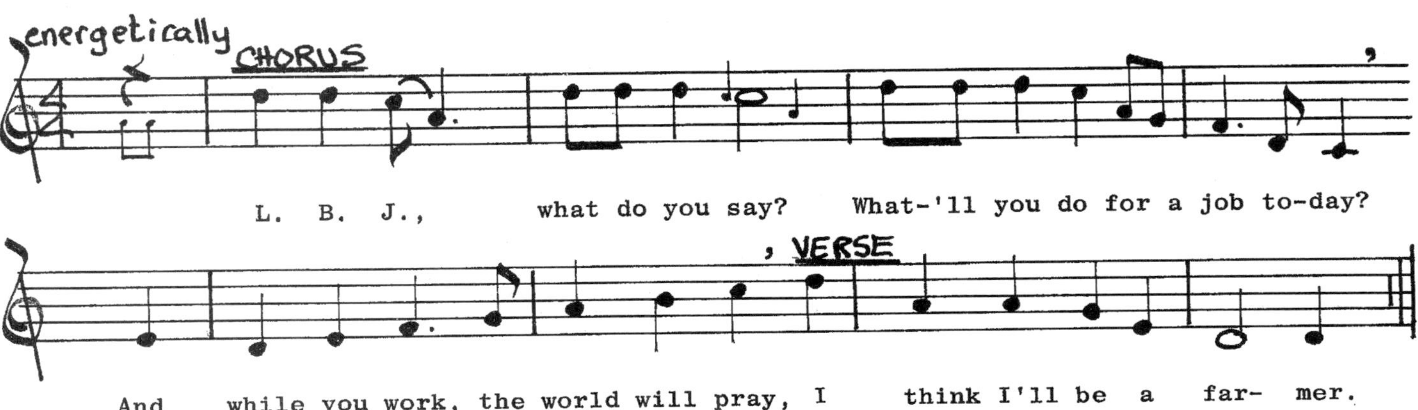

Chorus: L.B.J., what do you say?
What'll you do for a job today?
And while you work, the world will pray,

I think I'll be a farmer.
Give me a field, rich and calm,
I'll plough it up and sow napalm
To feed the kids of Vietnam,
When I become the farmer. *(chorus)*

I think I'll be a miner.
With a pick and shovel in my hand,
I'll hew and haul and sell for gain
The human gold of Vietnam
When I become the miner. *(chorus)*

I think I'll be a weaver.
Give me the warp of children's tears,
Give me the weft of women's fears,
I'll weave a shroud for the world to wear
When I become the weaver. *(chorus)*

I think I'll be a cowboy.
With Stetson hat and satin pants,
Them Asian steers don't stand a chance;
I'll round them up onto my ranch
When I become the cowboy. *(chorus)*

I think I'll be a doctor.
Give 'em bombs to make 'em well;
Call for the priest and ring the bell;
Promise heaven, give 'em hell
When I become the doctor. *(chorus)*

I think I'll be the banker.
When wages fall and profits rise,
Buy up stocks with human lives,
The world will be a booby prize
When I become the banker. *(chorus)*

I'll be the undertaker.
For the only job for a man like me
Is to make a corpse of liberty,
For them that's dead is surely free
When I'm the undertaker.

Music note: This tune used the first two lines of a traditional Scots song, "My Nanny-O," as a jumping-off point.

Billy and George

St. George and the Dragon: the mumming-play that still surfaces in the most unlikely places in Britain . . . descendant of all those magical plays and games in which Good (George, Spring, Jesus) dies at the hands of Evil (the Dragon, Winter, the Roman authorities) and is resurrected again. Ewan wrote a modern mumming play during the Vietnam War and the Critics Group took it on the road to folksong clubs, concert halls, and schools. Billy and Jack (I played Jack) were the facilitators who danced onto the stage, doing handstands and singing the bits of narration that were not acted by the players. George was played by Ted Culver, a butcher by trade. Tall, gangly, and decidedly London born and bred, he rode a Harley Davidson in real life and fused his own persona with that of the mythical hero, striding onstage in his helmet and leather biking clobber. Evil was a North American businessman-cum-politico, dressed in military uniform. Assorted supporting roles on both sides changed according to which goodies and baddies were in the news that day. One night we played at a Wolverhampton folk club that was habitually bedevilled by a group of noisy bikers who stood in the back, heckling. They were mesmerised by Ted's portrayal of St. George. They identified with him so completely that when Evil crept up behind him with a sword, they called "Look out, he's behind you!" and rushed the stage to assist their hero. It was good music, correct politics, and great fun.

tune: traditional Cornish ("Hal an Tow")
words and trad. arr.: Peggy Seeger
© 1992 Peggy Seeger (1)

There never was a winter yet
But spring could overcome him;
There never was a boaster born
But we could send him running.

Chorus: One, two, three,
Billy and George and me,
We dance and sing and welcome spring
To jovial company.

If spring is long upon the road,
It's up to us to find him;
Whenever he comes to wake the world
We're never far behind him. *(chorus)*

In April we're the gentle rains
That set the snow a-melting;
We follow the farmers down the field
To help them with the planting. *(chorus)*

In May the sun will never rise
Until we bring the day, O;
And should the wind be cold at noon
We send him on his way, O. *(chorus)*

When summer is a-coming in
And spring must needs retire,
We go beneath the earth and push
The leaves and branches higher. *(chorus)*

When David faced Goliath
We were standing there to guide him;
When Georgie killed the dragon
It was us that stood beside him. *(chorus)*

Of all the seasons of the year
The spring is always welcome;
And all the heroes ever fought
Had Billy and Jack to help them. *(chorus)*

Follow Harold round the Bend

Wilson had excellent credentials for a Labour Prime Minister. His trademarks were his pipe, his accent and his Gannex raincoat. He reigned from 1964 to 1970, then from 1974 to 1976, when he suddenly resigned, weary of politics and the state of the party. He was the Labour leader who took us into the Vietnam War (yet kept British troops out of it), who took us into the EEC with a referendum, who always seemed to be negotiating with an enemy, who manoeuvred a number of social reforms yet who never won the total allegiance of the left wing. He was somehow . . . disappointing. He was rewarded by the Queen with a peerage in 1983. One wonders what for. Lord Wilson of Rievaulx: an adroit, very clever politician who managed to leave behind him an extremely bland image.

tune: traditional Scots ("Rise and Follow Charlie")
new words and trad. arr.: Peggy Seeger
© 1992 Peggy Seeger (1)

We the ship and he the weather,
We the sheep and he our shepherd,
We the ass and he the tether,
Lead us, Harold, round the bend.

Chorus: Rally round and follow Harold,
Rally round and follow Harold,
Rally round and follow Harold,
Loyal even to the end.

Ancient ties are hard to sever,
Europe, we are yours forever;
Britain on the never-never,
Clever Harold needs a friend. *(chorus)*

Yankee pipes and Yankee drumming,
Lyndon singing, Harold humming,
Labour lemmings, are you coming?
Follow Harold to the end. *(chorus)*

Britain, land of hope and glory!
Britain, we are praying for ye!
Britain, land where even Tories
Follow Harold round the bend. *(chorus)*

In the olden days they shot 'em,
Sent them weighted to the bottom,
Dug their graves and danced upon 'em,
Harold's coming to the end. *(chorus)*

Song of Choice

With this song, I really began to feel like a songwriter. I was beginning to get original ideas and write songs from scratch. Up to now most of my songs (1) had been copies of Ewan's pieces, (2) had been set to pre-existing tunes, or (3) were based on folk forms. In "Song of Choice," the concept, the subject, the style, the tune and words were mine, all mine! Furthermore, the song could be adapted to changing situations. Just add a verse, subtract a verse and the song is once more contemporary. Ewan and I sang it and adapted it for years. It has been widely recorded in Norway and Sweden.

she bites

words and music: Peggy Seeger
disc 11, 19A, 24, 30, 31

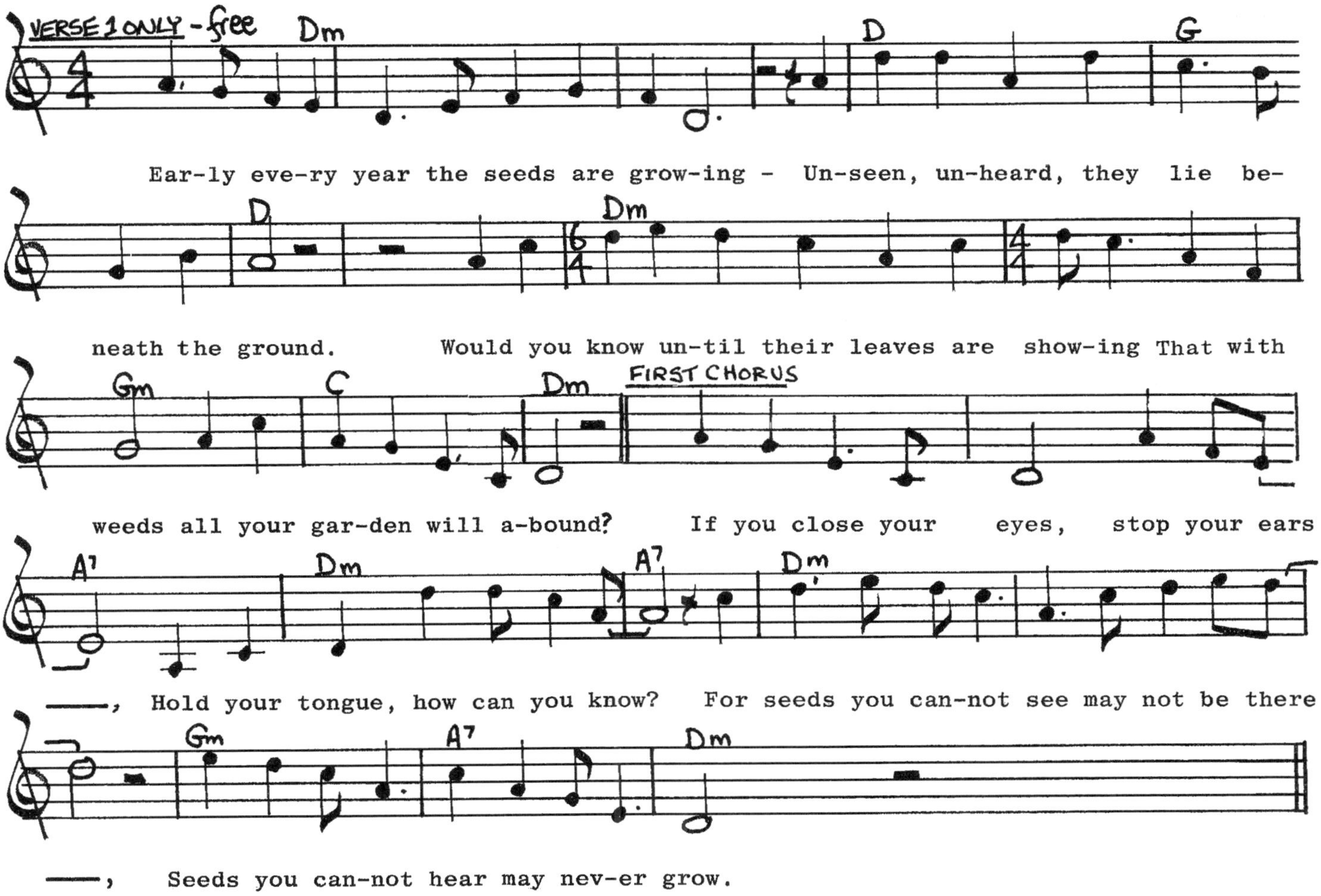
VERSE 1 ONLY - free
Dm D G
Ear-ly eve-ry year the seeds are grow-ing - Un-seen, un-heard, they lie be-
D Dm
neath the ground. Would you know un-til their leaves are show-ing That with
Gm C Dm FIRST CHORUS
weeds all your gar-den will a-bound? If you close your eyes, stop your ears
A7 Dm A7 Dm
——, Hold your tongue, how can you know? For seeds you can-not see may not be there
Gm A7 Dm
——, Seeds you can-not hear may nev-er grow.

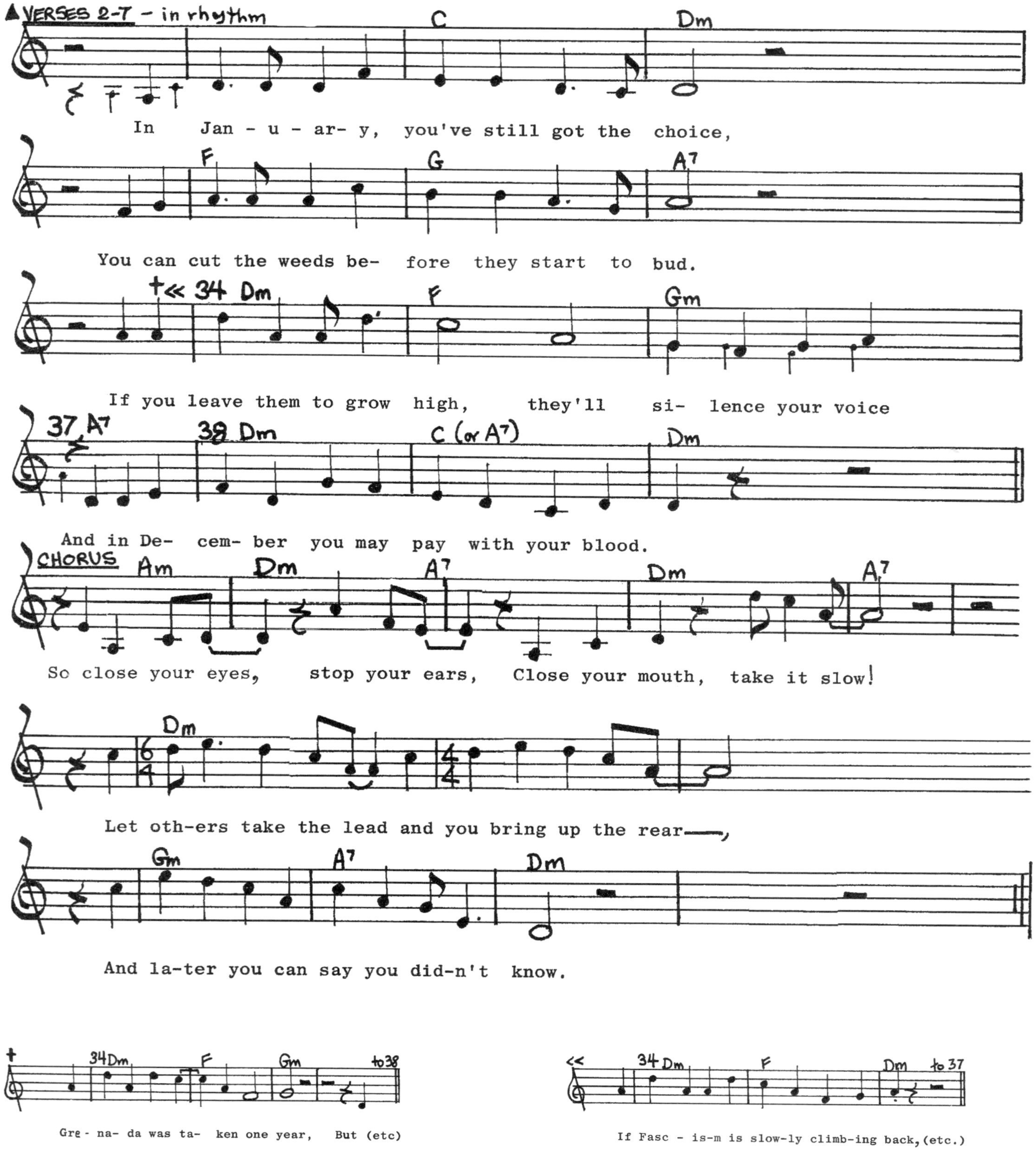

▲VERSES 2-7 – in rhythm

C Dm

In Jan - u - ar- y, you've still got the choice,

F G A7

You can cut the weeds be- fore they start to bud.

+<< 34 Dm F Gm

If you leave them to grow high, they'll si- lence your voice

37 A7 38 Dm C (or A7) Dm

And in De- cem- ber you may pay with your blood.

CHORUS

Am Dm A7 Dm A7

So close your eyes, stop your ears, Close your mouth, take it slow!

Dm

Let oth-ers take the lead and you bring up the rear——,

Gm A7 Dm

And la-ter you can say you did-n't know.

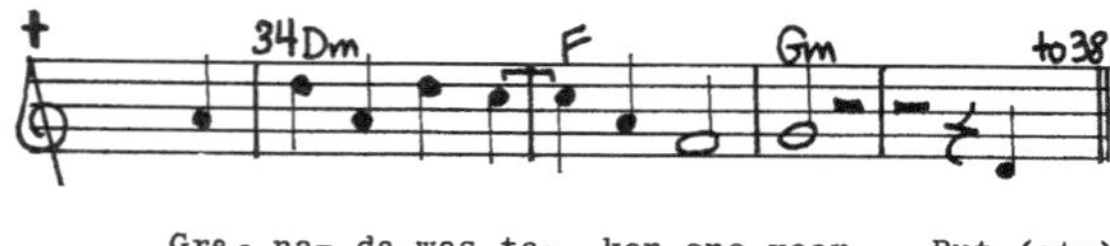
+
34Dm
F
Gm
to38
Gre - na- da was ta- ken one year, But (etc)

<<
34 Dm
F
Dm
to 37
If Fasc - is-m is slow-ly climb-ing back, (etc.)

Early every year the seeds are growing—
Unseen, unheard, they lie beneath the ground.
Would you know until their leaves are showing
That with weeds all your garden will abound?

Chorus (for verse 1 only):
If you close your eyes, stop your ears,
Hold your tongue, how can you know?
For seeds you cannot see may not be there,
Seeds you cannot hear may never grow.

Δ In January, you've still got the choice,
You can cut the weeds before they start to bud.
If you leave them to grow high, they'll silence your voice
And in December you may pay with your blood.

Chorus: So close your eyes, stop your ears,
Close your mouth, take it slow!
Let others take the lead and you bring up the rear,
And later you can say you didn't know.

Δ Every day another vulture takes flight,
There's another danger born every morning.
In the darkness of your blindness, the beast will learn to bite,
How can you fight if you can't recognise a warning? *(chorus)*

Δ Today you may earn a living wage.
Tomorrow you may be on the dole.
Though there's millions going hungry you needn't disengage,
For it's them not you that's fallen in the hole. *(chorus)*

Δ Today the soldiers took away one.
Tomorrow they may take away two.
† [Grenada] was taken one year,
But surely they will never take you. *(chorus)*

Δ It's all right for you if you run with the pack,
It's all right if you agree with all they do;
« If Fascism is slowly climbing back,
It's not here yet, so what's it got to do with you? *(chorus)*

Δ The weeds are all around us and they're growing.
It will soon be too late for the knife.
If you leave them on the wind that around the world is blowing
You may pay for your silence with your life.

Final chorus: So close your eyes, stop your ears,
Close your mouth and never dare!
And if it happens here, they'll never come for you
Because they'll know you really didn't care.

Abbey Wood Roads

Don Lange is one of my favourite songwriters. Twenty-five years ago he wrote me a long letter in which he talked about the importance of what he called *a sense of place*. He had recently moved to Solon, Iowa, and was methodically writing songs about the town, an activity which gave him a feeling of belonging. He felt that writing about the place you live in was vital to a songwriter and that it benefited the community. "Abbey Wood Roads" was written by and for a group of people who also needed that sense of belonging: the children of De Lucy School in Abbey Wood, southeast London. Now, Don Lange *chose* where he lived—the people of Abbey Wood did not. They were put there by the authorities when London needed a catchment area for its unhoused poor. Part of the ancient wood has been saved from developers, thanks to the proximity of the ruined Lesnes Abbey (after which Abbey Wood has been named). In the sixties, the huge housing estate was surrounded on three sides by sour wasteland, allotments and Ministry of Defence property. The fourth side comprised a busy thoroughfare connected to Abbey Wood by two roads, one leading in and another going out. The inhabitants had a plethora of churches but a dearth of secular amenities. I worked once a week with a class of eleven-year-olds, who felt that the estate was lacking in almost everything they wanted. They responded readily to the idea of a song about their warren of roads and houses. They roamed the streets for several days armed with notepads. I used their observations, added their desires and hopes and spiced it with their wonderful humour to make this song.

tune: traditional Irish ("Dublin Jack of All Trades")
new words and trad. arr.: Peggy Seeger
© 1992 Peggy Seeger (1)

cheerfully
D
A7
O, once I lived in London Town and that was ver- y crowd - ed,
D
A7
D
But now I live in Ab - bey Wood a - mong the coun- cil hou- ses;
(C)
C
D
A
It's clean and neat and eve- ry street has grass a- long the bor- der,
D
A7
D
A7
D
A7
D
And just in case you lose your way, I'll name the streets in or- der.

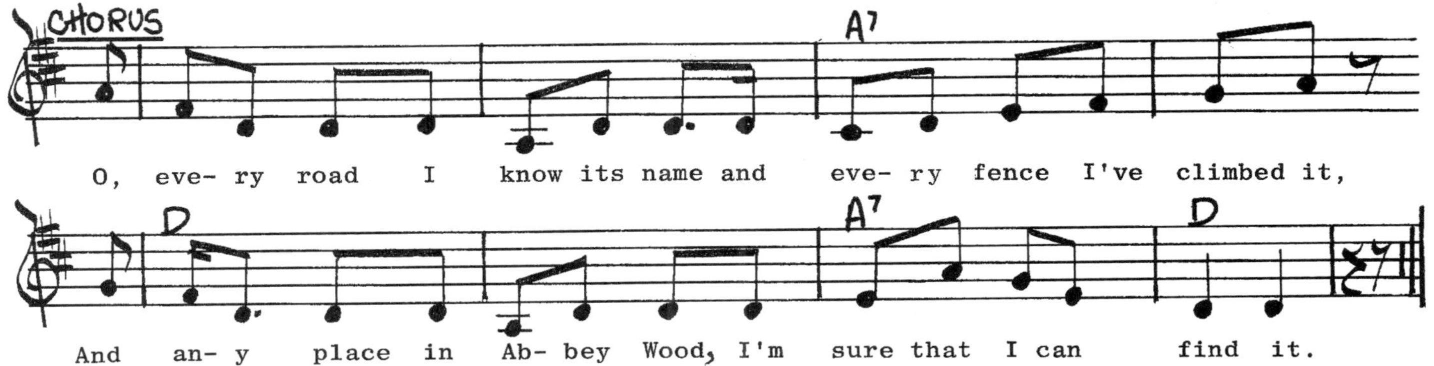

O, once I lived in London Town and that was very crowded,
But now I live in Abbey Wood among the council houses;
It's clean and neat and every street has grass along the border,
And just in case you lose your way, I'll name the streets in order.

Chorus: O, every road I know its name and every fence I've climbed it,
And any place in Abbey Wood, I'm sure that I can find it.

When you come over the railway bridge, take a right and then, sir,
Keep turning right and soon you'll find you're going out again, sir;
With only two roads leading in, I think we're safe from raiders,
Unless they're moles from underground, or Martian invaders. *(chorus)*

Mattisfont Road is on the south, there's a comprehensive school there,
By the time we're grown up we might get a chance to use the pool there.
Sewell Road is on the north, where there's a pumping station;
The smell that comes from Sewer Bank's the strongest in the nation. *(chorus)*

Church Manor Way is on the west, the allotments can be seen there,
There's War Department property (and cabbages and beans) there.
Harrow Manor's on the east, with caravans and gypsies,
And when The Pied Wagtail is open, someone's always tipsy. *(chorus)*

There's Tickford Close and Mountjoy Close with Andwell Close behind it,
There's Throwley Close and Pynham Close, but you have to look to find it.
On Rosedale Road you'll find some shops, on Cookhill Road are fences,
And if you want to rest your feet, in every road are benches. *(chorus)*

From Finchale Road to Manister Road to Devenish Road we wander,
Down Cookhill Road to Eynsham Drive to Woolwich over yonder.
The roads all lead to other roads, to other towns and places,
Where other kids in other schools have other names and faces. *(chorus)*

My name is [Mary Anderson], De Lucy is my school, sir;
I may not look so clever but I am nobody's fool, sir.
We're needing more than roads and houses for to make a nation,
Why should we go onto the streets to get our education? *(chorus)*

On Eynsham Drive a library, on Felixstowe some tennis,
On Finchale Road a rugby pitch and a good team to defend us.
On any road a youth club and a place to rendezvous, sir,
And when you've got it built for us, we'll start to build for you, sir. *(chorus)*

My Old Man's a Dustman

The *Times,* May 15, 1967: "Lord Howe, chairman of the Buckinghamshire County Education Committee, today appealed to a council dustman to return to teaching. The dustman, Mr. Martin Simonds, aged 24, father of two girls, left his art teacher's post at Watford Girls' Grammar School nine months ago to work on the dustcarts in Amersham. He said the reason was 'simply for money.'"

tune: Lonnie Donegan ("My Old Man's a Dustman")
new words: Peggy Seeger
© Tyler Music

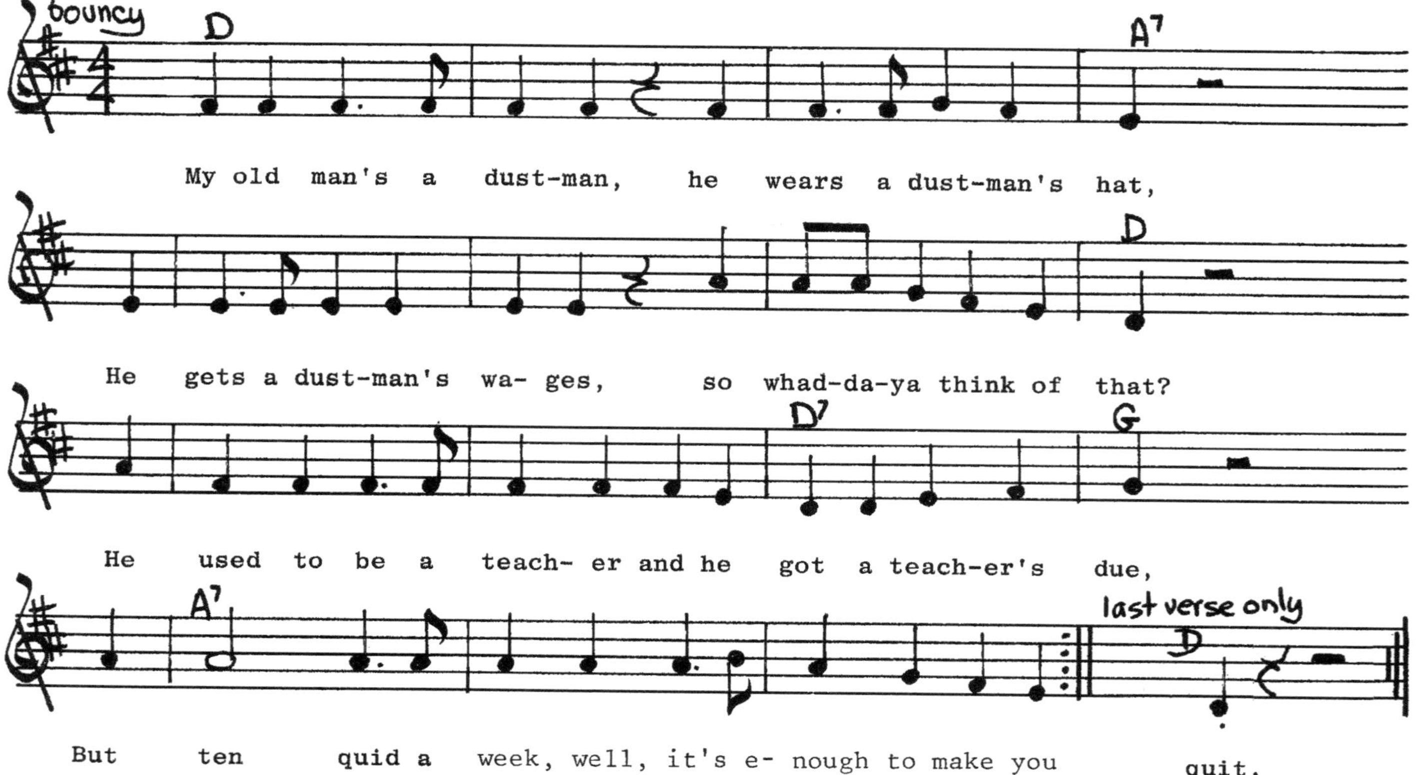
bouncy
D
A7
My old man's a dust-man, he wears a dust-man's hat,
D
He gets a dust-man's wa- ges, so whad-da-ya think of that?
D7
G
He used to be a teach- er and he got a teach-er's due,
A7
last verse only
D
But ten quid a week, well, it's e- nough to make you quit.

My old man's a dustman, he wears a dustman's hat,
He gets a dustman's wages, so whaddaya think of that?
He used to be a teacher and he got a teacher's due,
But ten quid a week, well, it's enough to make you

Stroll down to the broo, boys, and find a decent place,
Seventeen quid a week, boys, to wipe the public face.
He used to be a teacher, he used to teach 'em art,
But ten quid a week, well, it's enough to make you

Follow all the others. Go and serve the Queen.
Join the bleedin' army that keeps the city clean.
He used to be a teacher, he used to take a class,
But now he's been promoted and he wipes the public

AShes, teachers, bottles, junk—throw your rubbish in;
Here comes my old fella, carrying rubbish bins.
He used to be a teacher, but now he's seen the light,
Ten quid a week, well, it's enough to make you

SHiver in the winter, wear a patchy shirt,
Or double up your pay, boys, collecting all the dirt.
He used to be a teacher and he had the teacher's luck,
What a cheek! Ten pounds a week! He told 'em they could

FUnny how it used to be that teaching was a calling,
But now to get a living wage it's on your knees you're crawling.
He used to be a teacher, he loved his little flocks,
Well, the man who sets the wages, I hope he gets the

POpulation's rising, the kids are needing teachers,
And providing you're prepared to starve, it's got attractive features.
My old man was a teacher, he was in it heart and soul,
But ten quid a week, well, he said, "Stick it up your . . ."

WHOLEsome meals for school kids, served at every school,
And we'll bung you on the scrapheap if you don't work to rule.
He stuck it out for years and years, he really did his bit,
But he couldn't feed his family, and so he had to quit.

Music note: Go from the end of the fourth line to the first line of the following verse without a break.

Song of Myself

The interviews . . . those same questions, with the same old answers! Next time I'll sing them a *song* about myself. Apologies and thanks to Walt Whitman.

words and music: Peggy Seeger
disc 2, 19, 19A

I love those who labour, I sing of the farmers
And weavers and fishermen and miners as well;
Now all you who hear me, I pray you draw near me,
Before you grow weary I'll sing of myself.

I was brought up in plenty Δ until I was twenty,
A joy to myself as but children can be;
A joy to my father, a joy to my mother,
The pain of my country was nothing to me.

My schooldays being over, I became a rover,
To Russia and China, to France and to Spain;
I lived at my leisure, I lived but for pleasure
And so, none the wiser, to England I came.

I thought it no danger to follow a stranger,
But with time changing a friend he became;
For the joys of a lover can equal no other,
Forever anew, and yet always the same.

Good fortune attending, we don't lack a living,
Our children a treasure our joy to renew;
But to live amid plenty can only torment me
When the wealth of the country belongs to the few.

I join with the angry, I join with the hungry,
For long years of anguish the price will be paid.
To hate and to anger I am not a stranger,
I know there is danger and I am afraid.

For I fear the fate of the rebels and fighters
Who ransom the future with torture and pain.
As the trial comes near if I find I can dare it,
I'll willingly share it, no longer afraid.

For I've learned to be angry, I've learned to be lonely.
† I've learned to be many, I've learned to be one.
I've earned all my friends, even foes will commend me,
I stand with the many, I am not alone.

In the presence of fighters I find a new peace,
In the company of workers replenish myself;
Of miners and weavers, of rebels and dreamers,
When I sing of my comrades, I sing of myself.

Che Guevara

After the Cuban war for independence was won in 1958, Guevara was part of the new government. He reportedly found his work unrewarding and he strained at the leash of bureaucracy. He left and joined a small group of freedom-fighters in Bolivia. He was shot by Bolivian government agents on October 9, 1967, and buried in an unmarked grave in the jungle. In August 1997, his remains were unearthed in a secret mass grave near Vallegrande, Bolivia, from whence they were flown to Cuba. At the time of writing, a monument is being constructed in the square that bears his name in Santa Clara. His daughter Aleida said that he and his exhumed comrades "do not return vanquished—they come as heroes, always young, valiant, strong, and brave." He rests in the hearts of millions.

words and music: Peggy Seeger
disc 24, 31

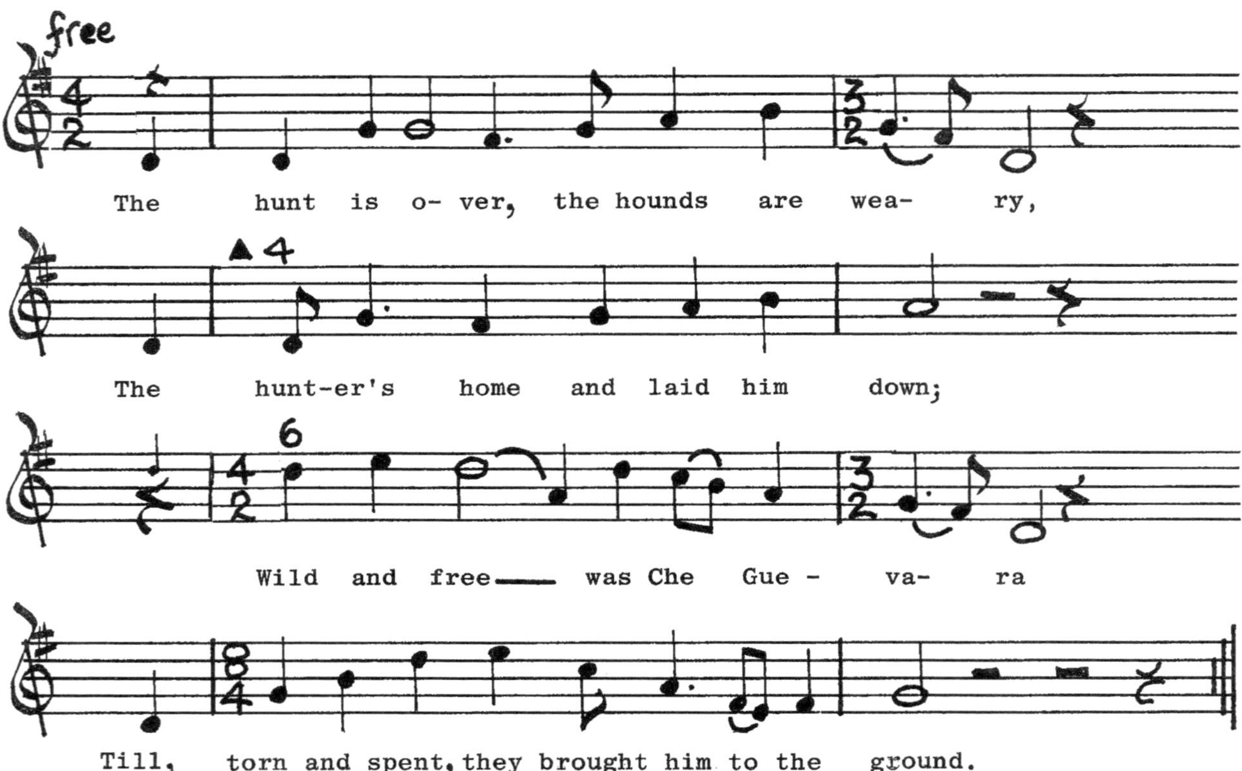
free
The hunt is o- ver, the hounds are wea- ry,
The hunt-er's home and laid him down;
Wild and free — was Che Gue - va- ra
Till, torn and spent, they brought him to the ground.

to 6
Hunt-er's moon stalks the emp-ty night;

The hunt is over, the hounds are weary,
The hunter's home and laid him down;
Wild and free was Che Guevara
Till, torn and spent, they brought him to the ground.

Stars are lost in the fields of darkness,
Δ Hunter's moon stalks the empty night;
Like a farmer walks Che Guevara,
Bearing suns to sow the world with light.

The way is dark and beset with danger,
The road may end in a prison cell;
A guiding hand is Che Guevara,
To lead us past the place at which he fell.

Brave ones show the way, and brave ones follow,
The earth bears heroes when a hero dies;
A hero's hero is Che Guevara,
Meeting death with morning in his eyes.

In jungle earth the hunters laid him,
No stone to mark a lonely grave;
Then farewell, comrade Che Guevara,
We will clear the trail that you have blazed.

Londonderry Down

This is obviously a song by an outsider (me) who knew little about Ireland, the Irish, or the Irish situation. It was written for *The Festival of Fools 1968* and did not really do justice to its subject. In October, police in Belfast routed demonstrators who were protesting about the discrimination against Catholics as regarded housing, jobs, and suffrage. The demonstration was nonsectarian—all shades of political opinion and age were represented. Although Stormont later created a government ombudsman and dealt partially with the housing and voting issues, 1968 was the year that marked the beginning of the present round of Irish "disturbances." Other countries have wars, insurrections, or revolutions. Ireland has The Troubles. For those not in the know, Orange signifies the Protestant faction, who refer to the town by its English name, Londonderry. Green refers to the Catholics who use the old name of Derry.

tune: traditional Irish ("The Jolly Tinker")
new words and trad. arr.: Peggy Seeger

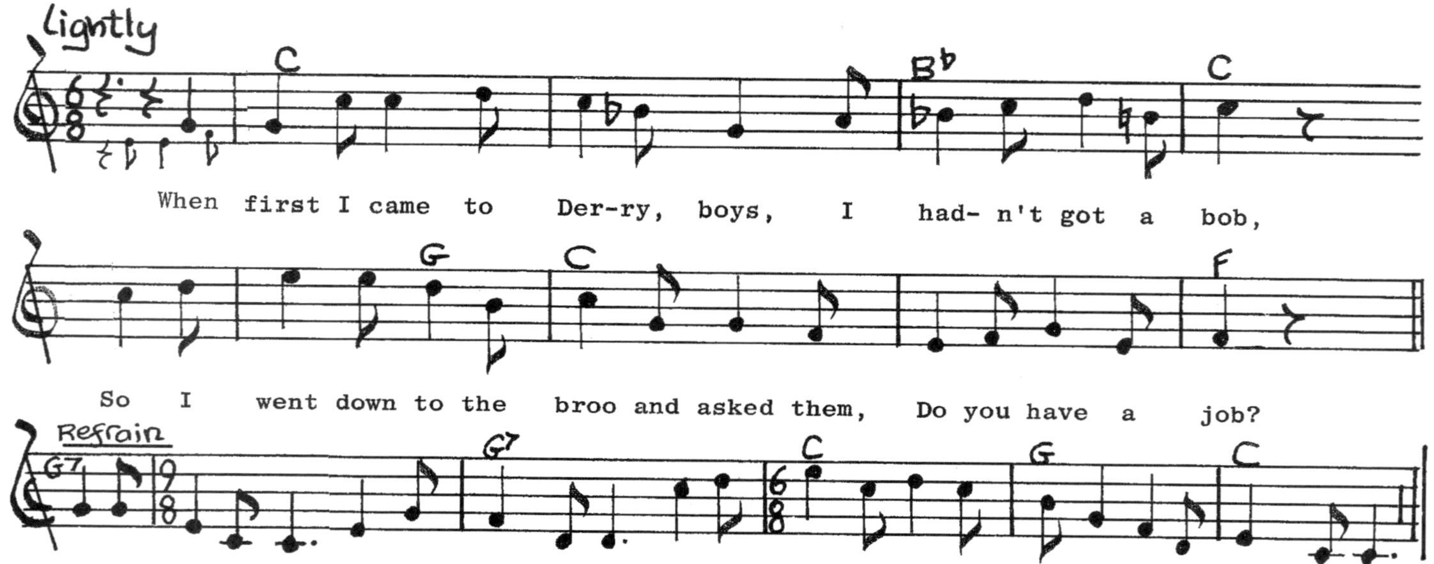

When first I came to Derry, boys, I hadn't got a bob,
So I went down to the broo and asked them, "Do you have a job?"

Refrain: O, indeed we do, don't you know we do?
With me right fa loo ra laddy, O, indeed we do.

We could put you on the rubbish carts, or else to sweep the street,
Or you *could* become a copper, for you've got the proper feet.
O, indeed you do, *(etc.)*

So when I got a job, I crossed meself, not thinking I was seen,
The gaffer roared and called me back. "Paddy, are you Green?"
    O, indeed I am, *(etc.)*

He says, "The Orange may be last to come, but Green's the first to go,
Go cross yourself with all your friends who're living on the dole."
    O, indeed they are, *(etc.)*

So I went into the street, me boys, me eyes were seeing red;
It was time for me to find a place where I could lay me head,
    O, indeed it was, *(etc.)*

But everywhere I went, me boys, and everywhere I tried,
Every bloody landlord spots the emerald in me eye,
    O, indeed he does, *(etc.)*

So I got me memory working, now, somewhere I have a cousin:
I tracked him to his lodgings—he was living there with a dozen.
    O, indeed he was, *(etc.)*

I expounded me predicament, they said that I could stay,
Providing I would not dissent upon the voting day.
    O, indeed I won't, *(etc.)*

"There's not a man can vote, but one that owns or rents a house,
"So most of us that's wearing the Green is quiet as a mouse."
    O, indeed we are, *(etc.)*

We've got a single vote between us, and as sure as I'm alive,
Our landlord is a single man, and he's got four or five.
    O, indeed he does, *(etc.)*

So on the tenth day of October, boys, I walked out in the rain,
I marched into the Diamond, boys, me purpose to complain.
    O, indeed I did, *(etc.)*

Three rows of gentlemen greets us, all dressed up in navy blue,
They treated us politely, like O'Neill told them to do.
    O, indeed they did, *(etc.)*

They put the boot into me groin and got me on the ground;
They dragged me to the wagon shouting, "Down, Derry, down!"
    O, indeed they did, *(etc.)*

Now, I may not have the vote, me boys, but I have got me voice,
And I'll march again to Duke Street—when I'm free to make the choice.
    O, indeed I will, *(etc.)*

It's All Happening Now

Effects: *(Church bells, shouts of "Happy New Year" and the sounds of celebration)*

Voice 1: New? *New?* What's new about it?

Voice 2: The blackest month of all the year
Is the month of Janiveer.

*** *(Lights up on Stage 1. Terry Yarnell with guitar.)*

Thus began the main body of *The Festival of Fools 1968*. Terry launched directly into this song to introduce the year's news. After a few verses the lights would fade on Stage 1 and go up on Stage 3 at the other end of the hall where I was sitting. I sang a verse of "The Children." Lights down on me and up on Terry for a few more verses, then back to me again until both songs were sung.

words and music: Peggy Seeger

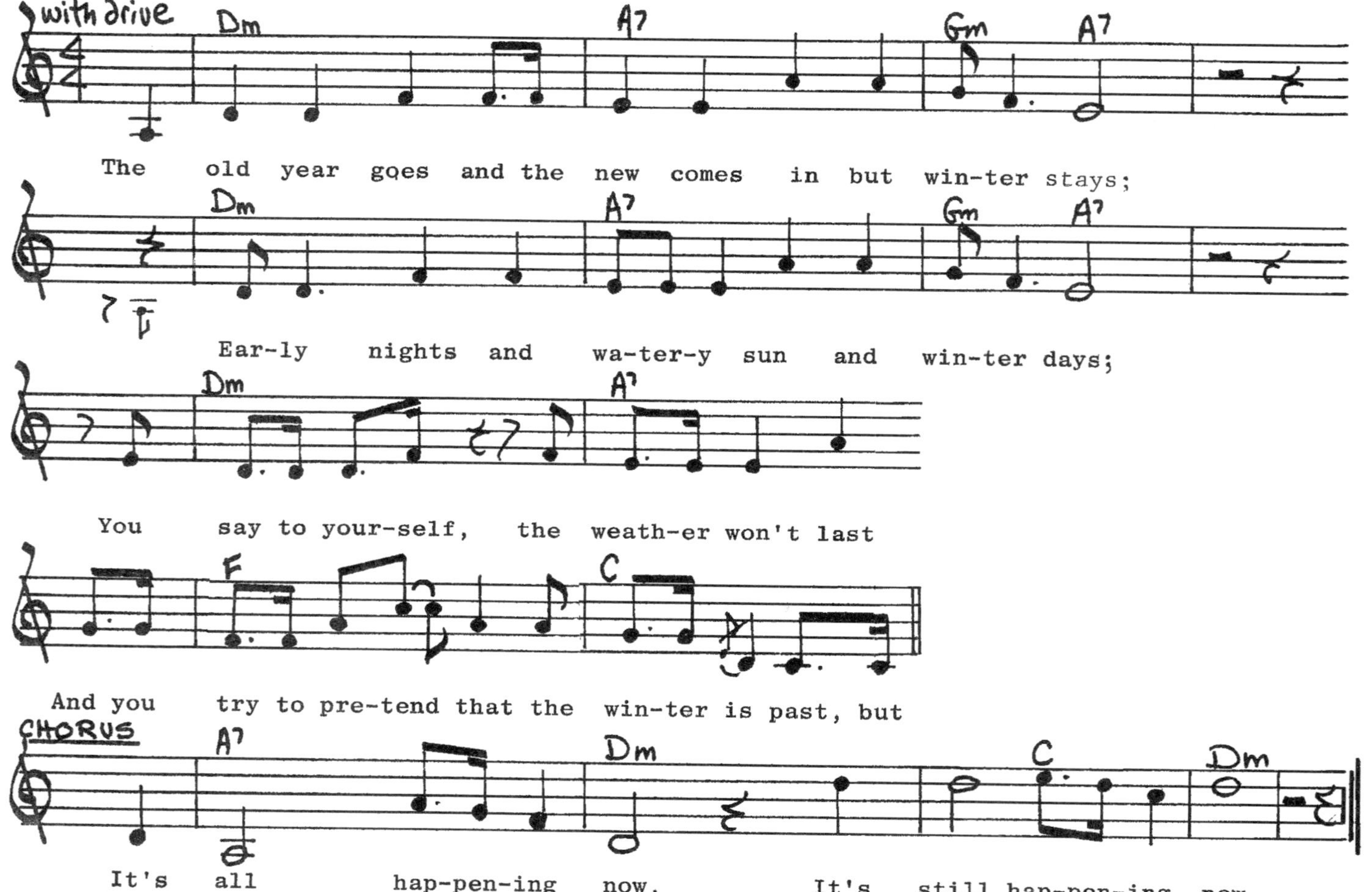
with drive
Dm A7 Gm A7
The old year goes and the new comes in but win-ter stays;
Dm A7 Gm A7
Ear-ly nights and wa-ter-y sun and win-ter days;
Dm A7
You say to your-self, the weath-er won't last
F C
And you try to pre-tend that the win-ter is past, but
CHORUS
A7 Dm C Dm
It's all hap-pen-ing now, It's still hap-pen-ing now.

The old year goes and the new comes in but winter stays;
Early nights and watery sun and winter days;
You say to yourself, "the weather won't last"
And you try to pretend that the winter is past, but

Chorus: It's all happening now,
It's still happening now.

There's a headline today, bold and black for all to see.
Tomorrow's news'll have it removed to page two or three;
Kicked hither and yon like an old football,
When the news gets old, you never see it at all, but *(chorus)*

In February of '65, the marines went in.
They had the tanks and the troops and the gas and the bombs and napalm sent in.
Three years later, do you find you can
Still get mad about Vietnam? But *(chorus)*

In Greece, the colonels are holding fast and they won't let go.
Rhodesia hangs black civilians, who says No?
South Africa, Malaysia, America, Spain,
It'll keep on going till we break the chain, for *(chorus)*

If you're backing Britain, you're backing Castle and the P.I.B.,
Porton Down, the Powell line, the C.I.D.
And if you can't get a job and you can't get a flat,
January First just won't change that, for *(chorus)*

There's flood and drought, heat and cold, calamity,
Infirmity, age, plague and death, eternally;
But of all the ills since time began,
The most and the worst are made by man, and they're *(chorus)*

There's interest, profit and rent: the Holy Trinity;
Recession, inflation, unemployment and monopoly.
The coupon-clippers and the revenue,
They're still running rings around me and you, for *(chorus)*

No use waiting and hoping when you know that the system stinks.
No use complaining and whispering the things you really think.
They've *got* to lose, we've *got* to win,
It'll just take longer if you don't join in, 'cause *(chorus)*

The Children

Unless our global lifestyle changes utterly, this song will always be contemporary.

words and music: Peggy Seeger
disc 19

The children are born, they bud and they bloom,
Four in a bed, eight in a room,
A tapestry woven on poverty's loom.
So build a wall where the children play
Till the welfare comes to take them away.

The children sit in the dust and stare,
Too hungry to move, too hungry to care;
Only their eyes beg us to share.
So build a wall and on it carve:
Behind this wall the children starve.

The children cry and crouch in the mud,
Pain in the belly and fear in the blood,
Fear is a torrent, but hate is a flood.
So build a wall when the bombers fly—
You needn't watch the children die.

Music note: Guitarists . . . try tuning your bottom string down to D. Play the song in A minor position. Slide the A chord up for the B♭ and the C, still using the open fifth string as a drone. Then wait to play the low D string until line 4, when the Dm chord first appears.

The Dead Men

September 4, 1968, the *Morning Star:* "Both Tory and Labour MPs, in defiance of their party leaders, yesterday made passionate appeals in the House of Commons that the government should immediately stop supplying arms to the Nigerian Federal Government [which at the time was in the process of trying to control Biafra, the stronghold of the Ibo people and, incidentally, the center of the country's oil production]." Commenting on the £300,000,000 investments in Nigeria, Mr. George Thompson, the Commonwealth Secretary, said . . . "You cannot do business in a cemetery."

tune: traditional Scots ("Little Sir Hugh")
new words and trad. arr.: Peggy Seeger
disc 24
© 1992 Peggy Seeger (1)

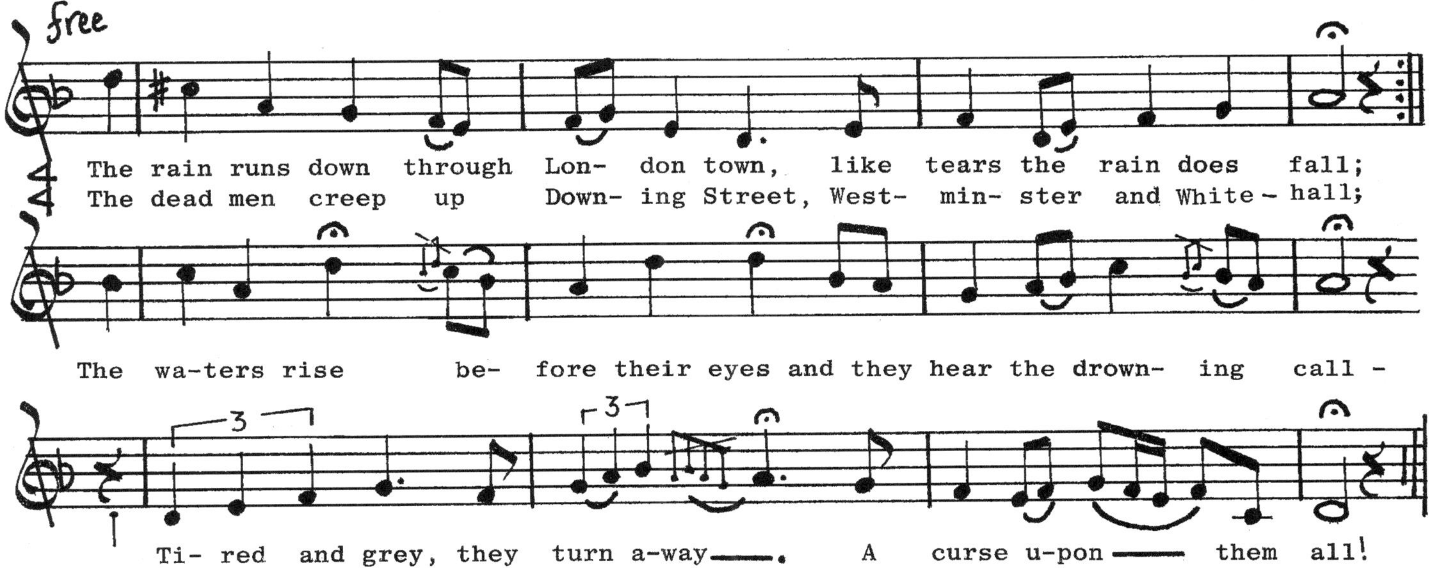

The rain runs down through London town, like tears the rain does fall;
The dead men creep up Downing Street, Westminster and Whitehall;
The waters rise before their eyes and they hear the drowning call—
Tired and grey, they turn away. A curse upon them all!

The dead men rise and open their eyes, ready to buy and sell,
To turn the wheels of English Steel, Vickers, Rolls-Royce and Shell.
They live and die for I.C.I. and from safe behind their wall,
They buy and they sell a vision of hell. A curse upon them all!

The dead men range the Stock Exchange, where every game is fair;
A throw of dice and the market price dividing the world in shares;
Row on row of carrion crows, they perch upon London Wall—
They flourish and thrive on flesh that's alive. A curse upon them all!

And you who stand and create with your hands the poison, the bomb, the gun,
Who drop your bob in the Oxfam box, after the killing's done;
Who draw your pay, then turn away from the ones up against the wall—
Go to your bed, and sleep like the dead. A curse upon you all!

The tears run down through London town, like rain the tears do fall;
The dead men stand with blood on their hands, the blood is upon us all;
[Biafra] dies before our eyes, and we weave her shroud and pall—
Write on her tomb: *We are your doom.* A curse upon us all!

Music note: The arms trade being what it is, this song is very contemporary. It sings like a clarion call when pitched fairly high in the singer's range.

Hello Friend

We were giving a week-long songwriting seminar in Birmingham. It rained the whole week and a cold front swept in. O.K., but it was July. At bus-stops and on church steps were bouquets of the bright, fluttering colours worn by Pakistanis, Indians, West Indians, and Africans, out in force to celebrate if not the Sabbath at least the day of no-work. The light fabrics were no match for an English summer day and many dark faces looked pinched and ashen with the cold. Enoch Powell (MP for Wolverhampton at the time) had just fired his first "rivers of blood" salvo across the bows of a multiracial Britain, advocating mass repatriation as the only way to salvage our traditional way of life. No matter that many stores were now stocked with an endless variety of new foods, textiles, and crafts that had arrived with the immigrants. No matter that these darker people filled menial jobs that lighter people were now able to forsake (much as men feel *above* a job category when women begin to habitually fill it). No matter that a number of incomer-nationalities were *not* targeted (North Americans, Canadians, Australians, New Zealanders, and Europeans). Ewan took the morning workshop while I wrote this song.

words and music: Peggy Seeger
disc 23

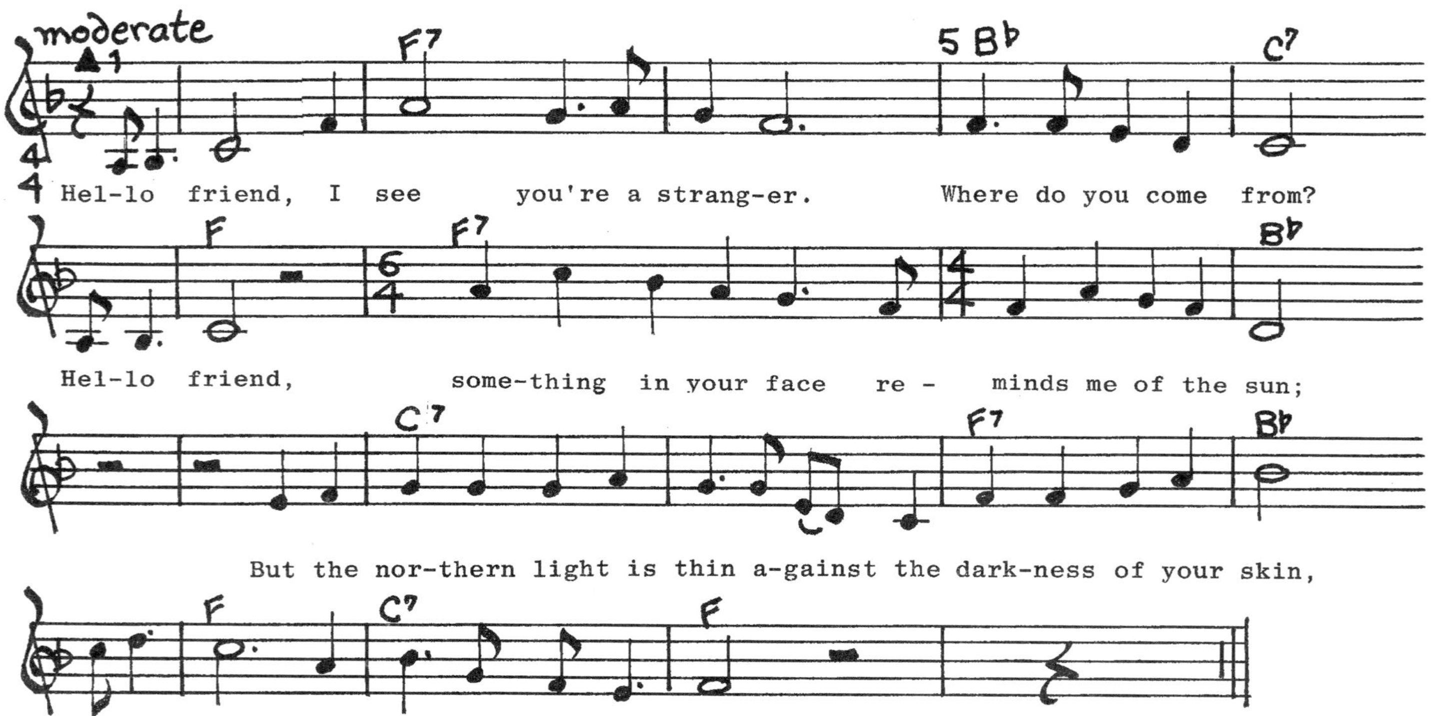
moderate
▲1
F7
5 B♭
C7
Hel-lo friend, I see you're a strang-er. Where do you come from?
F
F7
B♭
Hel-lo friend, some-thing in your face re - minds me of the sun;
C7
F7
B♭
But the nor-thern light is thin a-gainst the dark-ness of your skin,
F
C7
F
Hel-lo friend, I'm glad that you could come.

▲1
F
F7
to 5
I think I know what made you come here but what (etc.)

Hello friend, I see you're a stranger. Where do you come from?
Hello friend, something in your face reminds me of the sun;
But the northern light is thin against the darkness of your skin,
Hello friend, I'm glad that you could come.

When you talk, I hear the echo of the places you have been;
When you walk, colours all around you fluttering in the wind;
When I listen to your song, I feel you really do belong;
Am I the stranger, the one who's just come in?

Δ I think I know what made you come here but what made you want to stay?
Will you go if the weather and the welcome seem too cold and grey?
Do you feel you'll never find all the warmth you left behind?
Never mind—I hope you want to stay.

Did you find new friends to help you? Can you earn a living here?
Do you mind the smoke and grime around you and the warning loud and clear?
Or did your troubles just begin with the colour of your skin?
Never mind—I'm glad to see you here.

Did you come to climb a mountain and end up in a hole?
Have you won the right to join our people signing on the dole?
Can you be happy here amid suspicion and the fear,
Or will you run, and never more return?

Hello friend, all of us are strangers in this green and pleasant land.
Once again battle ranks are forming and we need a friendly hand.
Yours the fear and ours the shame, but our goal is just the same,
In the end this will be *our* native land.

Music note: I borrowed melodic ideas from this song to make "Old Friend."

Dustmen's Strike 1969

The "dirty jobs" strike began in Hackney on the 23rd of September and spread all over London. It involved 17,400 workers and the loss of 150,000 working days. Scab workers were employed to try to stem the tide of trash but they were amateurs. Rubbish piled up so quickly and the cost was so high that the government gave in after two months, its pay freeze policy broken. I wanted the song to be used, and used it was. We photocopied it and took it around to the strike meetings. As the strikers already knew the tune (and who *doesn't* know this tune?) they really enjoyed roaring along on the chorus and banging the dustbin lids. We turned the song into a broadsheet embellished with cartoons and jokes. These became . . . collectors' items.

tune: traditional British ("The Old Orange Flute")
new words and trad. arr.: Peggy Seeger
© 1992 Peggy Seeger (1)

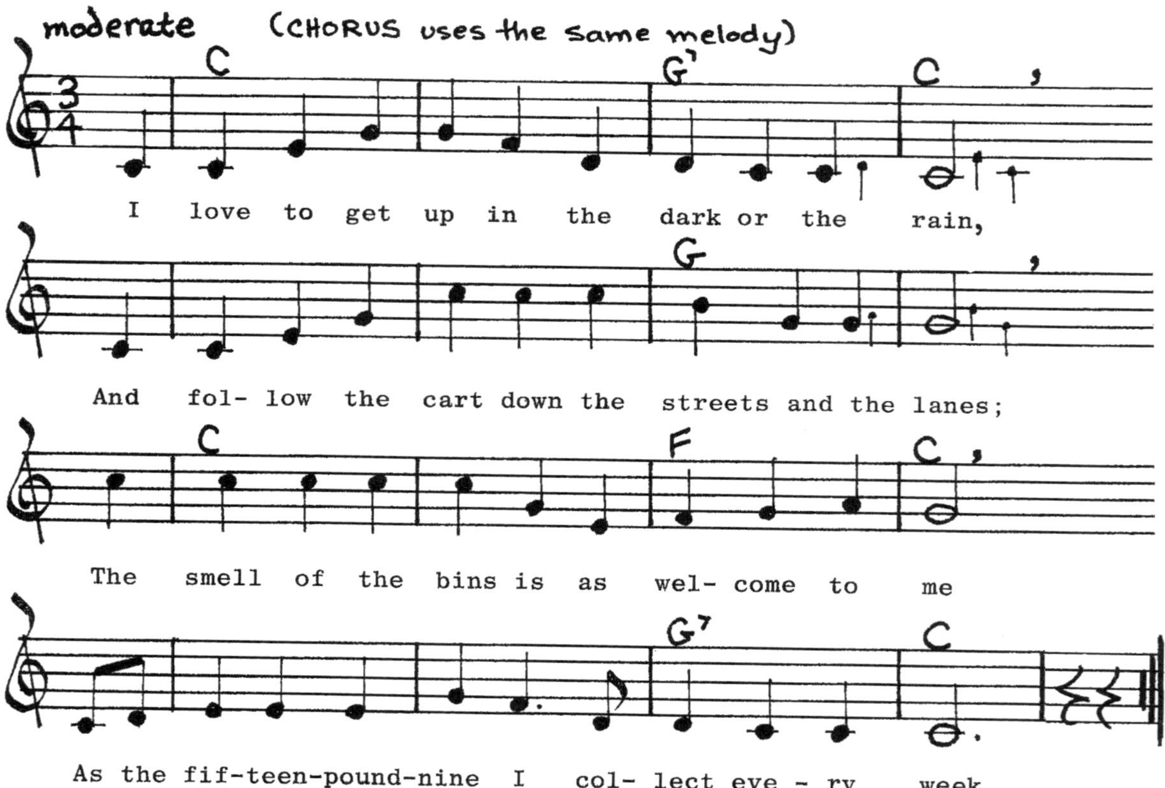

I love to get up in the dark or the rain,
And follow the cart down the streets and the lanes;
The smell of the bins is as welcome to me
As the fifteen-pound-nine* I collect every week.

Chorus: Roadsweepers, park-keepers, gravediggers and all,
Let's clear out the rubbish piled up in Whitehall;
Like Wilson and Castle and other antiques,
And the fifteen-pound-nine I collect every week.

Deductions, deductions, that's all I can see,
And when they are finished, I've thirteen-pounds-three;
That just about covers the grub and the rent—
So I'm only striking to show I'm content. *(chorus)*

Five quid a week you can add to my wages,
I ain't had an increase for ages and ages;
The toppers and coppers (who've had theirs) can yell,
But I'm going home till I get mine as well. *(chorus)*

The hotels and factories are hiring contractors
To take the leftovers of their manufactures;
The housewives are burning their rubbish forbye
(And sending smoke signals to us on the sly). *(chorus)*

So pile up your rubbish, just pile it up high,
So Whitehall can see that if they don't comply,
Instead of CONtractors, without any doubt,
They'll be needing EXtractors to winkle them out. *(chorus)*

For a couple of weeks now, I'll do as I like.
It won't be much longer till we win the strike.
Our motto is simple, it's just *C.O.D.*—
We'll *C*ollect—*O*n *D*elivery of twenty-a-week. *(chorus)*

**England's old currency: fifteen pounds and nine shillings.*

My Son

We were on our way to France—it was our first journey across the Channel by Hovercraft. Our vessel seemed to hover about two feet from the top of the water, so it didn't feel like water-travel . . . but when it hit the crests of the waves it didn't feel like air-travel either. It was rather like something in the Ray Bradbury sci-fi that I had just finished and that Neill (age eleven) was halfway through. At his age I, too, had been quiet and much given to reading and daydreaming. He was sitting next to me. The book lay opened in his lap, but his face was turned away, his forehead resting against the windowpane. These were exciting days: men had just landed on the moon . . . we were riding for the first time in a revolutionary form of transport . . . Bradbury had written about things like these.

It was one of those English days when you know the sun is up there, you just can't see it. The spume kicked up by the Hovercraft both hindered vision and turned the opalescent sky into something almost extraterrestrial. How wonderful, I thought, to be on the brink of adulthood with all this now and all that's to come! I was optimistic in those days about what was to come . . . I wondered what deep thoughts Neill was thinking. I won't ask. *I* wouldn't want to be asked if I were him. I held out for several minutes before I said softly, "Neill, what are you thinking?" He was asleep.

words and music: Peggy Seeger
disc 10, 19A, 24

free

When first I saw you, your life had just be- gun;
I was bound to love you, my ver- y soul was won.
But now the bonds are chang-ing, your child-hood's near-ly gone;
Soon you will go, my son.

When first I saw you, your life had just begun;
I was bound to love you, my very soul was won.
But now the bonds are changing, your childhood's nearly gone;
Soon you will go, my son.

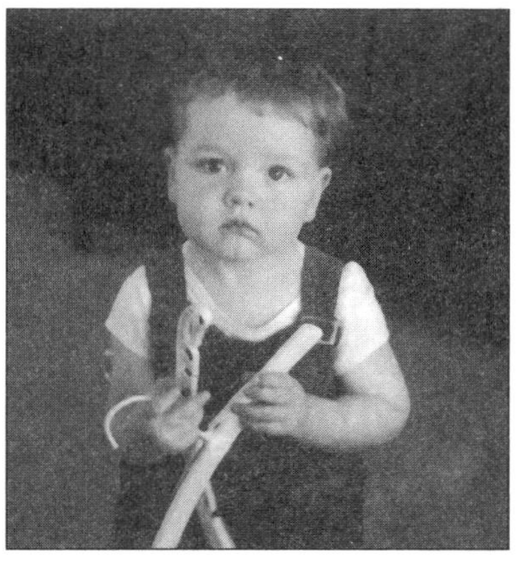

I fed your hunger, I suffered all your pain;
When you smiled, I'd answer. That made you smile again.
Are we becoming strangers, that once did breathe as one?
Who are you now, my son?

You wake in the morning, but you're dreaming all the day,
At school you sit and gaze at things so far away.
Where older hopes are fading, yours have just begun;
What do you dream, my son?

I've seen you watching, amazement in your eyes,
This world we've left you, a junkheap in disguise—
When you watch us, unbelieving, we older, wiser ones,
What do you see, my son?

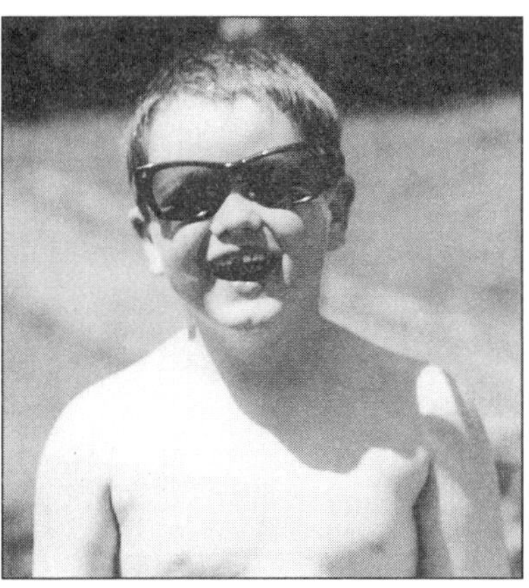

You ask a question: you wait for my reply,
But the world's so changed, sometimes you know as much as I;
In the new world that is coming, the old must ask the young;
Then where will you turn, my son?

You'll reach for loving, you'll learn that parents die;
You'll go on dreaming, once again you'll learn to cry.
And when you've joined our battle, when you've learned right from wrong,
Then you must go, my son.

Music note: The tune is based on a Northumbrian bagpipe air, "Lord Derwentwater's Farewell."

We Are the Young Ones

L-plates signify a learner driver in Britain. In 1968, some L-plate drivers got into the driving seat. It began in March in Paris. It spread rapidly to the Netherlands and Germany, where the student leader Rudi Dutschke was shot and wounded. It reached England by May and carried on in less violent forms for several years. In the early 1970s, we were singing at a student rally in a northern university (Lancaster? Leeds?). This song really appealed to them and they had to hear it over and over till they learned it. Soon it was time for the hall to close but the students wouldn't go back to barracks. The police were called. A dozen of the country's finest entered the hall and were immediately surrounded, much as a virus under the microscope is surrounded by antibodies in the blood. The students cheerfully promised to go home peacefully if the officers of the law would learn the chorus. By virtue of necessity, the officers learned it—kind of. The students then dispersed, still singing.

alternative title: "The Young Ones"
words and music: Peggy Seeger
disc 24

You sat us down in a schoolroom and gave us *John and Jane;*
For you we drew little houses with a garden and a lane;
We fought the Battle of Hastings, the invasion of the Gauls,
While outside our streets were crumbling and the rats ran through our halls.

Chorus: We are the young ones,
The learners, the readers, the writers,
The copiers, the reciters;
We are the L-plate subjects,
We are the young and small—
But we are the writing on your wall.

While we were adding two and two, you were counting pounds;
While we were learning chemistry, you were making bombs;
While we were learning medicine, you were digging graves—
And now you have the nerve to tell us how we should behave, but *(chorus)*

Thou shalt not rape thy neighbour's wife, seduce her if you can.
Thou shalt not steal his oxen, just defoliate his land.
Thou shalt not kill him face-to-face but bomb him from above—
But we won't let you take in vain the name of human love, for *(chorus)*

We're old enough to see that your world is wearing thin;
We're young enough to tear it down and build it up again;
We're bold enough to question, we're brave enough to fight;
We're strong enough to challenge you for what we know is right. *(chorus)*

We don't believe in profits. We don't believe in shares.
We don't believe in magic. We don't believe in prayers.
Turn around and face us! The future has begun—
From you we learned that power grows from the barrel of a gun. *(chorus)*

Music note: Compare this tune with that of "Women's Union."

Uncle Sam

The cost of the Vietnam War worked out to be about $3,000,000 an hour. If ever the United States gets a peace-loving, humanitarian government, the public purse will be full to bursting . . . and songwriters like me will have lost (as we did when Thatcher fell) a wonderful target.

tune: traditional U.S.A. ("Brown's Ferry Blues")
new words and trad. arr.: Peggy Seeger
disc 24

fast & busy ~ use same tune for verses
CHORUS
C7
F7
Un-cle Sam done changed his sta-tus, Im-pli-cate and de- pre- ci- ate us,
C
G7
Eve- ry where he goes there's a-noth-er war;
C7
F7
Sug-ar Dad- dy and Big Broth-er, With a dol-lar bill for a fath-er and moth-er,
C
F7
G7
C
Un-cle Sam just ain't no un-cle an- y more.

Chorus: Uncle Sam done changed his status,
Implicate and depreciate us,
Everywhere he goes there's another war;
Sugar Daddy and Big Brother,
With a dollar bill for a father and mother,
Uncle Sam just ain't no uncle any more.

Way back there in the Constitution
It says that the right of the revolution's
The right of the one who thinks that things are wrong.
That's the founding fathers' absolution
Of all the folks like Huey Newton,
Wonder why in the lovely world it took so long?

Chorus: Uncle Sam done changed his status,
Collaborate, circumstantiate us,
Everywhere he goes *(etc.)*

Uncle Sam's got ugly faces,
Pokin' 'em around in the strangest places,
But even in Alabama he's refined.
With the tear-gas bombs and the napalm jelly,
With a big red neck and a wobblin' belly,
Uncle Sam's got freedom-fightin' on his mind.

Chorus: Uncle Sam done changed his status,
Infiltrate and judiciate us, *(etc.)*

Uncle Sam's got lots of foes—
Santa Claus has a big red nose,
So one of his reindeer's in the C.I.A.;
But shootin' sittin' ducks is fun,
It's easier to aim if the duck don't run,
So only the ones who fight get a chance to get away.

Chorus: Uncle Sam done changed his status,
Speculate and appropriate us, *(etc.)*

Uncle Sam's got a wanted list
Of all the little places that Hitler missed,
He'll invade the Isle of Wight now one of these days.
At the top of the list is Chairman Mao
(He's dyin' to get him but he don't know how)
And even little Vietnam's gettin' away.

Chorus: Uncle Sam done changed his status,
Eliminate and annihilate us, *(etc.)*

To tell you the truth, it seems to me
Sam's lost touch with the family
And the U.S.A.'s kinda drifting over the sea.
If this continues I'm afraid
He'll have to send America foreign aid
And even at that he's bound to send it C.O.D.

Chorus: Everybody's changing status,
Liberate and beginning to hate us,
Everywhere we go there's another war;
But there's this one thing about Big Brother,
He can only beat us if we fight each other,
Uncle Sam just ain't my uncle any more.

Nightshift

Sheila Douglas, the Scots singer and songwriter, got the idea for this song and extended it beautifully in her "Too Much of a Good Thing." Although I sing in Scots in the shower, when I'm ironing or during long car journeys (to everyone's distress but mine), on stage I avoid songs in languages I don't speak fluently. So I put Sheila's song into English. The days-of-the-week song format is a common one both in folk and topical songmaking. Sheila's idea of juxtaposing the decreasing time element (in itself a lovely double meaning) with the progression of the weekdays is brilliant.

words and music: Peggy Seeger
disc 19

Lightly
F
C
Dm
On Mon-day night he came to my door and he made such a din:
F
Bb
F
Get up, get up, you dar- ling girl, and let your lov- er in!
Bb
F
Bb
C7
Well, I got up and I let him in and on me he did fall,
F
C7
F
It was five o'clock in the morn-ing be- fore I got an-y sleep at all!

On Monday night he came to my door and he made such a din:
"Get up, get up, you darling girl, and let your lover in!"
Well, I got up and I let him in and on me he did fall,
It was five o'clock in the morning before I got any sleep at all!

On Tuesday night he came to my door, the joys of love to tend:
"Get up, get up, you darling girl, before I go round the bend."
Well I got up and I let him in and in my arms he lay,
But he had to hear the stroke of four before he'd go away.

On Wednesday night he came to my door, a little bit late in time:
"I'd have been here sooner, you darling girl, but the hill was too hard to climb."
He wasn't long all in my arms before he let me be,
Then out of the house and down the road, but after the stroke of three.

On Thursday night he came to my door, so weary and so slow:
"Come, give me a drink, you darling girl, and then to work we go."
All night long he fought with it and I had to help him through,
And I heard him sigh as he rose to go: "It's only after two!"

On Friday night he came to my door, a-shaking in every limb:
"Get up, get up, you darling girl, and carry your lover in."
Well, I got up and I carried him in and I gently laid him down,
But barely could his spirit rise to reach the stroke of one.

On Saturday night he came to my door, he came on his hands and knees:
"O, don't get up, you darling girl, stay in and let me be!"
Well, I got up for to let him in and he fell down in a swoon,
And for all I tried to raise him up, he lay till Sunday noon.

Wasteland Lullabye

In 1962, Rachel Carson (*Silent Spring*) was a voice in the wilderness. People who talked about the end of the world were dismissed as lunatics or religious fanatics. Nowadays, terms like *deforestation, the environment,* and *ecology* are common even in the mouths of people who only pay them lip service. Most of the bookies in the country would probably give high odds on Britain's contribution to the end of the world, as our government is at present blocking practically every move to postpone Judgment Day (such as refusing to officially recycle waste, deregulating all sorts of industrial practices and products, denying the true severity of acid rain, maintaining high limits for acceptable radiation doses, hindering the control of CFCs, and so on). Now maybe if the government and the bookies got together . . .

words and music: Peggy Seeger
disc 24

Curl yourself up in your bed,
They've turned on the night-time below—
I'll tell you a wonderful tale:
The story of long ago.

The moon was the lamp of the night,
The sun was the light of the day—
Farmers went out on the land,
And children went out to play.

The green and the purple and gold,
The mist and the snow and the rain—
There was summer and winter and spring
That never will come again.

The oceans and rivers were full,
The forests were heavy with green—
There's a flower they called a red rose
That no one has ever seen.

Creatures crept out in the dark
In meadow and mountain and fen—
My grandmother once heard a lark,
It will never be heard again.

The earth was a present to those
Who used it and threw it away—
But tomorrow the air may be clear
And you can go up to play.

N is for Nobody

Richard Nixon, alias Tricky Dick, lost two presidential elections but finally made it in 1968. He won again in 1972 and resigned in 1974 rather than face impeachment proceedings (see "Watergate"). He was the first of our unbelievable presidents. You couldn't believe he'd be nominated. When he *was* nominated you couldn't believe he would ever be elected and after the election you couldn't believe he'd *won*. It's become a habit now. We went on to elect Reagan and Bush.

tune: traditional English ("The Sailor's Alphabet")
new words and trad. arr.: Peggy Seeger

N is for Nobody (Dick's his first name),
I is his Image (inept and inane);
X marks the spot where he buried his past
O-N for Old Nixon, he's made it at last!

Cheerily, wearily, so nearly came he,
Two times a failure (it should have been three).
Heave away, haul away, sweetly he sings
As he comes to Old England to pull all our strings.

Music note: I'm not including the tune for this song as it has the same format and melody as "The Housewife's Alphabet."

Darling Annie

A love song, written in fifteen minutes while sitting in the car on a rainy, cold morning by Loch Lomond in the Scottish highlands. In the afternoon I wrote "Jimmy Gray."

words and music: Peggy Seeger
disc 2, 19, 26A
© 1992 Peggy Seeger (1)

moderate
E B7 E B7
If you'll mar - ry me, I'll give you eve- ry-thing I have,
E7 A
You won't ev - er need to earn a pen-ny;
10 E B7 E B7
I will be your man, and the ring up -on your hand
13 A E B7 E
Will tell the world that you're my dar-ling An-nie —.
10 E B7 E A B7 to 13
We'll al - ways be free, me for you and you for me -

HE: If you'll marry me, I'll give you everything I have,
You won't ever need to earn a penny;
I will be your man, and the ring upon your hand
Will tell the world that you're my darling Annie.

SHE: Thank you love, I'll be glad to add your wages on to mine,
I can work and keep myself so handy;
You can be my man without a golden wedding-band,
And I'll tell the world that I'm your Annie.

Chorus (after each of her verses):
For it's love, love will hold us, love is everything,
Who could dream of anything that's better?
Not the vow, not the string, not the golden wedding-ring,
Just you, love, you and me together.

HE: If you'll marry me, I will give to you my name,
It will shield you from idle talk and envy;
For when you play the game you're secure from any blame,
Not ashamed to be my darling Annie.

SHE: Thank you love, I'm grateful for the offer of your name,
But my own will serve as well as any;
I don't like the game and the rules would make me tame,
Not the same girl you married, not your Annie. *(chorus)*

HE: If you'll marry me, we'll get a house and settle down,
A place to call our own, so neat and canny;
With a family and a home, love, you'll never feel alone,
Left on the shelf, a spinster, darling Annie.

SHE: Dearest love, we could surely find a place to call our own,
All we need is influence and money.
But I don't need a ring, or a house or anything
To become a mother or a granny. *(chorus)*

HE: If you'll marry me, I will be faithful unto death,
You will have all my love and my attention;
We will care, we will share life in sickness and in health—
And when I die you can draw the widow's pension.

SHE: I will live with you, and I'll be faithful unto death,
We will share all the burdens we must carry;
Δ We'll always be free, me for you and you for me—
But when we're old, love, maybe we should marry! *(chorus)*

Jimmy Gray

I occasionally write songs in twos, one right after the other. "Jimmy Gray" was written on the heels of "Darling Annie," during a trip to the Scottish highlands. It was a summer tour-cum-holiday and the weather was wet and freezing. We had hoped for some walking in the Grampians but the rain was so ferocious that we embarked instead on our British Weather Routine. We drove to where we knew there was a splendid (but invisible) view. We parked and got out the little Gilwell and the box of survival rations. We often cooked in the cramped back-seat footroom of our lovely second-hand maroon Citroën Light-15. The smell of bacon and eggs or liver and onions would linger in the upholstery for days, and subsequent passengers would enjoy our meal vicariously. Then we'd sit and wait, playing Scrabble, doing the *Guardian* crossword, talking, rehearsing, making plans for a future that always seemed present, writing songs . . . until the rain stopped and the view came into view.

words and music: Peggy Seeger
disc 19

lightly
C F C
It was in the month of sweet Ju- ly and a court- ship just be- gun,
D7 G7
They were both eigh- teen years old, but he was a lit-tle too young;
C F C
For when-ev-er she'd ask him to do a lit-tle job, he was al- ways heard to say:
C G C F C G7 C
Well, I would-n't know an-y thing about that, bet-ter go and ask Jim-my Gray.

It was in the month of sweet July and a courtship just begun,
They were both eighteen years old, but he was a little too young;
For whenever she'd ask him to do a little job, he was always heard to say:
"Well, I wouldn't know anything about that, better go and ask Jimmy Gray."

I have a field of early corn, it's waiting to be mown;
Love, would you come around with your scythe and help me to mow it down?
He said, "My scythe is rusty, too blunt for corn or hay.
For a mowing-machine the best to be seen belongs to Jimmy Gray."

I have a little sports car, but it drives me round the bend;
Would you come and fit me a new drive-shaft, or maybe some new big-ends?
He says, "If you'll take my advice, you'll phone up the A.A.—
But if you want a bang-up job better go and ask Jimmy Gray."

I have a lovely feather bed, it's big enough for two,
Nice and wide and strong beside, but the frame is split in two.
He says, "My drill needs sharpening and there may be some delay."
She turned around and went to the phone and called up Jimmy Gray.

He's fixed her bed, he's mowed her field and ground her corn to flour,
Fit a new drive-shaft and off they went at a hundred miles an hour.
So, fellas, if ever a woman asks, "Would you do a little job today?"
Just grab your tools and run like a hare, be there before Jimmy Gray.

I'm Gonna Be an Engineer

Nineteen ninety-four was the Year of the Family. Nineteen seventy-one was a year in which women were celebrated. (We also have an annual day, as Mothers! They bring us around in rotation regularly now, alternating us with Year for the Disabled, Year of the Children, Year to Combat World Hunger, and so on. Mind you, these do not displace Years of the Men—they simply accompany them.) So the *Festival of Fools 1971* concentrated on women. Ewan wrote the script at a stressful high speed. He was having trouble with a long musical section and I got involved in the writing of it. "Engineer" appeared so fast on the page that it almost seemed to write itself—you'd think I'd been brooding on discrimination and prejudice all my life. Not so. I had been encouraged personally, academically, musically, and sartorially to do whatever I wanted. And I never wanted to be a boy or an engineer . . . or operate a turret-lathe. Despite its complexity, the song took off quickly and a lot of women sing it now. It's even being used in some higher educational establishments as teaching material. It takes lung power, stamina, a large vocal range, a good sense of pitch, and quite a number of guitar chords.

alternative title: "Gonna Be an Engineer"
words and music: Peggy Seeger
disc 2, 5, 15, 19A, 24, 26A, 29

with spirit

G
When I was a lit- tle girl, I wished I was a boy,
(D7)
I tagged a-long be-hind the gang and wore me cor- du- roys,
(G)
Eve- ry - bod-y said I on- ly did it to an- noy
A7 D7
But I was gon- na be an en- gi- neer ——.
G A B7
Mom- ma told me, Can't you be a la- dy?

When I was a little girl, I wished I was a boy,
I tagged along behind the gang and wore my corduroys,
Everybody said I only did it to annoy
But I was gonna be an engineer.
    Momma told me, "Can't you be a lady?
    Your duty is to make me the mother of a pearl.
    Wait until you're older, dear, and maybe
    You'll be glad that you're a girl."

Dainty as a Dresden statue,
Gentle as a Jersey cow;
Smooth as silk, gives creamy milk,
Learn to coo, learn to moo,
That's what you do to be a lady now—

When I went to school I learned to write and how to read,
Some history, geography, and home economy.
Δ And typing is a skill that every girl is sure to need
† To while away the extra time until the time to breed,
Then they had the nerve to say, "What would you like to be?"
I says, "I'm gonna be an engineer!"
  No, you only need to learn to be a lady,
  The duty isn't yours for to try and run the world.
  An engineer could never have a baby!
  Remember, dear, that you're a girl.

She's smart (for a woman).
I wonder how she got that way?
You get no choice, you get no voice,
Just stay mum, pretend you're dumb,
And that's how you come to be a lady today—

Then Jimmy come along and we set up a conjugation,
We were busy every night with loving recreation.
I spent my day at work so he could get his education
And now he's an engineer!
  He says, "I know you'll always be a lady,
  It's the duty of my darling to love me all her life.
  Could an engineer look after or obey me?
  Remember, dear, that you're my wife."

Well, as soon as Jimmy got a job, I began again,
Then, happy at my turret-lathe a year or so and then:
The morning that the twins were born, Jimmy says to them,
"Kids, your mother *was* an engineer."
  You owe it to the kids to be a lady,
  Dainty as a dishrag, faithful as a chow;
  Stay at home, you got to mind the baby,
  Remember you're a mother now.

Well, every time I turn around there's something else to do,
It's cook a meal, mend a sock, or sweep a floor or two;
I listen in to Jimmy Young, it makes me want to spew,*
I was gonna be an engineer!
  Don't I really wish that I could be a lady?
  I could do the lovely things that a lady's s'posed to do,
  I wouldn't even mind if only they would pay me,
  And I could be a person too.

What price for a woman?
You can buy her for a ring of gold.
To love and obey, without any pay,
You get your cook and your nurse for better or worse,
You don't need your purse when the lady is sold—

Ah, but now that times are harder and my Jimmy's got the sack,
I went down to Vickers, they were glad to have me back,
But I'm a third-class citizen (my wages tell me that)
And I'm a first-class engineer.
    The boss he says, "We pay you as a lady,
    You only got the job 'cause I can't afford a man.
    With you I keep the profits high as may be,
    You're just a cheaper pair of hands."

You got one fault: you're a woman.
You're not worth the equal pay.
A bitch or a tart, you're nothing but heart,
Shallow and vain, you got no brain,
You even go down the drain like a lady today—

Well, I listened to my mother and I joined a typing-pool;
I listened to my lover and I put him through his school;
But if I listen to the boss I'm just a bloody fool
And an underpaid engineer!
    I been a sucker ever since I was a baby,
    As a daughter, as a wife, as a mother and a "dear."
    But I'll fight them as a woman, not a lady,
    Fight them as an engineer!

**Music note: I remade this line when I moved to the United States: "Holding out the potty when the baby wants to poo." I reworked much of the song when I was asked to sing it at the 1995 Knoxville celebration of the seventy-fifth anniversary of women's suffrage. The event was the result of the inspiration and work of a group of women lawyers. The new version, "I'm Gonna Be a Lawyer," outlines the problems that women have in the legal field. Opens up all kinds of vistas for female doctors, politicos, professors . . .*

I'M going to be a brain surgeon

Buffalo Holler

Buffalo Hollow in West Virginia is eighteen miles long. Eight thousand people lived along the creek: "whites," "blacks," Italians, Poles, Slavs. The valley was filled with coal mines, a few stores and thousands of homes. Almost everyone was a miner, a retired miner, or relative of a miner. The "dam" was not a dam at all. It was a slate dump—a slag heap—holding back millions of gallons of water. After the 1966 Aberfan disaster in Wales, the federal government commissioned reviews of all such dumps in the United States. The findings—and the geologists' warnings—were ignored. On February 26, 1972, the dam broke and a wall of water roared down the hollow. Several hundred people lost their lives. Most of the survivors lost their homes and their belongings.

The Buffalo Mining Company and Pittston Coal baulked every attempt to gain compensation and coöperated with the government (legally and otherwise) in demolishing the remaining houses and building a four-lane highway through the town, a project upon which the authorities had long had their sights set and which was now made easier by the flood damage. Eight of the ten mines were re-opened and working by the end of March. Business as usual. Paul Nyden, a West Virginia union official, sent me a taped interview with Minnie Chapman Cook, who had lost everything in the disaster. The song was made from her words.

words and music: Peggy Seeger
disc 19

moderate
C F G7 C
Born in West Vir- gin- ia, I've lived here all my life;
F G C
Six-teen years a mi-ner's daugh-ter, then a mi- ner's wife;
F G C
Raised in Lo- gan Coun-ty, when the creeks they all ran clear,
F G7 C
And Buf-fa-lo Hol-ler's been my home for more than fif-ty years.

Born in West Virginia, I've lived here all my life;
Sixteen years a miner's daughter, then a miner's wife;
Raised in Logan County, when the creeks they all ran clear,
And Buffalo Holler's been my home for more than fifty years.

I remember when Staviski came, the one they called The Pole;
And the Johnsons up from Georgia, their skins as black as coal;
Even the Italians came because the mines were here.
They been my friends in Buffalo Creek for more than fifty years.

Hunger took my baby girl in 1941.
Black lung got my husband, the army got my son.
But of all the troubles I have seen, the worst time I have known,
Was the day the towns were washed away, when the old gob hill came down.

Back in '65 they warned us, nobody made a will.
If you had the money you moved high up on the hill;
It was only poor coal miners who died that Saturday,
They can get plenty more like us, most any working day.

If your home was down the creek, you had time to get away,
But if you lived up by the dam, you had barely time to pray.
It only took one hour of the water roaring through
To take away everything I had, most every friend I knew.

Experts said the dam would go if we had a heavy rain.
The Bureau of Mines they wrote it down, and filed it down the drain.
The Governor made promises the year the elections ran,
Pittston called it an Act of God—I call it an act of man.

Don't wait for compensation, don't wait for them to care—
If you can't make that dollar sign, they just don't know you're there;
But I can't forget my Billy, who died in Vietnam,
Fighting for the system that made the old slate dam.

Lullabye for a Very New Baby

In December 1972, Kitty arrived to a full, busy house. For her first year she slept in the dining room and her nappies were changed on the dining-room table. Calum was ten at the time and he fed and changed and cuddled and sang to her. The smell of ironing, cooking, milk-fed baby, and baby-clothes warming on the radiators were the smell of home. I didn't write songs like this for my sons. This was probably due only to the fact that as a songwriter I was becoming more capable of dealing with deep, satisfying emotions without becoming maudlin. Kitty slept in her pram for the first six months—well, she didn't sleep very much. She was asleep for two hours, awake for one, asleep for three, awake for two, *etc.* Tiredness ran through my bones instead of marrow. I tried to hypnotise her into sleep by playing E-chord arpeggios on the guitar over and over while moving the pram with my foot, but that usually put *me* to sleep first. So I made up words to keep myself awake and, in the time-honoured tradition of lullabies, told Kitty just how I felt.

words and music: Peggy Seeger
disc 6, 26A

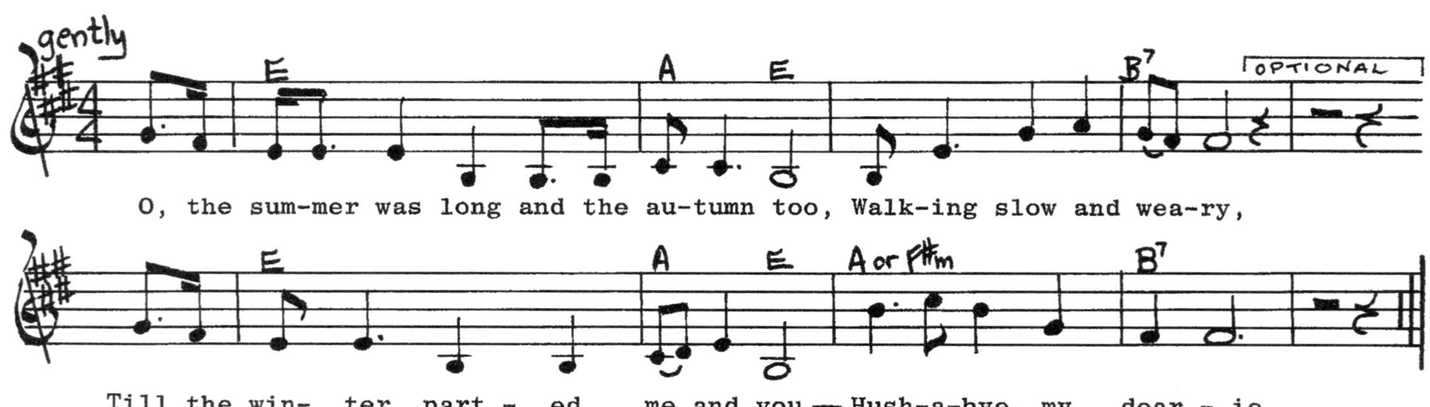

O, the summer was long and the autumn too,
Walking slow and weary,
Till the winter parted me and you—
Hushabye, my dearie.

When the time was come and the time was gone,
They laid you down so near me,
And together we slept the whole night long—
Hushabye, my dearie.

But my back is broke and my belly sore,
Your daddy can't come near me,
And it's up all night to walk the floor—
Hushabye, my dearie.

Though you keep me waking night and day
And your crying makes me weary,
You're welcome as a flower in May—
Hushabye, my dearie.

My darling girl, the world is wide,
I know it's going to fear me
To set you floating on the tide—
Hushabye, my dearie.

Music note: As monotony is one of the most important features of a lullabye, it can be very effective to keep a low E on the guitar droning right through all the chord changes.

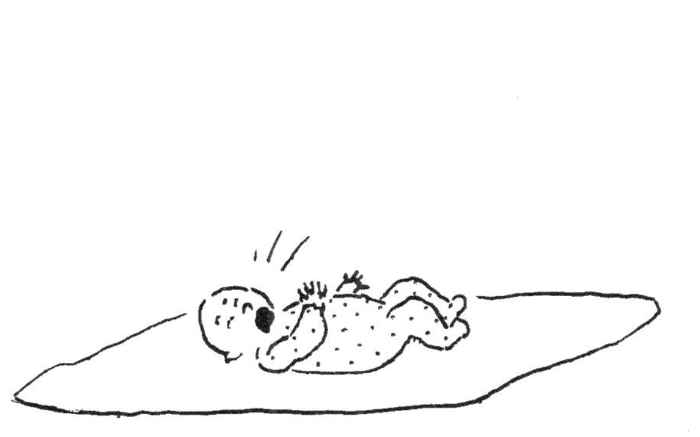

Watergate

First of all, I'd like to apologise to the animals in this song who are represented in a less than complimentary light. Revelations about the Watergate affair began spreading in March 1973 after allegations that President Nixon and some of his top aides had engineered a break-in at the Democratic party headquarters during the run up to the 1972 election. Impeachment was in the air and Nixon resigned in August 1974. He had made an election promise in 1968: "Let us begin by committing ourselves to the truth, to see it like it is and tell it like it is, to find the truth, to speak the truth and to live with the truth." True to that promise, he told the truth—even if it was only because someone else told it before he did.

words and music: Peggy Seeger
disc 31

a little bluesey
1 E
E7
4 A
Am
E
Here are words of wis- dom from a great man of our time:
F#7
B7
If you take a wood-en nick-el, chum, give back a plas-tic dime;
E
E7
A
Am
E
Nev-er give a suck-er an ev-en break, do an- y- thing to win;
A
E
C#
F#
B7
E
And don't jump in- to the wa- ter - hole be- fore you learn to swim.

1
E
to 4
(YA-HOO!) I'm wild as a bull, I'm

Here are words of wisdom from a great man of our time:
"If you take a wooden nickel, chum, give back a plastic dime;
"Never give a sucker an even break, do anything to win;
"And don't jump into the waterhole before you learn to swim."

Watch him when he makes a speech, it really is a treat.
The eyes are earnest and sincere, the voice is honey-sweet.
The honest mouth, heroic brow, the unstained face of youth,
This dandruff-crowned mediocrity is about to tell the truth.

Chorus: Water, water, everywhere, the gates are open wide.
Water, water, everywhere, he'll float out on the tide.
Napoleon had his Waterloo, Noah had the flood,
Nixon's below the water-line and somebody pulled the plug.

Being a politician's just like falling off a log;
First I got my wife and kids, then I got my dog;
Every twenty years or so I go down upon my knees,
And say, "I'm a liar, a cheat and a crook but folks, forgive me please!"

I been a pro at conning, I got training at the bar.
I been a secondhand salesman. Would you like to buy a car?
I been a Senator in my time, woulda been a Governor too,
But the hand of fate that guides us all struck me instead of you. *(chorus)*

I sure do love America, love all its people too,
'Cept for the poor, the reds, the blacks, the Democrats and the Jews,
The students, the women who want their lib, the reporters under my bed;
But I love the silent majority. Why? I love 'em because they're dead.

Δ *YAHOO!* I'm wild as a bull, I'm brother to the rat!
I'm so fast the White House staff never knows where I'm at.
I ride into town on Nader's back, pull Congress by the tail,
I'm a crew-cut Lifebuoy, Colgate cat and all of me's for sale. *(chorus)*

God bless everyone of you, the Law be with you all;
While I'm watching over you let not a sparrow fall.
I'm just an ordinary guy and I care about what you say,
And I know every goddamned word you said 'cause I'm listening night and day. *(chorus)*

Well, things are getting lonely now, I sure do miss my boys,
But single-handed I'll repulse the invaders from Hanoi.
By myself I'll struggle on in the War on Poverty,
And I'm never alone on the telephone 'cause I'm always bugging me. *(chorus)*

Music note: *The chorus is sung to the same tune as the verse. Because the song needs to be acted out, the musical notation has to be stretched, bent, expanded, varied, changed, etc. in order to fit the words. Like the subject of the song, be brash. Look innocent when you make mistakes.*

Big Man

The post-Vietnam years were strange ones—years of apathy, anticlimax, the same old strife on the home front. The Cold War crackled on. The forces of the Left grouped and regrouped, fragmented into smaller groups, like the road that turns into a lane, then into a path, then into a track, then into a squirrel run and disappears into a hole up a tree. But the United States kept on making fires without smoke and smoke without fires. I forget what incident made me write this song. It was popular at the time so it must have struck a chord in the communal consciousness. As a sworn subject of the most-infiltrated-by-the-U.S.A. nation in the world, I felt entitled to write such a song.

words and music: Peggy Seeger
disc 15

He's the big man—well, he sure looks big to me.
He's the big man—well, he sure looks big to me.
You find him everywhere, even the bottom of the sea.
He's got the long legs, big feet,
Walk across the water on the Seventh Fleet,
He's got the long arms, big hands,
Every finger stuck in a hole in the dam.

He's the kind man—well, he sure looks kind to me. *(2 times)*
Sell you anything, Coca Cola to I.T.T.
Got the nylon, plastic, elastic economy,
Little things to make your life sweet as a honeybee.
Tunnel underneath you like a goddamn mole
To get your country, heart, body and soul.

He's the good man—well, he sure looks good to me. *(2 times)*
Reads the Good Book—sells guns in Galilee.
Get you in trouble just to give you advice,
Then mop you up all tidy and nice.
He'll give you one hand when you think you're lost,
And with the other nail you up on the cross.

He's the new man—but he sure looks old to me. *(2 times)*
Been around so long, got invisibility.
Eye to the keyhole, ear to the wall,
Microphone, a camera, notebook and all;
He can torture and kill you, give you a smile,
That's Democracy, modern style.

He's the rich man—but he sure looks poor to me. *(2 times)*
'Cause everything he needs got to come from across the sea.
Black man, yellow man, where've you been?
Diggin' up my copper, oil, nickel and tin.
White man, boss man, what've you got?
A credit account and a dollar crop.

He's the strong man—well, he sure looks weak to me. *(2 times)*
Mister Universe, and he's built just like a machine.
Got a printed circuit, coil and mesh,
A-walkin' and a-talkin' like the human flesh;
See the little bitty wheels runnin' round and round,
Throw in a stone and he's flat on the ground.

He's the top man—and he sure smells high to me. *(2 times)*
And he got up there ridin' on you and me.
Everywhere the people play the profit game,
The man with the money, he's just the same,
We're all workin' just to fill his purse,
For him it gets better and for Δ us it's worse.

How long can we go on like this?
Lendin' a hand instead of makin' a fist?
For a thousand years we been givin' in,
But this world won't be worth † livin' in

TILL HE'S THE DEAD MAN,
TILL HE'S THE DEAD MAN,
TILL HE'S THE DEAD MAN.

Manner of the World Nowadays

John Skelton's poem "The Manner of the World Nowadays" has fifteen double verses dealing with much the same subject matter as I deal with here. An example:

So many cuckold-makers,
So many crakers, *[boasters]*
And so many peace-breakers,
Saw I never.
So many wrongs,
And so few merry songs,
And so many ill tongues,
Saw I never.

He, too, felt it was important not to leave the listener ready to jump under a coach-and-six:

Amendment
Were convenient,
But it may not be:
We have exiled veritie.
God is neither dead nor sick;
He may amend all yet,
And trow ye so indeed,
As ye believe ye shall have mede.
After better I hope ever,
For worse was it never.

He should see the old homestead now.

words and music: Peggy Seeger
© 1992 Peggy Seeger (1)

I'm gonna sing about things that are wrong,
Might sing it short, might sing it long;
Here's the chorus of my song:
    Saw I Never.

So many men who fight and fly,
So many women who sit and cry,
So many children born to die,
    Saw I Never.

So many rapists, thieves and thugs,
So many gentlemen pushing drugs,
So many victims, so many mugs,
    Saw I Never.

So much to learn, so few schools,
So many laws, so few rules,
So many waiting to win the Pools,
    Saw I Never.

So many battery cows and hens,
Additives added right up to the end,
Food for pigs fed to men,
    Saw I Never.

So many mackerel, herring and sprats,
Tuna and dolphins into the nets,
All for to feed pet dogs and cats,
    Saw I Never.

So many shoddy rags on racks,
So much bread that tastes like wax,
So many burdens on our backs,
    Saw I Never.

So many union men at a loss,
Because their leader's in league with the boss;
So many strikers counting the cost,
    Saw I Never.

So many laws to protect the rich,
Putting through deals with never a hitch,
Leaving the poor without a stitch,
    Saw I Never.

So many saints on Capitol Hill,
So many businessmen of goodwill
Supporting dictators in [Spain and Brazil,]
    Saw I Never.

So many homeless and nowhere to go,
So many bastards running the show,
So many victims who don't want to know,
    Saw I Never.

So many who know that something is wrong,
So many who know that many are strong,
Yet think to yourself I'm singing too long,
    Saw I Never.

Tomorrow there won't be time to think,
Tomorrow we'll have to swim or sink;
Δ Don't stop the fire, help it burn,
† Help the tide begin to turn,
Now's the time to watch and learn,
    Now or never.

was that the short version
or the long one?

Out of My Pocket

A down-home song, a little like "I Support the Boycott," a good kind of song to write when you have ideas and haven't got time, energy, or talent enough to create Undying Art. The verses can go in any order and they can be added or subtracted without damaging a storyline or sequence. The chorus can be warbled cheerfully, bawled out at the top of your lungs or sung in a miserable hangdog voice, depending on how short of cash you are and how you feel about it.

words and music: Peggy Seeger

vigorously
E E7 A E
I work all week as hard as I can and when I pay my bills
E F#7 B7
I feel like the time has come to sit down and make my will.
E A E
I'm hard- up by Mon-day morn-ing, I'm broke by Thurs- day night,
A E B7 E
But I can't af-ford to snuff it 'cause the cost would be too high.
CHORUS
B7 E
Out of my pock-et, out of my pock-et,
A E F#7 B7
Out of my pock-et, O, where does the mon-ey go?

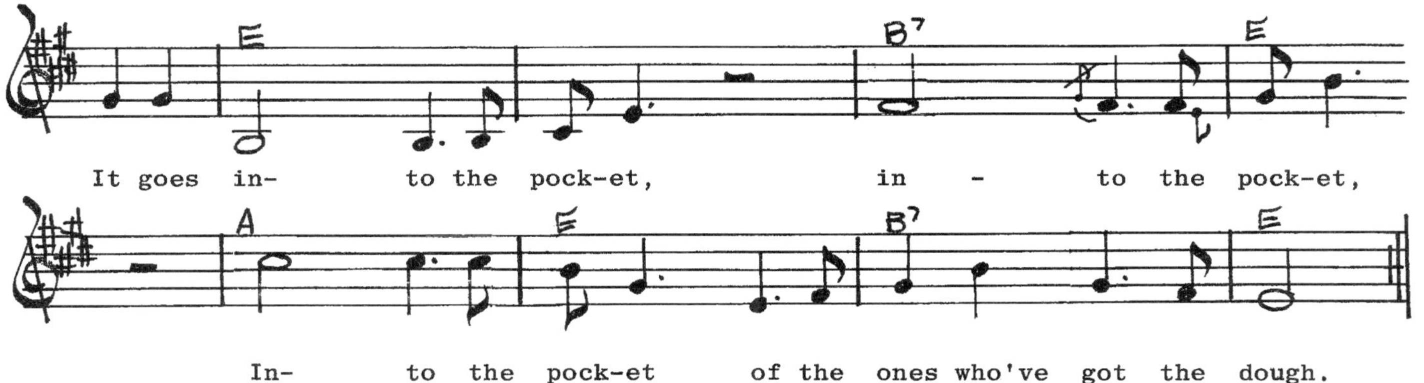

I work all week as hard as I can and when I pay my bills
I feel like the time has come to sit down and make my will.
I'm hard-up on Monday morning, I'm broke by Thursday night,
But I can't afford to snuff it 'cause the cost would be too high.

Chorus: Out of my pocket, out of my pocket,
Out of my pocket, O, where does the money go?
It goes into the pocket, into the pocket,
Into the pocket of the ones who've got the dough.

There's some who take off half a year to go on a southern cruise;
There's some that save up all the year just to buy a pair of shoes.
It doesn't seem quite right to me that I should dig so deep
When there's a guy who makes a half a million while he sleeps. *(chorus)*

When I go to buy my food it's just like Judgment Day,
Everything's a penny more than it was yesterday.
Half the shelves are empty, but on this you can depend:
They'll all be full tomorrow when the prices rise again. *(chorus)*

From Bromley up to Heathrow cost me nearly all my dough;
I took my seat and fastened my belt on the plane to Westward Ho.
But ticket prices rose again when the plane was in mid-air,
I couldn't pay the balance, so they dropped me halfway there. *(chorus)*

They tell me big monopolies own everything I see,
So I'll be on the market soon, 'cause they own most of me.
And after they have processed me and packaged me so nice,
I'll have to buy me back again at some godawful price. *(chorus)*

Song for Calum

When Neill was eleven, I wrote a song for him ("My Son"). When Kitty was born, I wrote one for her ("Lullabye for a Very New Baby"). Calum asked when it was his turn. He was—and is—a charmer: talkative, mercurial, and argumentative. At twelve-and-a-half, neither man nor boy, he was hard to write about because we didn't exactly hit it off at that time. I told him he was at a difficult age. He smiled, quick on the uptake as usual: "Well, let's face it, Mum, *you're* at a difficult age, too!" One day, just before Ewan and I were due to go on tour, Calum and I had a blazing argument. It was a Sunday, in April (statistics show that most of the violence within families takes place on Sundays and holidays). We had to leave in the middle of the turbulence. This song turned up in my head while we were barreling up the M6. It took fifteen minutes to decode. Calum wasn't too sure about it—he held out his hand, asking for a text, which he took to school. When he came home, he said, "It's O.K."

words and music: Peggy Seeger
disc 3, 19A
© 1992 Peggy Seeger (1)

quite free, not slow
O, I'm a young wom-an that's just hit-ting for - ty -
Three chil-dren we've borne, their young lives we've guard-ed,
I've a good lov-ing man who's both six -ty and young;
But they strain at the leash, ev-er read-y to run.
I could sing of a ba-by, her laugh-ter and prat-tle,
I could sing of a son who is near- ly a man;
I could sing of their fath-er, for- ev-er a lov-er,
But I'll sing of the boy who's just twelve- and - a - half.

O, I'm a young woman that's just hitting forty—
I've a good loving man who's both sixty and young;
Three children we've borne, their young lives we've guarded,
But they strain at the leash, ever ready to run.
I could sing of a baby, her laughter and prattle,
I could sing of a son who is nearly a man;
I could sing of their father, forever a lover,
But I'll sing of the boy who's just twelve-and-a-half.

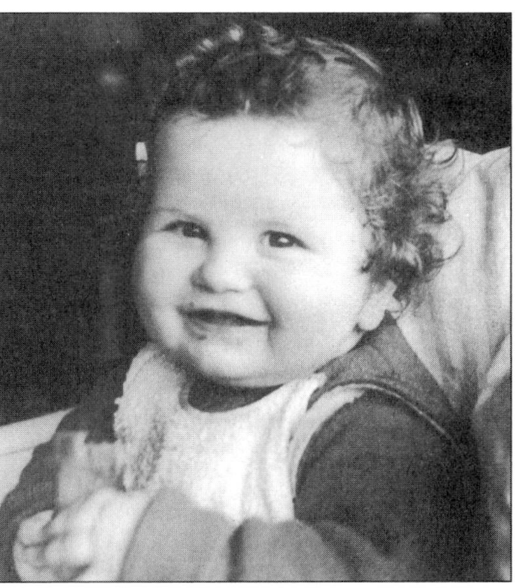

At running and jumping, at games of the season,
At swimming and football the best you have seen;
At arguing fine points of logic and reason
His method is one of a boy of thirteen.
The smile of his uncle, the face of his father,
The tongue of his granny and a mind of his own;
On every subject he holds an opinion
And he'll swear that he's right and the whole world is wrong.

He watches me closely and gauges my temper,
He knows just the moment to ask for a lend;
He'll wash the car and wipe all the dishes,
And then he'll complain about making his bed.
His face always mucky, his hands always dirty,
His shoes are unpolished, his jacket is torn;
His belongings are scattered from basement to attic
Yet he knows where they are like the crow finds the corn.

Son of my youth, so honest and open,
I'm proud of your will, your compulsion to fight.
Keep raising your voice, insist that you're counted,
And if you're wrong, the world sets you aright.
Son of my heart, thoughtful and loving,
The image of life and as elusive to hold.
Today I am weary so man-child, please hear me:
No doubt you're right but—*do as you're told!*

Music note: *As the tune is a collation of a hundred Irish airs, the song may be sung with the casual, offhand delivery employed by so many fine Irish singers. I usually speak the last four words emphatically.*

Nine-Month Blues

When I wrote "I'm Gonna Be an Engineer" I unwittingly hit a subject that was not an integral part of my life. Back in the early seventies, I was invited to women's gatherings specifically to sing it—but I had no other feminist songs to go with it. So I set myself a project (which eventually culminated in the disc *Different Therefore Equal*): to write a song about each of the main issues on the feminist agenda at that time. I was abysmally ignorant on these subjects so I started reading and talking to feminists. (Later, in 1992, I took the Women's Studies Course at the Open University.) I tried to make different types of songs so that the disc would be interesting to listen to. This song is a light, somewhat flippant way of dealing with contraception, based in part on some of my own experience. I had tried everything, including the Lippes Loop I.U.D., which not only gave me chronic thrush but which came with a warning that it wasn't one hundred percent foolproof. They were right—it wasn't. Compare this song with "The Judge's Chair."

words and music: Peggy Seeger
disc 2, 5, 26A

not too fast
(A) B7 E7
If you can't be care-ful, try to be good. Well, we cared & we cared as much as we could;
A D7 G7
We al-ways agreed, me and my man, We said, Some-day we'll try the fam-i-ly plan.
C7 F
Well, the first thing we tried was Nothing at All, 'Cause an amateur rider never thinks she'll
A7 Dm D7 G7
fall; We charted my tides & followed my moon, But then Someday came a lit-tle too soon.
CHORUS
C B7 E7 (F7) E7 A
I got the nine- month blues —— Too much to gain, too much to lose, But
D7 E7 C7 B7 A
he was kind-a hap-py when he heard my news- I got the nine- month blues ——.

If you can't be careful, try to be good.
Well, we cared and we cared as much as we could;
We always agreed, me and my man,
We said, "Someday we'll try the family plan."
Well, the first thing we tried was Nothing at All
'Cause an amateur rider never thinks she'll fall;
We charted my tides and followed my moon,
But then Someday came a little too soon.

Chorus: I got the nine-month blues—
Too much to gain, too much to lose,
But he was kinda happy when he heard my news—
I got the nine-month blues.

There was him and me and the baby made three,
But we made up our minds to stay that way
With little bitty things made of rubber and such,
And 'cause we were friends we decided to go Dutch.
When we said "I do" it was a solemn oath,
So we did and we did and it pleased us both.
Still can't figure out what went wrong,
But that's the first line of the nine-month song,

Chorus: I got the nine-month blues—
Too much to gain, too much to lose,
Get out The Dress and The Sensible Shoes—
I got the nine-month blues.

I says, "This time around I'm gonna cast my stone,
I'm gonna have a chance to call my life my own."
But the S.P.U.C. and the F.P.A.
They said, "Keep that child, don't fling it away!"
The doctor said he had the right to refuse;
The law says if you want to beat the noose
You gotta be rich or near to your grave,
So away I went again on my nine-month rave,

Chorus: I got the nine-month blues—
Too much to gain, too much to lose,
But this time around, I got 'em in twos—
I got the nine-month blues.

The next thing we tried was the capital P-
And I-L-L is what that made me;
My head bust open and I nearly went crazy
And my moon started risin' every fourteen days;
I says, "I may be sick, but I'm safe and free."
So we started making honey like a coupla bees.
But one May morning I musta forgot;
Dropped me right back into the nine-month slot.

Chorus: I got the nine-month blues—
Too much to gain, too much to lose,
Won't my old man be happy when he hears my news?
I got the nine-month blues.

I got the kids everywhere, two, three, four, five—
I just can't swim without taking the dive.
I went for advice, and they says to me,
They said, "The next thing to try is the I.U.D."
But the small print allows that the Loopity-Loop
Has a margin of error, then you're in the soup.
But your kid'll be normal so don't you fret,
Even though you're leased for your nine-month let,

Chorus: I got the nine-month blues—
Too much to gain, too much to lose,
I better get my old man to disconnect his fuse—
I got the nine-month blues.

I love that man, I love my kids,
But if I have any more I'm gonna blow my lid!
It's not just the forty weeks on my mind,
It's also the washin' hangin' on my line.
It could be the worry on the old man's face,
Or thinking of the future of the Earthly Race.
It all began with the loving and laughter,
Then so much care for such a long time after

Chorus: Every nine-month blues—
Too much to gain, too much to lose,
Now don't you think we ought to have the right to choose,
To sing the Twenty-Year Blues?

IMMACULATE
CONTRACEPTION
you ninny

Housewife's Alphabet

In the 1960s, Folkways Records put out an entire disc of alphabet songs: alphabets for fishermen, loggers, students, A & R men . . . obviously an easy format to write in. I took this tune and the idea from an East Anglian sea song, the chorus of which is:

> Merrily, cheerily, so wearily are we,
> No mortal on earth like a sailor at sea;
> Heave away, haul away, hey do a down,
> Give a sailor his grog and there's nothing go wrong.

This is my soft housewife song. For the hard one, see "Lady, What Do You Do All Day?"

tune: traditional English ("The Sailor's Alphabet")
new words and trad. arr.: Peggy Seeger
disc 10, 25, 26

Smoothly

A is for al-tar where we go a- stray, B for the bills that be- gin the next day;

C for the cuffs & the col-lars of shirts,& D is for dish-es and dust-ing and dirt.

E is my en-ergy drain-ing a-way on F is for floors to be swept eve-ry day;

G for girl-hood, gaw-ky and gone, & H,fed-up house-wife that's sing-ing this song.

CHORUS

Wea-rily, it's mer- e- ly a good wom-an's day,

Cook-ing and clean-ing and tid-y-ing a - way;

G
F
C
If ev-er you fin-ish, re- mem- ber that when
G7
C
You wake up to- mor- row it all starts a- gain.

final verse
G
F
C
If this song was house-work, you'd sing it and then You'd go back where you
G7
C
F ad infinitum C
Fm
C
start-ed and sing it a-gain And a-gain and a-gain and a-gain and a-gain.....

A is for altar where we go astray,
B for the bills that begin the next day;
C for the cuffs and the collars of shirts, and
D is for dishes and dusting and dirt.
E is my energy draining away on
F is for floors to be swept every day;
G for girlhood, gawky and gone, and
H, fed-up housewife that's singing this song.

Chorus: Wearily, it's merely a good woman's day,
Cooking and cleaning and tidying away;
If ever you finish, remember that when
You wake up tomorrow it all starts again.

I is for ironing for kids in their teens,
J is for jerseys and jumpers and jeans.
K is the kitchen, for years upon end
I've lived with **L**eftovers and **L**aundry for friends.
M is for mending, there's mile upon mile,
N for the nappies in a big stinking pile.
O for the odd jobs, the odd one or two
Like **P**ushing the **P**ram or un**P**lugging the loo.
(chorus)

Q is for quarrelling of chicks in my nest,
R is for referee and a one-minute rest.
S for the shopping, in snow, sleet or rain,
And **T** for that toilet, it's stopped up again!
U is for underwear, grimy and soiled,
V for those things that you peel, chop and boil.
W for woman and washing machine,
We both need attention (you know what I mean).
(chorus)

We've got no union, it's eight days a week—
They're crammed into seven, I'm out on my feet.
So much to do—where should I begin?
But I've got all my lifetime to finish it in.
W for wings, if I had them I'd fly,
X marks the spot where I sit down and cry . . .
Y-Z for yours truly, I've gone on too long,
And so has the system, and so has this song.
(chorus)

Δ If this song was housework, you'd sing it and then
You'd go back where you started and sing it again
And again and again and again and again . . .

Music note: The chorus takes a while to teach to an audience but it is well worth it. Use the Pete Seeger method of singing a line and inviting them out there to sing it after you. Listen critically to their rendition. Do not accept second-best. If they do it well, reward them with the verses. If they don't, invite them to try again and again and again and again . . .

and N is for
not bloody likely

Thoughts of Time

At one point there should have been a Government Health Warning stamped on me. The kids liked us to be home overnight, so if we were singing within 200 miles of home we would drive back in the early hours when there was less traffic. I usually did the night-driving. If the journey was by motorway I would settle down in the driver's seat as if at my desk at home. In my lap would be a shorthand spiral notebook and a pencil. I could write without taking my eyes off the road: one idea per page, then just turn the page over. The speed limit was seventy mph but I often went faster because the roads were virtually empty in the small hours of the morning. I tremble to think of it now . . . I'd arrive home with an entire notebook of pages filled on both sides: words, phrases, bits of tune in alphabet shorthand, ideas, all jumbled up. Type up the notes next day, make units or order of some kind, melt them down for a while, run through several drafts and then pour them into a tune-mould. That's how this song got written. It was three years before Ewan's first heart trouble, but we'd been talking about things. . . .

words and music: Peggy Seeger
disc 3, 16, 19A
© 1992 Peggy Seeger (1)

contemplative
G7 C ▲5 C7
When first we loved and when our life was new,
F 7 C
Time lay be- fore us like the space a-round a star;
G7 C F
But time moves fast- er than it used to do -
C G7 C
Thoughts of time will break my heart.

▲5
F to7
me, For-ev-er twin-ing our-

When first we loved and when our life was new,
Time lay before us like the space around a star;
But time moves faster than it used to do—
    Thoughts of time will break my heart.

We've been through every weather, you and Δ me,
Forever twining ourselves together till death will us part;
But death seems nearer than it used to be—
    Thoughts of time will break my heart.

We know our children will take wing and fly,
Ties will be broken and a circle torn apart;
But to know our children will grow old and die—
    Thoughts of time will break my heart.

When our time is gone and others' time begun,
Our lives swept aside and others' lives about to start;
Then we'll join the past as countless more have done—
    Thoughts of time will break my heart.

If we joined our dream, my love, we joined the fear
That one will be left behind, the other will depart;
But we've been in love for more than twenty years—
    Thoughts of time will break my heart.

Our dream is old, our dream is always new,
A dream ever with us, it was with us from the start,
† The dream that all could live as lovers do,
« A dream coming nearer though it always seems afar—
But to die before we see our dream come true,
    Only that could break my heart.

Emily

The Forest Hill refuge for battered women was a huge old Victorian house, with hardly any soft furnishings. The kitchen had no pots and pans and there was one well-worn sitting room. Each large bedroom housed six or seven people; *i.e.,* two or three small families or one larger one. Emily came to the Forest Hill sanctuary with her four children in the summer of 1977. She didn't speak for four months and she only went out to take her children to school or to do her shopping. When she did begin to speak it was in totally articulate short sentences. It was as if her experience had been etched into her consciousness with a diamond stylus, much as Kafka's wrongdoer had his crime carved on his breast. I recorded her, put her short sentences in order and made a tune. Emily was a very small Irish woman who had married a very large English man. When she was rehoused three doors down the street from him, he would make a point of *coming to see her* or walking frequently and slowly past her front door. Once again, she retreated into her shell, going out only when it was absolutely necessary. Her husband was then served with an injunction to keep more than 100 yards away from her home and *he* was rehoused—across the street so that a dual carriageway now separated them. He would sit out on his front stoop staring at her house for hours and watching her as she came in and out, taking the children to school and going shopping. She was a bundle of nerves when I took the song to her for her final approval. She was pleased with it but was afraid her husband might hear it. . . .

words and music: Peggy Seeger
disc 4, 26

Once we were single, once we were young,
And once we were happy, husband and wife;
But fourteen years married, thirteen years harried,
Now I don't care what comes of my life.

The first time he lifted his hand against me,
He knew the blow was wicked and wrong;
He put his arms round me, said he was sorry,
Sorry, love, sorry all the night long.

The next time he lifted his fist against me,
I thought I'd provoked him, I was to blame;
The next time, the next time and the time after,
I told no one 'cause I was ashamed.

When anything crossed him I got his fist,
If dinner was late he slapped me around;
With begging and pleading, stitches and bleeding,
Nothing would do till I'm on the ground.

My mum come in, she seen I been crying,
Seen I was cut and bruised round the eyes;
My husband turned round, all smiling and charming,
Says, "All she does is spend and tell lies."

He said I was out with men every day,
He locked me indoors and tore up my clothes.
My friend heard me screaming, never come near—
Why did I stay with him? God only knows.

If I go quiet, that makes him rage,
If I turn and run, he's hunting me down.
I says, "Why do you hit me?" He hit me for asking;
Whatever I do, I'm down on the ground.

Each afternoon, my heart would start trembling,
I followed his journey all the way home.
His step at the door would nearly dissolve me;
When he walked in, my judgment was come.

I know there's two sides to every question,
I may be wrong, he may be right.
But he's got just two ways to settle a quarrel:
One is his left, the other his right.

The doctor says he needs my understanding,
The police seldom challenge a man in his home.
Everyone knows him, no one defends me,
After the altar, a wife's on her own.

I wander, I cry, I pray I may die,
I walk up to strangers to talk in the road.
Three kids and no money, how can I leave him?
I lose my kids if I've got no home.

The last time he hit me, he nearly killed me,
I thought I was dead and glad to be free.
I gathered the kids up and went to a refuge,
He grabbed a crowbar and come after me.

When I go out I see him behind me,
Three times we've moved, he's found us again.
If I kill myself at least I'll die easy,
At least I'll know why, at least I'll know when.

The refuge is bare, the floors and walls echo,
Nothing reminds me of comfort or home.
But here I can sleep, and here I can rest,
Here I have friends, I'm no longer alone.

Music note: On disc 4, the song is sung unaccompanied in $\frac{5}{4}$. *On disc 26, we have experimented with singing it in a slow* $\frac{6}{8}$.

Pay-Up Song

There is a strict ritual governing the collection of money at benefit concerts. It always occurs just before the first interval, after the entertainment and before the audience (see **Glossary**) has the chance to spend their money on drink and refreshment. Collection speakers come in all shapes, sizes, and qualities. Over the years I've seen them coax a whole range of responses from an audience: shouts of support, rowdy laughter, cross-eyed boredom, snoring, premature exits. Then the buckets go around . . . a noisy business which can take anywhere up to a half an hour while the speaker plays on our competitive and exhibitionist instincts and waxes warm about the superiority of paper currency to metal coins. Whatever you do, get the song in before any of this ritual starts. End your spot with it in the first half, or else end the whole concert with it, hopefully causing those last pennies to leap from their hiding places—pockets and purses—into the pail.

words and music: Peggy Seeger
disc 4, 31
© 1992 Peggy Seeger (1)

with energy
Mon-ey is a use - ful thing, takes a long time to earn.
Mon-ey is a pow-er-ful thing, does-n't take long to learn.
Mon-ey can ar-rest you, put you in jail; Mon-ey pays fines, mon-ey pays bail;
Some-times the court-house is up for sale, But mon-ey is-n't all we need.
CHORUS
So if you give a penny, give at least 20, After all, it's on-ly money you're giving away;
And the five - P, ten - P fifty-P pie-ces Won't buy much with the prices to-day.

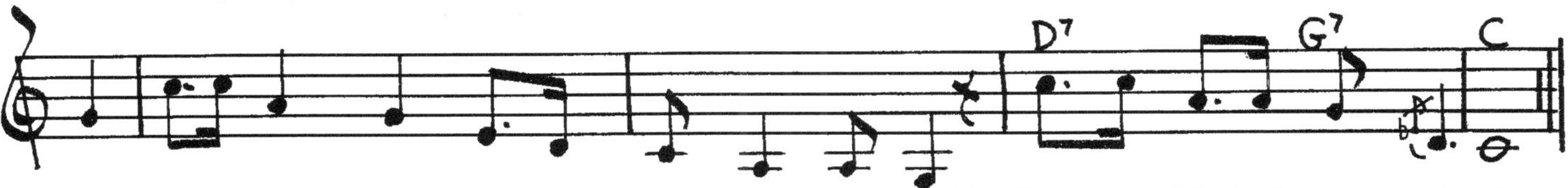

Money is a useful thing, takes a long time to earn.
Money is a powerful thing, doesn't take long to learn.
Money can arrest you, put you in jail;
Money pays fines, money pays bail;
And sometimes the courthouse is up for sale,
But money isn't all we need.

Chorus: So if you give a penny, give at least twenty,
After all, it's only money you're giving away;
And the 5p, 10p, 50p pieces
Won't buy much with the prices today.
A pound from each of you would save our neck
But if you got no cash just write out a cheque.
If all you got to give is your own two hands,
We'll find a job for you—
'Cause if you can't stand in the front line yourself,
Stand behind the ones who do.

Time is a costly thing, so put it to use.
Time is a precious thing, we haven't got much to lose.
I took the time out to sing you a song,
You took the time tonight to come on along,
But it takes more than time to make us strong,
So time isn't all we need. *(chorus)*

Thinking is a wonderful thing, try and do it all the time.
Thinking is a beautiful thing, some folks call it a crime.
Thinking helps you see what's wrong and what's right,
Thinking makes you mad so you just want to fight,
But it won't make Utopia happen tonight,
So thinking isn't all we need. *(chorus)*

Doing's an affirmative thing, takes a positive person to *do*.
Doing is the logical thing, it could happen to you.
* A nurse spends her life doing what's right,
* That's why the nurses are out on strike,
And that's why you're giving money tonight,
'Cause doing is the only thing. *(chorus)*

Now—if you like my song, don't keep a penny back.
Giving is a loving thing—have you got the knack?
Give a little more than you think you ought,
Give us your time, your money and thought,
* The health of the nation has got to be bought,
So giving is the thing for you. *(chorus)*

**Music note: The starred lines can be altered according to the issue for which the benefit is being given. When I moved to North Carolina, I remade the song to help with fundraising for National Public Radio.*

Money is a useful thing, takes a long time to earn.
Money is a wonderful thing, doesn't take long to learn;
Money can take you anywhere
Money can show you really care
Money will keep us on the air
So money is the thing we need.

Chorus: So if you give a penny, give at least twenty
After all, it's only money you're giving away
And the dimes and the quarters and the pesky little nickels
Won't buy much with the prices today.
A dollar from each of you would save our neck
Credit card, cash, or write out a check
If all you got to give is your own two hands
We'll find a job for you.
Even if you don't go on the airwaves yourself
Stand behind the ones who do.

We know you listen every day, sometimes through the night;
Do you know how hard we work to keep all the programs right?
The stories, the music, the chat, and the news,
We keep you in touch, we keep you amused—
Now you can keep us from singing the blues
Your money sends the blues away. *(chorus)*

Now—if you like my song, don't keep a penny back;
Giving is a loving thing—have you got the knack?
Give a little more than you think you ought,
Give us your time, your money, and thought,
It's a shame but freedom has got to be bought
So give in and call right now.

Here's the number: *[here the number of the radio station is given] (chorus)*

Talking Matrimony Blues

This is a talking blues, in which

- the ordinary type is spoken in rhythm against a rhythmic accompaniment
- THE UPPERCASE TYPE IS SPOKEN FREELY, CONVERSATIONALLY
- *the italics signify a sung section*

To my mind, it is an easy and rewarding form to write in because you can make your own rules. As long as the guitar keeps going throughout (usually in 4/4) and you speak more or less in rhythm, you can set your own poetic form, throwing in instrumentals, song lines, and comments when you want. The only real temptation is that if you have a lot to say you can just keep going and going and going and going . . .

words and music: Peggy Seeger
disc 5

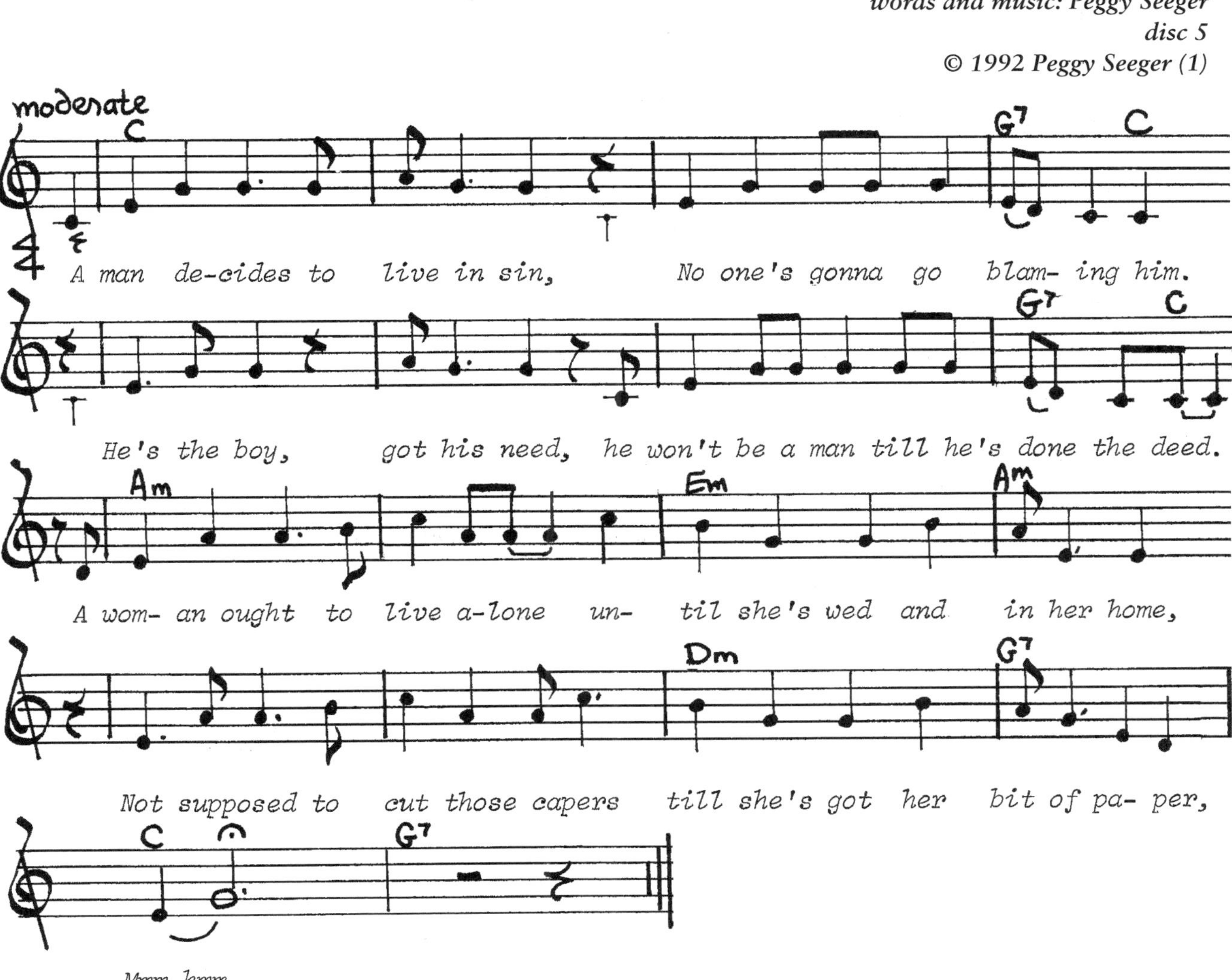

Girls, don't hanker for bouquets and veils,
They soon turn to cabbage and nappies in pails.
The joys (and the sorrows) of conjugal life,
All these can be yours without being a wife.
Yes, a good life can come to fruition,
You don't need a license to give you permission,
    YOU DON'T HAVE TO MARRY. YOU NEVER GET COMPLETELY FREE CHOICE ANYHOW. TOO MANY PEOPLE YOU *CAN'T* MARRY FOR A START. I ALWAYS FANCIED PAUL NEWMAN.

A man decides to live in sin, no one's gonna go blaming him.
He's the boy, got his need, he won't be a man till he's done the deed.
A woman ought to live alone until she's wed and in her home,
Not supposed to cut those capers till she's got that bit of paper,
Mmm-hmm . . .

Now, there are places in this world,
Where they tell the young men and young girls,
"Before you hit your marriage-bed,
"Indulge yourselves, go ahead.
    "ELIMINATE THE CRUDER FORMS OF SEXUAL EXPRESSION FROM YOUR MATRIMONIAL SELECTION."

But civilised folks, despite our climates,
Fancy we're above those primates.
Scorning prenuptial intercourse,
We favour marriage . . . then divorce.
    THE SINGLE MOTHER AND HER CHILDREN ARE A LEGALLY INCOMPLETE UNIT. UNCLAIMED ASSETS.

Marry for safety, marry for gain,
Marry to give the little bugger a name,
Marry by custom or marry by chance,
But don't kid yourself, what we call "romance"
    ENDS AT THE ALTAR. MARRIAGE IS A LEGAL CONTRACT. YEAH, THAT'S WHAT I SAID: A LETHAL CON-TRICK.
    TWO EQUALS GET MARRIED AND THEN—HEY-PRESTO!—THEY'RE *UN*EQUAL.

A married man goes out each day, he's the one who earns the pay.
His life may just be work and bed, but in the family he's the head.
A wife remains at home all day or else goes out for part-time pay.
Kids and housework all her life—but every family needs the wife,
Mmm-hmm . . .

Now, marriage don't have to be one-to-one,
The alternative systems since time begun
(Like polygamy, polyandry, or marriage-in-groups)
Wasn't invented by nincompoops
    BUT BY ECONOMIC NECESSITY. INFANT BETROTHAL . . . CHILD BRIDES . . . WIFE-STEALING . . . JUST DIFFERENT METHODS OF TRANSFERRING PROPERTY.

'Cause a wife has a place in the eyes of the law,
She's as much a possession as a house or a car.
You're a dependent now, you once was a bride,
And he's your voice to the world outside.
Meet the wife.
    (SAY SOMETHING TO THE FOLKS, DEAR.)

A husband's rights are his by law, whether it's Rome or Arkansas,
The system ain't no parvenu, it uses him to manage you.
A wife has rights: her husband gives her food to eat and a place to live,
After that what he bestows is up to him, and no one knows,
Mmm-hmm . . .

Now, even if you get on great,
He'll collect your rent rebates.
And even if you get on fine,
Your legal papers are his to sign.
And even if he's your bosom friend,
You may have to beg for money to spend.
And even if your love is true,
He can open anything addressed to you,
    AFTER ALL, IT'S GOT HIS NAME WRIT RIGHT THERE ON THE ENVELOPE.
What's yours is his,
What's his is yours, but
You're his.

If you don't like marriage you can, of course,
Throw in the towel and go for divorce,
But that little old knot (so easy to tie)
Just won't unravel or lay down and die.
Think of the cost. Think of the shame.
Think of the kids. Think of the blame.
Think of the men who'll call you fair game.
    WE DIDN'T ALL MARRY DONALD TRUMP. MARRIAGE IMPLIES:
A most difficult and delicate adjustment
Of a passionate, emotional relationship
    WITH DOMESTIC AND ECONOMIC COÖPERATION . . . SO DOES DIVORCE.

A man goes off and starts again. He may be sad and hurt, but then
He's got his job, got his skill; a weekly cheque will pay the bills.
A woman's left with kids to mind, a life to mend and a job to find;
Got no training, got no skills, got no way to pay the bills,
Mmm-hmm . . .

So, love him, live with him, make your own vows,
It don't matter when or where or how,
'Cause just being a woman's a challenge for life.
Why complicate things by becoming a wife?

I suppose you think I'm being cynical,
But social surgery's got to be clinical.
Marriage is really to safeguard the kids,
'Cause without a mother they'd be on the skids.
Who better to feed 'em and wipe their little bums
Than good old dependable, stay-at-home Mum?

And marriage is really to safeguard the man,
Send him off to work well-fed, spic and span,
It's not only *his* labour he's a-going to sell
But that of his wife and his kids as well.
    TWO CAN EARN CHEAPER THAN ONE.

So marriage is really to safeguard the boss,
'Cause without a workforce he'd make a loss,
* And how could he rob 'em and screw 'em and twist 'em
Unless he had marriage to uphold the system
That supports the class
That exploits the man
Who exploits the wife
Who bears the kids
Who live in the house that Jack built . . .
    AND JILL CLEANS.

**Music note: At this point the song speeds up—then slows down on the penultimate line.*

The Invader

In 1957, there was an enormous release of radioactivity at the Windscale nuclear complex on the Cumbrian Coast. The enquiry into this incident (as they now call such events) took place twenty years later. In 1981, Windscale was renamed Sellafield (an apt name) in an effort to wipe out the memory of the accident. Sellafield is a source of constant environmental concern. Greenpeace has targeted it for direct action due to the massive pollution of the Irish Sea and the prevalence of child leukaemia in the villages surrounding the plant. In current media-speak, Sellafield is "one of the safest plants of its kind in the world" . . . this could mean either that it is among the very safest of all nuclear establishments or that it is one point less deadly than the most deadly. The waste that such plants produce is travelling all over the world—in the words of the famed boll weevil, "just a-lookin' for a home." I wrote "The Invader" after discovering that consignments of these lethal materials passed by rail within a half a mile of my home in Beckenham, heading for west London where they sat overnight in a shunting yard.

words and music: Peggy Seeger
disc 1A, 4, 14A

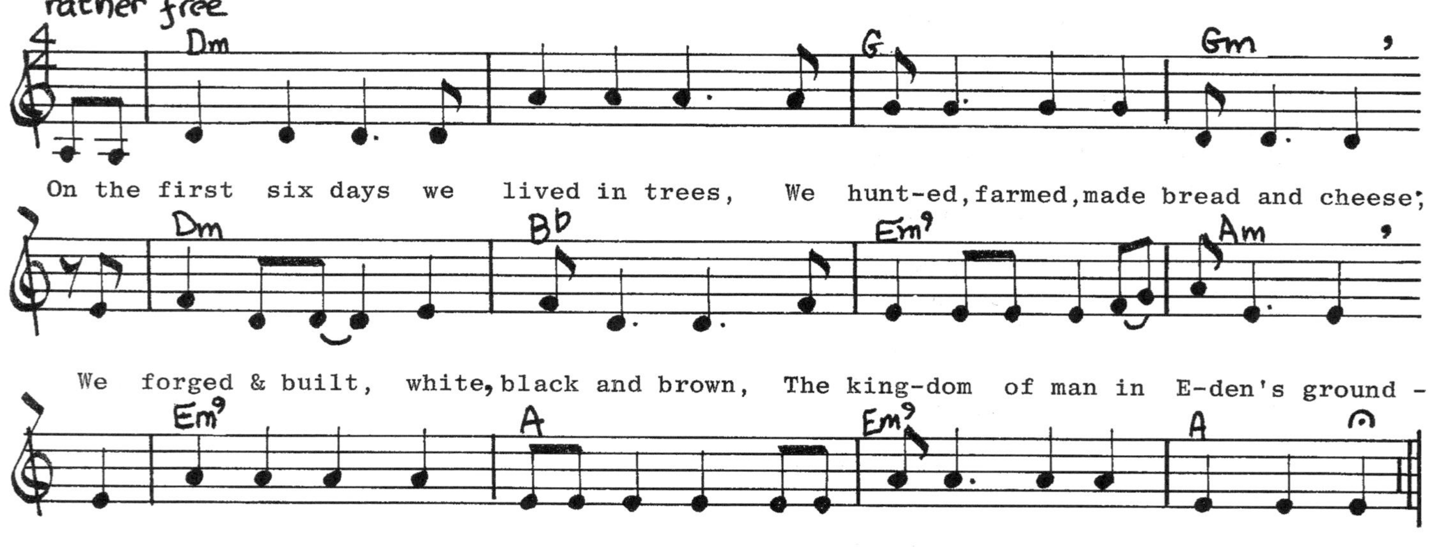

On the first six days we lived in trees,
We hunted, farmed, made bread and cheese;
We forged and built, white, black and brown,
The kingdom of man in Eden's ground—
And when we'd made our heaven and hell,
On the seventh day we killed ourselves . . .

On the first six days we fought with rocks,
With slings and bows and firelocks;
Eye for an eye, pound for a pound,
We took our wars to another man's ground—
On the seventh day our kith and kin
Welcomed the dread invader in . . .

He has no sight, no sound, no smell,
No reason at all on earth to dwell;
He has no mind to call his own,
His nature is made by man alone—
You need a machine to know he's there
In wind and water, food or air . . .

He does the work of coal and oil,
But no one wants him on their soil;
He is not made in nightly stealth,
He's made to increase worldly wealth—
And when his useful life is done,
They'll pay the earth to see him gone . . .

He comes by ship, he comes by plane,
He comes in trucks, he comes by train,
We all take tablets every week
In case they crash or they find a leak—
The children know about spent fuel
Even before they go to school . . .

Police and soldiers everywhere,
You're never alone, anywhere,
They watch your post, they tap your phone,
They check your past, and they search your home—
They give us a pass, forbid us arms,
In case we mean the invader harm . . .

The invader lives where jobs are few,
It runs itself, little to do;
Our men work there because it's near
Replaced by the death rate every year—
The poison gases overhang,
Then blow away to another man's land . . .

They pack him into glass and steel,
Then away in secret to conceal
In ocean, mountain, desert holes,
As if they were hiding their own black souls—
But someday, somewhere, he'll get out
And bring his maker to account . . .

On the seventh day we've proved our worth
As a nuclear dustbin for the earth;
* A fitting end, to set the pace
For a way of life that depends on waste—
When our children's children bear the scar,
They'll curse us for the fools we are. . . .

*Music note: *When I sing this, I tune the sixth string of the guitar down to low D. Throughout the whole song, I never play that D until the starred point in the last verse.*

Union Woman II

In August 1976, 160 workers at the Grunwick film processing plant in west London struck for the right to join a trade union (APEX). A large proportion of the strikers were Asian ladies (they do not call themselves *women*, for that is what the British and their *ladies* called native females in colonial times). In the course of the struggle, Mrs. Jayaben Desai, a Kenyan Asian immigrant, was thrust into the role of strike leader—her first experience as a political activist. APEX failed to call for a mass picket and pitched battles took place on the picket lines. ACAS (the official mediating body), the Labour Party, and the Trades Union Congress were equally reluctant to come to the aid of the strikers. After fourteen months of bitter fighting, the strike was lost. I recorded Mrs. Desai three times at the strike headquarters in Southall. She was extremely intelligent and sensitive—"cultured" is probably the appropriate word—and her leadership gave the strike an extra dimension. She apologised for not speaking "high" (*i.e.*, correct) English. In fact, her English was very colourful because it was *not* strictly correct. Many of her words and phrases, direct translations from her native tongue, are to be found in this song. Her comment, upon hearing the final draft, was, "I hear myself talking."

words and music: Peggy Seeger
disc 5, 26A, 31

Born rich in the womb,
As you say "with a silver spoon in the mouth."
Born female,
Learned early to work but never had to labour.
The luxury life is a knife in the heart and mind,
Every day, all day, any day,
Nothing to do but waste your time.

Time to marry, time to mould the life.
Father and mother choose husband and wife.
Met him, liked him, married him, love him,
Lucky.
God gives some the peaceful and loving life.

Gone the easy time, come the children,
Love the children, teach the children.
Hit your children now, they hit you later when you're old.
Find the good road, the natural life—
Good politics start at home.

Moved to England, love England.
Like to live among, learn from all manner of people.
Find a new home—the English move away;
Don't know why, the English move away.

Don't cry for the old life,
Work brings independence, self-respect and pride.
But Grunwick wants slaves and silence.
The watchdog creep behind you, white man.
Brown woman, like a schoolchild, ask to leave the line.
Children could be crying—or dying—at home,
You got to do overtime.

Management bleed, they bleach, they trample.
They hire neither man nor woman, just a worker.
A pair of hands for the wage.
The heart opens.
One, then twenty, then forty, a hundred-and-sixty,
Calling, "Union!"
Calling, "Union!"

Back the English came,
English miners, English students—and English policemen.
More than a year, every day, all day,
Late in the night and in dark morning.
Learn to think, learn to speak the English, join the English.
Don't like the fighting, inside crying—
Now the husbands are proud to see the sari on the picket line.

What matter that the strike was lost,
The enemy showed his face.
Employers, management, labour and union leaders.
Ambition and secret, scheming and shame,
APEX was low, low—unworthy of its name.

What matter that the strike was lost,
The fighting is further on.
The ladies take the lesson home to husband and children.
The crime: to ask for a real life.
The judgment: blacklisted.

Defiant, still organising, still in the union.
Employers know her name, her face, her tongue, her scorn.
But woman is patient. Her world is young, like a child,
Rich in the womb and fighting to be born.

Music note: The tune for this song is improvised so that every verse is different (see music note for "Missing"). I cast the melody into the Dorian mode and accompanied it on the five-string banjo in mountain-style playing. Mrs. Desai commented on the melody as being "very like our music."

Little Girl Child

I was at home more by the time Kitty was born and spent more time with her than I had with the boys. She was my little companion right into her early teens. I still miss her company. There she is in her overalls . . . in her school uniform . . . then flanked by the books she is forever reading . . . and trying on my glasses. Ewan, Kitty, and I went on a lot of holidays and long drives. Kitty preferred stuffed animals to dolls. She and I would sit in the back teaching Panda to read or singing Mousie to sleep. This song was written on such a drive, when Kitty was six. I really like it. Like many of my songs, it's rather wordy. But you'll have trouble cutting verses out because the last line of each verse rhymes with the second line of the following verse.

words and music: Peggy Seeger
disc 5, 19A, 26A

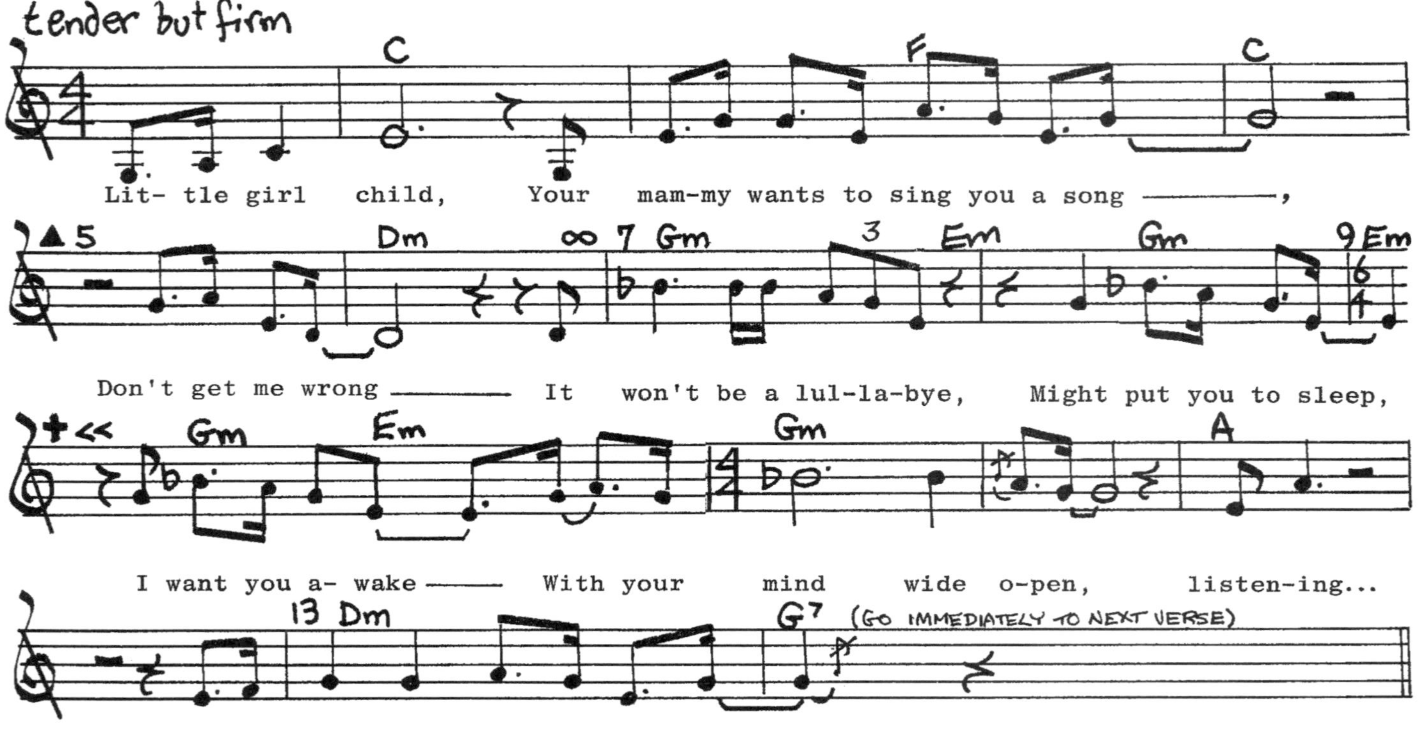
tender but firm
C
F
C
Lit- tle girl child, Your mam-my wants to sing you a song ——,
5
Dm
7 Gm
3
Em
Gm
9 Em
Don't get me wrong —— It won't be a lul-la-bye, Might put you to sleep,
Gm
Em
Gm
A
I want you a- wake —— With your mind wide o-pen, listen-ing...
13 Dm
G7
(GO IMMEDIATELY TO NEXT VERSE)
But I don't mind sing-ing it twice ——.

5
Dm
C
to 7
Not be-cause you're mine, 'Cause you're yours.

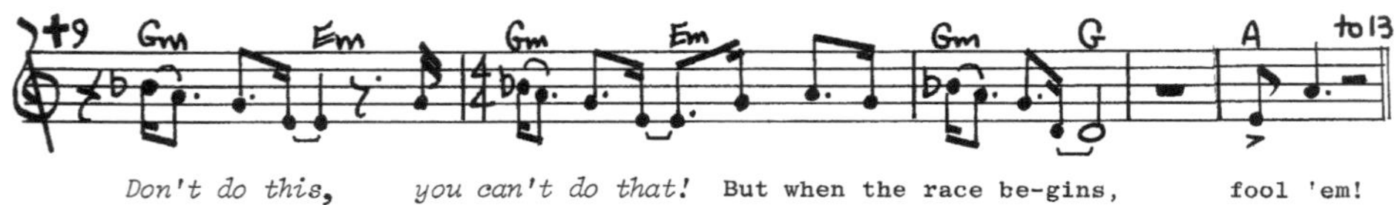
9
Gm
Em
Gm
Em
Gm
G
A
to 13
Don't do this, you can't do that! But when the race be-gins, fool 'em!

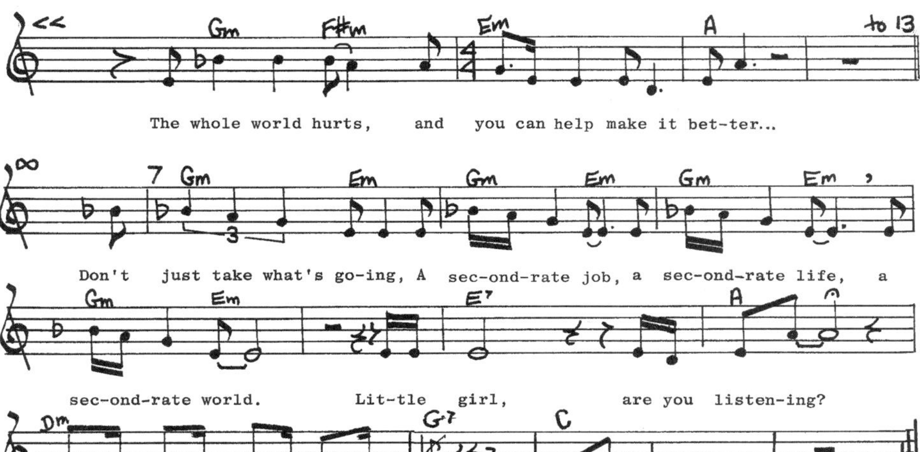

Gm F#m Em A to 13
The whole world hurts, and you can help make it bet-ter...
7 Gm Em Gm Em Gm Em
Don't just take what's go-ing, A sec-ond-rate job, a sec-ond-rate life, a
Gm Em E7 A
sec-ond-rate world. Lit-tle girl, are you listen-ing?
Dm G7 C
Guess I'll have to sing it a- gain—— to- mor-row ——.

Little girl child,
Your mammy wants to sing you a song,
Don't get me wrong—
It won't be a lullabye,
Might put you to sleep,
I want you awake
With your mind wide open, listening . . .
But I don't mind singing it twice.

Little girl child,
Your mammy wants to give you advice,
Don't be too nice—
'Cause the world isn't made for a lady,
Take what you reckon is yours,
'Cause while you're asking politely
Someone'll grab your toys.

Little girl child,
I want to hear you making a noise,
Loud as the boys—
Anything they can do you can do too,
You can be rough or smooth,
You, too, can get your hands dirty,
You don't have to toe the line.

Little girl child,
Your mammy wants you dressed up fine,
Δ Not because you're mine,
'Cause you're yours.
Nothing wrong with looking good,
Care for yourself and you'll care for others,
Ready for life and loving . . .
Nobody lives alone.

Little girl child,
Your mammy wants you to roam,
You don't have to stay home—
'Cause you're a girl they'll hold you back,
† *Don't do this, you can't do that!*
But when the race begins, fool 'em!
You can be out of sight.

Little girl child,
Your mammy wants to see you right,
Teach you to fight;
Not just for yourself
Or for the ones you love,
« The whole world hurts, and you can help make it better . . .
We'll try to show you how.

Little girl child,
I want to hear you making a vow
Starting right now;
∞ Don't just take what's going,
A second-rate job, a second-rate life, a second-rate world.
Little girl, are you listening?
Guess I'll have to sing it again tomorrow.

Music note: I've only notated the extreme variations. It would be best to listen to the recording of this one if you are having trouble fitting the words in.

you don't look
like a feminist

WATCH OUT -
we DISGUISE ourselves
as human beings
until DUSK

Lady, What Do You Do All Day?

(1) Billy's comment as he sits down with the paper reminds me of a programme I saw on the drought in the Sahel desert. The fields are burnt out. Stock is dead and dying. Children sit with distended bellies, starving. The camera catches glimpses of men sitting in groups, hunkered down and talking. The commentary burbles on, ". . . and the women have to walk miles for water. . . ."

(2) In February 1994, the Legal and General insurance company set the amount of £349 as the sum required to pay people to do the weekly work of a housewife.

(3) The *1965 Dictionary of Occupational Titles* (put together by the Department of Labour) ranks 22,000 occupations according to the complexity of skills involved. It rated HOMEMAKER at the lowest possible level, along with shovellers of poultry shit, rest-room attendants, and parking-lot attendants.

words and music: Peggy Seeger
disc 5, 19A

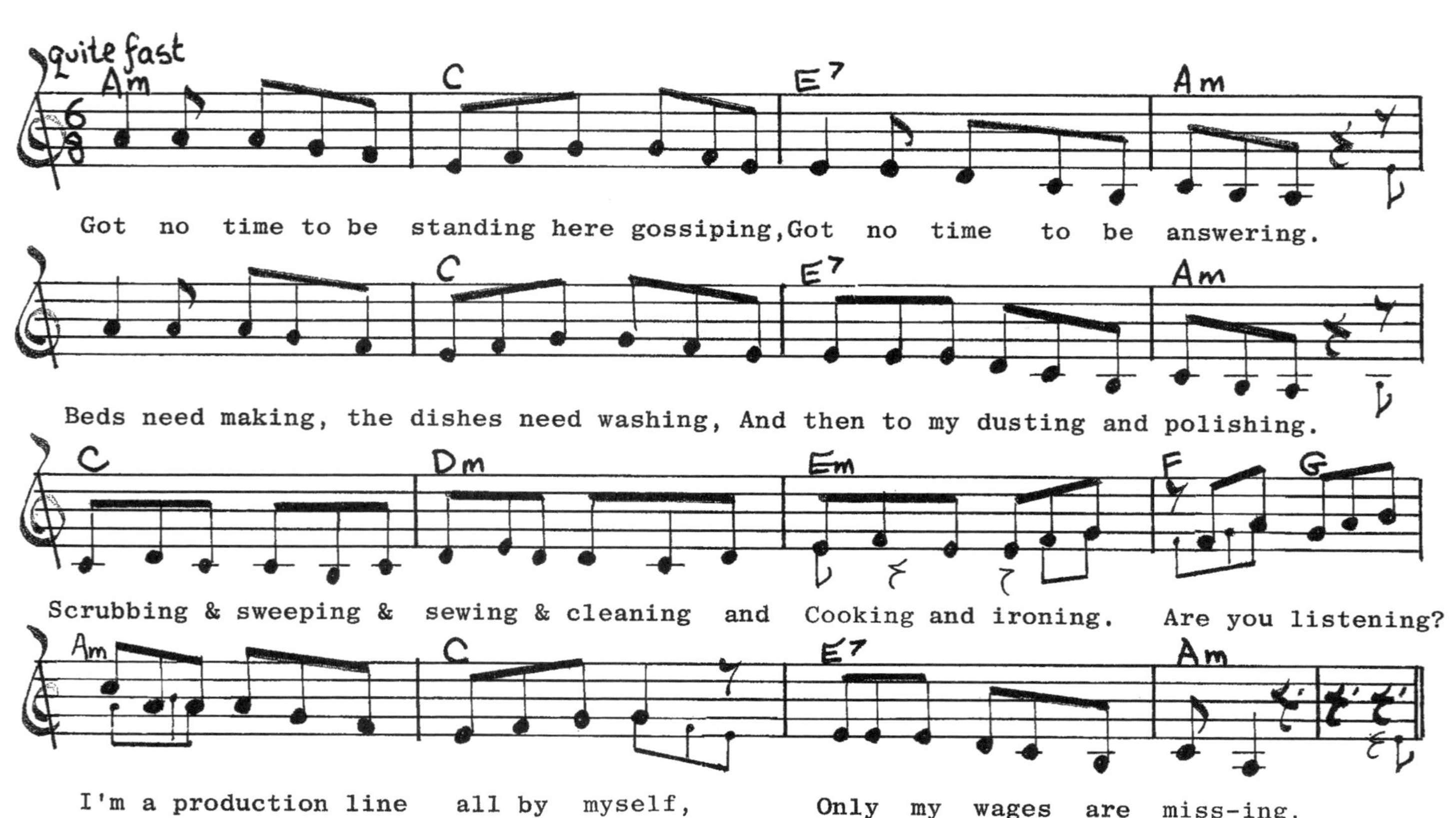
free
LA-DY - WHAT DO YOU DO ALL DAY? LA-DY - HOW DO YOU SPEND YOUR TIME? LA-DY -
quite fast
Am C E7 Am
Got no time to be standing here gossiping, Got no time to be answering.
C E7 Am
Beds need making, the dishes need washing, And then to my dusting and polishing.
C Dm Em F G
Scrubbing & sweeping & sewing & cleaning and Cooking and ironing. Are you listening?
Am C E7 Am
I'm a production line all by myself, Only my wages are miss-ing.

Give me my wa- ges, give me my due, I'm opt- ing out of the sys- tem.
Give me bo-nus-es, overtime, sick-leave & paid holidays and a pension. Then I can
(accompaniment halts...)
(then begins again)
strike, work to rule, or go slow, Or ob- ject to conditions and
hours For wages will give me the pow-er To have a say in a world Where a per-son who
slow down
hap-pens to be fe-male is s'posed to be hap-py To spend all her time as a
fast again
Ba-by-mind-er, sock- find-er, Ba-con-fry-er, dish-dry-er, Floor-sweep-er,
light slee-per, Brow smooth-er, mend the Hoo-ver ... Nap-py-fold-er, hand-hold-er,
On-ion-chop-per, mess-mop-per, But-ton-sew-er, to-and-fro-er, Ti - dy-up- per,
(spoken)
(any chords or unison octaves)
(What's for sup-per?) Mon-ey-stretch-er, run-and- fetch-er .. Cake-bak - er,
speed up
Back- ach-er, Ear-ly wak-er, Bed- mak-er, Break-fast-mak-er, Lunch- mak-er,
(free)
Tea-mak-er, Sand-wich-mak-er, LA-DY - WHAT DO YOU DO ALL DAY? LA-DY - IT'S YOUR
(spoken)
ON- LY LIFE! WHEN THEY ASK YOU, WHAT DO YOU SAY——? O,
I don't work. I'm noth-ing but a house-wife.

(free)
LADY—WHAT DO YOU DO ALL DAY?
LADY—HOW DO YOU SPEND YOUR TIME?
LADY—

(in rhythm)
Got no time to be standing here gossiping,
Got no time to be answering.
Beds need making, the dishes need washing,
And then to my dusting and polishing.
Scrubbing and sweeping and sewing and cleaning and
Cooking and ironing. Are you listening?
I'm a production line all by myself,
Only my wages are missing.

Three kids of eight and seven and two,
Leisure is just a mythology.
When it's over my head, I can't go to bed,
It's temper or else psychology.
Mary's bedwetting and Tommy is jealous
Of Baby, his yelling is driving me crazy,
A nurse and a nanny until I'm a granny
But why is it nobody pays me?

I care for a lovely old mother-in-law,
She's eighty-seven and cranky.
Husband's home with a feverish cold,
Run for the tea and the hankies,
The hot-water bottle, the telly, the paper,
And now the kids have it (it must be contagious),
So now I'm the family medical staff,
But where the hell are my wages?

If wives and mothers all took to their heels,
You'd soon be needing an army;
And paying them all their union wages,
I bet it would drive you barmy.
All eyes and ears, all hands and feet,
My sign is Gemini (should have been two of me),
I do the work of a dozen a day
But where are the wages due to me?

With wages so low and prices so high,
Budgeting must be meticulous.
The hours I spend in looking for bargains
And cooking 'em's really ridiculous.
And though my man's doing all that he can,
What he brings home isn't making ends meet
And I'll have to go out for a wage myself
If the family's going to keep eating.

So it's up in the morning before all the family,
Get the grub on the table.
Beds need making, the dishes need washing,
It's everything done on the double.
Drop the kids off at the school then run for my bus,
Don't you think it's outrageous?
I'd more than enough with my Labour of Love
Now I'm doing another for wages.

The boss is as good as a boss can be
But the office is just like a nursery.
Smoothing his life, soothing his troubles,
Remembering his anniversary.
Reminding, hurrying, scurrying, worrying,
Into the frying pan, out of the cage
And it's home from home wherever I roam,
But at least I'm getting the wages.

On my way home I shop for the dinner
And then have a tidy around.
Billy comes in, sits down with the paper,
Says, "Girl, don't you ever sit down?"
Men of the world, would you think it was strange,
Think it was right, think it was funny
To slog every night at a job for free
After slogging all day for your money? So—

Δ Give me my wages, give me my due,
I'm opting out of the system.
Give me bonuses, overtime, sick-leave
And paid holidays and a pension.
Then I can strike, work to rule, or go slow,
Or object to conditions and hours
For wages would give me the power
To have a say in a world
Where a person who happens to be female
Is s'posed to be happy
To spend all her time as a
    Baby-minder, sock-finder,
    Bacon-fryer, dish-dryer,
    Floor-sweeper, light sleeper,
    Brow-smoother, mend the Hoover . . .
    Nappy-folder, hand-holder,
    Onion-chopper, mess-mopper,
    Button-sewer, to-and-fro-er,
    Tidy-upper, (What's for supper?)
    Money-stretcher, run-and-fetcher . . .
        Cake-baker,
        Back-acher,
        Early waker,
        Bed-maker,
        Breakfast-maker,
        Lunch-maker,
        Tea-maker,
        Sandwich-maker,

(freely)
LADY—WHAT DO YOU DO ALL DAY?
LADY—IT'S YOUR ONLY LIFE!
WHEN THEY ASK YOU, WHAT DO YOU SAY?

(spoken) O, I don't work.
(sung) I'm nothing but a housewife.

Music note: As catalogue songs have to be sung almost automatically, it's a great temptation to get enthusiastic and sing this song far too fast. Sing it like housework, methodically and thoroughly.

and to demonstrate the biological differences between the male and the female of the species, you can see that the male is almost entirely brain whilst the female is shaped like a pram

Twenty Years

This is a foil to the previous song. It is the philosophy as opposed to the physical actuality of the housewife.

words and music: Peggy Seeger
disc 5, 26A

Twenty years to teach her all she needs to learn
To take that sweet mysterious journey past the point of no return;
Overall or apron, single girl or wed,
Learns first to use her heart and hands, then to use her head—
She's not a trueborn woman if she can't make a bed.

Twenty years to show her what seems her only way,
She won't know until too late the price she'll have to pay;
If she don't want to settle down she must be running wild,
Her body tells her "Go ahead," her head says "Wait awhile"—
But she's not a trueborn woman if she don't want a child.

Twenty years to teach her to want to be a wife,
To find and hold another human who must keep her all his life;
Because she works for nothing he'll get a lower wage,
If she were not dependent they might fly out of their cage—
She starts out as a lover and may end up as a slave.

Twenty years we train her to work for love alone,
You can define a woman: she works in the home.
If everyone who loves their job shouldn't ask a fee,
Then everyone who hates their job should get the wage of three—
She's not a trueborn woman till she wants to work for free.

Twenty years we train her to give away her time,
So when she works outside the home she'll keep the men in line,
Underselling, underpaid, home-piecework when she can,
Becomes the perfect lever for the boss against her man—
And for a trueborn woman that's hard to understand.

All her life we nurture, we mothers and the men,
That sweet mysterious nature of the cow, the mouse, the hen;
Diligent in heart and hand, lazy in her mind,
And not till every trueborn woman sees this as a crime
Can every trueborn human leave the past behind.

Music note: Try singing this song interlaced with the previous one. Its soaring, free melody, against a continuous ripple of accompaniment, makes a wonderful contrast to the energetic, busy housewife.

Winnie and Sam

Winnie was another one of the inmates of the Forest Hill sanctuary (see "Emily"). She shuttled from refuge to refuge because whenever she was rehoused with her children her husband would discover their whereabouts and make their lives impossible. She had a wonderful sense of humour—until she started talking about her marriage. Then her whole body went still and her speaking delivery became terse and unemotional. It is from this body language that I have derived the style of the song. She asked a lot about *my* life, which is unusual in my experience of interviewing. She was well educated and appeared to have been well off before she'd flown the marriage coop. Her experiences in a number of safehouses had given her a personal perspective on the battering man. Her view was that working-class men generally struck out in fury, aiming for any part of the body that they could reach; middle-class men would batter more carefully, aiming for parts of the body that would be covered by clothing. "That gave him a lot of scope," said Winnie, "because I was fond of long sleeves, turtlenecks, and trousers." The more money in a house, she claimed, the more mental and less physical the violence became. Into this song, which is Winnie's life, I interjected some of the universal reactions that battered women report from the police, the medical/social services, and the law.

words and music: Peggy Seeger
disc 5, 26A

Here's a little song about Winnie,
Married Handsome Sam;
He called her "my own little wife,"
She called him "my man."

Wasn't it a lovely wedding?
A hundred guests or more.
Before the honeymoon was over
He'd knocked her to the floor.

Wasn't it a lovely marriage?
He never left her alone.
She always wore a high-necked blouse,
She must've been accident-prone.

Whenever the neighbours heard the noise,
The cops come rollin' along.
Saw his fist and her black eye,
Hullo, is there anything wrong?

Casualty always patched her up,
Sent her right back home.
Said, "Our job is to heal the sick.
"Not to ask *how come?*"

The GP he was a family man,
Didn't want to intercede;
A bottle of pills, a bit of advice:
A baby is what you need.

So on Saturday he beat his own little wife,
Sunday he bashed the kids;
One Monday morning, Winnie woke up:
This union is on the skids.

She went to the Marriage Guidance
But she had to go alone.
Handsome Sam wouldn't go with her
So they guided her right back home.

A social worker come onto the case,
She found Winnie in tears.
Says, "You're not as bad as some I've seen,
"And it proves that he loves you, dear."

The Housing Department turned her away
After filling in all those forms.
"We just got no place to put you, dear,
"Afraid you'll have to go back home."

Well, maybe the Homeless Persons Act
Might be applicable here;
But can you define—and be exact—
How hard does he hit you, dear?

Well, after eleven heavenly years,
To make a long story short;
One day Sam went a little too far—
Winnie took Sam to court.

O, what a lovely trial!
Sam got the shock of his life.
He stood in the dock, stared at the judge,
"You mean I can't beat my wife?"

Do you think my song is funny?
Well, it was not meant to be,
'Cause the world believes it when a man says,
"Honey, you belong to me."

Does it only happen to a poor man's wife
Or a so-called "lower degree?"
Winnie is a lawyer's daughter,
Sam's got a Ph.D.

Marriage is a feudal custom,
Women are one of the props;
Women help to make it go
And women got to make it stop.
We all got to make it stop.

Music note: I've given no chords because I usually accompany this entirely in A position (here capoed up to C). The constant A in the bass, with fairly monotonous single-note figures above it, will provide all you need as accompaniment.

Different Therefore Equal

The premise contained in this title should apply not only to human females, but also to the air, the mountains and waters, and to all the flora and fauna of the world we live in.

words and music: Peggy Seeger
disc 5, 26A

lightly, terse
Is a fa - ther Bet-ter than a moth-er?
Is a sis-ter Bet-ter than a broth-er?
One's con- cave. One's con- vex.
OPTIONAL
Does that make one sex Bet-ter than the oth-er?

▲ verse 5 only
Is black bet-ter than white, Day bet-ter than night?
With-out ei - ther There'd be nei - ther.

Is a father
Better than a mother?
Is a sister
Better than a brother?
One's concave.
One's convex.
Does that make one sex
Better than the other?

Ajax' shoulders
Moved boulders.
Helen's hips
Launched ships.
Opposites favour
Their opposites' nature.
Adam and Eve are
Fish and chips.

The world needs us
So the world breeds us,
From the ant and the elephant
To the little rhesus monkey.
Every creature
From the anteater
To the mooses
Has its uses.

A dog don't sing.
A bird don't bark.
So which is the best thing,
A poodle or a lark?
It's ridickless
Comparing
One who's prickless
To one who's hairy.

Δ Is black better than white,
Day better than night?
Without either
There'd be neither.

Some we-mens
Try to be she-mens
Then say that he-mens
Are worse than demons.
Nature gives us
Equal chances,
And to get 'em,
You shouldn't have to wear pantses.

Let's be like moles,
Or does or rabbits
And try and control
Unsocial habits,
And things that turn us
Against each other,
And don't learn us
To be sister and brother.

If her and him are
Indispensable,
Treatin' em similar
Is only sensible.
Reason gives us
The logical sequel:
We're different,
Therefore equal.

Music note: *The singing style of this song is almost conversational. Nearly every verse has a different melody, sung in different rhythms. It's a song you can have fun with. Don't be afraid of silence and syncopation, of adding and subtracting beats so long as the rhythm stays steady and continuous. I find the best accompaniment to be a foot-tap alternating with a hand-clap.*

Reclaim the Night

It is the winter of 1994. I have rented a small renovated stable in the North Country. Here I will put the bulk of the song notes together. The countryside in this part of Yorkshire is wonderful, despite the three thermal power stations that ring my western horizon. The land is flat—there are few trees and the Derwent river slides quietly between the dykes. It is a wet winter and occasionally the fields are flooded. The 180-degree skies are a revelation, especially at dusk. I walk several miles every day on long, lonely country roads and across huge expanses. It is now a feature of life in Britain that a lone female is in a potential danger situation *vis-à-vis* males. We can be insulted, assaulted, raped, and murdered *anywhere:* in our homes, in our places of work, in the cities, in the countryside—anytime. I thank the friends who gave me a walking stick for Christmas, not because they were worried about my solo excursions but because they figured if I got it before I needed it then I wouldn't feel so bad about getting it later on when I *do* need it. I resent the fact that my stick reassures me when, on my walks, a man with a dog approaches, or a car stops to ask directions. I would love to walk at night but I don't, for rather than walk with fear as a companion I will not walk at all. Here, where I want to greet the dark and the stars, I understand completely the feminist slogan "Reclaim the Night": reclaim the *right* to go *where* we want and *when* we want—alone. I have only once in my life been the recipient of violence—and that fairly mild—at the hand of a man. Yet I have apprehension permanently imprinted on my circuit now—and I am angry.

words and music: Peggy Seeger
disc 5, 26A, 31

free

Though Eve was made from A-dam's rib, nine months he lay with- in her crib;

How can a man of wom-an born there- af- ter use her sex with scorn?

For though we bear the hu-man race, to us is given but sec-ond place;

And some men place us low-er still by us- ing us a- gainst our will.

Though Eve was made from Adam's rib, nine months he lay within her crib;
How can a man of woman born thereafter use her sex with scorn?
For though we bear the human race, to us is given but second place;
And some men place us lower still by using us against our will.

If men can't be trusted on the streets at night

If we choose to walk alone for us there is no safety zone,
If we're attacked we bear the blame, they say that we began the game;
And though you prove your injury, the judge may set the rapist free;
Therefore the victim is to blame. Call it nature—but rape's the name.

Chorus: Reclaim the night and win the day,
We want the right that should be our own,
A freedom women have seldom known:
The right to live, the right to walk alone without fear.

A husband has his lawful rights, can take his wife whene'er he likes,
Δ Though courts uphold, time after time, that rape in marriage *is* a crime.
The choice is hers, and hers alone: submit, or lose your kids and home.
When love becomes a legal claim, call it duty—but rape's the name.

And if a man should rape a child is it because his spirit's wild?
Our system gives the prize to all who trample on the weak and small;
When fathers rape, they surely know their kids have nowhere else to go.
Try to forget, don't ask us to forgive them: they know what they do. *(chorus)*

then why aren't THEY kept in?

When exploitation is the norm, rape is found in many forms:
Lower wages, meaner tasks, poorer schooling, second class.
We serve our own and, like the men, we serve employers. It follows then
That body's rape is nothing new but just a servant's final due.

We've raised our voices in the past † and this time will not be the last.
Our body's gift is ours to give not payment for the right to live.
Since we reject the status quo, we claim the right to answer NO!
If without consent he stake a claim, call it rape—for rape's the name.

Music note: A group of women singing this in unison, unaccompanied, is powerful. It takes a lot of practice but it's worth it.

Harry's Eats

This song is dedicated to the gentleman cook who put up the sign HARRY'S EATS at the 1979 Winnipeg Folk Festival and proceeded to make mealtimes the main attraction of the weekend for the performers and staff. At the 1993 festival he accepted my proposal, but it was too late. He'd given up cooking.

words and music: Peggy Seeger
© 1992 Peggy Seeger (1)

happily
D G D Bm
Har-ry Paine's no friend of mine, Ad-ded two in-ches to my waist-line;
D G D A7 D
Three on the thigh, four on the hip, On-ly three days and my clothes don't fit.
G D E7 A7
We came in leaps, we came in bounds, Danc-ing through the gates of the Fes-ti-val Grounds,
D7 G D A7 D
Look at us now, stuck to our seats, Too full to move. It's Har-ry's Eats.

LAST TWO LINES ONLY
D G D G D
But if ev-er I come out west a-gain, Please won't you mar-ry me, Har-ry Paine?

Harry Paine's no friend of mine,
Added two inches to my waistline;
Three on the thigh, four on the hip,
Only three days and my clothes don't fit.
    We came in leaps, we came in bounds,
    Dancing through the gates of the Festival Grounds,
    Look at us now, stuck to our seats,
    Too full to move. It's Harry's Eats.

Honey and cheese, cookies and cake,
Turkey and ham and the charcoal steak;
De Danaan couldn't even murmur "Good on ye!"
Their mouths were too full of Harry's lasagne.
    They come up through the ground, drop out of the sky,
    Just to get a sniff of that rhubarb pie;
    They walk on their hands, run on their feets
    Just to get a helping of Harry's Eats.

I bet you think I'm Peggy Seeger
Or a real folksinger. Nope, I'm neither.
I ripped off a banjo, bought me a wig
Just to get a taste of that sucking pig.
    O, they come from Peoria, Prague and Penang
    Just to get a nibble of lemon meringue.
    Even a corpse would shake off the sheets
    Just to get a morsel of Harry's Eats.

With grub like that, you don't need wine.
But don't just eat—sit down and *dine*;
And every time a meal comes rolling along,
Add another verse to this damn fool song.
    O, we all learned bluegrass, boogie and ballad
    Just to get grabs at the 'taters and salad;
    Even a Shakespeare, Chaucer or Keats
    Couldn't pay proper tribute to HARRY'S EATS.

Δ But if ever I come out west again,
    Please won't you marry me, Harry Paine?

the way to a
woman's heart...
chocolate mousse

Four-Minute Warning

The 1955 Defence White Paper recommended massive retaliation as the proper defence policy for Britain. Four minutes was the length of time that we would have between warning of a (Soviet) nuclear attack and the attack itself. The Four-Minute Warning became a catch-phrase that struck terror to the heart, that filled the ranks of CND and formed the subject of apocalyptic films and documentaries. A small report in the *Guardian* (October 1980) used concentric circles drawn around the centre of London to show what one nuclear bomb would do to our capital city and its environs. My tower is the British Telecom Tower (previously the Post Office Tower) which was itself closed to the public after being bombed in October 1971. With the use of a compass I drew similar circles and wrote this song according to the predictions in the article.

words and music: Peggy Seeger
disc 6

Imagine a city. Imagine a tower
Whose crown turns around fully once every hour.

North, south, east and west, see the heath and the river,
With Chelsea on one side, Mile End on the other.

Imagine that city! Imagine that morning
In summer, imagine the Four-Minute Warning.

Panic, then wait, or kneel and start praying—
Four minutes to make your god hear what you're saying.

Look towards home, no time for leave-taking,
The sound that you hear is twelve-million hearts breaking.

There's a circle around you, six miles to the rim,
From Acton to Poplar, from Finchley to Balham.

Dulwich to Hendon, it's the heart of the nation,
Not a blade of grass standing, complete devastation.

There's a circle beyond, where firestorms roar,
From Redhill to Hornchurch, from Hemel to Slough.

Weybridge to Harlow, too wounded for crying,
Half the folk dead and the other half dying.

Two minutes are gone, the fall-out drifts over
To Banbury, Winchester, way beyond Dover.

Ipswich to Brighton, radiation is high,
The ones who are left may take ten years to die.

The rulers are sheltered, but God has gone under,
Victim perhaps of a technical blunder.

The vermin survive disease and starvation,
To witness the end of a civilisation.

No air safe to breathe, no land remains fertile,
While our bombs home in on some other circle.

There's no one to help you, there's no medication.
This bomb was one part of proposed saturation.

If your children survive, they may carry mutations
To the next and the next and all next generations.

A half-minute to go, you won't see another.
Twelve-million children are crying for mother.

Open your eyes: tomorrow comes morning,
You have been hearing a Four-Minute Warning.

Music note: The song should last exactly four minutes.

'dig a hole and jump into it'.
RIP

Plutonium Factor

One morning in the late seventies a leaflet on nuclear power was dropped through our letterbox. It was one of a series of excellent little documents put out by ECOROPA, an environmental and political information service. I read it over breakfast and took it with me to the crowd of mothers who gathered daily around Kitty's school gate where, within days, nuclear waste, nuclear transport, nuclear *anything* became a daily subject of conversation. When we discovered that spent fuel was travelling daily a half mile from the school, we formed the Beckenham Anti-Nuclear Group (BANG) and I was put in charge of its programme. I knew nothing about nuclear power, but by immersing myself from Wednesday to Monday in what we later referred to as "The Big Blue Book" (*No Nukes,* by Anna Gyorgy and friends) I managed to sound sufficiently authoritative at the Tuesday evening meetings. When we had more information at our fingertips, we lectured at schools, leafletted the neighbourhood and petitioned Number Ten in white boiler suits. This piece is the BBB, telescoped and put into poetry. The music is too complicated to include here. For years I witheld a percentage of my electricity bill as an objection to nuclear power—*i.e.*, when the latter provided eleven percent of the supply, I witheld eleven percent of the bill. When I finally *had* to pay or be cut off I would write the cheque out on a door, on a rotten egg, on a cake, or on a small coffin-shaped dulcimer case. One similar objector in Dorset wrote his cheque out on the side of a cow and led the cow into the bank to pay the bill! All cheques have to go through a system of checking, stamping, filing, and being sent back to the originator. My "cheques" came back to me by courier. The egg was *very* gently presented to me on my doorstep. The cake never came back. I had sent a note with it, requesting the bank staff to eat it. I found out later that two of them refused. Perhaps they thought it might be damaging to their health?

words and music: Peggy Seeger
disc 6

The problem is elemental, easy to understand:
Uranium's incidental, lying beneath the land.
Find it, mine it,
Enrich and refine it—
No matter its use,
A demon is loose,
Plutonium's left, long after the death of man.

Energy is reactive, easy to understand:
Uranium's radioactive, unstable and quick to expand;
Send a neutron to enter,
Splitting the centre
Of 2-3-5,
Fission brings it alive;
Atoms are broken,
Heat is the token we take.
More neutrons are made,
More atoms invaded,
The element vanishes—but in its wake
Plutonium's left.
Thus was the world betrayed.

The core broods like the heart of the sun,
Cool gas or water for a cage,
Guarded by fallible gods.
If natural force overrun its course
Who would be keeper then?
No one.
Not the expert, the backer, the builder, the worker,

No one knows what would happen then.
In that split second of endless time
Will we, in the name of heaven,
Remember a time when it wasn't too late,
Russia in '58, Harrisburg '79?

The problem is elemental, easy to engineer:
The process is fundamental, once it is set in gear.
The fuel is old,
Too lethal to hold,
If no one steals it,
Wheel it through city and town.
Re-make it, break it,
Windscale it down
Or use it again, it won't disappear;
Fast-breeder excreting more shit than it's eating,
Plutonium's made—thousands of pounds a year.

Disaster is not a notion, it's easy to be foreseen,
Whether by movement of ocean or land, failure of man or machine.
Fallout or leakage,
Dumping or breakage,
Caesium . . . tritium . . . curium . . . krypton-85,
And anything alive begins to be dead.
But plutonium's made—
Plutonium never dies.

The core broods, unconcerned, unaware,
Unseen, won't stay in a cage.
Touch it, you die.
Stand near it, you die.
Breathe it, you die.
Live near it, you die.
Cremated, you burn—your bones fill the air,
Who breathes it will die.
As long as it's there,
Someone,
Something, will slip out of line.
In that split second of endless time,
When the clocks stop and the dial clicks,
Will we, falling into the void,
Remember Detroit
'Way back in '66?

The problem is monumental, but easy to understand:
Someone is raking in profits, hand over hand over hand.
Too many cracks in the system.
Too many flaws in the plan.
Too many pounds of plutonium missing,
Too many fools among men.
The game's nearly up, we're playing it now,
Eeny meeny miney moe—

(chanted rhythmically, like a children's counting-out game)
Sizewell, Bradwell, Chapel Cross, Heysham, Hunterston, Dungeness, Calder Hall started it all,
Trawsfynydd, Winfrith, Hinkley Point, Berkeley, Oldbury, Hartlepool, Springfields, Capenhurst,
Dounreay, Wylfa, Windscale, YOU!

We have the power to close them down,
Or just be a unit in the body-count,
A citizen of the Plutonium State.
Now is the moment of endless time,
Turn around and step out of line—
Tomorrow will be too late!

Music note: *This is a production piece, almost Brechtian. It needs several voices and an adventurous instrumental arrangment to put it to full effect. Writing down the simple melody line here would not really have given much of an idea of its potential. Try to get hold of the disc.*

Song for Charles Parker

Charles was the kind of man who stood at military attention, saluting, at the end of films when "God Save the Queen" was played. He was the kind of person who, when everyone in the car was starving with hunger, would secretly pop chocolates into his mouth from the little paper bag in his breast pocket. That's the kind of person he was before he changed. Mao Zedong would have been proud of Charles Parker's personal transformation. He was an established, establishment radio producer, on his way up in the BBC until he got the idea that inspired the first radio ballad (see "In Particular"). He and I came into contact with Ewan at roughly the same time and we developed along parallel lines, although Charles was sixteen years my senior. We three were the leaders of the radio ballad team: Ewan, a writer with singing and theatrical background; Charles, a superb producer and tape-editor; and myself, capable of dealing with the instrumental and musical end of things. Charles revolutionised his politics but when he tried to apply them at the BBC he lost his job. He continued to immerse himself in the working-class movement and was one of the founders of Banner Theatre in Birmingham. He had learned how to share himself—and his chocolates—tirelessly with friends and collaborators. He was well on the way to making his heart and his mind work together when he died at the age of sixty-one, on December 10, 1980. We had our differences—but I remember him with love and admiration.

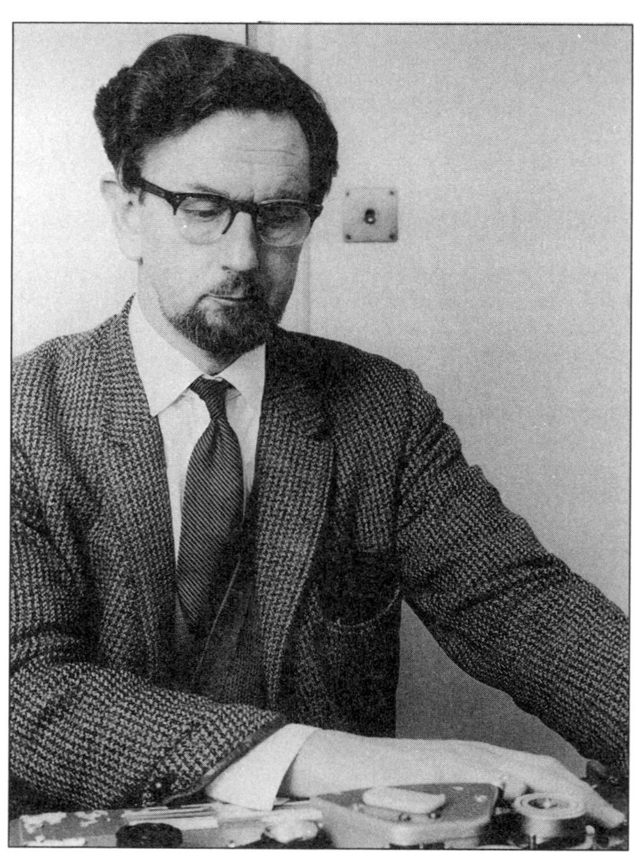

words and music: Peggy Seeger

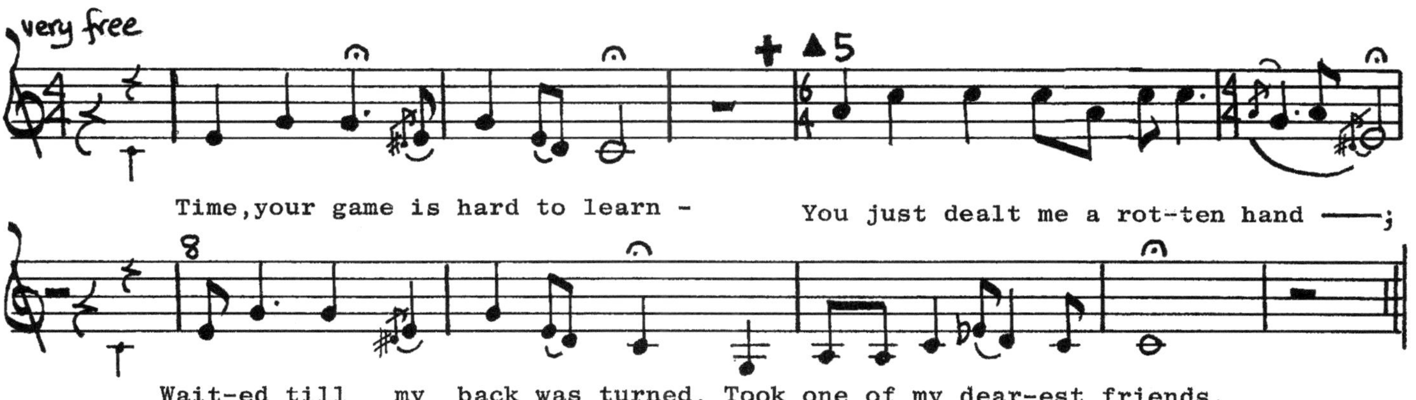

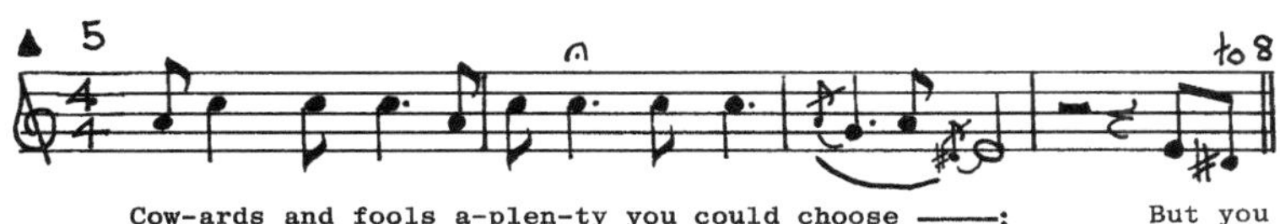

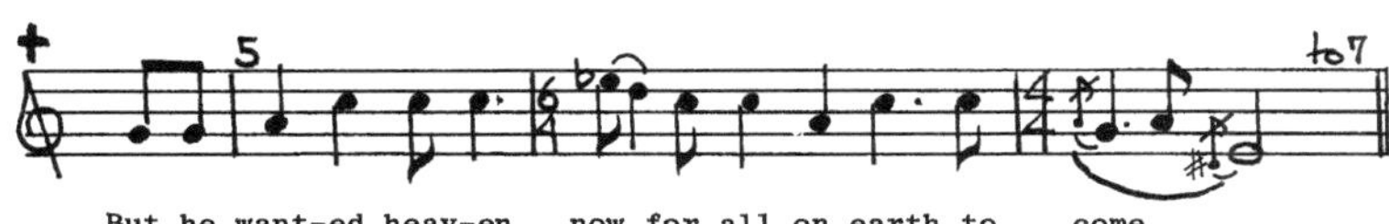

Time, your game is hard to learn—
You just dealt me a rotten hand;
Waited till my back was turned,
Took one of my dearest friends.

Many others that you might take,
Δ Cowards and fools aplenty you could choose;
But you took a friend so hard to make
And harder still to lose.

He could have sold out, denied his soul,
† But he wanted heaven now for all on earth to come.
A good, skilled man, he died on the dole,
He chose the race he run.

Time, tide me over a few more years,
Please allow my comrade's friends to thrive;
We're part of all that he held dear—
We keep our friend alive.

Enough Is Enough

I took seven pieces of blank paper. At the top of each I put the subject of a verse of this song, in the form of a question:

1. What do you worry about?
2. What do you spend your money on?
3. What is wearing out in your life?
4. What are some great projects that have gone wrong?
5. What are the ways in which one can die?
6. What would you most hate to lose in your life?
7. What are the solutions to the world's problems?

I walked around with this sheaf of papers for weeks, asking friends, acquaintances, and family members to just scrawl something on each page. As a method it worked beautifully. They came up with ideas and ways of expressing them that I would never have hit upon. It made the song appeal to a wider variety of people. It also made the song much longer (if that's possible) than it would have been had I been left on my own . . . and the song became less regular and more interesting. So I wish to thank all the contributors, wherever you are. As the text printed here has recently been North Americanised, I am acknowledging folks on both sides of the ocean.

words and music: Peggy Seeger
disc 16

fast but not too fast

C F
Some-thing al-ways keeps you scur-ry-ing with prob-lems and with wor-ry-ing, There's

C D7 G F
ad-di-tives in the vit-tles and there's poi-sons in the air. There's kids with prob-lem

C A1 2 G C A1
pa-rents and you can't i-ma-gine where You'll get the mon-ey to pay the bills, You're

(REPEAT THESE BARS FOR ITALIC TYPE) 1 2 D7 G
get-ting old, get-ting fat (etc). . .that You've got no mat-ches for the gas. Your

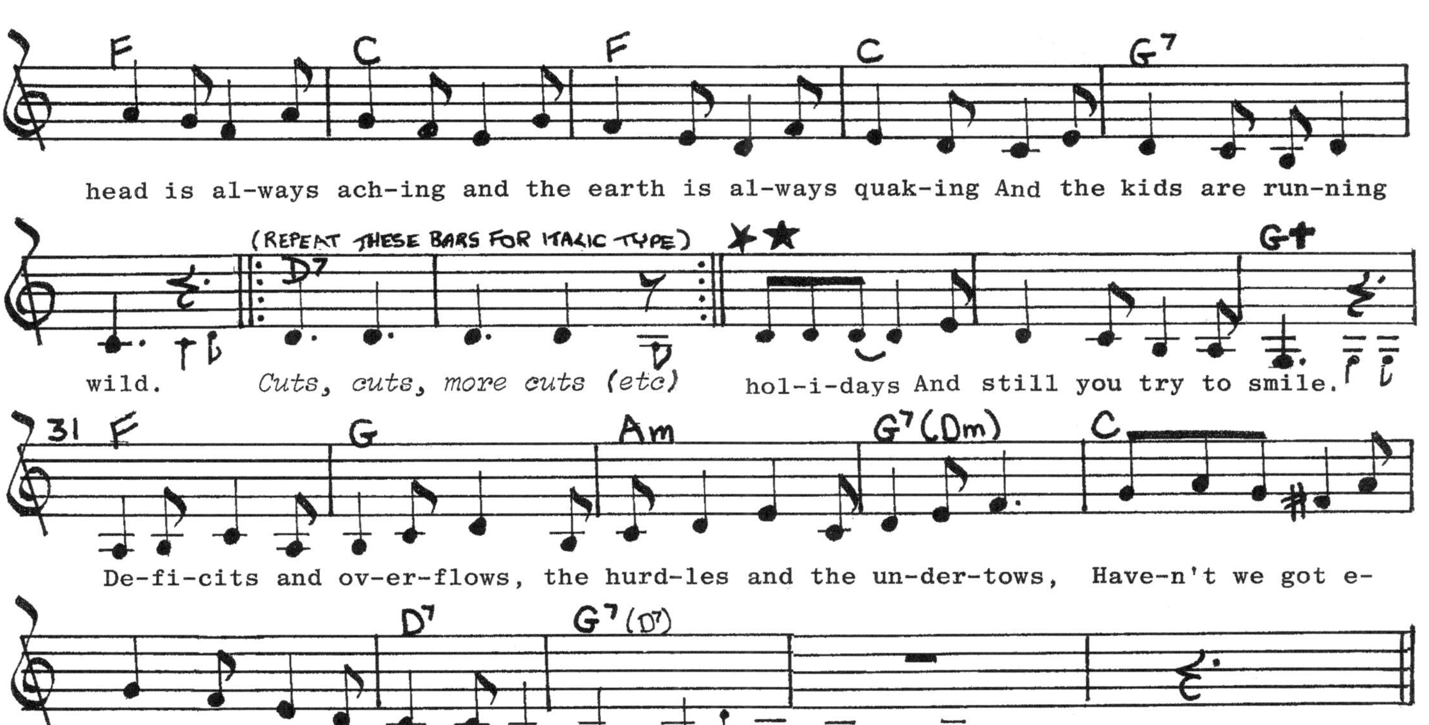

Something always keeps you scurrying with problems and with worrying,
There's additives in the vittles and there's poisons in the air.
There's kids with problem parents and you can't imagine where
You'll get the money to pay the bills,
You're *getting old, getting fat,*
Behind the Joneses, lost your job, and to top *that
You've just run out of gas.
Your head is always aching and the earth is always quaking
And the kids are running wild.
Cuts, cuts, more cuts, Survivalists, Separatists, cholesterol,
Traffic jams, you've missed your plane, it's raining on your **holidays
And still you try to smile.
Deficits and overflows, the hurdles and the undertows,
Haven't we got enough without a nuclear sideshow?

You're always courting Lady Luck and shelling out another buck,
On legal fees and medicine, the insurance, and the rent.
Your kid is going to college: it's a ruinous event.
Matrimony, alimony, you've *just confessed to the IRS*
And before the turn of the century
The *Portuguese'll be sending foreign aid.
You pay to read the news about inflation and the nation
Doesn't buy the kids their shoes.
Laxatives and dental floss, a drop of booze and little things
Like clothes, food, heat, light, **AND . . . your Mediterranean cruise.
Plenty of ways to lose your pence from dire need to extravagance,
Haven't we got enough without the nuclear expenses?

Everything without a doubt is wearing thin and wearing out,
Gas and oil are giving out, the bar runs out of beer.
Your teeth are full of fillings and the Δ peace talks disappear
Along with the strike negotiations, re-*lations with your relations,*
Cities *crumbling, there's holes in all the sheets;
Your marriage needs repairing, lots of billy clubs wearing out
With hitting folks between the ears.
Broken-down machines combine to wear you down
**More than the passing of your years.
Whatever it is that's getting you down by breaking up and breaking down,
Haven't we got enough without a nuclear meltdown?

The finest plans of men and mice often don't turn out so nice,
Thalidomide, the microwave, a drop of Beaujolais;
Getting married can be great until the second day.
DDT, CFCs, the *Hindenberg, Challenger,*
Concorde, join the *army, don't forget your Dalkon Shield.
Enlargements of the bosom or electing folks like Jesse
Or the disaster known as Newt.
Tobacco, the automobile, malls, kudzu . . .
They even built a hospital **with an enema room without a loo.
Guinea pigs of every nation, let's announce our abdication
Haven't we had enough without a nuclear miscalculation?

You can die of suffocation or go up in a conflagration,
If you're fond of transportation you can die among the wheels.
There's drowning, falling down the stairs, and choking on your meals.
Cigarettes and drugs or *guns and clubs and knives,*
In the hands of *thugs and mugs and husbands and their wives.
There's suicide and cancer or there's falling off a cliff,
Or just an overdose of flu.
Dying of shock on Budget Day, drinking all your cares away,
Cholera, diphtheria, hysteria, or **snakebite in the jungles of Peru.
Plenty of ways of getting faster to the day you breathe your last,
O, haven't we got enough without a nuclear disaster?

All the things you like to do, the very things you'd hate to lose,
Lovers, kids, the dog, the cat, cooking, playing cards.
Being a couch potato or dabbling in the arts.
Bacon and egg and books . . . *flowers . . . clouds . . .*
Gardening and fishing,
Sleeping in, and wishing for a lottery *win
Or simply gazing into space.
Once upon a time, a loaf of bread, a double bed,
A glass of wine, my love, and you.
I've *even heard it said that women get their kicks from*
Watching waves of **Sani-Flush rippling down the loo.
All the good things that attract you, don't forget that it's a fact that
All of it could be lost because of a nuclear reactor.

There's answers everywhere you look, they could be in the Holy Book,
There's power in the wind and water, power from the sun.
There's energy from outer space from now to Kingdom Come.
Insulation, conservation, con-*trol the population,*
Make MacDonald's with a soya bean, and all things geothermal
*(They're in-**fernal 'cause no profit can be made).
Of course we could share out the wealth
But some would say it ruined their health,
They'd have to take the bus.
Or walk—or go cycling—and recycling
All the plastic and the glass, the Enquirer, the metals,
*And the unbiode-***gradable things we dump down in the drains.
† There's reforming of our institutions, maybe a little revolution,
Just remember that the nuclear way may any day turn out to be a
Very Final Solution.

Music note: *This song looks daunting at first glance. At second glance, a pattern emerges. At third glance, it makes absolute sense. Any words that are in italics are sung to an endless repetition of the same note, the section covered by the repeated bars in the notations. The stars and double stars tell you when and where to swing back into the set melody tune. The nice thing about the piece is that you can add or subtract topical items and ideas to make the song of a more local flavour or of contemporary relevance. Don't be afraid to leave spaces and change the* $\frac{6}{8}$ *to* $\frac{9}{8}$ *when you fancy. It's satisfying—and impressive—when you memorise it and rattle it off blithely.*

Please, Mr. Reagan

December 13, 1981: The *Guardian* carried a small article which declared that "by the end of the decade there will be about 80,000 nuclear warheads in the great arsenals, aimed at virtually every town in the northern hemisphere . . . but there are simply not enough military targets to meet the number of warheads. . . ." Little Bookham actually exists. Everything else in the song is pure fiction, including Reagan.

words and music: Peggy Seeger
disc 16

If you go to Little Bookham, go beyond the Rose and Crown,
Take a left, the second right until the road goes down
A little hill and then turn left again, beyond the willow tree;
There's a house, a dog, a cat, two kids, and my old man and me.

I saw it in the paper, so I know it must be true.
They've got more bombs than targets and they don't know what to do,
There's SS-20s aimed at Yeovil, even Clacton-on-the-Sea,
But no one nowhere's ever aiming anything at me.

Chorus: Δ So please, Mr. Reagan, I'm missing all the fun,
The other players in the game have pieces, I've got none;
I don't want to live beyond my time, be left here all alone;
Please, let me have a little missile of my own.

It must be great to live in London, in Hamburg, or in Cannes,
You know how many bombs you'll get and what you've got in hand;
I think the Great Atomic Battle should be shared by all mankind—
And Little Bookham's very, very, very far behind.

I feel so insignificant, it's just like I was poor;
Even *Dallas* cannot raise my spirits any more;
I've got a dandy little shelter and a great survival kit;
But with a shield, without a sword, how can I do my bit? *(chorus)*

If I had a missile I could hold it on my lap,
And someone on the other side would put me on their map,
And I'd be part of Our Defences, I could press my button too;
Then I'd be as good as them, and half as good as you.

Now I come to think of it, one is not enough.
The enemy is all around, about to call my bluff;
So please, Mr. Reagan, won't you send me two?
One to aim at Thatcher, and the other at you.

Music note: The opening line of the tune is the same as that of a toothpaste advert from the years when I was a teenage radio-addict.

Carry Greenham Home

Greenham Common Peace Camp: symbol of the power of women against the juggernaut of patriarchy and military might! At first we called ourselves Women for Life on Earth, firmly dedicated to the fight against nuclear weapons in general and Cruise missiles in particular. Men and women marched with their children from Cardiff to Newbury during the summer of 1981, calling at military installations along the way. Ewan and I sang for them at Marlborough, a raggle-taggle bunch of exhausted families who, thank goodness, fell asleep during the concert . . . a well-earned rest. When they arrived at Greenham they chained themselves to the railings of the main gate at the air base. It began as a mixed camp but it soon became a women's crusade. Donations of food, blankets, clothing, and tents flooded in. Women handled it like a military operation with education classes for participants and constant speedy communiqués between the seven gates, which were named for the colours of the rainbow. The press consistently implied that we were a bunch of bedraggled lesbians, but thousands of women of all sexual and political persuasions continued to come and go. Hundreds stayed permanently.

In December 1982 there was a "Circle the Base" demonstration, of which the intention was to join hands around the nine-mile perimeter. Thirty thousand women and girls came. There were *two* circles—eighteen miles—of clasped hands. The chain-link fence was festooned with photographs, swatches of children's clothing, poems, hanks of hair, wool-woven pictures, jewellery, and news clippings. When the authorities tried to remove them with flame-throwers, they found that the plastic coating on the fence also got terminated. So they sent local children out to unpick the fence of its howls of grief, triumph, joy, and love.

Now after more than half a century of military occupation, Greenham Common Airfield is to be restored to its original owners: the public. Although the Common was compulsorily requisitioned for wartime use, Newbury District Council is paying £7 million for its return.

words and music: Peggy Seeger
disc 9, 22, 26A

Hand in hand, the line extends
All around the nine-mile fence,
Thirty-thousand women chant,
    Bring the message home.

Chorus: Carry Greenham home, yes,
Nearer home and far away,
Carry Greenham home.

Singing voices, rising higher,
Weave a dove into the wire,
In our hearts a blazing fire,
    Bring the message home. *(chorus)*

No one asked us if we cared
If Cruise should be stationed here,
Now we've got them running scared,
    Bring the message home. *(chorus)*

Here we sit, here we stand,
Here we claim the common land;
Nuclear arms shall not command,
    Bring the message home. *(chorus)*

Singing voices, sing again,
To the children, to the men,
From the Channel to the glens,
    Bring the message home. *(chorus)*

Not the nightmare, not the scream,
Just the loving human dream
Of peace, the everflowing stream,
    Bring the message home. *(chorus)*

Woman tiger, woman dove,
Help to save the world we love,
Velvet fist in iron glove,
    Bring the message home. *(chorus)*

Music note: The tune is based on the Scots melody "Mari's Wedding."

Tomorrow

I've only been arrested once, and that was when I was involved during the 1980s predominantly with feminist and nuclear issues, which were merged by the Greenham Common Women's Peace Camp. In 1983, Cruise missiles were due to arrive at Greenham from the U.S.A. and an enormous demonstration assembled at the Houses of Parliament on November 15. Then came the news that the missiles had actually arrived several days earlier and were now ensconced at the base. The demo reacted accordingly. Thousands of us just sat down at rush hour in Parliament Square. I was right at the gates and was arrested with several hundred other people. The details of the arrest and of the next twelve hours is another story. So many people were rounded up that night that criminals had a field day as all the police and police stations in London were taken up with nuclear demonstrators (see "Villains' Chorus"). My trial was held in February 1984. I wrote this song to sing in court as part of my defence, the substance of which was that my action had been carried out because I was in fear of my life. Before I got through one verse I was sent out for contempt of court and taken down to the cells by the very policeman who had originally arrested me. It wasn't as dramatic as it sounds—but I got fined more than the two fellows who bravely climbed Big Ben to put antinuclear slogans across his clock-face.

words and music: Peggy Seeger
disc 8, 22

free

I know where my pleas-ures lie, for plea-sures I have man-y,

Hopes and dreams that car-ry me through dai- ly care and wor-ry;

But eve- ry plea-sure's touched with grief, eve-ry hope blight- ed with sor-row,

Night-mare ov-er - takes the dream- I fear I've lost to- mor-row.

I know where my pleasures lie, for pleasures I have many,
Hopes and dreams that carry me through daily care and worry;
But every pleasure's touched with grief, every hope blighted with sorrow,
Nightmare overtakes the dream—I fear I've lost tomorrow.

There it is, deep in my mind when I wake in the morning—
I'm waiting, trembling, listening for the dread Four-Minute Warning.
When I watch the children play and only see annihilation,
Then I know fear has now become a normal part of living.

Nature trains us to survive, protect our children's children;
We break the first of human laws preparing now to kill them.
Peace is what they say we have—it feels more like a poisoned arrow
Pointing at our deepest dream—the promise of tomorrow.

You know where your pleasures lie. Will you have time to use them?
Hopes and dreams are empty joys if we're prepared to lose them.
You who stand and shake your head and judge us that we act in error,
Ask yourself, deep in your heart: Do you, too, live in terror?

My spirit's dying day by day, murdered by warmongers;
That is why I'm here, for I can't bear it any longer.
I'm not here to waste my time, I'm not here to beg or borrow,
I'm here to demand what's mine. I've come to claim tomorrow.

The Villains' Chorus

The style of policing employed in the 1984–85 Miners' Strike was something which had never been seen since the formation of the police service in the early 1800s. The forces of the law no longer operated only at the scene of the dispute. All over the country, vehicles were being stopped for roadside interrogations. If you were the wrong occupants, you could be turned back or arrested. And who were the wrong occupants? Anyone who looked like a striking miner, whatever that is; anyone who looked as if they might be going to support a picket line; men of all kinds: young men, older men, men in overalls and suits, men in minis, and men in Rovers. (The police paid little attention to women, so that many members of the less visible sex followed Norman Tebbit's advice and got on their bikes. See note for "Women's Union.") Criminals had the scene of the crime to themselves because all the police were . . . (see note for "Tomorrow"). "I think your police are *won*derful," is one of our English stock mottoes. It was probably said quite a while ago in all seriousness by a stranger to these shores. Nowadays, it is usually delivered in a high, mock-posh voice with the hands flapping and the eyes directed upward.

alternative title: "I Think Our Police Are Wonderful"
words and music: Peggy Seeger
disc 12
© 1992 Peggy Seeger (1)

relaxed
D
A7
6/8
Shall we go down to Bar- clays Bank, the Mid-land or Nat West?
D A7 D
Got no need to make an-y plans or de- cide which one is best.
D7 G
Plen-ty of time to hold 'em up then scar-per to Ar- gen-ti-na,
D A7 D
No long arm of the law a-round —— since the wom-en went to Green-ham.
CHORUS
A7 D7
I think our po- lice are won- der- ful, won-der- ful, won-der-ful,

Shall we go down to Barclays Bank, the Midland or Nat West?
Got no need to make any plans or decide which one is best.
Plenty of time to hold 'em up then scarper to Argentina,
No long arm of the law around . . . since the women went to Greenham.

Chorus: I think our police are *won*derful, *won*derful, *won*derful,
So join us in the chorus.
We don't have to pay 'em to stay away . . .
The government does it for us.

You can stand on the corner any day without a fear or worry,
And advertise your merchandise that fell out of a lorry.
The boys in blue won't bother you, they're all down in Brixton
Picking up black fellas there . . . and taking 'em in to fix 'em. *(chorus)*

Pickpockets, hit-men, gangsters, thieves, petermen, racketeers,
Forgers, murderers, hooligans, thugs, for Thatcher give a cheer!
No coppers creeping round our pad to spoil our concentration,
They're bashin' 'em in Trafalgar Square . . . at a nuclear demonstration. *(chorus)*

He got away in the getaway car, after he made the haul,
But driving up the motorway they got him after all.
They flagged him down and searched his car and him and his attire;
They thought he was a miner go . . . ing to picket in Nottinghamshire. *(chorus)*

I'm going to leave the underworld and join the constabulary;
There's lots of laughs and plenty of kicks and the perks are extraordinary.
My mates have been in the force for years, so I'll be with my friends
Who like the long arm of the law . . . with its boot at the other end. *(chorus)*

Music note: *This song bounces along until you get to the word followed by three dots. Then you raise your glass and hold the note and sing loud and long . . . until you bounce into the rest of the line.*

Votecatcher in the Rye

Did the American Irish fall for it? It was a hoot from beginning to end and the Irish Irish had a laugh-in. Reagan visited Ireland in June 1984 to Put Flowers on His Great Ole Gran'daddy's Grave, God bless him. Many comedians need a straight man. Reagan did both jobs himself.

tune: traditional Irish ("The Old Orange Flute")
new words and trad. arr.: Peggy Seeger

Every four years an election comes round.
Among Yankee Paddies there's votes to be found.
To Ronnie a wink's just as good as a nod—
He's developed a yearning to see the Owld Sod.

Debrette's found an instant owld Family Tree:
Great-grandpappy Ryan from Tipperary.
'Twas a slip of handwriting, sure, no one's to blame,
REAGAN was really owld grandpappy's name.

The White House said, "Galway," but Ronnie said, "Cork."
Nancy said "I'd rather visit New York."
The PR men dressed them in emerald green
And delivered them (Eire-mail) to Ballyporeen.

What masses of soldiers, what hordes of police;
They searched all the bushes and hired more trees.
They checked out the cow-pats (their time was well spent—
That's where gunmen lie waiting to kill presidents).

A distant hand waving was all the crowd saw,
A glove on a stick poking out of the car.
The real hand's too precious, its fingers are for
The pushing of buttons to start the next war.

He studied at Galway from two until three,
Thus earning a fine honorary degree;
A few folks objected, but only a few:
The staff and the students (to name one or two).

With bodyguards round him and gunmen behind,
The Illinois boyo to speak did incline;
Both houses of Parliament in Dublin did hear
The following message, profound and sincere:

"Dear friends, I'm so glad to be home, home again,
"Bejasus, begorra, cor blimey, goddamn!"
Nancy gave Ronnie a kick on the shin,
"Why can't you remember what country we're in?"

Killarney and Blarney and owld Galway Bay,
And why can't you controwel your owld I.R.A.?
Schultz whispered a warning, but Ronnie, enraged,
Said, "McGinty, it's *my* show, so get off the stage!

"It's been a great honour for my wife and me
"To earn a few votes in your lovely country.
"I've learned to speak Welsh and to smoke a dudeen,
"And I'm leaving my heart here in Ballyporeen.

"Now Maggie and I have friendship to renew,
"And Nancy looks spiffing in red-white-and-blue.
"So top of the morning!" And with his police
He steamed off to Shannon like lightning that's greased.

This tired old tune's worked without a complaint,
And Ballyporeen's got a new coat of paint;
Ronnie's seeking his roots and we all gather round
And hope that he finds them—six feet underground.

Music note: This song uses the same tune as "Dustman's Strike 1969."

Items of News

El Salvador: from the early 1970s there were burgeoning peasant organisations and popular armed movements such as the People's Revolutionary Army. These were matched by growing official and unofficial repression. Nineteen seventy-five saw the reappearance of death squads and in March 1977 the first priest was murdered. This production piece was assembled from a small pamphlet simply entitled *El Salvador.* The opening poem is by Ewan MacColl.

The typefaces help to divide the units of the piece:

- Ordinary type signifies conversationally delivered spoken text.
- *ITALIC CAPITALS SIGNIFY WHISPERED PASSAGES.*
- **Sung text is in bold lowercase, in ABCB quatrain form.**
- ORDINARY CAPITALS SIGNIFY RHYTHMICALLY OR DRAMATICALLY DELIVERED SPOKEN TEXT.

alternative titles: "El Salvador"
words and music: Peggy Seeger
disc 8
© 1992 Peggy Seeger (1)

steadily
C G7 3 C
When my great-grand-fath-er's sons were young,
G7 C
Like us, they were poor-er than the poor;
F
Like we, half-dead with hun-ger, they had one road to choose,
G7 C
Tell the sto- ry of El Sal-va-dor

LIVING BY PROXY IN THE HALF-LIGHT,
ITEMS OF NEWS SLIP BY LIKE FLAKES OF FOOD IN A FISHTANK.
BETWEEN THE UNSEATING OF A ROYAL JOCKEY
AND THE BLAND INSINCERITIES OF TALKING HEADS
WE SEE, FOR AN INSTANT, THE AWKWARD DEAD,
HEAPED CARELESSLY AT THE CORNER OF A STREET
LIKE BRUSHWOOD PILED FOR BURNING.

THIS WOOD IS GREEN, UNSUITABLE FOR FIRING.
SAP STILL OOZES FROM THE STRICKEN LIMBS OF STRIPLINGS,
BROKEN BOYS AND GIRLS
WITH FACES MADE ANONYMOUS BY DEATH.
ONLY A TEAR IN THE KNEE OF A PAIR OF JEANS,
A SHOELESS FOOT UNNATURALLY BENT,
A RUCKED-UP SWEATSHIRT REVEALING PITIFUL FLESH,
REMINDS US THAT THEY ONCE POSSESSED A SINGULARITY
BEYOND THE COMPREHENSION OF THE KILLERS
WHO STARE AT THE CAMERA LENS WITH EYES
AS BLANK AS BOTTLE-TOPS.

It's not a long story—unless you had to live it yourself—but it began many times. With gold . . . or with coffee, that grain of gold that convinced fourteen families that the country belonged to them . . . oil, cotton, sugar, tobacco . . . *any* excuse will serve for land appropriation (as war is sometimes called). In Scotland it was pasturage for sheep. In the United States it was land—and that most elusive of crops, Freedom And Democracy, in supposed search of which victims of one civilisation made victims of another.

O, BELOVED CHILD,
WAIT UNTIL THEY'RE GONE—
I'LL LET YOU DIE.

You can reach any part of the country by air in an hour. Only a little bigger than Massachusetts—part of North America's back yard, you might say. Needs tidying up. Clearing out. Freedom And Democracy can be very house-proud. In 1932, 30,000 people were tidied up.

THEY DIDN'T COME AT NIGHT,
THEY CAME IN BROAD DAYLIGHT.
MORE OF US THAN THEY,
LESS OF THEM THAN WE.
THEY HAD STEEL—
WE HAD STICKS AND STONES.

O, BELOVED CHILD,
WAIT UNTIL THEY'RE GONE—
I'LL LET YOU DIE.

Then 1944, 1947, 1957, *etc.* The Fourteen spring-clean regularly, with northern approval in the shape of advisers, economic control—and goodies from the imaginative arsenals of the Land of the Free.

When my great grandfather's sons were young,
Like us, they were poorer than the poor;
Like we, half-dead with hunger, they had one road to choose,
Tell the story of El Salvador.

Listen, maybe you heard us calling,
We and all the ones who went before;
Our dead come forward with us, ever striving to speak,
And tell the story of El Salvador.

Four-and-a-half-million people. A fifth of them live in San Salvador and a fifth of *those* live in paper and cardboard huts. Two percent of the population own sixty percent of the land. Half the children die of malnutrition and diarrhoea before they are five. But statistics are boring. Unless you are one of them.

Listen, surely you hear us calling,
Or did you hear and did you choose to hear no more?
Four million voices sound together as one:
They tell the story of El Salvador.

HOPE!

In 1979 a dictator flees and a popular front military group takes over.

COINCIDENCE?

1980: state of siege and all free speech, freedom of the press, the right to form trade unions, the right to public assembly, the right of *habeas corpus* are suspended for the entire country. The Right cancels other rights.

THEIR SAFEGUARDS?

Destruction of newspapers, radio stations, libraries, educational institutions, hospitals, clinics. And, of course, people. Collaborate, "disappear," or

A hundred, then a thousand, then a million,
And each of them knows what they're fighting for.
Peasants join the workers and an army is formed,
Tell the story of El Salvador.

ONE GUN AMONG THREE
THE INNOCENTS FACE THE ENEMY.

O, BELOVED CHILD,
WAIT UNTIL THEY'RE GONE—

It's what they call "logistical support." It really starts with us, who can be against such . . . adventures . . . but our taxes can be *for* them. They pay for the new military command in Key West, the Rapid Deployment Forces, the heavy artillery, the mortars, airplanes and Huey helicopters. Thus the land is freed—of its occupants. Those who are caught are freed more slowly. Torture is routine and inventive.

We fighters move with all our people around us,
Young and old remind us what we're fighting for;
Pharaoh's Sons cannot defeat us though they surround us,
Tell the story of El Salvador.

Fifty-percent illiteracy—maybe they won't know *how* to fight a modern war. Vietnam was just a fluke. Can't even speak English!

I cannot read, yet I know of Vietnam,
I know this has all been done before.
I cannot write, yet with my life proclaim my hope and my love,
Tell the story of El Salvador.

Are these men Pharaoh has sent against us?
They take our lives, our land, and still they crave for more.
They even fire in the dark at babies crying for food,
Tell the story of El Salvador.

The rebels overestimate the humanity of the enemy. An old man cowered by a tree trunk, seeking protection from the machine-gun fire. He whispered to the American journalist, "Isn't it too bad Reagan isn't here? Wouldn't he be sad, too, if he saw this? Will you tell him about it?"

THE AGRARIAN REFORM:
DESIGNED AND DIRECTED BY . . . WHO?

The soldiers come and take the land.

ARMS FOR THE JUNTA PROVIDED BY . . . WHO?

Thirty thousand murdered and not *one* person brought to trial.

WHO? . . . WHO?

She was nine. The soldiers raped her. She was only nine and they cut off her hands and cut out her tongue and threw her like a little red rag doll at her mother's feet.

O, BELOVED CHILD . . .

Friends, surely you hear us calling.
Your silence brings their victory to our door.
Take our story with you and wherever you go,
Tell the story of El Salvador,
Tell the story of El Salvador.

Music note: This is a scripted skit. It is most effective when performed by several speakers and singers. It offers great scope for instrumentalists.

A Lovely Little Island

October 27, 1983: U.S.A. invades Grenada. Reagan gave several reasons for attacking, from the construction of a new airport which could be used for military jets to the protection of U.S. citizens living on the tiny island. The move was thought to be inspired by the presence of Cuban troops on Grenada. It was widely construed as a message to other small Latin American countries that North America would not tolerate Marxism in its backyard (an area that is often someone else's front yard). It was a great victory, even greater for the fact that the two sides were well matched. We in Britain have (at last count) thirty-three Yankee military bases on our soil.

words and music: Peggy Seeger

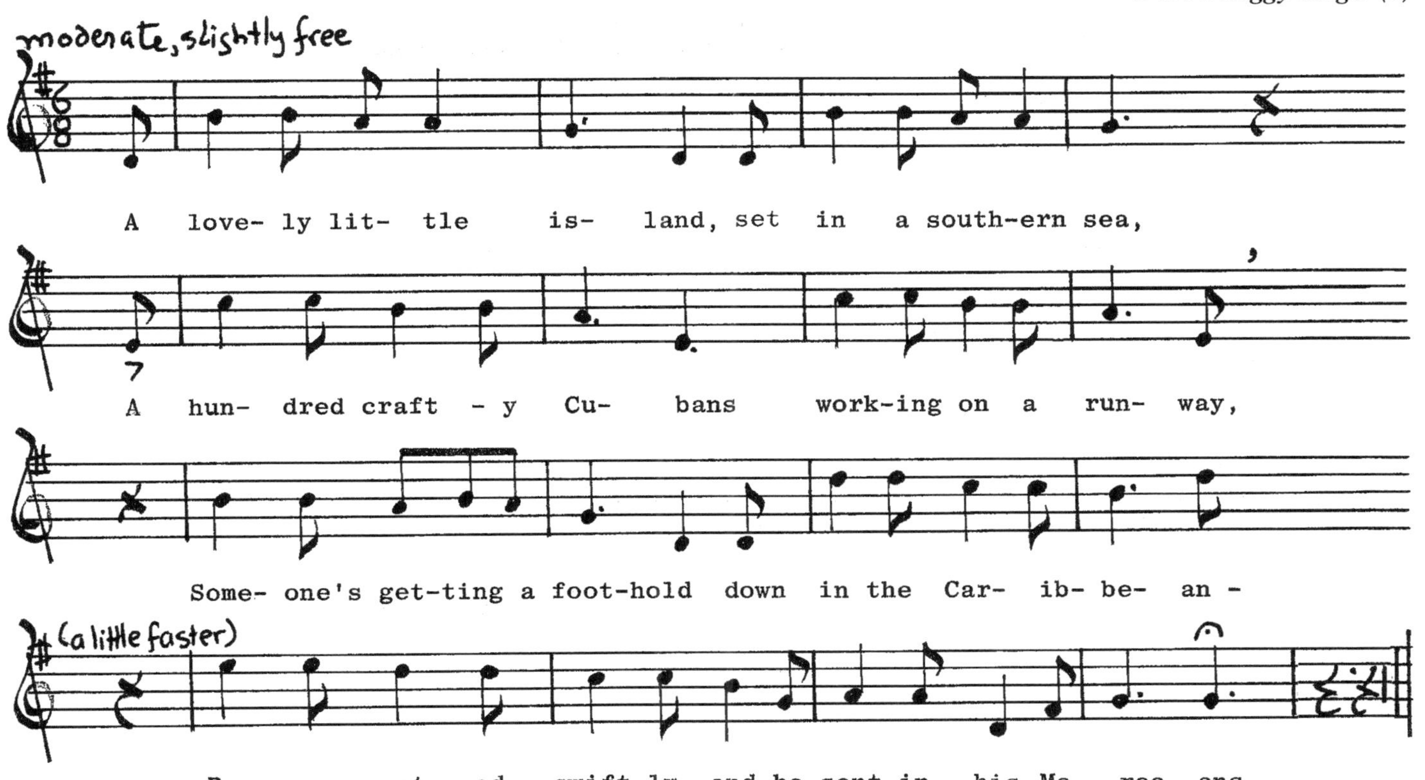

A lovely little island, set in a southern sea,
A hundred crafty Cubans working on a runway,
Someone's getting a foothold down in the Caribbean—
Reagan acted swiftly and he sent in his Marines.

Another little island, set in a northern sea,
Thirty thousand crafty Yanks working on their runways,
Someone's getting a foothold now that Cruise has made it—
Russia, come and save us quick, I think we've been invaded.

1985

Belfast Mother

There were several huge issues that I wrote almost nothing about, notably Vietnam and Northern Ireland. With Vietnam, it was probably the unspeakable enormity of the war. In the case of Northern Ireland, however, I think it was the mind-boggling complexity of its history—books, treatises, essays, plays, poems, critiques, documentaries (*etc.*) were written on this subject. In 1973, Parliament enacted that certain offences committed by "terrorists" (such as murder, arson, riot, *etc.*) should—*in Northern Ireland*—be tried without a jury. This gave rise to the Diplock Courts, named after Lord Diplock who headed the commission of enquiry. Political prisoners fought long and hard for the right to be treated differently from criminals, to be housed separately and to not have to don prison uniforms. In 1981, protesters added the hunger strike to their other tactics: the *blanket protests* (living with only a blanket as covering) and the *dirty protests* (in which prisoners allowed their cells to become completely covered in excrement and waste). This song is dedicated to Bobby Sands and to those who followed his example in Northern Ireland. Although I feel the song is strong, it was however written by an Anglicised Yankee.

words and music: Peggy Seeger

very free

Her voice rang out from the Di- vis Flats, from Cross-ma-glen to the far Bog-side;

It was heard way out at Belle- vue where the teen - a-gers go on joy-rides;

It was heard by eve - ry mother and wife from the Falls Road to the Shan-kill:

My Pat -rick's joined the hun-ger-strike and he's dy - ing on the blan-ket.

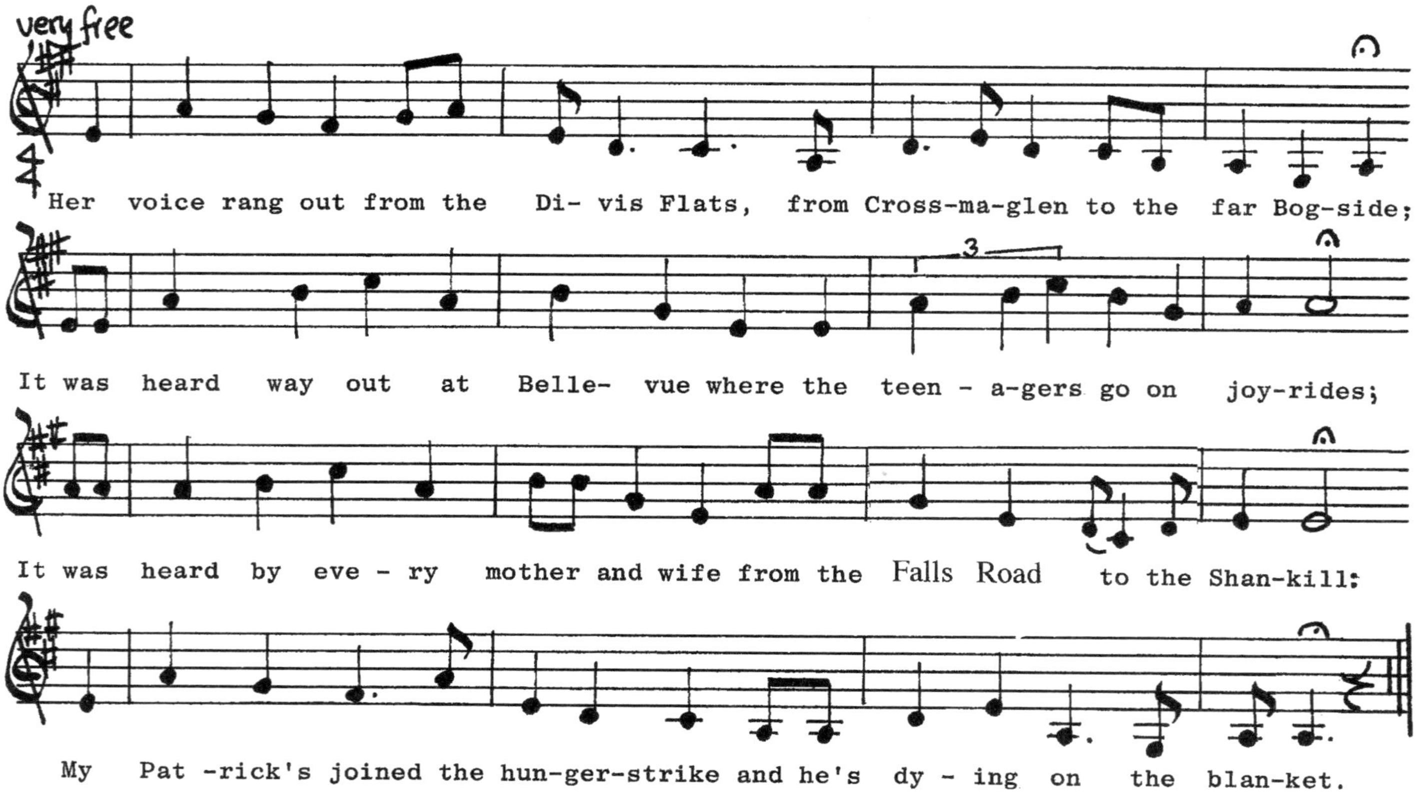

Her voice rang out from the Divis Flats, from Crossmaglen to the far Bogside;
It was heard way out at Bellevue where the teenagers go on joyrides;
It was heard by every mother and wife from the Falls Road to the Shankill:
My Patrick's joined the hunger strike and he's dying on the blanket.

He was only nine when the Brits came in, he was only ten when the raids began;
At eleven he stoned the Saracens and at twelve he called himself a man.
They lifted him when he was seventeen, with a Diplock court they jailed him.
At twenty-nine his youth is gone and the hunger strike will kill him.

Nothing's too bad for a blanket man, no treatment too inhuman,
But before he'd wear the prison shirt they'll have to nail it on him.
They've worn him down to skin and bone, he's alone and naked all the time.
For love of freedom's become a war and love of country's become a crime.

The battle ground of Belfast town, the burnt out buses and broken glass;
Valium soothes your sleepless nerves and drinking helps the time to pass—
Not the endless raids, not the children crying, there's nothing hurts my heart and mind
Like my Patrick's eyes when the visit's over and the screws all gather behind him.

The British say they won't bend the knee, but neither will the Irish.
They say that if the army leaves the blood will rise and drown us.
Leave us alone to rule ourselves with no RUC or Paisley,
No skeleton sons behind the wire, no invaders from across the sea.

You feel like taking yourself away to any other place but Belfast—
Sometimes I feel I could take my life but my heart's too full of love for that.
Ten men died to win five demands, now the rest of us can fight for one:
And we'll fill the streets, the courts and jails, and blood will flow till the Brits are gone.

Music note: The tune is a collation of a number of traditional tune-types.

Forty-five, Eighty-five

There was the 1984–85 Miners' Strike . . . then the Printers' Strike . . . then the rate-capping issue and the poll tax . . . and the continual privatisation of public assets . . . and all the endemic ills of the Thatcher days. The fact that the opposing sides were coming out so violently against one another clarified and restated once more the history of class warfare in Marxist terms, making 1985 feel quite fresh. Nineteen forty-five was a comparable time, when the desire to wipe the slate clean, start again, and draw the lines clearly swept Labour into power with a landslide vote. It seemed obvious to twin the two years. In spite of all that, the terminology of this song and some of its assumptions about British society give it an old-hat flavour. The *struggle,* the *movement*—we need new ways to talk about it, write about it, sing about it, and keep our involvement in it ever-fresh and stimulating.

words and music: Peggy Seeger

In '45 the time was ripe, the war was at an end,
Time to wage that other war we've fought since time began.
With Labour in and Tory out,
The enemy had been put to rout,
Fair shares for all, not all for a few: the world turned upside down.

What a dream, a glorious dream, a dream for the brave and bold!
Plenty for the poor and hungry, care for the sick and old.
The message rang out clear and loud:
NO EXTRAS FOR THE CHEQUE-BOOK CROWD!
Foundations shook as Labour took the winter into spring.

A nightmare for the idle ones who lost both goods and land;
Steel and coal and transport passed into the public hands.
All over Europe, jubilee!
We held elections, filled the seats;
The bosses nursed their bank accounts and settled down to wait.

For the dreamers only dream at night, they wake up in the day;
But social change is like true love, you got to go all the way.
The people cried, "No holds barred!"
The leaders cried, "That's much too far!"
And bit by bit the thieves crept back to bring us down to par.

They've stolen steel and Telecom, the NHS is next,
We're turned into warmongers with the eagle in our nest.
They feed us slowly, piece by piece,
To NATO and the EEC,
And bit by bit Four Freedoms change to bingo and TV.

Our taxes go for Trident, for the Falklands, and the rest;
For the sick and hungry, young and old and poor, there's nothing left.
They've tried to wreck the welfare state,
And now they want to cap the rates,
The peacetime looters never sleep, they're always on the make.

In '85, the time is ripe, the war has never stopped;
The enemy's in the open now, the velvet glove has dropped.
Every gain is dearly bought,
Every issue must be fought—
If we give an inch they'll take a mile—and then the bloody lot!

A Matter of Degree

The media had a ball. Prime Ministers always get an honorary degree from *somewhere,* but usually it is offered. Mrs. Thatcher went in search of it, followed by reporters and television cameras. We watched her pilgrimage from Oxford to Peradeniya (in Sri Lanka) to Galway—where Reagan got his honorary degree (see "Votecatcher in the Rye")—to Middlesex Polytechnic to the Hendon Business School to Finchley Girls'. The "Letters" sections of the major newspapers were inundated with suggestions as to where she might look next. The Quest caught everyone's imagination, including mine. During her political career, Thatcher cut education funds viciously—lower education suffered badly. It was obvious that she was distressed that her Grail was so elusive—and it was satisfying to her opponents that she couldn't say on this occasion (as she had at a Commonwealth conference against tighter sanctions on South Africa): "If it is forty-eight against one, I feel sorry for the forty-eight."

words and music: Peggy Seeger

wry

Am
Ma-dam, can you spare a mo-ment? I've a re-quest to make,

G Am
Come lis-ten to my sad tale,'t would make your heart to break.

G
It's of a gal-lant fe-male who has served her coun-ter- ee,

Am Em or E7 Am
She thinks it's time that she re-ceived an hon- or- ar- y de- gree.

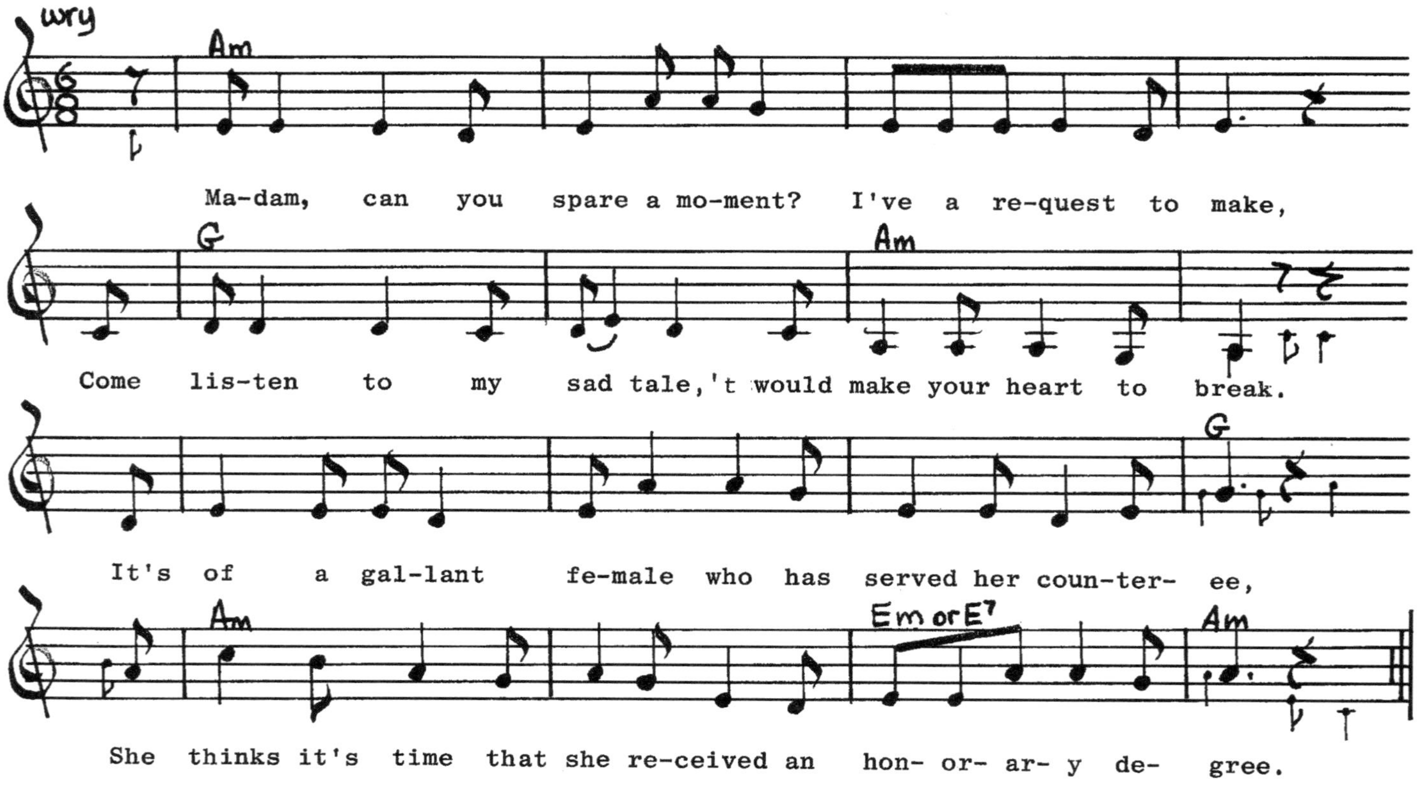

Madam, can you spare a moment? I've a request to make,
Come listen to my sad tale, 'twould make your heart to break.
It's of a gallant female who has served her counteree,
She thinks it's time that she received an honorary degree.

She trotted up to Oxford, but the students and the staff
Said, "Oxford is the place for wheat and not the place for chaff."
She blinked her eyes, she clutched her bag and clenched her tiny fist,
And jabbed her index finger at the next one on the list.

Peradeniya, a famous school, with courses that delight:
Degrees in animal husbandry and the study of parasites.
"As I want a country full of sheep, it's just the place," said she,
"And as for parasites, I'm one myself, so let's have that degree."

Middlesex Polytechnic was the next one to be tried,
And then the Hendon Business School and several more besides.
I hear she's been to Galway, for she's often heard to sigh:
"Wherever my dear Ronnie sucks, there suck I."

She tried her luck at Finchley Girls', but the ball's still in their court.
And now, ma'am, I'll come to the point, for you're our last resort.
You knew her as a snotty tot a-sitting on her stool;
We're sure you'd grant her a degree from her old nursery school.

The teacher wiped her streaming eyes and shook her hoary head,
Folded her hands and wiped her specs and sorrowfully she said:
"You know, I'd like to help you, and I'm really glad you asked,
"But due to education cuts her Alma Mater's axed."

And so the lady's killed the goose that laid the golden egg;
One day she'll axe the lamp-post where she likes to cock her leg;
But she's passed out at the College of Official Thievery,
Where liars, thieves, and businessmen have granted her degree.

It's in the *Guinness Book of Records* on page eighty-three,
The first PM who *couldn't* get an honorary degree;
But if she gets what she deserves and earns all that she's got,
The college up on Holloway Road would have her like a shot.

If You Want the Bomb

We know about the direct links between the atomic bomb and the nuclear power station. We know about the danger and the costs. They know we know and still they deny it or play it down. We know they play it down and we still allow nuclear waste from power stations to be transported across and reprocessed in our tight little island. They know we know they know . . . and by the millennium, the British public will be paying thirty-three percent more on its electricity bills to cover the cost of decommissioning all those power stations. We know about the direct links between (*etc.*). They know we know (*etc.*).

words and music: Peggy Seeger
disc 8

bright & cheery
C
Dm
If you want the Bomb, One of your ver-y own- i- um,
G
8 D7
G7
Not the or- di- na- ry kind But one made of plu- to- ni- um,
10 C
C7
F
C dim.
You got to have a place, A kind of pow-er sta- tion-
C
G
C
It's the on-ly place plu- to-ni-um's made.

8 D7
G7
to 10
(The cost is quite spec- tac- u- lar), When (etc.)

If you want the Bomb,
One of your very ownium,
Not the ordinary kind
But one made of plutonium,
You got to have a place,
A kind of power station—
It's the only place plutonium's made.

If you want the Bomb,
Build a station that is nuclear,
Johnny Doe will foot the bill
Δ (The cost is quite spectacular),
When atoms work for peace,
Electricity bills increase—
But it's the only way plutonium's made.

If you want the Bomb,
Turn your lights on with uranium,
(How to explain away the cost
Is straining many a cranium),
Shut down the plants that toil
On gas and coal and oil—
Then you'll *have* to get plutonium made.

If you want the Bomb,
Say goodbye to civil liberties,
Atoms ain't compatible
With freedom and democracy,
'Cause unions and the like
Are apt to go on strike
Just when you want to get plutonium made.

If you want the Bomb,
Don't expect to have the niceties,
Hospitals and schools and things
And people's paradi-cities,
Kick Britain up the ass,
Put the miners out to grass—
But at least you'll get plutonium made.

(spoken) On the other hand . . .

(sung)
If we really get the Bomb,
We won't need no amenities—
NHS for corpses is somewhat of an obscenity;
So Maggie may be right
Cutting everything in sight—
Except the way plutonium's made.

New Spring Morning

By 1985, it was obvious that Ewan was not going to get well again. He'd never been what I would call a *healthy* person. He was a smoker and he loved good wines, cheese, fatty meats, and cream on his desserts; he was a type-A compulsive worker and didn't do enough exercise. Every year he would come down with some dire ailment that would confine him to bed. It all caught up with him in 1979. In the ten last years of his life, he suffered from chronic bronchitis; diverticulitis; arteriosclerosis; hiatus hernia; gout; several heart problems; and Old Fateful, his slipped disc. Every now and then he succumbed to a rogue illness that would plunge him into fearfully high fevers, drenching sweats, and hilarious delirium.

Each passing year a new malady appeared to drain his body and besiege his mind. At first these afflictions drew us together but gradually, as the song says, we drifted. . . . The prospect of losing him haunted me for at least five years before his death. Each time he got ill, I would prepare myself yet once again . . . not realising that I would never be really prepared. "Thoughts of Time" was a tranquil generalised contemplation of our separation by the death of one of us. "New Spring Morning" was my realisation that within a decade he would be gone.

Summer 1956

words and music: Peggy Seeger
disc 9, 15A, 20, 21

We were a new spring morning,
You and me and the rising sun;
We were a new day dawning,
Our loving had only begun.

How soon the morning's over,
How soon the sun shines overhead,
But summer rain brings seedling trees,
And children were blessing our bed.

From noon to early evening,
Always together yet drifting apart;
Hold fast the bonds that bind us,
Companion of my heart.

Can it be the day is ending,
Our harvest gathered, our fledglings have flown;
Would you leave me in the autumn, love,
To live out my winter alone?

O, far-off new day dawning,
Far off summer and rising sun—
Be with me in the morning, love,
When the lonely nights are done.
    Come back to me in April, love,
    When the long, cold winter is gone.

Autumn 1984

The Mother

I have heard that Eskimo sculptors don't regard themselves as the main moving force in their art. They believe that they merely release the image that is caught in the stone. Sometimes they will keep a stone for years before starting on it, waiting for the shape to make itself known. I did the same with this tune which I carried in my head for two years. One day, in the parking lot of the West Wickham swimming pool, the text of the song made itself known to me. I could hardly write fast enough. A work session with Irene finished it.

alternative title: "Love Song to the Earth"
tune: Peggy Seeger
words: Peggy Seeger with Irene Scott
*disc 8, 26**

slow & steady
G
Slow-ly, slow-ly she turns o-ver through the night,
D7
G
Turns her love-ly face to- wards the morn-ing light.
G7
C
Al-ways turn-ing, turn-ing, turn-ing —
D7
G
On her long and end-less jour-ney through the sky.

* *These are two different mixes of the same recording.*

Slowly, slowly she turns over through the night,
Turns her lovely face towards the morning light.
Always turning, turning, turning—
On her long and endless journey through the sky.

Slowly, slowly she turns over through the day,
Flowers bloom and seed and die and fade away.
Seasons turning, turning, turning—
Till tomorrow's just a memory of today.

Virgin water tumbling, tumbling down the hill,
First the storm and then the time when all is still.
All will follow, follow, follow—
All in balance when the earth does as she will.

Who invades the sky to bring the goddess down?
Who's laid poison in her body, in her bones?
The earth is trembling, trembling, trembling—
Is she waiting for the deadly, final wound?

Wanton man, beware the power of the tide,
Learn to answer to the Mother's warning cry.
Learn to follow, follow, follow—
Live with all that live on earth—or all will die.

Bill

Irene is Belfast born and bred. We were talking one day about why any white (less-black?) person would want to move to South Africa. She told me about a Belfast street bully who'd done just that. He was now the owner of a large suburban house with ten servants to service his family and as many dogs to patrol his grounds. I decided to change his nationality to English and place him in London, for such people have become *un vrai type.* The 1980s were the heyday of the skinheads: young urban men (usually less-black or, surprisingly, very black) who shaved their heads, wore Dr. Martens, and cruised in gangs in search of Asians. Paki-bashing refers to a pastime that many skinheads still indulge in: the seeking out of Pakistanis and giving them a once, twice, or three times over with fists, footwear, and anything else appropriate to what is often a one-sided conflict. The Elephant and Castle area of South London has been a popular meeting place for roughs, toughs, and aggro-seekers since Shakespeare wrote, "Hie thee to the Elephant."

words and music: Peggy Seeger
disc 13

laconically
Am Bb Am Bb Am E7 Am
This is the sto-ry, the real-life sto-ry, sto-ry of a guy named Bill;
Cm G7 Cm G7 Cm G7 Cm
I used to get bad dreams a-bout him, I think I al- ways will;
E7 Am E7 Am
A-bout four-foot wide, he stood six-foot-four- and- a-half in his stock-ing feet,
G Am Dm Am B7 E7 Am
And all he had un- der- neath his hat was a lump of bone and meat.

This is the story, the real-life story, story of a guy named Bill;
I used to get bad dreams about him, I think I always will;
About four-foot wide, he stood six-foot-four-and-a-half in his stocking feet,
And all he had underneath his hat was a lump of bone and meat.

When he was a kid he kicked the cat, later he kicked the dog;
He was so thick he had to work hard to learn to fall off a log;
Ran with the skinheads, Paki-bashing, in the boots and the drainpipe jeans,
Scrapped and lounged on every street from the Elephant to Bethnal Green.

His mother and his sister and his wife and kids never had a peaceful day;
The neighbours went in when Bill came out, hoped he'd move away.
One day he did—and for a year or two we never heard a word about Bill;
Then I turned on the news and there he was—I wish I was dreaming still.

Seems he'd answered the call of the wild, decided to go down south;
Now he's got black servants and a swimming pool and a great big ten-room house,
With the barbed-wire fence and the Doberman dogs to keep all the riff-raff out,
Joined the Johannesburg *nouveau riche*. Bill's got it all worked out.

Seems they weighed and measured him up, saw he was big and mean.
Looked for his brain with a microscope, found it was in his spleen.
Now he sits on a truck, patrols Soweto, looking for blacks to kill.
He's King for a Day (till they blow him away)—then goodbye, Bwana Bill.
He's King for a Day (till they blow him away)—then goodbye, Bwana Bill.

No More

There are some people in this book about whom it has been unnecessary to write a note and who will not appear in the glossary because they are on a global honour roll. They are people who seem larger than life, whose purpose and courage defy any description other than a string of superlatives. This piece is dedicated to such a person: Nelson Mandela who, on February 11, 1990, walked away free, whole, and sane from twenty-four years in a South African prison.

words and music: Peggy Seeger
disc 13

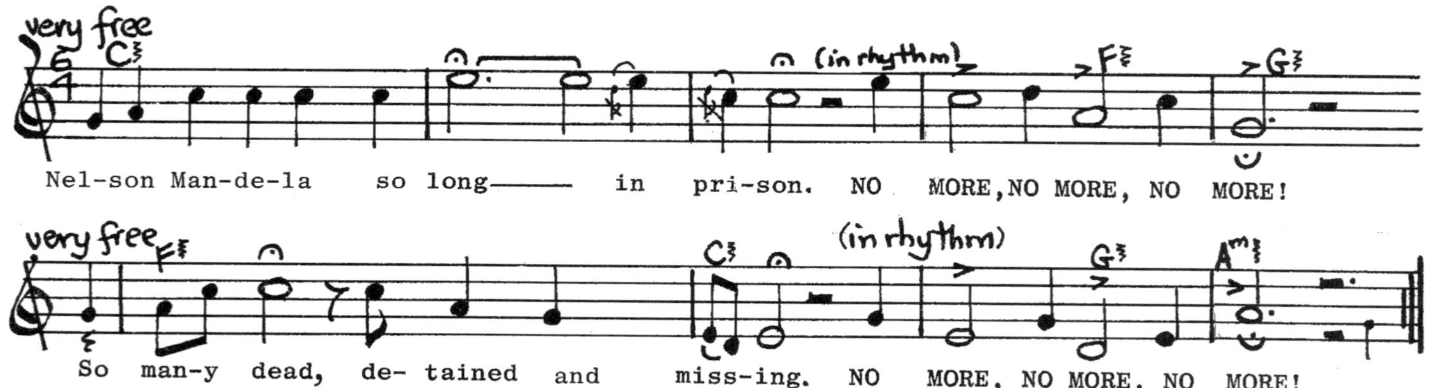

Nelson Mandela so long in prison.
    No more, no more, no more!
So many dead, detained and missing.
    No more, no more, no more!

For some, the rich and fertile land.
    No more *(etc.)*
For others, the desert homelands.
    No more *(etc.)*

This boy goes to the mine and factory. *(etc.)*
That one wields sjambok and kiri. *(etc.)*

Black woman in the field and kitchen.
Children learn apartheid's lessons.

Police wherever black people meet.
Dogs and soldiers in every street.

Live and work and die in misery.
Glory of the white man's history.

They think they hear the lion sleeping.
It's the sound of dead children weeping.

Sing louder, for they haven't heard you.
They've gone too far, now no further.

Music note: Each line is to be sung as a complete thought. The melody tends to change slightly from verse to verse.
I feel that this song is best sung unaccompanied and have only given chords as a guide to vocal harmonies.

Prisons

Songs like this are often called 'philosophical songs', embodying as they do a set of observations and conclusions set in relatively formal language. "Prisons" is most effective when sung totally unaccompanied as the starkness of the lone voice sets off the minimalism of the poetry.

words and music: Peggy Seeger
disc 13

Poverty's prison has no bars,
It holds the blacks wherever they are;
No lock, no door, only walls—
South Africa's homelands are prisons all.

The law is a prison with movable bars,
It favours the whites whoever they are.
It waits for blacks with open jaws,
Their last resort is to break the laws.

The prison's a kingdom where terror reigns,
No practice forbidden, no limit to pain.
No beast would act as man does to man,
As the white to the black South African.

The state is a prison, the whips are all poised,
The guns are in place, the armies deployed.
The whites are caged also, all the time,
By fear and prejudice, self-confined.

Apartheid enslaves in every degree;
When one leg is shackled, neither is free.
Until the whites are willing to share,
The country's a prison for everyone there.

Women's Union

I first met Iris Preston at a women's benefit concert for the striking miners in late 1984. A Yorkshire woman, she was working as an usher in the courts by day and running messages for the miners by night. Her son was a miner and his job was at risk, but that was incidental as regards Iris's commitment. She lived and breathed, ate and slept the strike. She had an ingenious method for smuggling messages through police lines on her little moped. I won't detail it here, because (like the printed instructions for making nuclear bombs at home) it might fall into the wrong hands. The Miners' Strike launched Iris into a whole new world of meetings, picketing, public speaking, and thinking for herself. She kept her support committee going after the strike was over, helping other strikers to develop similar groups. I recorded the women she worked with and made this song out of their words. The only thing they found wrong with my text was the word 'union'. They felt that the word represents a woman-unfriendly type of organisation. They wanted another word but couldn't come up with one. Any suggestions?

words and music: Peggy Seeger
disc 9

Women left the kitchen sink, left the beds unmade,
Women left the school and shop to join the barricade;
Women came from everywhere like we never had before,
To join the miners in the strike of 1984.

Chorus: We're in the Women's Union, we're all together now,
We're fully paid up members and we've taken the union vow.
We know where we're going and we know the reason why,
We're the Women's Union and we're aiming for the sky.

Way back in the good old days, when men went out to picket,
Women scraped for food and coal wherever they could get it;
We greeted scabs with dustbin lids, then with lifelong silence,
And we were there—always there—the women and the miners. *(chorus)*

I'll never forget the fourteen months of 1984;
A penny was like a pound at home, MacGregor was at the door;
We ran soup-kitchens, spoke at rallies, rattled collecting tins,
Faced the cops on the picket line and always fought to win. *(chorus)*

Men, learn to cook and wash. Children, learn to sew.
Stand there at the kitchen door and watch the women go;
We're going where the action is, to carry on the fight,
Though the miners' strike is over, long live the miners' strike! *(chorus)*

When [teachers] strike for better pay: join the picket line!
When [printers] hold the boss at bay: join the picket line!
When workers strike to win their rights: join the picket line!
And we'll be there—always there—on the picket line! *(chorus)*

Music note: I borrowed this tune from myself, from "We Are the Young Ones," and made a new chorus. The [bracketed] words were always changed to fit whatever issue was topical at the time the song was sung.

Polonium 2-1-0

I am blessed with friends all over the world who send me things they know I will be interested in. One day a sheaf of half-a-dozen pages arrived, photocopied from the *American Scientist*, Volume 63. No letter, no note, just the article: "Tobacco, Radioactivity and Cancer in Smokers," by Edward A. Martell. Tobacco has a myriad of harmful elements in it but it became aggressively carcinogenic when we started forcing its growth with phosphate fertilisers. The latter actually contains uranium, which degrades into americium then into radon and finally into polonium 210. This little-known radioactive element attaches itself, Velcro-like, to the tobacco plant. It holds on—right through all the industrial processes of cigarette-making. It holds on—right through the smoking ritual, so that a smoker is inhaling radioactivity and exhaling it into secondary smokers. It holds on—till many active and passive smokers deposit it, with themselves, back into the earth where it continues to hold on . . .

words and music: Peggy Seeger
disc 8, 15A, 20, 21

vigorous
F (B♭ in verse 4)
B♭
F
Look at him there, the lit-tle boy, got to do his grow-in' yet;
G7
C7
A flick of the hand & he's a Big Man, light-ing that cig - a- rette;
F C#7 F C#7 F C#7 F
Mom's smo-kin', Dad's smo-kin', Gran's smo-kin', so I'M smo-kin';
A7
A moth a-round the flame——
B♭ D7 G7 C7 F
The fall guy eag-er to take the fall, the lo-ser who loves the game.

This is the sto-ry of a hot lit-tle a-tom, spit-tin' out al- pha rays;
The to- bac- co plant just laps it up and sends it on its way.
Ex - hale, ex- hale! Then we all play touch - and - go,
'Cause eve - ry bod- y near you gets to meet Po - lo - ni - um 2 - 1 - 0.
He could-a lived to be a hun - dred (they of - ten do, y'know)

I

(in spoken verse)
If you want to grow tobacco, and get a king-size yield,
You gotta grind up rocks—phosphate rocks—to fertilise your fields.
Them rocks is rich in something else, uranium is the name . . .
It hits the air with radon gas and it's never the same again,
(Neither the air or the radon gas).

Now, in nature, nothing disappears, and the next act in the show
Is a real bad guy with a short half-life: Polonium 2-1-0.
That lung-shakin', nucleus-breakin' radioactive bum
Has a yen for the young tobacco plant, who thinks Polonium's fun.

So they have their fun and they make their pad
In any part of your lungs that they can grab.
An easy berth, free bed and board,
And you're headed straight for the cancer ward.

So beat it, sucker, time to blow!
Make room—for Polonium 2-1-0.

II

(sung)

1 Look at him there, the little boy, got to do his growin' yet;
2 A flick of the hand and he's a Big Man, lighting that cigarette;
3 Mom's smokin', Dad's smokin', Gran's smokin', so *I'm* smokin';
4 A moth around the flame—
5 The fall guy eager to take the fall, the loser who loves the game.

1 Look at her, ain't she pretty, walkin' down the street?
2 Cigarette odour in her hair, nicotine on her teeth.
3 Emma's smokin', Clare's smokin', Samantha's smokin', so *I'm* smokin';
4 She'll be the star of the show—
5 It's a knock-down, drag-out tragedy called *Polonium 2-1-0.*

6 This is the story of a hot little atom, spittin' out alpha rays;
7 The tobacco plant just laps it up and sends it on its way.
8 Exhale, exhale! Then we all play touch-and-go,
9 'Cause everybody near you gets to meet Polonium 2-1-0.

1 Just a poor little helium nucleus lookin' for a home,
2 Runnin' through your red lights till you look like a honeycomb.
8 Inhale, inhale! Then the very next thing you know,
9 It's R.I.P., courtesy of Polonium 2-1-0.

1 Look at him, he's his own man with his old tobacco tin.
2 All his life he's rolled his own and now it's rollin' him.
10 He could'a lived to be a hundred (they often do, y'know)—
5 But he died in his youth at forty-two of Polonium 2-1-0.

1 I wrote this song 'cause I don't like breathing radioactive smoke.
2 I made it light so you won't walk out before the end of the joke.
6 But there ain't no laugh when the payoff comes and you're six feet underground,
7 And the tobacco companies count the cash and eagerly look around
10 For the next poor kid who thinks a smoke is a ticket to the grown-up show,
9 And nobody tries to stop him—but Polonium 2-1-0.

Music note: The numbers at the beginning of each line in the sung verses refer to numbered lines in the music notation. The mixing and matching of the various lines makes for a good mixture between major and minor parts of the tune.

Give 'Em an Inch

It was a delightful cartoon. The midwife had a look of wonder on her face as she held the baby boy in one hand and pinched his tiny protuberance with the other. It is a wondrous appendage. It arrives in inches and becomes the yardstick by which so much manhood is measured.

words and music: Peggy Seeger
disc 15A, 21

free, slow
Am G F G Am
The man wait-ed, the wom-an groaned, She was lost in la-bour's toil. For-
G Am E D (a little faster)
got-ten for now the long nine-month, The act of pas-sion and joy. Ten fin-gers,
Am Bb Am Bm
ten toes, Two eyes, two ears, a mouth and a nose, And that one inch of flesh that pro-
B7 Em (slower) B7 Em Bm Em
claims IT'S A BOY! The mid-wife in-spect-ed his bel-ly and bum, Coun-ted ap-
Am Em Am Em E7
pen-da-ges one by one. Took his sweet wil-lie twixt fin-ger and thumb, Looked
A A7
at it in won-der and said:

in rhythm, moderate
D A7 D G D
Does this lit-tle spike of flesh de- fine the strong-er sex?
G D Em A7
Will this lit-tle plea-sure rod put this ba-by next to God?
G D
Is this the thing that gets him high-er wa ——— ges,
E7 A
That's kept him up on top through-out the a ——— ges?
Bm Em F#7
Will these round thing-a-ma-bobs get this child a bet-ter job?
Bm Em
A pi - lot, not a stew-ar-dess; a doc- tor, not a nurse;
A7 D
Pro- fess-or, not a teach- er; a chance to get there first -
G D A7 D
The scep-tre that makes king-doms, the key that o-pens doors,
Em E7 A E7 A7
The rea- son why this ba-by won't be scrub-bing kit-chen floors.

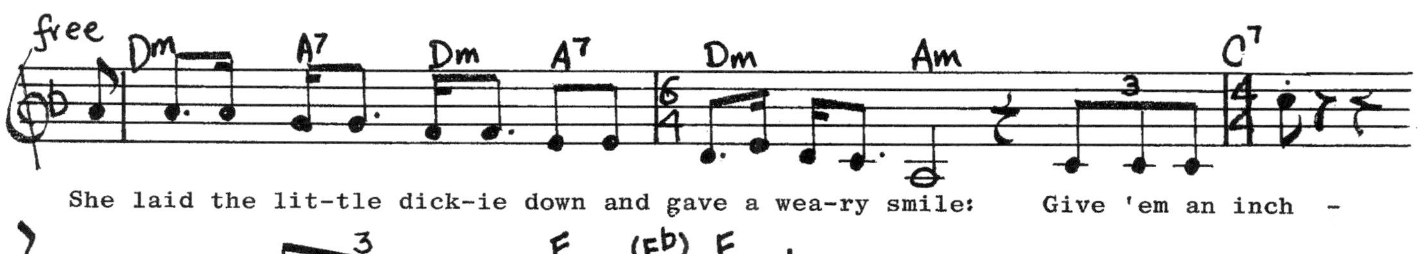

(free, slow)
The man waited, the woman groaned,
She was lost in labour's toil.
Forgotten for now the long nine-month,
The act of passion and joy.
Ten fingers, ten toes,
Two eyes, two ears, a mouth and a nose,
And that one inch of flesh that proclaims IT'S A BOY!
The midwife inspected his belly and bum,
Counted appendages one by one.
Took his sweet willie twixt finger and thumb,
Looked at it in wonder and said:

(in rhythm, moderate)
Does this little spike of flesh define the stronger sex?
Will this little pleasure rod put this baby next to God?
Is this the thing that gets him higher wages,
That's kept him up on top throughout the ages?
Will these round thingamabobs get this child a better job?
A pilot, not a stewardess; a doctor, not a nurse;
Professor, not a teacher; a chance to get there first—
The sceptre that makes kingdoms, the key that opens doors,
The reason why this baby won't be scrubbing kitchen floors.

(free)
She laid the little dickie down and gave a weary smile:
"Give 'em an inch—and they'll take a mile."

Missing

I met Berenice Dockendorff at a benefit for Chilean refugees in 1987. She came backstage after the concert to tell me about her sister, Murielita, who had been "disappeared" at the age of twenty-two by the Pinochet government in 1974. I visited Berenice and her mother, Ana Maria Navarrete, who spoke almost no English and felt lost in Britain. The interview was harrowing. 'Disappear' is a very exact term for what happens. The authorities remove every official trace of a person's existence: hospital records, school reports, driver's license, birth certificate, exam results, degrees, and so on. Pinochet himself told Ana Maria that she was deluded—that she had really only borne one daughter. For seven years, Berenice and Ana Maria followed what came to be a routine for the relatives of vanished people. They went every Sunday to demonstrate at the Moneda, the main government building in Santiago. They carried Murielita's photograph pinned to their clothing, showing it to people in bus queues and shops with the question, "Have you seen this woman?" They followed rumours that led them to prisons and hospitals all over Chile but Murielita was never found. In 1980 it became too dangerous and they moved to London. Ana Maria now works at a medical centre for Latin American women. In 1992 she was interviewed for a television documentary in which she said, "The other day I was watching a comedy programme and for the first time ever, I understood an English joke. Can you imagine? I was so pleased!"

The melody is improvised anew each time I sing it—it is impossible to notate.

alternative title: "Murielita"
words and music: Peggy Seeger
disc 9, 26A
© 1992 Peggy Seeger (1)

I had a little sparrow, my little bird, Murielita;
I held her in my womb, my heart sang to her;
I opened my hand, she flew into the daylight, singing—
Now my little bird is gone.

The hunters caught her, caged her, Murielita;
They held her in their hands and still she sang of dawn;
They closed their hands, they closed their hands—
My little bird is gone.

I went to San Miguel, I stood and stood and stood outside the cage.
The prisoners have seen her, the soldiers have seen her,
But the jailers say she never flew, she never sang, never was she born, she never was—
Where are you, where are you, little bird?

Seven years have I followed the echoes and whispers, Murielita,
Can you hear me, little bird?
And still we come to the Moneda, we stand, we wait, we ask, we plead,
Have you seen my little bird?
    See, here is her photo, Murielita;
    His picture, Carlos, Manuel;
    Her likeness, Violeta, Rosario, Maria;
    Give me back my little bird!

My child, your clothes are ready, your books are still open;
We seek you by day, by night we call your name.
Everywhere we hold your picture high, that someone may see and tell us who took you,
But the answer is the same: no one saw, no one heard, no one knew.
No one knew.

I had a little sparrow, her hair was golden brown, my heart was in her hands.
She sang of tomorrow, but will she see tomorrow?
The generals tore off her wings, my little sparrow fell,
And even God—even God—even God cannot find her—
Chinita, little girl, Murielita . . .
I will sing your song for you, I will sing—
Can you hear me, little bird?
    Can you hear me little bird?

Music note: *This song posed a unique problem. I had heard a Sicilian folksong which consisted of an ever-changing melody backed by a recurring pattern of four chords. I knew I was going to set the new song into this format. When the text of "Missing" was more or less finalised, I placed the song in E minor and used the Sicilian chord pattern in* $\frac{4}{4}$*: one bar each of D, G, B7, and Em. I thought it would be simple to just play the chords and let the voice wander. It wasn't. I just couldn't do the two together. So I recorded five minutes' worth of the chord pattern: D, G, B7, Em over and over again. I put the cassette into the car stereo and every time I got into the car I switched it on and improvised a tune with the text. When I started this routine, I frequently found myself driving to places I hadn't planned to go, but when I could both reach my planned destination and the end of the song without mishap, I thought "Fine. Now I can sing it." But when I picked up the guitar to play the chords, I lost the ability to improvise the singing. Not fine. So I decided to read the newspaper out loud while playing the chords, making sure that I really understood what I was reading, thus divorcing my mind from my fingers. I held conversations while playing the chords, then graduated to reading poetry while playing the chords. After a month I was finally able to sing the song while playing the chords. I shouldn't think the guy who sang the Sicilian song had all that trouble.*

See also "In Particular," the "Radio Ballads" section.

R.S.I.

Even as I type this book out on the word-processor, I am aware of the dangers of repetitive strain injury. Is my chair high enough? Is the screen at eye-level? I set my little timer at hourly intervals to remind me to get up and stretch or make the bed or play the guitar. For me it is a little too late—too much word-processing and the Chopin Study in A-flat (Opus 25, No. 1) left me with a mild form of R.S.I. My left wrist and my right shoulder will never be the same. For Joy, a West London VDU operator, it was far too late. Her arms from the elbow down were swathed in bandages to keep her wrists from moving. When they moved it was excruciatingly painful. She was philosophical: "It seems to have stabilised at this point. It used to be worse. It spread up to my neck." Obsessed with efficiency, her boss had hired a firm of experts who stood over the staff timing each work process. Their recommendations cleared the office of everything that necessitated exercise or a variety of movements. Eight out of its nine female staff developed R.S.I. Joy was glad to tell me all about it but she didn't want either her surname or the name of her boss mentioned as she and the rest of the office were busy suing him.

words and music: Peggy Seeger
disc 9, 26A

fairly fast, rhythmically
Mis-ter Wad-leigh, I'm leav-ing, But I'm tak-ing my sto-ry with me. Mis-ter
Wad-leigh, you'll nev-er see me a-gain. You brought in the time-and-mo-tion men,
Took a-way my golf-ball, my I B M; She ran with the sound of a run-a-way mare,
Made me swear,— but I loved her. Mis-ter Wad-leigh, you used me!
Got-ta be ef-fi-cient is what you said, And we're gon-na be ef-fi-cient till we're dead;

Em Bm Em F#m
You took a-way the cop-i-er, moved the phone, We sit in one place all day long -
G F#m Em C# Em C#
Nine 'girls' in the of-fice and each a-lone With her Gol-den Reed... That's
Bm F#7 Bm 3 Cm
all we need, you said. You put your head-phones on -
C#m Dm D#m
Start to roll - Hold your arms out straight - Your hands like that -
Em E7 Am 4
Key and touch, touch and key - And that's all, No more. Miles and
Bb Am Bb E7 Am Dm
miles of words and words, Days and days of num-bers, Till you're all wound up and
Am E7 Am
all worn down, Then you be-gin to won-der If some-one knew all a-long,
Am Dm C Bm 5 D Am
Some-one -- knew it'd turn out wrong. Mis-ter Wad-leigh, we're leav-ing!
D G D A7 D
'Cause there's not just me, there's Den-ny and Brid and Kate and Sue and Mar-y's kid;

We're the walk-ing wound-ed, R. S. I! The talk-ing wound-ed, R. S. I!, The
par-a-lysed wound-ed, R. S. I!, The out-raged, weep-ing wound-ed, R. S. I! Who
won't do the de-cent thing and die And spare your con-science.
THE WORLD'S NOT BIG ENOUGH FOR CONSCIENCE AND the PROFIT MOTIVE.
6
Mis-ter Wad-leigh, I'm leav-ing,
But I'm tak-ing my sto-ry with me. Mis-ter Wad-leigh, you'll nev-er see me a-gain.
Chap-ter Two. Nine lit-tle ro-bots work-ing for you. Touch and key, key and
touch, Nev-er thought a bod-y could hurt so much. Shoul-ders burn, my el-bows ache,
7
Arms so sore I think they'll break. Key and touch, touch and key, Gol-den Reed
made a mess of me; State-ments, briefs, re-ports and wills, Let-ters, memos, notes and

bills. Hands all numb, weak and cold – I'm on-ly thir-ty but I feel so old!
I love typ-ing, I love my work, But I sleep in pain and I wake up hurt ...
Mis-ter Wadleigh, on a Fri-day I col-lect my dole two blocks a-way from you;
I got a big felt pen, write me a sign, I'm gon-na be a so-lo pick-et line With a
card on a stick! I'll pick-et your place And tell your cli-ents face to face:
You're a bas-tard! And one of these days, one of these days, I'll climb in
through the tran-som, Smash up all the Gol-den Reeds and hold you all to ran-som.
And while you stand there wet-ting your pants, I'll say: Mis-ter Wad-leigh, your
last chance to tell me, While I count to ten:
WHERE'S MY

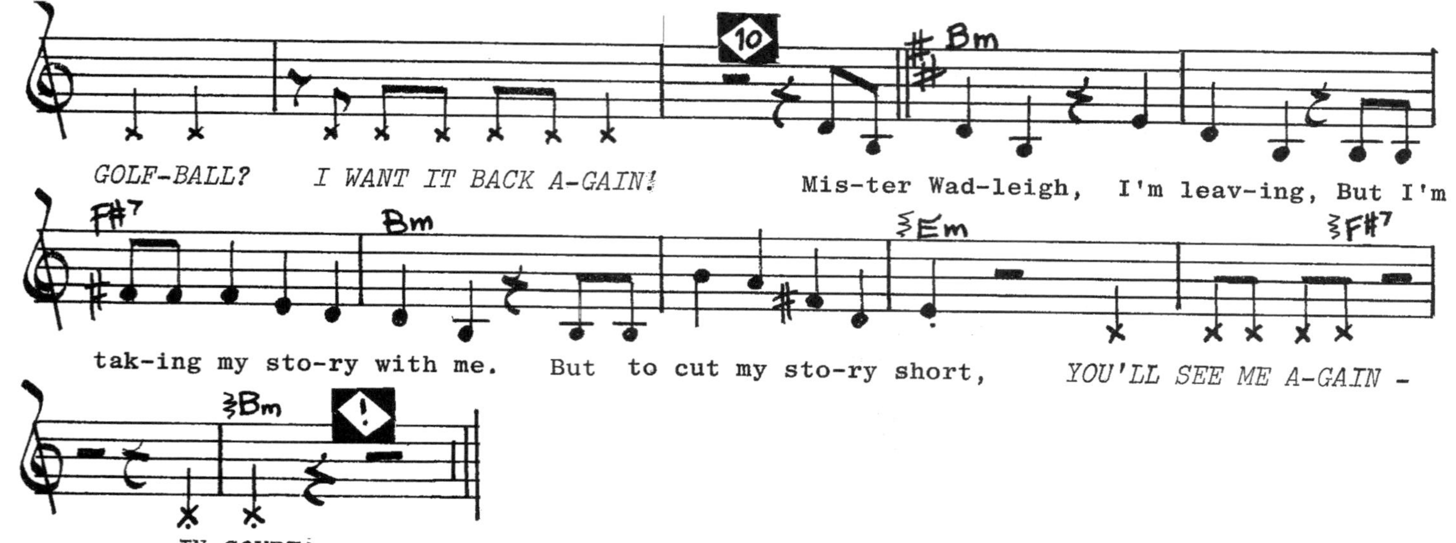
10
Bm
F#7
Bm
Em
F#7
Bm
GOLF-BALL? I WANT IT BACK A-GAIN!
Mis-ter Wad-leigh, I'm leav-ing, But I'm
tak-ing my sto-ry with me. But to cut my sto-ry short,
YOU'LL SEE ME A-GAIN -
IN COURT!

1 Mr. Wadleigh, I'm leaving,
But I'm taking my story with me.
Mr. Wadleigh, you'll never see me again.
You brought in the time-and-motion men,
Took away my golf-ball, my IBM;
She ran with the sound of a runaway mare,
Made me swear, but I loved her.

2 Mr. Wadleigh, you used me!
"Gotta be efficient" is what you said,
And we're gonna be efficient till we're dead;
You took away the copier, moved the phone,
We sit in one place all day long—
Nine "girls" in the office, and each alone
With her Golden Reed . . .
That's all we need, you said.

3 You put your headphones on—
Start to roll—
Hold your arms out straight—
Your hands like that—
Key and touch, touch and key—
And that's all,
No more.

4 Miles and miles of words and words,
Days and days of numbers,
Till you're all wound up and all worn down,
Then you begin to wonder
If someone knew all along,
Someone—knew it'd turn out wrong.

5 Mr. Wadleigh, we're leaving!
'Cause there's not just me, there's Denny and Brid
And Kate and Sue and Mary's kid;
We're the walking wounded, R.S.I.!
The talking wounded, R.S.I.!
The paralysed wounded, R.S.I.!
The outraged, weeping wounded, R.S.I.!
Who won't do the decent thing and die
And spare your conscience.

(spoken)
THE WORLD'S NOT BIG ENOUGH FOR CONSCIENCE AND *THE PROFIT MOTIVE.*

6 Mr. Wadleigh, I'm leaving,
But I'm taking my story with me.
Mr. Wadleigh, you'll never see me again.
Chapter Two.
Nine little robots working for you.
Touch and key, key and touch,
Never thought a body could hurt so much.
Shoulders burn, my elbows ache,
Arms so sore I think they'll break.

7 Key and touch, touch and key,
Golden Reed made a mess of me;
Statements, briefs, reports and wills,
Letters, memos, notes and bills.
Hands all numb, weak and cold—
I'm only thirty but I feel so old!
I love typing, I love my work,
But I sleep in pain and I wake up hurt . . .

8 Mr. Wadleigh, on a Friday
I collect my dole two blocks away from you;
I got a big felt pen, write me a sign,
I'm gonna be a solo picket line
With a card on a stick!
I'll picket your place
And tell your clients face to face:
You're a bastard!

9 And one of these days, one of these days,
I'll climb in through the transom,
Smash up all the Golden Reeds
And hold you all to ransom.
And while you stand there wetting your pants, I'll say:
Mr. Wadleigh, your last chance to tell me,
While I count to ten:

(spoken)
WHERE'S MY GOLF-BALL? I WANT IT BACK AGAIN!

10 Mr. Wadleigh, I'm leaving,
But I'm taking my story with me.
But to cut my story short,

(spoken)
YOU'LL SEE ME AGAIN—IN COURT!

Music note: *I think that a solo female singer alternating with a female group is the best combination for this song. There is lots of scope for instrumentalists who want more than the three or four chords per song that permeate this book. The chords given here are just a very basic guide. Neill and Calum were accompanying me when we recorded "R.S.I." and some of the chords they play don't even have names. So either embellish on mine or make your own.*

Woman on Wheels

When the camp was first established at Greenham (see "Carry Greenham Home"), there was only a flimsy picket fence surrounding the base. As time passed the presence and behaviour of the dangerous peace-women obliged the military to construct a veritable obstacle course of barriers, walkways, rolls of barbed wire, and guardhouses. By 1987 the fence was eight feet high but quite easy to topple: just apply a strong push to the concrete posts, followed by a hefty pull and the chain-link fence sagged to the ground where you could walk over it. Of course, cutting the fence made for an easier entry, to say nothing of the deep satisfaction gained from hearing the lovely, soft, sensual *scrunch* produced by a good set of bolt cutters. That's what we were doing on Circle the Base Day (see "Carry Greenham Home").

Bolt-cutters are very heavy and Jennifer Jones couldn't handle them on her own. So her friends helped her to hold them, bracing them against the armrests of her wheelchair. She wanted to feel that *scrunch* herself. That was how I first saw her and I immediately wanted to write a song about it. Where angels feared to tread, this songwriter fought her way through the screaming, milling mass of women and police. I broached my subject but she didn't even look up. She just said, "I'm busy," and went on scrunching. I got her name and called her a week later at her home in North London. She's an architect who developed multiple sclerosis in her mid forties. She lives on her own in a house she's designed for herself and for her wheelchair. She welcomed me and my recording machine and gave me hours of time and patience. She also volunteered details and incidents from her life, things that I could never have dredged out of my own imagination (such as the fact that the police had told her at Greenham that her wheelchair status rendered her ineligible for arrest. She found this insulting.) Jennifer Jones—the Woman on Wheels.

words and music: Peggy Seeger
disc 9, 26A

with spirit
D
G7
D
I'm a wom-an on wheels, but I still got my brain,
Bb7
A7
Bb7
A7
D
I'm gon-na tell you how it feels to be your own rail-way train.
G7
D
Roll down to the corn-er, put on your brakes,
Bb7
A7
G7
D
I'm gon-na tell you what it takes to be a wom-an on wheels.

Bb7 A7 G7 D
I'm gon-na tell you what it takes to be a wom-an on wheels.
17 D7 G A7 D
Roll on! O-ver the holes, the bumps and cracks, roll on!
Em * an expandable section A7 Bm
Re- mem-ber that day we were run-ning for the train and my tyre went flat?
A Bm D6
Roll on!
17 D7 G A7 D
Roll on! With the deaf and blind, the lame and halt, roll on!
D7 G E7
There's mon-ey a-round to help us all, It's a crip-pled sys-tem holds us back,
A7 G D
Keeps the people on wheels off the main - line track!

I'm a woman on wheels, but I still got my brain,
I'm gonna tell you how it feels to be your own railway train.
Roll down to the corner, put on your brakes,
I'm gonna tell you what it takes to be a woman on wheels.
Roll on!
Over the holes, the bumps and cracks, roll on!
Remember that day we were running for the train and my tyre went flat?
Roll on!

That man over there—the one under the hat,
Trying so hard not to stare—you get used to that.
Still, it's better than looking, then looking away,
You get that every day, you're a woman on wheels.
Roll on!
Pity me and I'll pity you, roll on!
All they want to do is talk about things that I can't do.
Roll on!

When it comes to kerbs, when it comes to stairs,
I got my special words, and I don't mean prayers.
When it comes to the shops, to reach the merchandise
Is a major exercise for the woman on wheels.
    Roll on!
    I want a chair that can levitate, roll on!
    Race up ramps, roll down stairs, wouldn't that be great?
    Roll on!

I went down to Greenham and I was cutting the fence;
Cops pulled me out of the way, then they waded in;
Said, "You'll never get arrested, a little lady like you."
I says, "Who are you talking to? I'm a woman on wheels."
    I said, "Hold on!
    "I got my rights to demonstrate!" Roll on!
    Next time I went down I took a dozen bolt-cutters and a dozen wheelchair mates,
    Roll on!

I want to be alone, but I'm always under care,
I've got that urge to roam, me and my chair;
We're together for life, not together for love,
And there's things I need more of. I'm a woman on wheels.
    Roll on!
    So many places I can't go, roll on!
    I want to lie in a field with the flowers . . . or run on a beach with the sand between my toes,
    Roll on!

Well, I need you—but you need me
To tell you 'bout a different view of the world you see,
About the pain I feel, about the fight I've won,
About how to do some little things you think can't be done.
Δ   Roll on!
    With the deaf and blind, the lame and halt, roll on!
    There's money around to help us all,
    It's a crippled system holds us back,
    Keeps the people on wheels off the mainline track!

B-Side

Most men seem to have difficulty addressing the subject of male violence against women. To them we say, "Look at it this way . . ."

alternative title: "Dangerous Women"
tune: Peggy Seeger
words: Peggy Seeger and Irene Scott
disc 9, 26A
© 1992 Peggy Seeger (1)

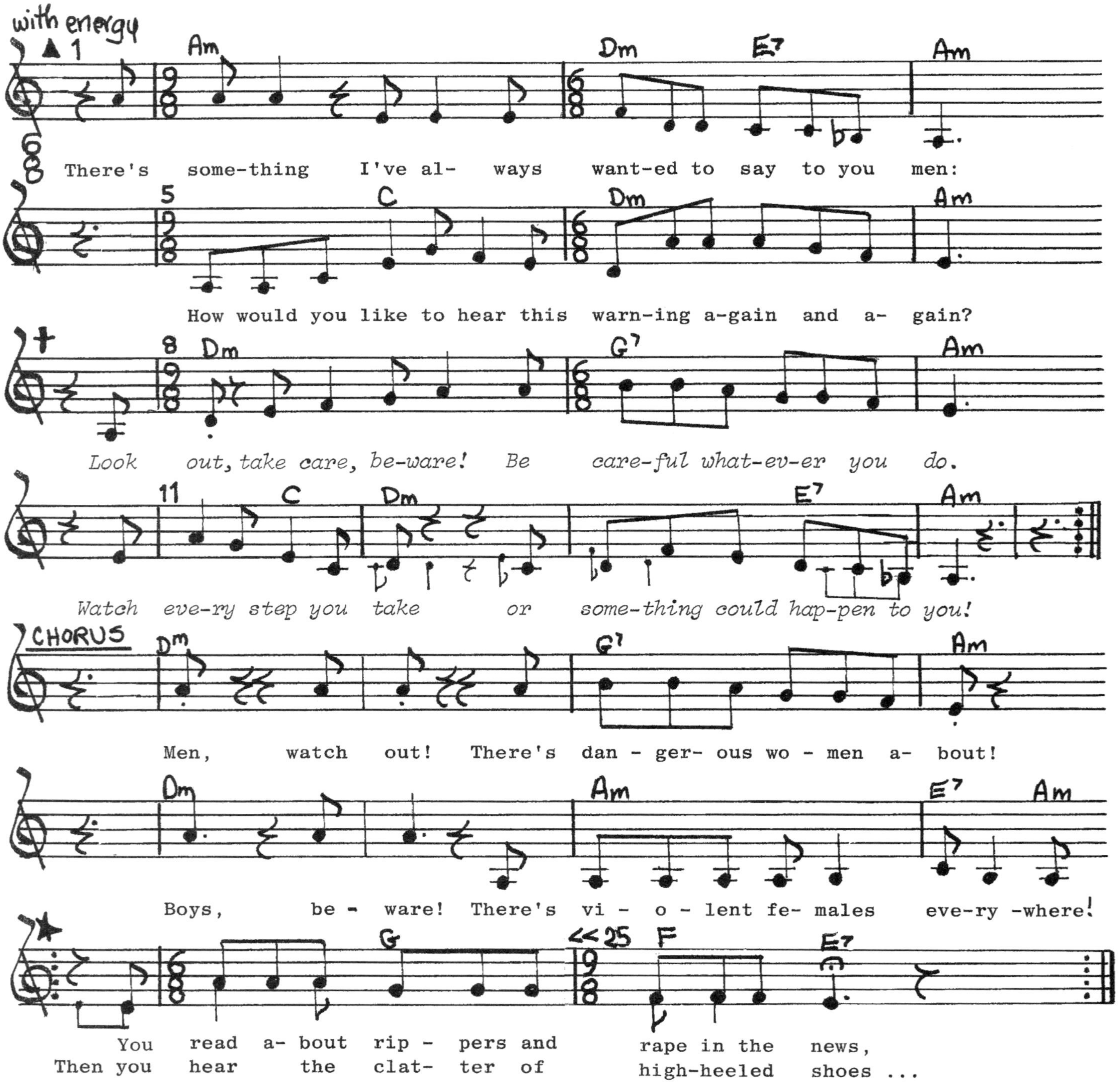
with energy
Am Dm E7 Am
There's some-thing I've al- ways want-ed to say to you men:
C Dm Am
How would you like to hear this warn-ing a-gain and a- gain?
Dm G7 Am
Look out, take care, be-ware! Be care-ful what-ev-er you do.
C Dm E7 Am
Watch eve-ry step you take or some-thing could hap-pen to you!
CHORUS
Dm G7 Am
Men, watch out! There's dan - ger- ous wo - men a- bout!
Dm Am E7 Am
Boys, be - ware! There's vi - o - lent fe- males eve-ry -where!
G F E7
You read a- bout rip - pers and rape in the news,
Then you hear the clat- ter of high-heeled shoes ...

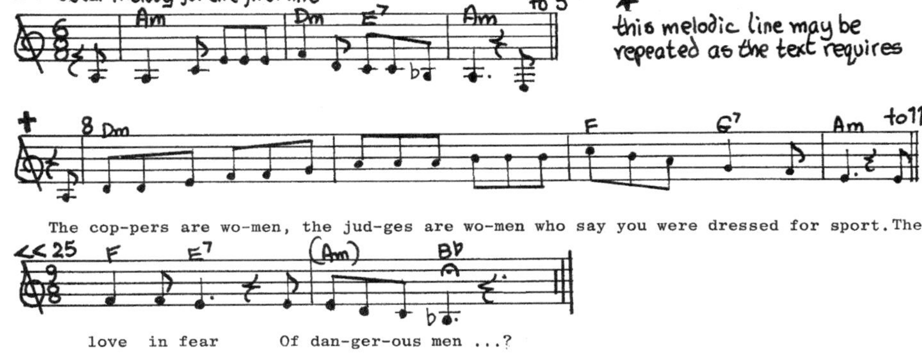

There's something I've always wanted to say to you men:
How would you like to hear this warning again and again?
"Look out, take care, beware! Be careful whatever you do.
"Watch every step you take or something could happen to you!"

Δ Suppose that boys were made of sugar and spice,
And girls were snails and puppy dogs' tails and nothing that's nice;
They'd turn into women whose needs would be terribly hard to control—
So you'd have to dress and behave like prisoners out on parole.

Chorus: Men, watch out! There's dangerous women about!
Boys, beware! There's violent females everywhere!
You read about rippers and rape in the news,
Then you hear the clatter of high-heeled shoes . . .

Δ Females are easily roused to passion and lust;
You're asking for trouble waiting alone at night for a bus.
She could be the one Miss Right, the one you can't live without;
She could be one of those ones your daddy warned you about.

Δ It could be a friend who threatens your body and life;
It could be your teacher, your lover, your mother, your sister, your wife.
She's used to the fact that you don't fight back or run or shout,
She's one of the ones your daddy never warned you about.

Chorus: Men, watch out! There's dangerous women about!
Boys, beware! There's violent females everywhere!
They crawl along kerbs in their Mercs and Jags,
They goggle at porn and toy-boy mags,
* They go to the football, riot and then
* Sing "Cigarettes; whiskey; and wild, wild men! . . ."

Cover your legs, remember to button your shirt,
For if you're attacked or abused and you take the woman to court,
† The coppers are women, the judges are women who say you were dressed for sport.
The doctors are women, the lawyers are women who say you were asking for it.

Δ Every day you open the paper and it's
Another man battered or raped or murdered and dumped in a ditch.
Babies and boys and old, old men, when will it end?
Degradation and fear and pain that women inflict on the men.

Chorus: * O, what a crime, what a bloody disgrace,
* To have to fear half of the human race . . .

(*slightly free*)
Δ But look around, the lovely women about
Outnumber the dangerous, menacing ones, there's never a doubt.
Do *they* raise their voices or try and find the cause or the cure?
No, they only say, "I'm not one of the dangerous ones, for sure."

Chorus: Men: for girls, there is no joke in this song.
Boys: for women, oppression has gone on far too long.
Could you bear, as we do here,
To walk and live and « love in fear
Of dangerous men? . . .

Music note: Considerable variation is needed to adapt the written tune to the words. It is one of those songs whose singing style evolves with repeated performances.

* *These are repeated chorus lines.*

I learnt some of it at self-defence and the rest I made up myself

The Presidential Bodyguard

In the early 1990s, I went into helpless hysterics in a bookshop in Ann Arbor, Michigan, while reading the *Quayle Quarterly,* a publication dealing exclusively with the utterances of Bush's second-in-command. J. Danforth 'Potatoe' Quayle's difficulties with (among other things) politics, social situations, and basic English produced such gems as:

- To a hall of Republicans: "My friends, we can and we will never, never, never surrender to what is right."
- To a passing funeral cortège: "Have a nice day."
- To a meeting of Western Samoans: "You all look like happy campers to me. Happy campers you are . . . and as far as I am concerned, happy campers you will always be."
- When questioned about the Holocaust, he replied that it was "an obscene period in our nation's history." When asked to elaborate, he said, "We all lived in this century—I didn't live in this century."

His greatest contribution to world politics, however, was to catalyse American humourists, whose contributions filled the *Quarterly*. They echoed, in cartoons, jokes, puns, quotes, and scathing comments, the six presidential words that not only America but the world feared most: "Dan, I don't feel very well."

tune: traditional Irish
words: Peggy Seeger
© 1992 Peggy Seeger (1)

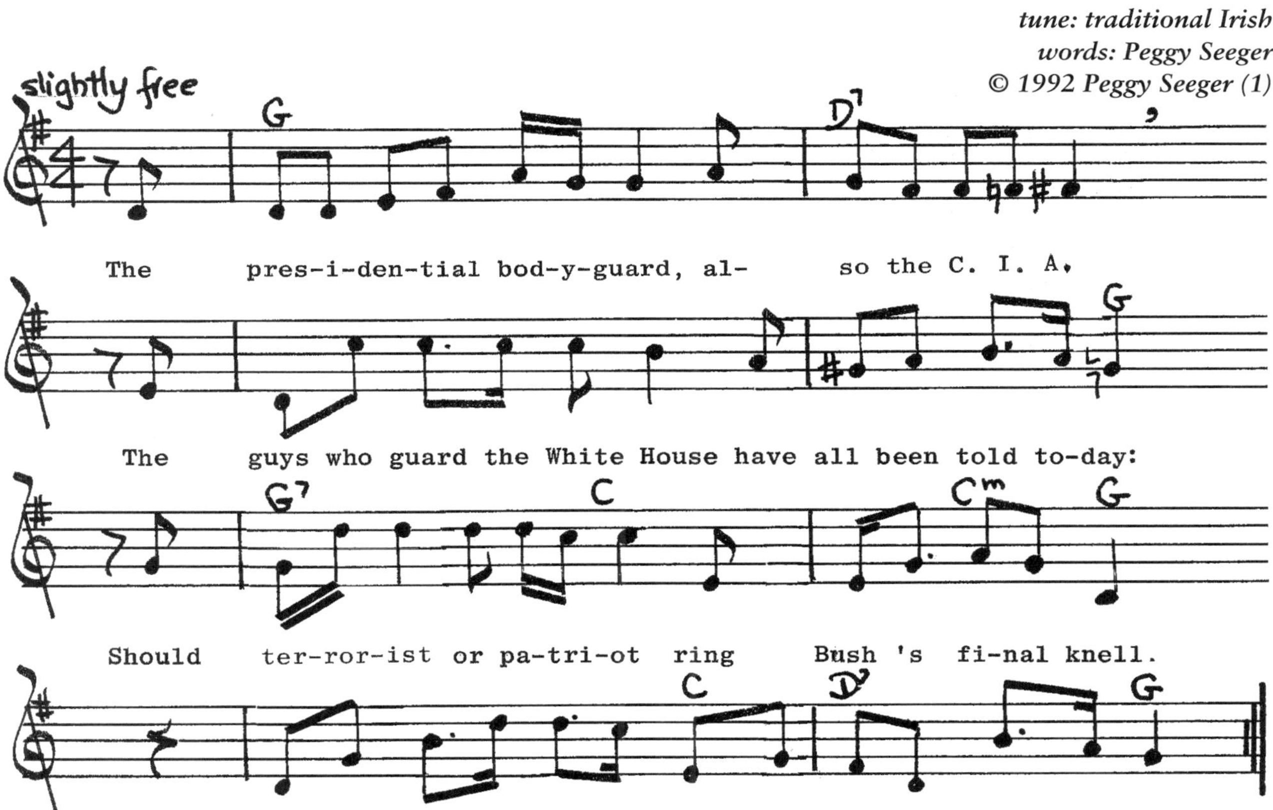

The presidential bodyguard, also the C.I.A.,
The guys who guard the White House have all been told today:
Should terrorist or patriot ring Bush's final knell,
Just take off the safety catch and get Dan Quayle as well.

Turn Up the Music

You could hear the bass thumping halfway down Bromley High Street. It was heavy metal, with drums like a rhythmical earthquake. It should be called *male music,* as it is almost entirely made by men. I was unfortunately walking in its direction and my irritation and distress increased the closer I got to it. It was emanating from a shop that had a gaggle of young women standing out front in the cold, clutching their skimpy cardigans. I had to pick up a parcel from the shop, so I entered. One of the women followed me in. The music was absolutely ear-splitting and I had to shout out the name under which the package had been left. When she followed me out again, I asked why they were all standing outside in the cold. "Can't stand the music," she said. Who decides on the music? "The management." May I speak to the manager? "He only comes in between nine and ten o'clock." *The staff* have no say. *I* have no say. Who *does* have a say? Have we *asked* for music everywhere we go? This is just part of normal everyday life in a big city. How do we cope with all these assaults on the body and soul? Some of us can't.

words and music: Peggy Seeger
disc 9

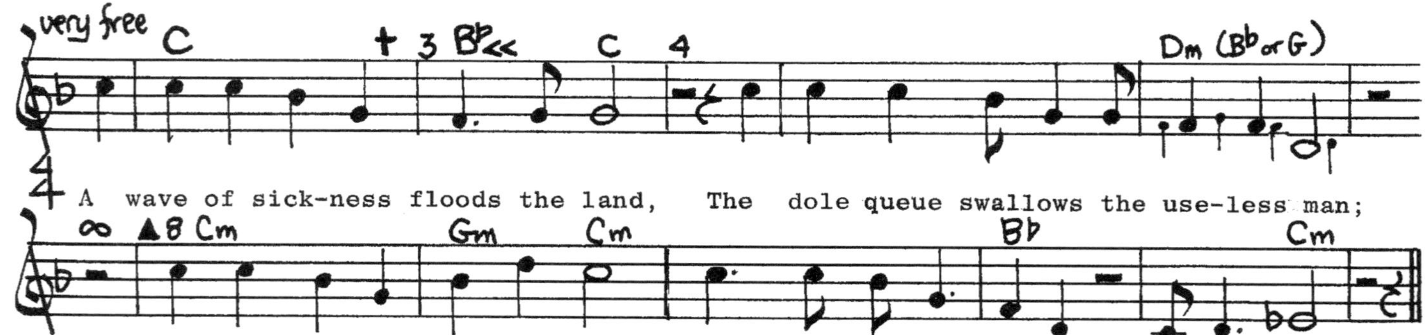

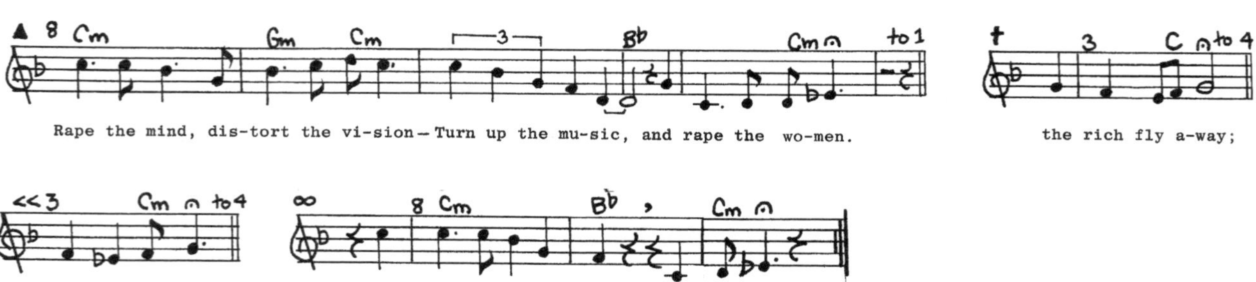

A wave of sickness floods the land,
The dole queue swallows the useless man;
Aimless days and endless nights—
Bruised and battered children, battered wife.

Rape the land and kill the seas,
Butter mountains, starving legions;
Δ Break the mind, distort the vision—
Turn up the music, and rape the women.

The poor get poorer, † the rich fly away;
Kids learn that learning doesn't pay;
Join the mob, buy and sell the world—
Turn up the music and murder little girls.

The system teaches « rape and murder;
People turn against each other;
Make a man feel less than human,
∞ He'll turn upon himself—and women.

Music note: I like to sing this freely over a very fast, rippling accompaniment.

Different Tunes

This song is partly autobiographical and partly put together from conversations with other mothers and their teenage daughters. Most of the mothers said the same thing: at somewhere between eleven and sixteen, their daughters turned into monsters. The majority of the daughters referred to their mothers as ferocious, interfering, dictatorial, judgmental, *etc.—i.e.,* monsters. It sometimes seemed as if the better the pre-teenage relationship had been, the worse it became once that age-corner had been turned. I have seen a number of these pairs of females since, and most of them report that the earlier relationship re-established itself within three or four years—as mine seems to have done.

words and music: Peggy Seeger
disc 9, 26A

1 MOTHER - freely
My moth- er was ex- ot- ic, she was like a gyp- sy queen;
I'd pre-tend she was- n't mine when I was fif-teen ———;
Her voice was loud, she wore men's shoes, she braid- ed up her hair;
Men would stop and stare.
Her clothes were few and sel- dom new, she was al- ways out of style;
She was al- ways nag- ging me, she would treat me like a child;

Some - times I wished I had a moth-er like the rest-
Some- times she was so love- ly that it took a- way my breath.

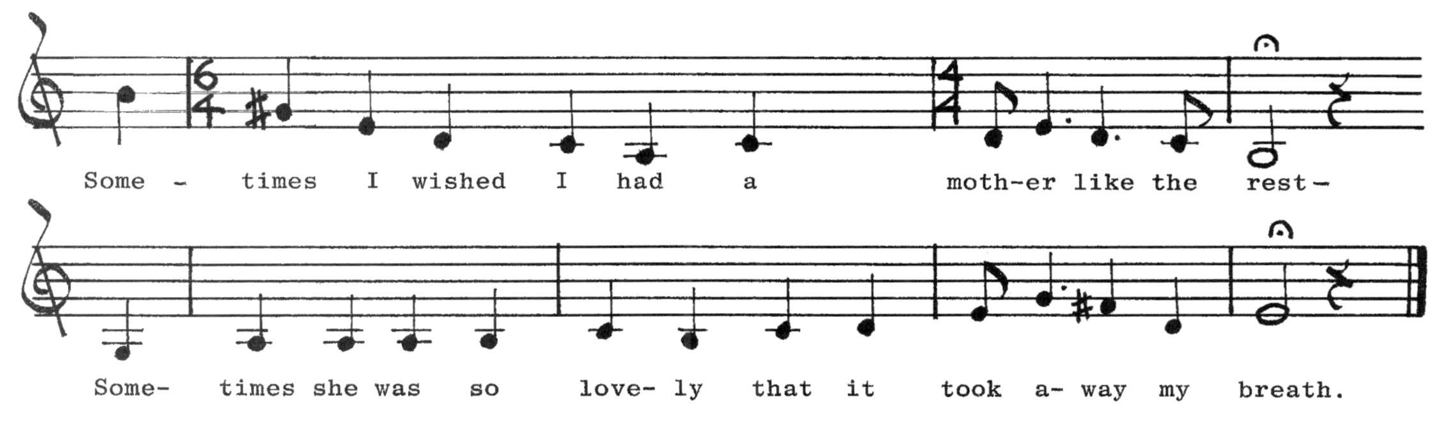

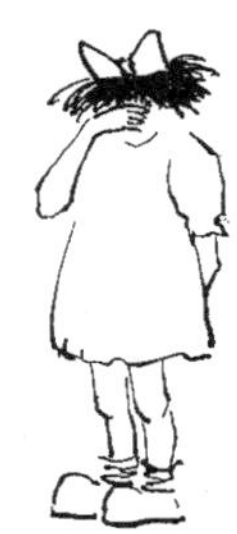

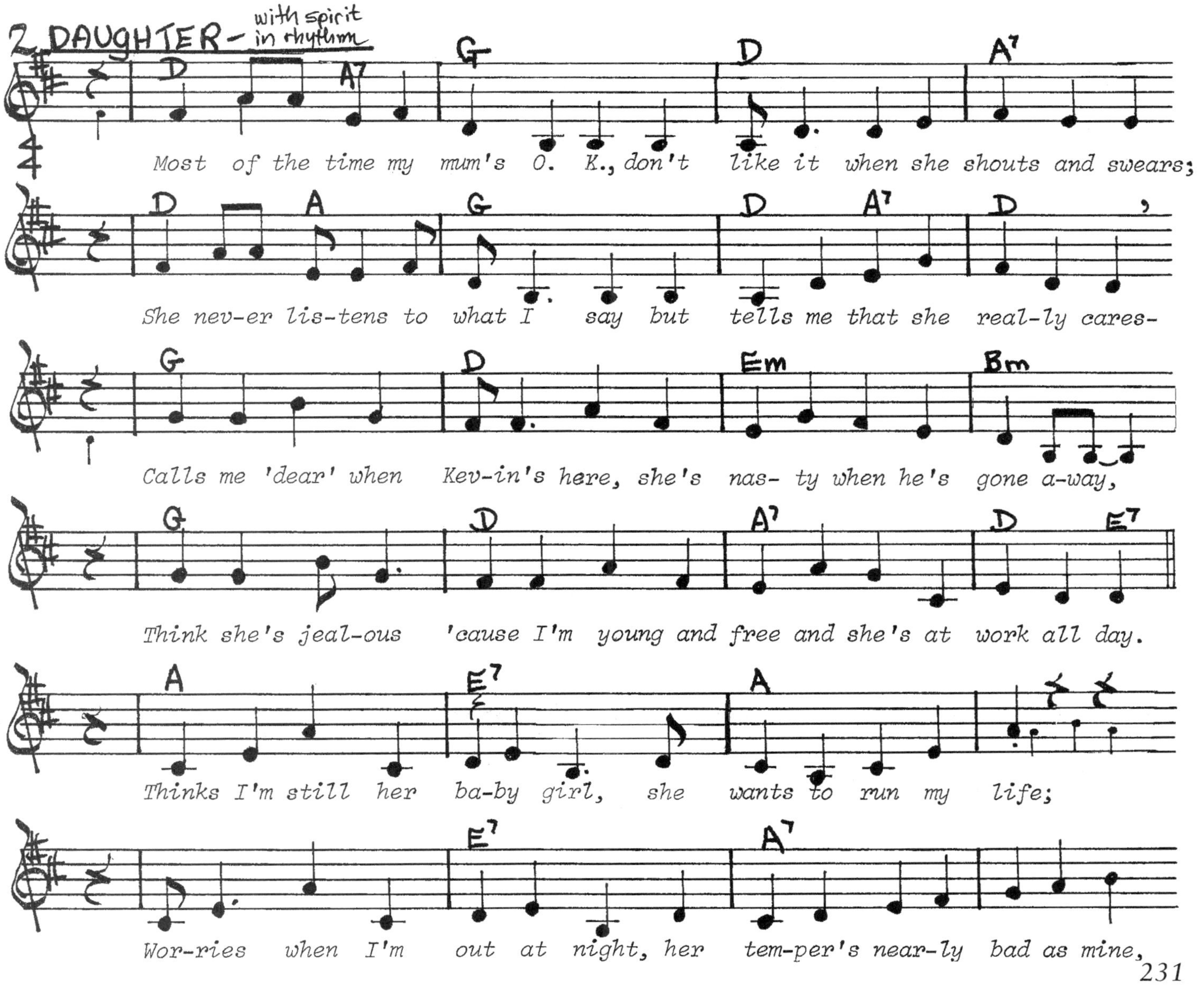

2. DAUGHTER- with spirit in rhythm
Most of the time my mum's O. K., don't like it when she shouts and swears;
She nev-er lis-tens to what I say but tells me that she real-ly cares-
Calls me 'dear' when Kev-in's here, she's nas- ty when he's gone a-way,
Think she's jeal-ous 'cause I'm young and free and she's at work all day.
Thinks I'm still her ba-by girl, she wants to run my life;
Wor-ries when I'm out at night, her tem-per's near-ly bad as mine,

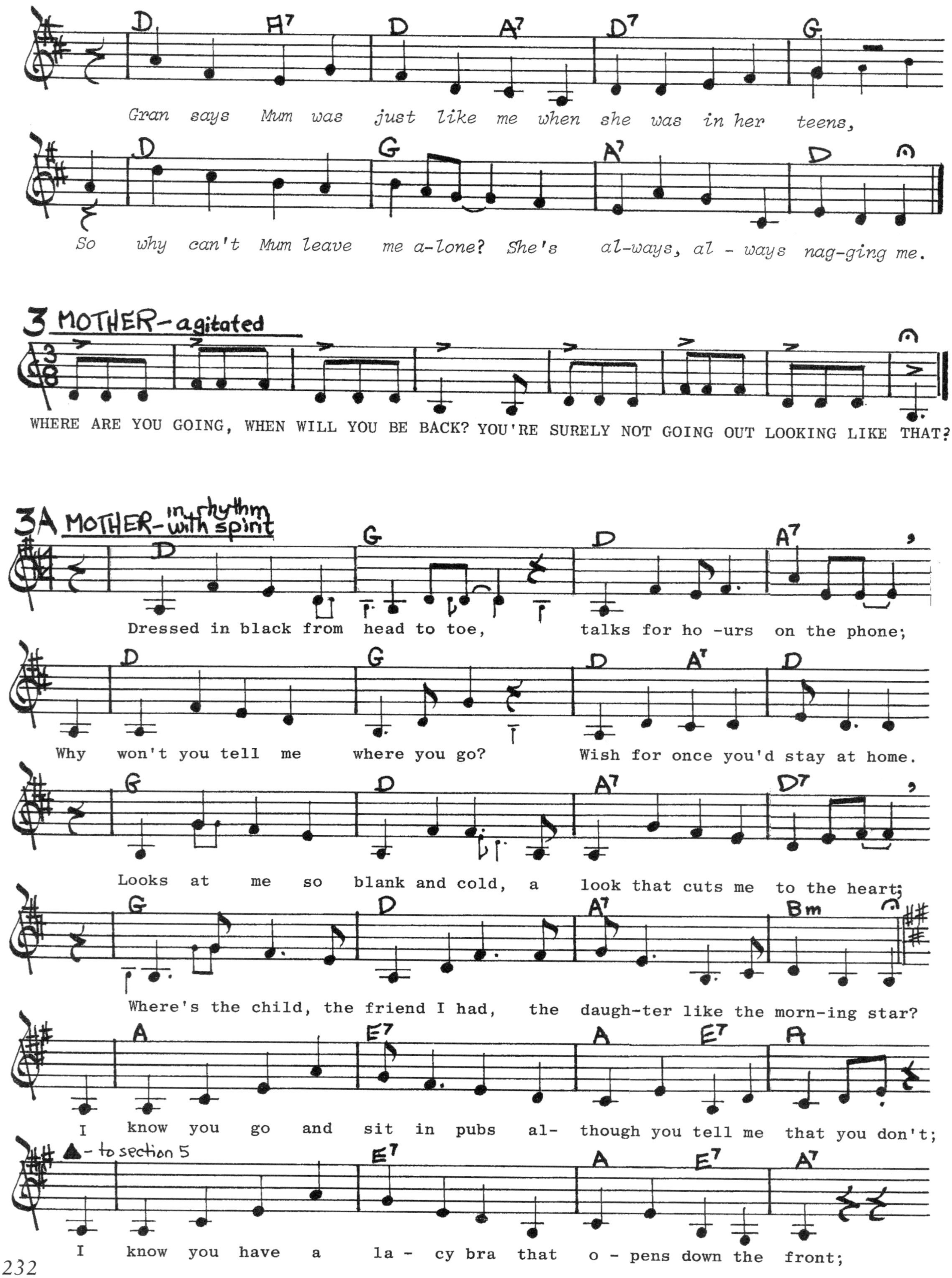

3A MOTHER – in rhythm with spirit

D G D A7
Dressed in black from head to toe, talks for ho -urs on the phone;

D G D A7 D
Why won't you tell me where you go? Wish for once you'd stay at home.

G D A7 D7
Looks at me so blank and cold, a look that cuts me to the heart;

G D A7 Bm
Where's the child, the friend I had, the daugh-ter like the morn-ing star?

A E7 A E7 A
I know you go and sit in pubs al- though you tell me that you don't;

▲ – to section 5

E7 A E7 A7
I know you have a la - cy bra that o - pens down the front;

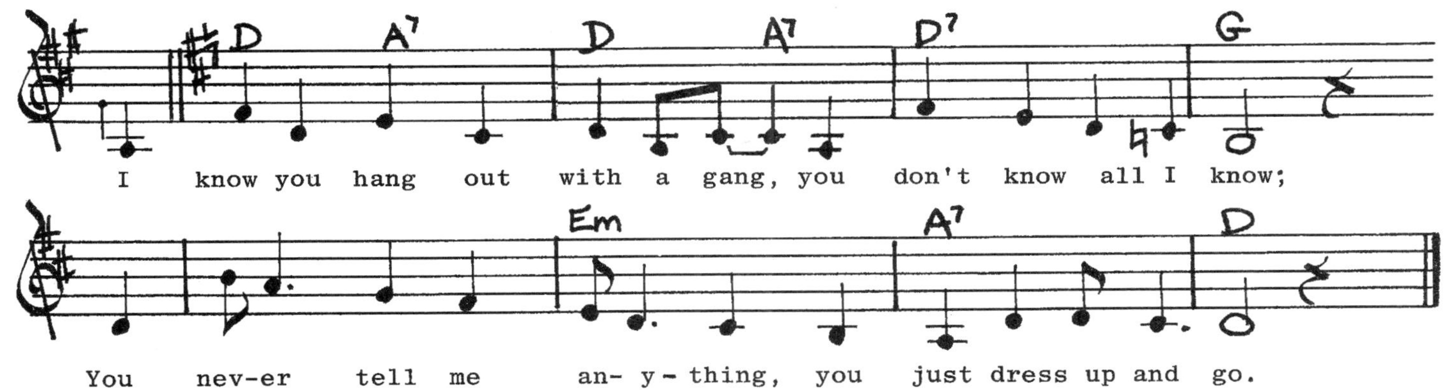
D A7 D A7 D7 G
I know you hang out with a gang, you don't know all I know;
Em A7 D
You nev-er tell me an- y - thing, you just dress up and go.

4 DAUGHTER - agitated
WHY SHOULD I TELL YOU? I'LL GO WHERE I WANT, I'LL DO WHAT I WANT AND SAY WHAT I WANT...

4A DAUGHTER - free
When I have a kid I'll let her do her home-work when she wants to do it;
Tell her how it was for me, and how my moth-er put me through it;
(speed up slightly)
I won't wait till her dad comes home and tell him all she's said and done -
(free again)
And I hope that I won't have to work so hard and wor-ry, like my mum.

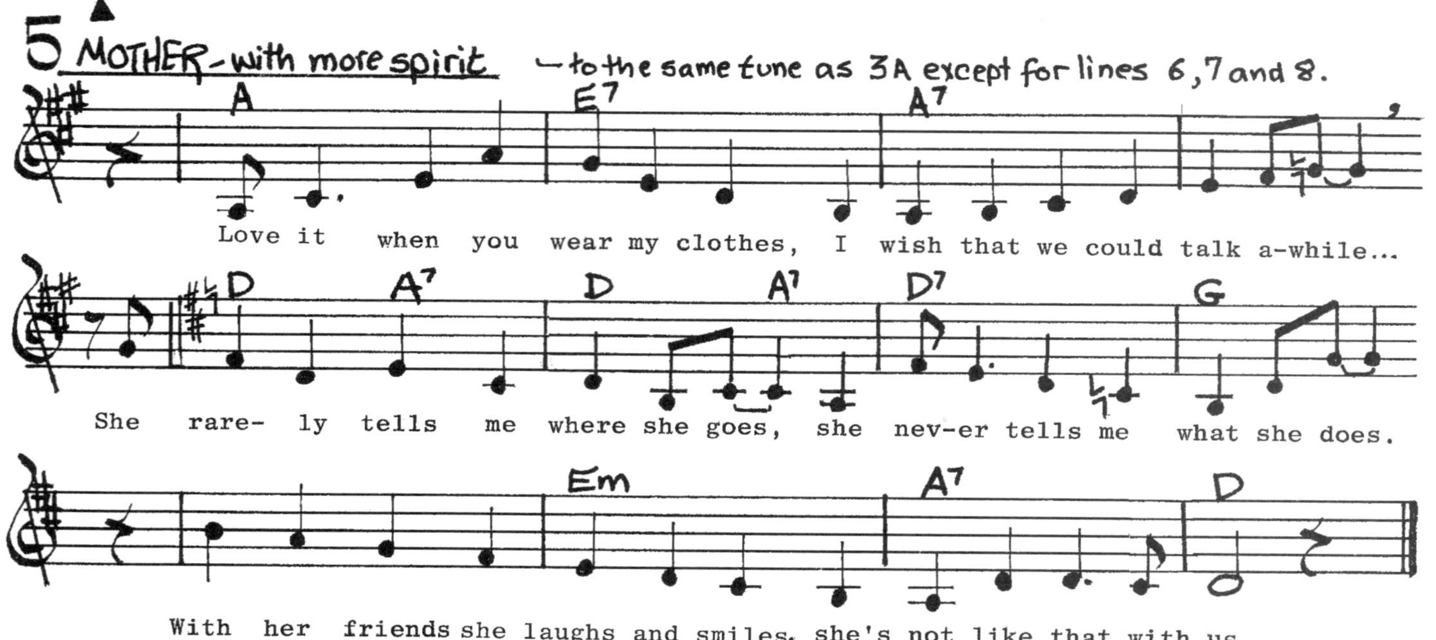

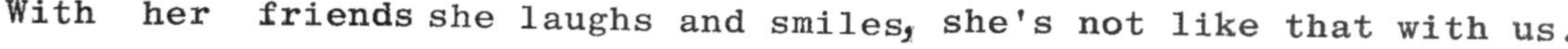

I CAN TAKE CARE OF MY-SELF, YOU KNOW, I'M NOT A BA-BY NOW, LEAVE ME A-LONE...

6A DAUGHTER - very spirited - to the same tune as 2

WHERE ARE YOU GOING? WHEN WILL YOU BE BACK?
WHERE ARE YOU GOING? WHEN WILL YOU BE BACK?
(mocking) WHERE ARE YOU GOING? WHEN WILL YOU BE BACK?

7 DAUGHTER - free
Some - times I'm a stran-ger in my own skin.

MOTHER
I'm los- ing pow- er, giv-ing in.

DAUGHTER
She taught me to shop and to man - age the house.
MOTHER (D7) (G) (D7) (G)
She taught me how to put make-up on and frowns when I wear my low-cut blouse.
DAUGHTER (A)
My mum's there, when I need her she's there...
MOTHER
Eve-ry - one needs some-thing secret, Some-thing they don't have to share.

7A DAUGHTER
D A7 G D A7
Don't make jokes in front of my mates, you look so sil- ly when you do.
MOTHER
D G D A7 D
You won't come and I won't fol-low, don't know how to get through to you.

DAUGHTER

Most of the time my mum is right, but I'm not going to tell her so.

MOTHER

She copes with the world much bet-ter than I did, she knows things I'll nev-er know.

DAUGHTER

Gran says you were just like me, and I say you're the same as her.

MOTHER

Good- bye, ba- by, good- bye, girl. Wel- come, wom-an, to the world.

DAUGHTER

Why do you make me feel so guil- ty, eve- ry- thing I say and do?

MOTHER

Those are the words of my old song, love, you're just sing-ing a dif'rent tune.

1 **MOTHER** *(sung freely)*
My mother was exotic, she was like a Gypsy queen;
I'd pretend she wasn't mine when I was fifteen;
Her voice was loud, she wore men's shoes, she braided up her hair;
Men would stop and stare.

Her clothes were few and seldom new, she was always out of style;
She was always nagging me, she would treat me like a child;
Sometimes I wished I had a mother like the rest—
Sometimes she was so lovely that it took away my breath.

2 **DAUGHTER** *(in rhythm)*
Most of the time my mum's O.K., don't like it when she shouts and swears,
She never listens to what I say but tells me that she really cares—
Calls me "dear" when Kevin's here, she's nasty when he's gone away,
Think she's jealous 'cause I'm young and free and she's at work all day.
Thinks I'm still her baby girl, she wants to run my life;
Worries when I'm out at night, her temper's nearly bad as mine,
Gran says Mum was just like me when she was in her teens,
So why can't Mum leave me alone? She's always, always nagging me.

3 **MOTHER** *(agitated)*
Where are you going, when will you be back?
You're surely not going out looking like that?

3A *(in rhythm)*
Dressed in black from head to toe, talks for hours on the phone;
Why won't you tell me where you go? Wish for once you'd stay at home.
Looks at me so blank and cold, a look that cuts me to the heart;
Where's the child, the friend I had, the daughter like the morning star?
I know you go and sit in pubs although you tell me that you don't;
I know you have a lacy bra that opens down the front;
I know you hang out with a gang, you don't know all I know;
You never tell me anything, you just dress up and go.

4 **DAUGHTER** *(agitated, fairly fast)*
Why should I tell you? I ll go where I want,
I ll do what I want and say what I want . . .

4A *(sung freely, slower)*
When I have a kid I'll let her do her homework when she wants to do it;
Tell her how it was for me, and how my mother put me through it;
I won't wait till her dad comes home and tell him all she's said and done—
And I hope that I won't have to work so hard and worry, like my mum.

5 **MOTHER** *(in rhythm)*
Shakes me off when I try to touch her, throws herself at all the boys,
Just can't think with her music blaring, she can't live without that noise,
I'm in the kitchen making dinner, washing dishes, in the dirt,
Mum, have you seen my satin blouse and fixed the zipper on my skirt?
I wish that I had looked so pretty, wish that I had had your style,
Δ Love it when you wear my clothes, I wish that we could talk awhile . . .
She rarely tells me where she goes, she never tells me what she does.
With her friends she laughs and smiles, she's not like that with us.

6 **DAUGHTER** *(angry)*
I can take care of myself, you know,
I m not a baby now, leave me alone . . .

6A *(in rhythm)*
My mum goes out to work all day, when she comes home I make her tea,
I can cook and sew and clean, none of my mates do that but me;
Mum goes all coy about the boys, she thinks I do more than I do,
She never tells me what she does, but she's too old for that, I know.
Wish that I was . . . eighteen, wish that I lived on my own,
When she gets that suffering look I try and think of what I've done,
Wants to hold me, wants to keep me, wants me in by half-past ten,
Every time I stand my ground, the same old chorus starts again.

6B MOTHER
WHERE ARE YOU GOING? WHEN WILL YOU BE BACK?
WHERE ARE YOU GOING? WHEN WILL YOU BE BACK?

DAUGHTER *(mocking)*
WHERE ARE YOU GOING? WHEN WILL YOU BE BACK?

7 BOTH *(alternating, singing freely)*
Sometimes I'm a stranger in my own skin.
I'm losing power, giving in.
She taught me to shop and to manage the house.
She taught me how to put make-up on and frowns when I wear my low-cut blouse.
My mum's there, when I need her she's there . . .
Everyone needs something secret, something they don t have to share.

7A BOTH *(in rhythm, alternating, each using her own tune forms)*
Don't make jokes in front of my mates, you look so silly when you do.
You won't come and I won t follow, don't know how to get through to you.
Most of the time my mum is right, but I'm not going to tell her so.
She copes with the world much better than I did, she knows things I'll never know.
Gran says you were just like me, and I say you're the same as her.
Goodbye, baby, goodbye, girl. Welcome, woman, to the world.
Why do you make me feel so guilty, everything I say and do?
Those are the words of my old song, love, you're just singing a different tune.

Music note: *The mother sings all the lines in ordinary type, the daughter sings those in italics. The lines in capitals are meant to be* AGITATED, EMPHATIC. *Parts of the song are meant to be sung unaccompanied. The rhythmic sections of Mother and Daughter dovetail melodically and harmonically and can be lilted simultaneously without words. The tune uses thematic material from "The Dead Men."*

and what are you going to be
when you grow up, little girl?
HORRIBLE

That's How the World Goes On

About work and play, when to give up and when to keep going.

words and music: Peggy Seeger
disc 9

waltz tempo
E E7 A E
When a mi - ner gets old, he leaves the coal- face,
F#7 B7
A- ban-dons his work and the tools of his trade;
E E7 A E
The mine was his life but the life got too tough,
B7 E
When a min - er gets old, they pen-sion him off.
A (E) E
Now he looks to his gar- den, walks down to the pub,
F#7 B7 OPTIONAL BAR
Goes out with the wife, plays darts at the club.
E7 A E
A strong young mi- ner is fill-ing his tubs-
(B7) B7 E E7
That's how the world goes on.

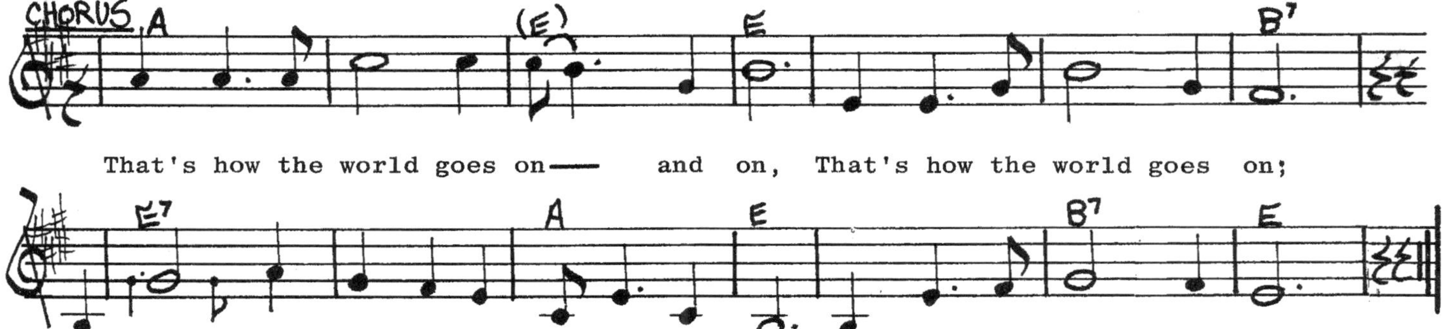

When a miner gets old, he leaves the coal-face,
Abandons his work and the tools of his trade;
The mine was his life but the life got too tough,
When a miner gets old, they pension him off.
    Now he looks to his garden, walks down to the pub,
    Goes out with the wife, plays darts at the club.
  * A strong young miner is filling his tubs—
    That's how the world goes on.

Chorus: That's how the world goes on and on,
That's how the world goes on;
A strong young miner is filling his tubs—
That's how the world goes on.

When a seaman gets old, he retires to land,
Leaving the skills that were at his command;
He dreams of his ship and it's hard to be free,
When a seaman gets old, he's not welcome at sea.
    Now he sits on a bench and he cracks with his mates,
    Hangs around harbours and dockyard gates.
  * A strong young seaman has taken his place—
    That's how the world goes on. *(chorus)*

When a lover grows old, he's tempted to spurn
The knowledge that took him a lifetime to learn;
But a woman is more than a mine or a ship—
My lover's grown old and I won't let him quit.
    You've still got the job, you've a garden to tend,
    No pension for lovers, just toil to the end.
  * It's time to clock on, love, so kiss me again,
    That's how the world goes on. *(chorus)*

**This line becomes the third line of each following chorus.*

My Friend Pat

This really happened to Gina, a feisty friend of mine. She is a wonderful raconteuse, laughing at herself and her experiences and acting out all the parts, including that of her friend Pat. The last verse reminds me of a recording session with a splendid strong woman, Frances Willard, whose work in trade unionism and politics was the subject under discussion. I think she was seventy-four at the time and almost too busy to see me. We talked for three hours. At the end of the session, I asked if I could come back next week and talk some more. With her eyes absolutely alive and a wide smile on her face, she dropped her voice two octaves and said, "Yes. And next time we'll talk about my love life."

words and music: Peggy Seeger

with spirit
I did-n't know ver-y much a-bout men un- til I mar-ried my hus-band;
I did-n't know ver-y much a-bout life when I prom-ised to love and trust him:
I did-n't know how to cook or clean, No one ev- er taught me;
But Pete just laughed and said it's not for house-work that he got me.
My friend Pat knows where it's at, said, You did-n't need an-y urg-in',
But I feel sor-ry for poor old Pete, he went and mar-ried a vir-gin.

I didn't know very much about men until I married my husband;
I didn't know very much about life when I promised to love and trust him;
I didn't know how to cook or clean, no-one ever taught me;
But Pete just laughed and said it's not for housework that he got me.
    My friend Pat knows where it's at, said, "You didn't need any urgin',
    "But I feel sorry for poor old Pete, he went and married a virgin."

I maybe didn't know very much about sex, I soon found out about babies;
Then Pete went a little bit funny on me, just like I'd got the rabies.
He bought me a car but wouldn't let me take the driving lessons,
Bought me a brand new washing-machine—to help cure my depression.
    My friend Pat's no diplomat, says, "Pete's a clever fella;
    "Leaves you out in the rain, my girl, then buys you a new umbrella."

The kids shot up and I shot off, back to full-time typing;
Pete took off to beer and golf and soon we'd started fighting;
The atomic household on its way to good old family fission,
I quit my job to work for free, getting Pete's commissions.
    My friend Pat says, "Look at that, she's gone and dumped her pension!
    "You'll save him several grand a year. Just thought it's worth a mention."

One night he tried new tricks in bed, I asked him, "Who's been teaching?
"You never tried that way before." Then I found out he's cheating on me;
Moved the family down to Spain then shipped me back to Eltham,
Filed a suit down in Madrid, told the judge I'd left him.
    My friend Pat came in to chat, says, "Nothing could be neater:
    "Wife down the drain, divorce in Spain, then marry a señorita."

We couldn't afford to live apart, for years we lived in silence;
He never laid a hand on me, they call it "mental violence";
He stripped our joint account and turned our daughter dead against me;
Sold my rings and the china tea-set that my mother left me.
(go immediately to next verse)

Smashed the pictures, spiked the mixer, slashed my little sofa;
Looked like Ali Baba and his boys had done us over;
Telly, hi-fi, pots and pans, the fixtures and the fittings;
Then it finally dawned on me: my Pete was splitting.
    My friend Pat says, "That's that! Possessions? You don't need 'em.
    "You're going Dutch, and that ain't much to pay to get your freedom."

He talks to me through a lawyer now, we're going fifty-fifty
On house and garden, curtains, carpets, all that he's not lifted.
That leaves me with my health, my wits, and me at the age of sixty;
A sense of humour saw me through, and that's been always with me.
    Me and Pat, we have a little laugh, to think of all he's losing:
    A loyal wife, a slave for life who, after all, did choose him.

There's a couple of fellas a-coming around, I love 'em all for trying;
They're great old guys, and I'm a great old girl, and I'm not going to sit here crying;
They come and chat up me and Pat, some nights we go out dancing;
Then I come home and live alone—but after the romancing.
    My friend Pat, she's a bit of a cat, and whenever we're divergin',
    Says, "I feel sorry for poor old Pete—he went and married a virgin."

Garden of Flowers

When I like a tune I hum it, whistle it, lilt it without words, either in fragments or *in toto*, for days. For weeks. It is a source of keen irritation to my family and friends. It's one sure way to win at cards though, to whistle the same tune throughout the game. This tune was hummed, whistled, and lilted at *me* for several weeks by Ewan and Kitty on a trip through the Scottish highlands in 1986. It was one of many songs sent to us on a cassette by a Sicilian friend and it imprinted itself indelibly on all three of us as we drove up one side of Scotland and down the other. We never knew what the words meant—but we carried the melody with us for three years before I put this set of words to it during that terrible summer when Ewan was so ill.

tune: traditional Sicilian
new words and trad. arr.: Peggy Seeger and Irene Scott
disc 15A, 19A, 20, 21

They live in the garden of flowers,
They live in the garden of flowers
    By the riverside.
They tend it every hour,
They tend it every hour
    That it may never die.

He sings to her in the morning,
He sings to her in the morning
    From the riverside.
The river tells the story,
The river tells the story
    To the waiting sky.

She held him while he was sleeping,
She held him while he was sleeping
    In the light of day.
When he awoke she was weeping,
When he awoke she was weeping
    And she turned away.

Δ Tears flow into the river,
The tears flow into the river
    Through the winter garden.
She carries flowers with her,
She carries flowers with her
    And lays them in his hand.

She sings to him in the morning,
She sings to him in the morning
    From the riverside.
When the song is over,
When the song is over
    She will sing the song again.

Music note: *The whole of verse 4 is sung in F minor. You modulate from D minor to F minor via a transitional C7 chord and modulate back from F minor to D minor via an A7 chord.*

Sellafield Child

Ewan was in hospital again. At visiting time, he described being wheeled, horizontal, on a trolley late the previous evening, down endless corridors past ward after ward. As he was trundled past rooms of old men watching TV or listening to the radio on their headsets, he heard the thin cry of a baby wailing. He described it so vividly, the ceiling overhead, the cracked plaster of the walls . . . I projected this scenario onto another situation, the clusters of leukaemia children around so many of the nuclear power plants in the world. Sellafield, in Cumbria, is our most notorious site for this phenomenon but the song could apply to the environs of any nuclear installation, many chemical plants and numerous inner cities. (See also "The Invader" and "Plutonium Factor.")

words and music: Peggy Seeger
*disc 14 and 26**

slow

Am · E7 · A7 · D

The trol-ley goes fast, Life goes slow, Takes you where You don't want to go;

Dm · Am · <<8 F7 · E7 · 10

Wait-ing for morning All your life; Be-fore you were born They turned out the light.

CHORUS Dm · Am · Dm · Am

Baby, you've got to cry, They'll hear you bye and bye;

Am · E7 · Am

Baby, you've got to move Or they won't see you.

Dm · D7 · Am · E7 · Am

Ba-by, cry, they think you're dead, Ba-by, cry in your hos-pi-tal bed.

*These are two mixes of the same recording.

The trolley goes fast,
Life goes slow,
Takes you where
You don't want to go;
Waiting for morning
All your life;
Before you were born
They turned out the light.

Chorus: Baby, you've got to cry,
They ll hear you bye and bye;
Baby, you've got to move
Or they won't see you.
Baby, cry, they think you're dead,
Baby, cry in your hospital bed.

The trolley goes fast,
Lights go by,
Neon stars,
Plaster sky,
Turn them off
One by one,
Baby lives
In a hospital room. *(chorus)*

Poisoned water,
Poisoned air,
Poisoned thinking
Brought you here.
Cry, baby,
They won't mind,
Δ Walkman, talkman,
† Deaf and blind,
Δ Old men sit
† With headphones on,
« Baby's dead and gone. *(chorus)*

Music note: I could have saved space by typing the verses in longer lines, but the singing technique is one of terse, short lines. Seeing it in short lines helps to keep you from vocalising too much.

We Remember

I am proud of this song even though I didn't write the tune. There is power in a name—*Rumplestiltskin* is more than a simple fairy-tale. Repeating the names of political activists makes me feel good about the human race and I need to feel good as I daily confront the desecrations wreaked by man against humanity and man against nature. This is one of those songs that can be constantly updated. These are the names we are singing at the time of writing. I hope many of them will be well known to you, although some of them have been taken from the honour roll of "ordinary" hero(in)es who have disappeared or been incarcerated during wars, revolutions, and political actions—like Kazim Arli (Turkey) and Juan Hernandez (Mexico). These names are *not* fictional.

alternative title: "Naming of Names"
tune: traditional Scots Gaelic
new words and trad. arr.: Peggy Seeger
disc 4
© 1992 Peggy Seeger (1)

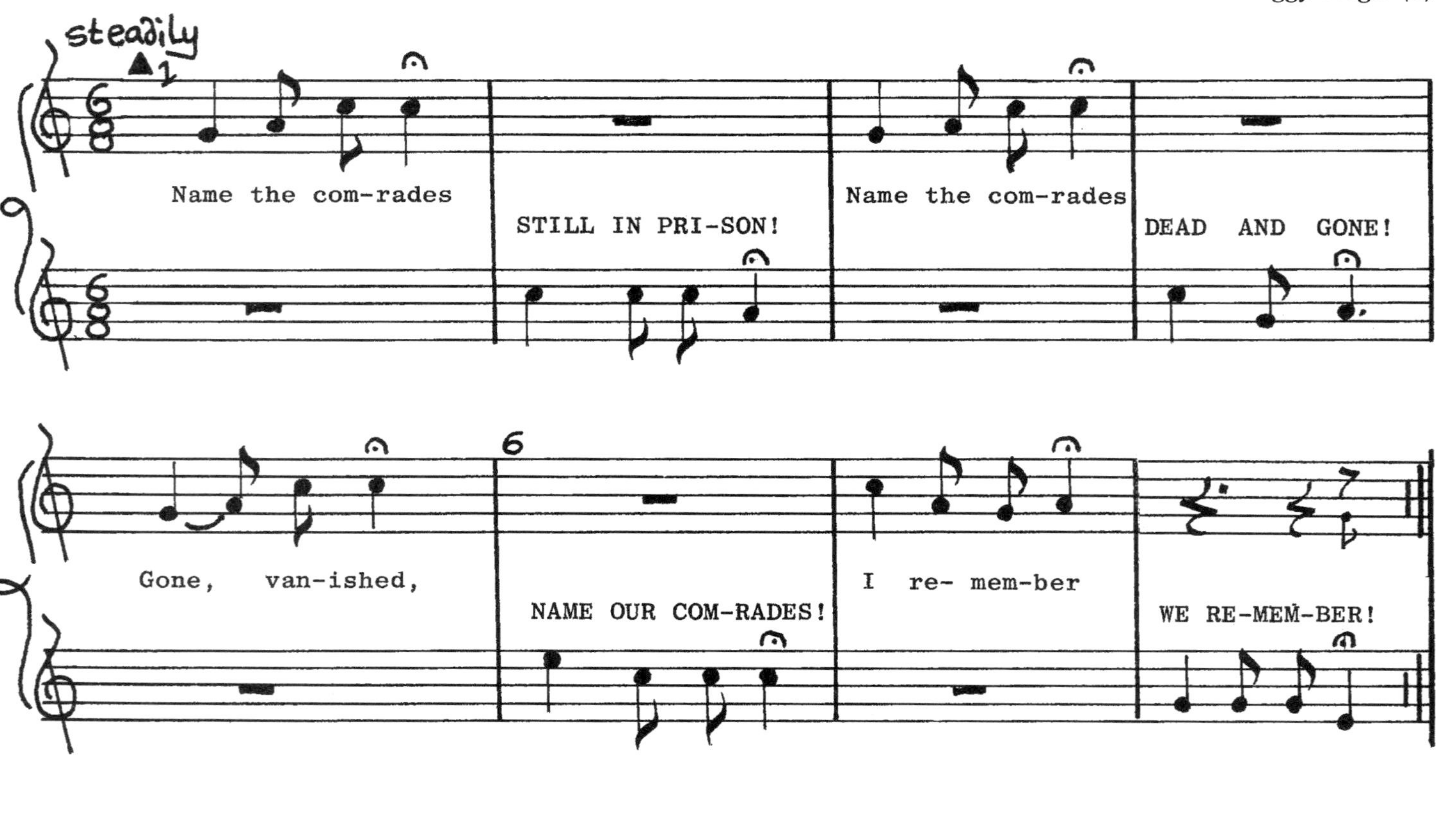
steadily
Name the com-rades
STILL IN PRI-SON!
Name the com-rades
DEAD AND GONE!
Gone, van-ished,
NAME OUR COM-RADES!
I re- mem-ber
WE RE-MEM-BER!

Ernst Tael-mann DIED IN PRI-SON! Bob-by Sands DIED IN PRI-SON! John Mac-Lean (etc.)
to 6

Music note: *The lowercase type is for a solo singer, and* THE UPPERCASE TYPE IS FOR A SMALL GROUP. *Some of the phrases cross over or dovetail. Just keep singing—it all fits. The original tune was that of a 'waulking song'. Waulking is one of the processes used in the manufacture of fine tweeds. It is usually a task performed by a group of women, who sit on either side of a lipped table or trough. The cloth is lifted out of a bath of urine in which it has been soaking. The women lift the cloth and bang it onto the table to size it and season it. All the movements are done in rhythm with the song, which is virtually a cloth-making shanty. The soloist makes up new lines ad infinitum to keep everyone entertained as the work progresses. In our song, names can be endlessly added for, to quote a songwriter, "The earth bears heroes when a hero dies."*

Name the comrades
Still in prison!
Name the comrades
Dead and gone!
Gone, vanished,
Name our comrades!
I remember
We remember!

Kazim Arli
Still in prison!
Karen Silkwood
Dead and gone!
Juan Hernandez
Gone, vanished!
Don't forget them
We remember!

Nelson Mandela
Long in prison!
Joe Hill
Long gone!
Murielita
No one knows!
Don't forget them
We remember!

Δ Ernst Taelmann
Died in prison!
Bobby Sands
Died in prison!
John MacLean
Died in prison!
Nameless millions
Died in prison!

Wallace, hung and
Drawn and quartered!
Carmen Quintana
Set on fire!
Scholl and Shehr and Schwartz
Beheaded!
Victor Jara
Died singing!

Patrice Lumumba
Garçía Lorca
Kobayashi
Mother Jones
Karl and Rosa
All murdered!
Don't forget them
We remember!

Sing with pride
Sing with joy
Sing today
Sing tomorrow
Sing them down
Sing them down
Brave comrades
We remember!

We remember
Cesar Sandino
We remember
Manuel Quisqina
We remember
The Birmingham Six
And Tom Mooney
We remember

Sing their names
Eduardo Mondlaine
Sing their names
James Connolly
Sing their fame
The nameless comrades
I remember
We remember!

(all singing)
We remember
Those in prison!
We remember
Those who died!
Don't forget them
We remember—
They died for us
They live forever!

The Judge's Chair

I was determined to have only planned children. I had a son at twenty-four and a backstreet abortion shortly afterward. I went alone, came home alone, picked Neill up from Fay Tracinsky's house, haemorrhaged alone through the night, took Neill back to Fay the next morning and went to the TV studio where I was helping to provide music for a program on racism in London. Where was Ewan? Working as well, but in Scotland. Neither of us had known an abortion could be that bad. The next three terminations, alternating with two more children, were different. I have never forgotten that first one: that sordid little room, the pain, the trip home, the blood, the isolation, and above all, the fear.

All the countries in the world are run by a majority of men. Britain is no different, with women forming about one-seventh of its MPs. Control of the means of production is one of capitalism's Ten Commandments. So every few years, Parliament tries once again to control *re*production by making abortion on demand yet more difficult for women. We even have foreign fundamentalists besieging our abortion clinics now . . . as if we didn't have enough native ones.

tune: Peggy Seeger
words: Peggy Seeger and Irene Scott
disc 26

free
I don't want the boy with the long brown hair,
I don't want the one with the curls.
I want Jim-my with the de-vil- may -care,
Jim-my's good with the girls.

1 I don't want the boy with the long brown hair,
I don't want the one with the curls.
I want Jimmy with the devil-may-care,
Jimmy's good with the girls.

2 He took the girl with the long brown hair,
He took the one with the curls.
He took me, and the devil may care,
And Jimmy's good with the girls.

3 Come and walk in the autumn woods,
Come and walk in town;
She walked with him to the end of the earth
And together they lay down.

4 Annie, the light that's in your eyes
Tells your lover's name;
Annie, the hope that's in your heart
Will turn to grief and shame.

5 Sunday, Monday passing by,
Thursday, Friday too;
Annie walks in the winter sun,
A week past she was due.

6 Two weeks, three weeks passing by,
Three and four and five;
Annie walked in the winter sun
And wished that she could die.

7 December past, the New Year gone,
Judgement Day has come;
The doctors sat in the judge's chair
And the judges turned her down.

8 Jimmy won't walk, Jimmy won't talk,
Jimmy won't come around;
Annie's gone to a backstreet woman
To bring the baby down.

9 Pain floods into that place
Where love has come and gone;
Close the door, and close the door
And Annie's walking home.

10 Slowly, slowly up the stair
Into her childhood room;
Her bed filled up with red, red blood,
Annie died alone.

11 She won't have the boy with the long brown hair,
She won't have the one with the curls;
She got Jimmy and the devil-may-care,
And Jimmy's good with the girls.

12 MEN SIT IN THE JUDGE'S CHAIR—
WE ARE UP ON TRIAL.
WOMAN, IF YOU CONCEIVE
YOU MUST BEAR YOUR CHILD.

Music note: *This should be sung ballad-style, plain and without histrionics. The last verse is to be sung almost heroically—the range in which the tune has been placed will help that. Be sure you begin the song fairly low, otherwise you'll find yourself straining in the last verse. The verses have been numbered because there is an analysis of this song in the section "In Particular" (Models).*

Maggie Went Green

Red is the colour of the Labour Party rose. Blue is the colour of the Conservatives. Margaret Thatcher was indifferent, nay hostile, to environmentalists and everything having to do with their environment until September 27, 1988 (at about 9:30 in the evening at a Royal Society dinner), when she suddenly saw the light, repented, and confessed that she was really green at heart. She may have paid little attention to the advice of her Cabinet ministers, but she did heed Saatchi and Saatchi, the fashionable advertising firm that fashioned (after a fashion) the Conservative image and handled her (or should I say, "handed her the"?) 1979 election.

words and music: Peggy Seeger
disc 14

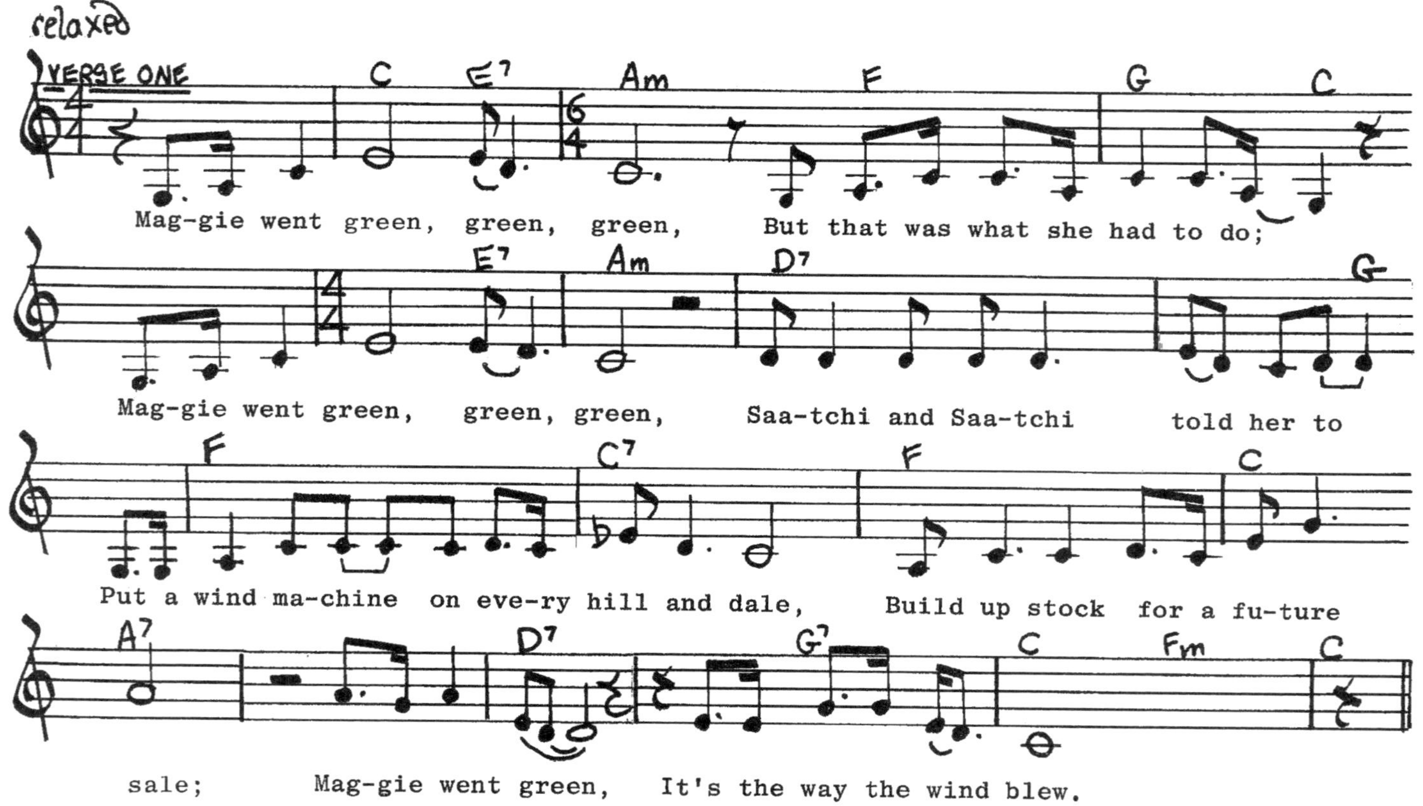
relaxed
VERSE ONE
C E7 Am F G C
Mag-gie went green, green, green, But that was what she had to do;
E7 Am D7 G
Mag-gie went green, green, green, Saa-tchi and Saa-tchi told her to
F C7 F C
Put a wind ma-chine on eve-ry hill and dale, Build up stock for a fu-ture
A7 D7 G7 C Fm C
sale; Mag-gie went green, It's the way the wind blew.

and pigs
can fly

Maggie went green, green, green,
But that was what she had to do;
Maggie went green, green, green,
Saatchi and Saatchi told her to
Put a wind machine on every hill and dale,
Build up stock for a future sale;
Maggie went green,
It's the way the wind blew.

If Maggie is green, green, green,
It's the green of the slime on a stagnant pool;
To learn the meaning of green,
She'd have to go back to school
And learn that green is a natural hue,
It'll mix with red if the red is true—
Maggie's not green,
She's a royal navy blue.
. . . And she'll tread on you with her blue suède shoes.

Just the Tax for Me

See notes for "Fifteen Ways to Beat the Poll Tax" and "Can't Pay, Won't Pay."

tune: traditional English ("In and out the Windows")
new words and trad. arr.: Peggy Seeger
disc 14

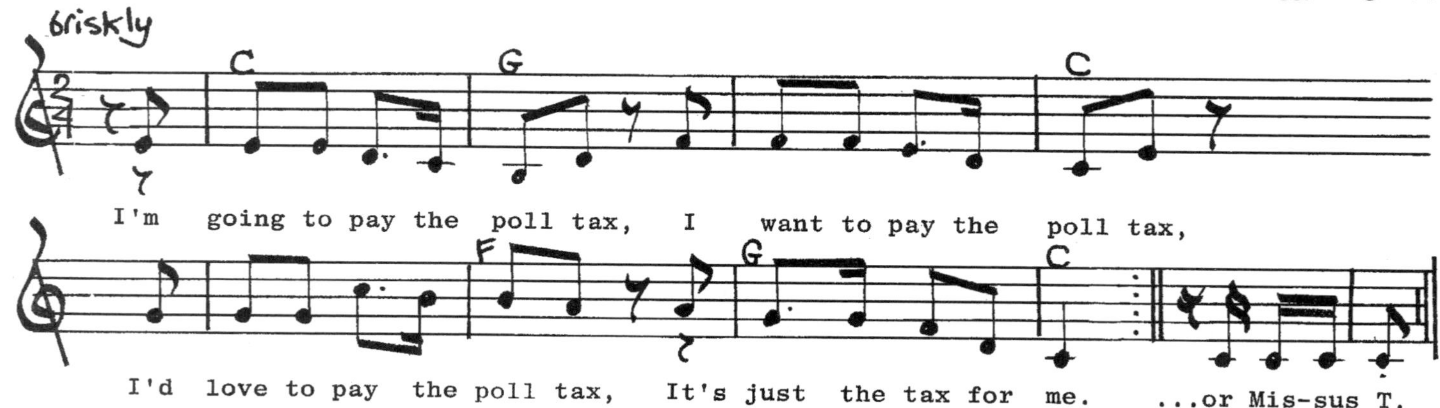

I'm going to pay the poll tax,
I want to pay the poll tax,
I'd love to pay the poll tax,
It's just the tax for me.

My gran will pay the poll tax,
My kids will pay the poll tax,
My cat will pay the poll tax,
And so will you and me.

MPs will pay the poll tax,
VIPs will pay the poll tax,
Mrs. T. will pay the poll tax,
So it's the tax for me.

Hand or foot or thumb tax,
Elbow, knee, or bum tax,
Inane, insane, or dumb tax,
It's any tax for me.

I would pay a rain tax,
A train, a grain, a drain tax;
But if they make a brain tax
It won't apply to me
. . . or Mrs. T.

Music note: To be sung like a children's chant.

One Step, Two Step

Despite the fact that Neil Kinnock was a seasoned politician, he did not inspire confidence among the electorate. He took over the leadership of the demoralised Labour Party in 1983 and began to move it to the right by purging it of its dissident elements. He continued by abandoning many policies that he had endorsed before taking office. He made the party electable but somehow was never considered electable himself. For seven years his Parliamentary sentence ran concurrent with Thatcher's. He spoke confidently and well, with a colourful Welsh accent, but never quite seemed to be a match for Thatch. The Prime Minister and her shadow slugged it out daily in Parliament—*Question Time* on the radio was a veritable lesson in the meaning of the term 'pecking order.'

words and music: Peggy Seeger

One step, two step, Kinnock's little dance,
Abandoning his promises whenever he gets the chance;
One step forward, a valiant move,
Then two steps backward so he can prove
That he can waltz with Maggie in time to Maggie's tune.

Once Again

Ewan died in hospital in London on October 22, 1989. We scattered his ashes on Bleaklow Stones in Derbyshire in May of the following year.

words and music: Peggy Seeger
disc 15A, 20, 21

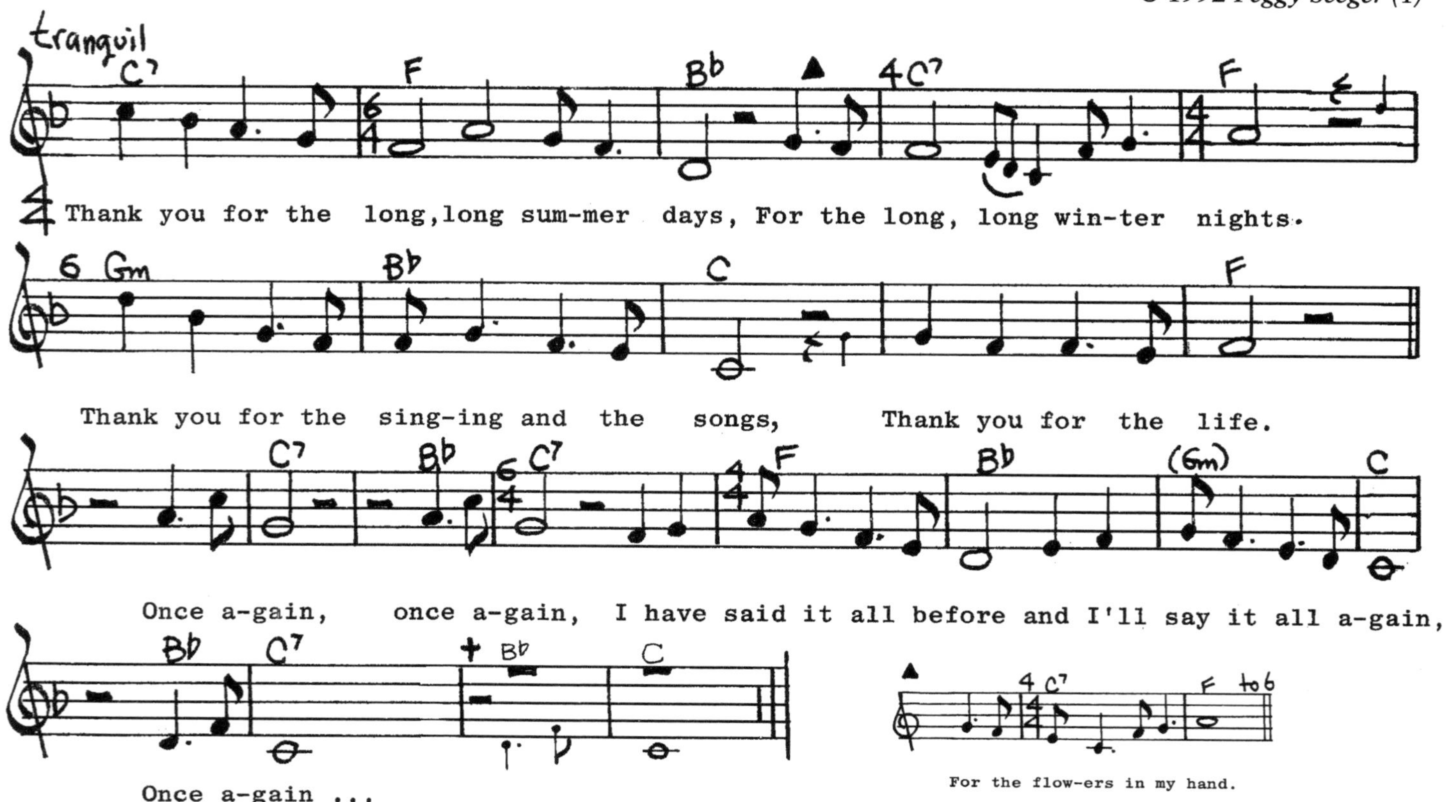

Thank you for the long, long summer days,
For the long, long winter nights.
Thank you for the singing and the songs,
Thank you for the life.
    Once again,
    Once again,
    I have said it all before
    And I'll say it all again,
    Once again . . .

Thank you for the sharing and for the faith,
Δ For the flowers in my hand.
Remember every time and every place,
Thank you once again.
    Once again,
    Once again,
    We have lived it all before
    Now I'll live it all again,
    Once again . . .

Thank you for the children, the gift of love,
Gotten when our life was full and strong;
Thank you for the hope and for the joy,
And thank you for the songs.
    Once again,
    Once again,
    We have sung them all before
    And we'll sing them all again,
    Once again,
† Once again . . .

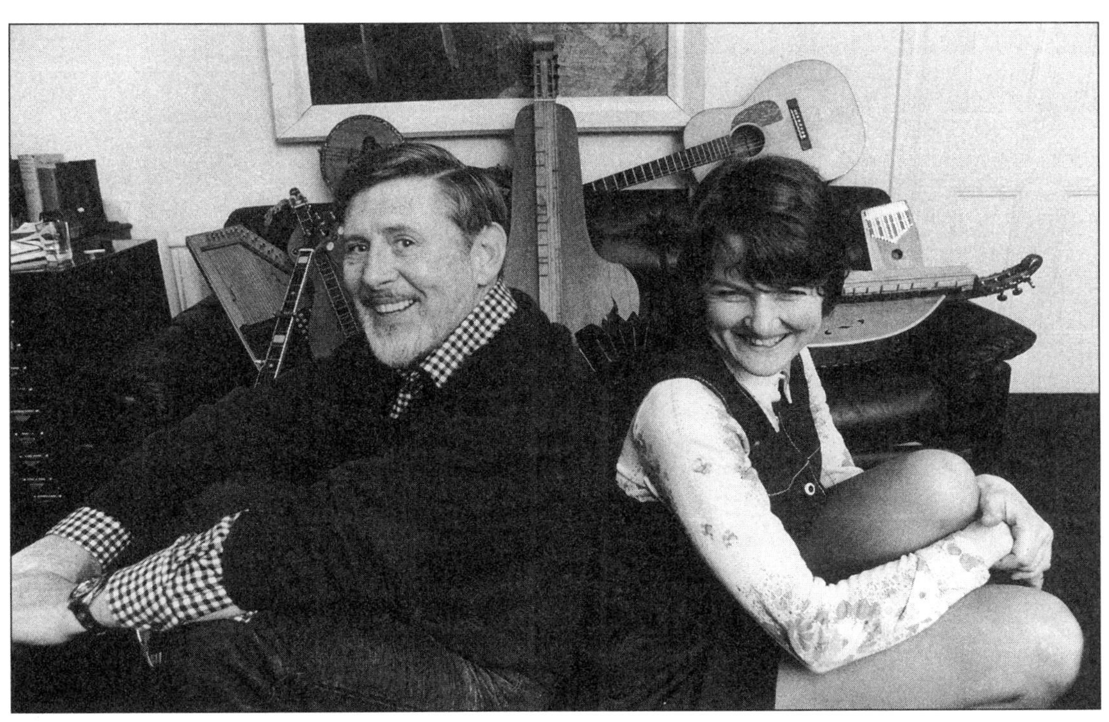

Lost

When Ewan died, I lost a fellow singer and working partner. I lost a lover who knew me when I was young. I lost the father of my children. I lost the companionship of his mind, for it was only his body that betrayed him unto Death. I became the sole custodian of our joint memories. I could no longer turn and say, "Do you remember when . . . ?" I was lost. I kept on singing and writing songs but the burden of grief was heavy and I was sick for a long time. I find this song hard to sing, even now.

words and music: Peggy Seeger
disc 26
© 1992 Peggy Seeger (1)

Lost, I lost my virgin treasure
While that I was sleeping;
Losing it was pleasure
So it wasn't worth the keeping.

I lost a coin from round my neck,
It sank into the Norfolk sand;
I lost a ring, a lover's gift,
It slipped from off my hand.

A coin, a ring, a loving heart
Are often by a stranger found
Then lost again. From hand to hand,
They come and go the Δ world around.

I found my love, then lost he wandered
Calling down the shadow glen;
And though I see him everywhere,
I'll ne'er find him again.

I was frozen
Grief thawed me
Hot anger, warm self-pity
Tepid remorse and regret
I lay outside his work-room
Beating the floor and crying.

I no longer feared dying
But he lived so deep within me
That to die would mean twice-death for him.

Kaleidoscope of memory
Projects bright fragments onto the face of time
Old patterns, new patterns, no patterns.
The pieces are whole.
The mirror is broken.

Happily-ever-after?
The fairy tale is a true lie.

Bread and Wine

It was a lovely summer morning with all the trimmings: cloudless, blue skies and warm, dry air. We seem to get so few of these in England these days. Irene and I were travelling to London by car with a studio picnic and a boot full of musical instruments. We had to keep the windows of the car shut because the exhaust fumes were so heavy and the sound of traffic drowned our conversation. We turned on the radio. On came the news: People with asthma were advised not to go out; people with AIDS were advised not to drink the water. We are both old enough to remember long days of lazing around in the garden and visits to a countryside where there are still remnants of a lifestyle (and an environment) that the spirit can accept. The main tune of this song always reminds me of summer holidays in southern France.

tune: Peggy Seeger
words: Peggy Seeger and Irene Scott
disc 15A, 20, 21
© 1992 Peggy Seeger (1)

smoothly
The wheat is read-y in the field, The grape is read-y on the vine,
Boys and girls are sing-ing, play-ing, Wait-ing for the bread and wine.
CHORUS
PROCEED DIRECTLY TO NEXT VERSE
Let the small rain fall, Let the sun shine on me, Let the days go by, sweet as hon-ey,
(inset verse)
Con-crete or-chard, fields of trash, Met-al moun- tain, walls of glass,
A-cid rain on stun-ted grass – Stink-ing air, man- made time,
End-less traf-fic, noise and grime, Pow-er, prof-it, hun-ger, crime ...

★this chord should be a G⁷ when you return after the inset verse

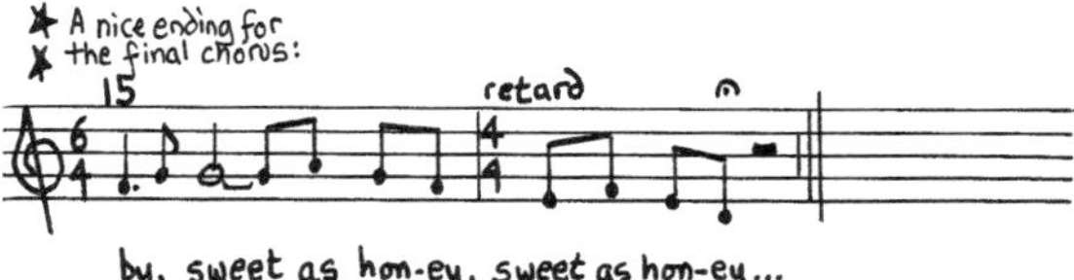
A nice ending for the final chorus:
retard
by, sweet as hon-ey, sweet as hon-ey...

The wheat is ready in the field,
The grape is ready on the vine,
Boys and girls are singing, playing,
Waiting for the bread and wine.

Chorus: Let the small rain fall,
Let the sun shine on me,
Let the days go by, sweet as honey,

Mother lays her baby down,
Old women greet the end of day,
Old men sit and dream of youth
And lovers kiss the night away. *(chorus)*

Ploughing of the stubble field,
Pruning of the winter vine,
Old and young will gather in the harvest,
Making of the bread and wine. *(chorus)*

Concrete orchard, fields of trash,
Metal mountain, walls of glass,
Acid rain on stunted grass,
Stinking air, man-made time,
Endless traffic, noise and grime,
Power, profit, hunger, crime . . .

The wheat is ready in the field,
The grape is ready on the vine,
Old and young will gather at the table,
Sharing out the bread and wine. *(chorus)*

Music note: The inset verse is meant to be quite different from the others. A change of vocal style or using a different instrument can produce this effect.

It's a Natural Thing

Hugh Callaghan, Patrick Hill, Gerrard Hunter, Richard McIlkenny, William Power, John Walker: six Irish U.K. residents, accused in 1975 of the Birmingham pub bombings, in which twenty-one people died and 200 were injured. They were found guilty and served sixteen years till their convictions were quashed by the Court of Appeal in March 1991. This song was made to sing at a benefit for their release. The media and the authorities are fond of bunching individuals together under a single name, immediately giving the impression that they were *acting* together towards a mutual goal: the Maguire Seven . . . the Guildford Four (about whom *In the Name of the Father* has been made) . . . the Birmingham Six. In the case of the latter, forensic evidence was inconclusive, and statements and confessions were forged. All of these cases caused deep concern as to the nature and procedures of our legal system and police methods, prompting the establishment of a Royal Commission on Criminal Justice.

words and music: Peggy Seeger

with spirit
If you want to see (IF YOU WANT TO SEE)
In the mid-dle of the night (IN THE MID-DLE OF THE NIGHT)
You turn on the light, (YOU TURN ON THE LIGHT)
Yes, you turn on the light. (YES, YOU TURN ON THE LIGHT)
'Cause it's a nat-u- ral thing (IT'S A NAT- U - RAL THING)
GO IMMEDIATELY to NEXT VERSE
To turn on the light. (TO TURN ON THE LIGHT.)

If you want to see (IF YOU WANT TO SEE)
In the middle of the night (IN THE MIDDLE OF THE NIGHT)
You turn on the light, (YOU, *etc.*)
Yes, you turn on the light. (YES, *etc.*)
'Cause it's a natural thing *(etc.)*
To turn on the light. *(etc.)*

When you get hungry (WHEN YOU GET HUNGRY)
You know it's right (YOU KNOW, *etc.*)
To go and get a bite,
Yes, to go and get a bite,
'Cause it's a natural thing,
To go and get a bite.

When you get cold
You try to get warm.
That's not wrong,
To go and get warm.
'Cause it's a natural thing
To go and get warm.

When you need love,
You turn to a friend;
It's a natural thing,
Yes, it's a natural thing.
'Cause you know that love
Is a natural thing.

When everything's wrong,
Don't moan and sigh,
Don't sit down and cry,
Don't lay down and die.
'Cause when life hits hard
You gotta hit harder,
Δ When it's gone too far
† You gotta go farther.

Well, we're here to fight
For the Birmingham Six,
Against all the tricks,
All the dirty tricks!
And we're gonna fight
And we're gonna fight harder,
Δ And we're gonna go far
† Then we're gonna go farther.

Δ 'Cause it's a natural thing,
† Yes, a natural thing.
(etc., ad infinitum)

Music note: This is a group participation song. The group repeats every line that the soloist sings. Lines may be added to suit practically every and any occasion, time or place.

Can't Pay, Won't Pay

Margaret Thatcher got a bright idea (the same idea that, when it was first implemented, brought on the Peasants' Revolt of 1381). It was called the *poll tax,* and it levied varying amounts of flat-rate local tax on every adult in the country except for certain exemptions (see "Fifteen Ways to Beat the Poll Tax"). This new tax meant that the wealthy now paid the same—and sometimes less—than the less-wealthy. The system it replaced was quite fair: It was called *rates,* and it levied a scaled local tax on propertied people. From the day the poll tax was introduced in England (on April Fool's Day, 1990), it was hated and fought because twenty-five percent of the population who had never paid local taxes now had to do so—and (understandably) they disliked the idea. There were jokes, cartoons, poems, songs, pamphlets, diatribes, committees, meetings, demonstrations, and—finally—riots, the violence of which shocked the nation. In 1993, John Major's government replaced it with the *council tax*, which (like the rates) is property-based. *This* was denounced as unfair by many householders who had paid less under the poll tax! You can't win no matter how you cheat. The poll tax was one of the issues that brought the Thatcher government down.

tune: traditional U.S.A. ("Pick a Bale of Cotton")
new words and trad. arr.: Peggy Seeger

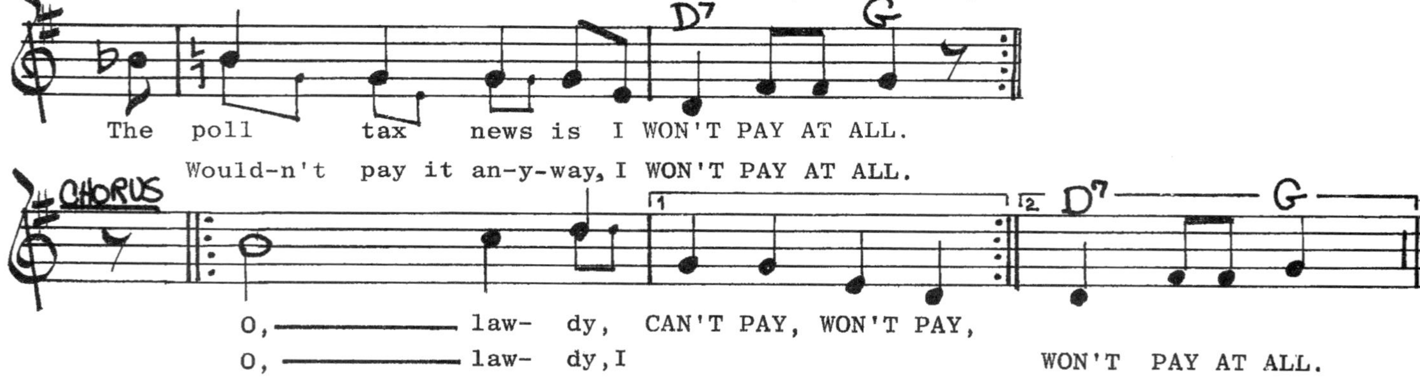
emphatically
G
The poll tax blues is CAN'T PAY, WON'T PAY,
Won't pay, can't pay, CAN'T PAY, WON'T PAY,
D7 G
The poll tax news is I WON'T PAY AT ALL.
Would-n't pay it an-y-way, I WON'T PAY AT ALL.
CHORUS
O, law- dy, CAN'T PAY, WON'T PAY,
O, law- dy, I
D7 G
WON'T PAY AT ALL.

The poll tax blues is
    CAN'T PAY, WON'T PAY,
The poll tax news is
    I WON'T PAY AT ALL.
Won't pay, can't pay,
    CAN'T PAY, WON'T PAY,
Wouldn't pay it anyway,
    I WON'T PAY AT ALL.

Chorus: O, lawdy,
    CAN'T PAY, WON'T PAY,
O, lawdy,
    I WON'T PAY AT ALL.

The first thing to say is
    CAN'T PAY *(etc.)*
The next thing to say is
    I WON'T PAY *(etc.)*
Won't pay tomorrow
    CAN'T PAY *(etc.)*
I won't pay the next day,
    I WON'T *(etc.) (chorus)*

Wat Tyler said, *(etc.)*
His pal, John Ball, said, *(etc.)*
A peasant and a serf say, *(etc.)*
Go and tell the king that *(etc.) (chorus)*

Momma says, Poppa says,
Sister and a brother say,
He says, she says,
They say, we say, *(chorus)*

A lot of the Scots say,
A lot of the Welsh say,
A lot of my friends say,
Most of my family *(chorus)*

I didn't say I couldn't pay,
I only say I wouldn't pay,
The main thing I can say,
Is even though I can pay, *(chorus)*

What you gonna say now?
What you gonna do now?
What you gonna say now?
What you gonna do now? *(chorus)*

Music note: Lowercase lines are to be sung by a solo singer.
UPPERCASE LINES ARE FOR A CHORUS.

yes means YES
and no means
NO
I expect you'll want that repeating

Fifteen Ways to Beat the Poll Tax

From the moment of its inception, the poll tax was almost impossible to implement. Of course, not everyone had to pay. Among those exempt were the Queen, spies and traitors, certain citizens living abroad, some of the clergy, those who were certified incurably insane or institutionalised ill, and so on. The majority of adults, however, had to cough up whether or not they were able. Citizens shared a growing pool of information and ways of circumventing payment: You messed up (or claimed to be confused by) the forms and paperwork; you were never at home to receive official mail, or had your mail redirected to fictional addresses; you wrote out cheques and never signed them or signed them without filling in the amount; you made endless phone calls to local tax offices with questions, complaints, suggestions, *etc.*—many people simply took to the road and couldn't be found by the authorities at all. A new body of folklore came into being, involving tales of hassle, bravado, and tragedy. Support committees and advisory bodies were formed to help those who were carrying their protest right to the end—the end being a court trial followed by a fine or a spell in jail.

During the reign of Queen Elizabeth I, someone invented a gallows that would hang forty people at once. Our poll tax courts, besieged with thousands of cases, also dealt with people in batches. My case was tried with nine other defendants. The Dartford Unemployed Group put out a humorous pamphlet entitled *Twenty Ways of Not Paying the Poll Tax.* The little book joined Paul Simon in giving me the approach to "Fifteen Ways."

Re. verse 5: When the time came to vote the poll tax in, the attendance in the House of Lords was the highest in living memory. Members who hadn't attended or voted for decades turned up in droves—some of them in ambulances and wheelchairs and some too senile to even know what was going on (see also "Just the Tax for Me"). Callaghan (ex–Prime Minister, Labour) and Young had recently been knighted.

Re. verse 10: This song was written at a time when precious body organs of unsuspecting foreigners (especially Turks) were being removed surreptitiously and clandestinely re-homed in needier (*i.e.,* rich or native British) people.

Music note: This is a kind of rap or talking blues. I usually accompany it with percussion, interspersed with sung parts (in italics) in any key you want. At the starred point (*) in verse 8, I begin a talking blues guitar in D Minor and continue it, with judicious chord changes, through to the end. It begins with rhythmic speaking. The following short pieces of music are inserted at indicated points.

words and music: Peggy Seeger

...stand on the corn-er and pre-tend to be a tree And fool the tax man. (etc.)

Dm
A7
Dm
Go and tell your dad And your mum that you dis-own them 'cause you want to be the

A7
Dm
C
Bb
A
Gm (free)
Queen, Or re-tire to a ha-ven where a tax is nev-er seen. Be-come a Rus-sian

(in rhythm)
spy and get ex-pelled! But there's a catch: (etc.)

(freely)
Gm
A7
Dm
And AXE THE TAX! Ya - hoo! That's just fif-teen ways to beat the poll tax.

Can't pay your poll tax, don't know what to do?
Time's running out and they're coming after you;
But if you're going to have a battle choose your own battleground
And there's way's of getting past, ways of getting round
  The problem.

Well, it may sound silly, but you could emigrate,
Take a pint of oil with you, start your own Emirate
On a rock out in the Channel where there's no one but you.
But it would be more sociable to organise a coup.

Gather all your family, round up your friends,
Take over the government, the media, and then
Let the whole world know what the poll tax means!
Or maybe you'd prefer to paint yourself green

And Δ *stand on the corner and pretend to be a tree*
And fool the tax man. But I'm sure you will agree
That as a tax-evasion strategy it's not what it appears.
Dogs pee on your leg—and in the autumn of the year
  Your hair falls out.

You could become a Lord, but then you'd have to make
A little visit down to London where you'd have to stay awake
Just long enough to vote yourself a monumental sum.
(Mind—you'd have to fraternise with Callaghan—and Young.)

If you're single get married. If you're married get divorced
Then reverse the situation every seven days and force
The tax officers to fill another form in every month.
. . . They'd give up and go to lunch.

Declare your house the embassy of somewhere like Atlantis,
Park your Rolls on the zigzags. They'll understand it.
They'll even ask you down to Number Ten to take tea,
And the diplomatic bag'll bring you goodies (tax free).

* Get into the habit, be a monk or be a nun,
There's the music and the wine and every Sunday there's a bun!
Get certified insane. Nope—anyone who's mad
Would pay the tax without a murmur. *†Go and tell your dad*

And your mum that you disown them 'cause you want to be the Queen,
Or retire to a haven where a tax is never seen.
Become a Russian spy and get expelled! But there's a catch:
A state visit's in the offing. No escape from Mrs. Thatch.

Be continually ill, that'd do the trick,
'Cause the state of NHS is making everybody sick,
But be careful if you're Turkish, mark your kidneys with your name,
That's how they get the pee in the Poll Tax Game.

In reality, there's two ways to circumvent the tax:
You can die (it's drastic, you won't be coming back)
The other way's to join with other people like you
« AND AXE THE TAX! YAHOO!

That's just fifteen ways to beat the poll tax.

Heseltine

Michael R. D. Heseltine (a.k.a. 'Tarzan' and 'Goldilocks') is famed for his flowing mane of hair and his two styles of rictus smile, one with lips open and one with lips zipped. He is a magazine-publishing millionaire who has been in British politics longer than anyone cares to remember. He was junior Minister in the Heath government and held senior posts under (please note the preposition) Thatcher until the Westland affair, when he resigned after kicking out her props (one of which he turned out to be). He returned to challenge her for the leadership, forcing *her* to resign but not gaining the position himself. He has been known to hold up John Major's props but occasionally lets it be known (by denial) that he would not be averse to an upward move. Apparently one of his party tricks is an impression of Clint Eastwood playing Mussolini.

tune: traditional U.S.A. ("Clementine")
new words and trad. arr.: Peggy Seeger
© 1992 Peggy Seeger (1)

In a cavern, in a canyon,
Excavated for a mine,
Dwelt a minor party-liner
And he lived in Number Nine.

In a cottage at the pit-head,
Just a stone's throw from Big Ben,
Dwelt the grocer's blue-eyed daughter
And she lived in Number Ten.

Now her dearie got so wearie
Of waiting in the line
That he stole out and dug the coal out
And she fell into the mine.

O me darling, O me darling,
O me darling Clementine,
You will soon be gone forever—
What was yours will now be mine.

There's a moral to the story:
Never live above a mine,
In case a minor party-liner
Wants to move from Number Nine.

O me darling, O me darling,
O me darling Valentine,
You are lost and gone forever,
Dreadful happy Heseltine.

Heseltiny Moon

Cartoonists often portrayed Margaret Thatcher as an active aspirant to the throne. Her home is in Dulwich, a select estate in South London. One day she sailed out onto her balcony to greet her subjects . . . and there was a little pig-in-a-wig below, huffing and puffing and blowing her house down (see note for "Heseltine").

words and music: Peggy Seeger

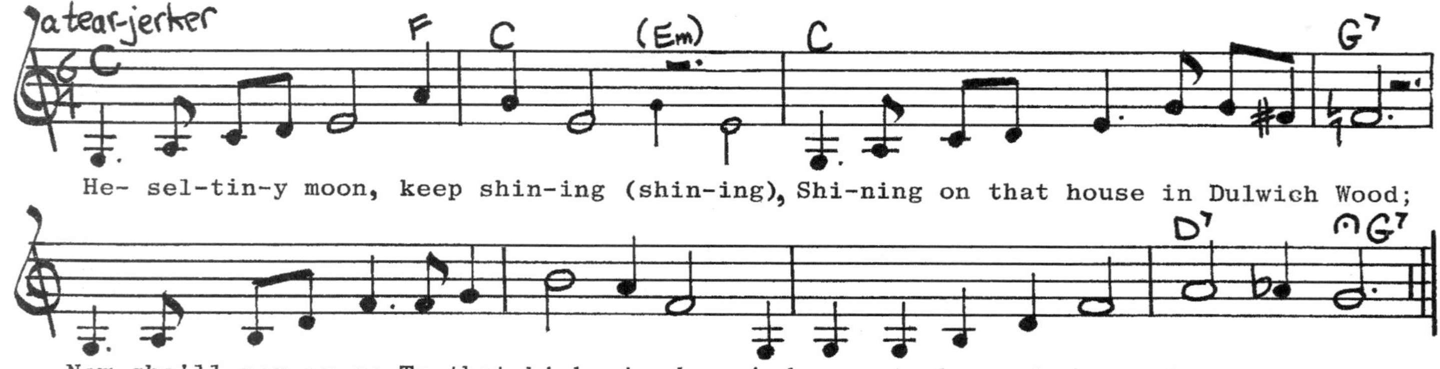

Heseltiny moon, keep shining (shining),
Shining on that house in Dulwich Wood;
Now she'll never go
To that high window
And wave to her subjects down below.

Goodbye, Maggie

Margaret Thatcher had a science degree from Oxford, where it was forecast that she would make "a perfectly good second-class chemist." A 1948 I.C.I. personnel report observed that she was "headstrong, obstinate and dangerously self-opinionated." As Prime Minister (1979–90) she had a reputation that Dracula would have envied. The Miners' Strike, the poll tax, the privatisation program, education and health service cuts, the Falkland War, disastrous policies regarding monetarism, Northern Ireland, the European community and South Africa . . . she set Britain on a steady downhill course. She left Downing Street for the last time on 28 November with tears streaming from her eyes. There was so much she had left to do . . .

tune: Peggy Seeger
words: Peggy Seeger and Irene Scott
© 1992 Peggy Seeger (1)

Goodbye, Maggie, now you're leaving,
One last word before you go.
Are we crying, are we grieving,
Are we sorry? NO, NO, NO!
The Party's waiting at the station,
The boys are standing in a row,
It's an end to your scheming,
Your lying and your queening,
Maggie, GO, GO, GO!

They Sent a Boy to Downing Street

The *Guardian*, November 28, 1990:

> TO MARGARET AND THE TORY PARTY A SON AND HEIR.
> After a prolonged and painful labour, the Conservative Party last night announced that it had given birth to a new Prime Minister—a baby boy called John. The new-born leader emerged in Downing Street to utter his first words. . . . "It is a very exciting thing to become leader of the Conservative Party," he said in such a flat voice that he might have just come first in the school egg-and-spoon race.

I seem to remember that egg-and-spoon races were exciting . . .

tune: traditional English ("Tottie")
new words and trad. arr.: Peggy Seeger
© 1992 Peggy Seeger (1)

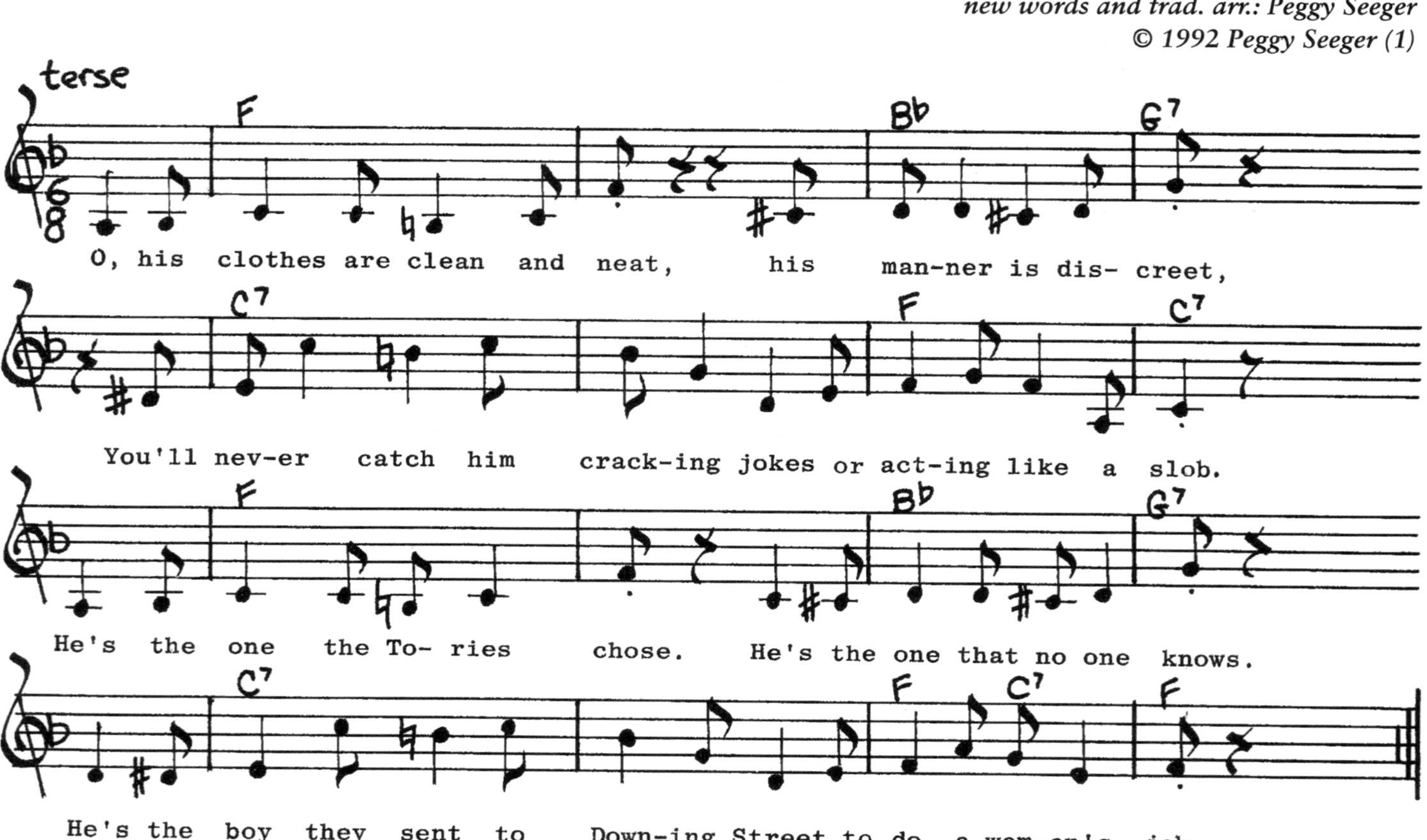

O, his clothes are clean and neat, his manner is discreet,
You'll never catch him cracking jokes or acting like a slob.
He's the one the Tories chose.
He's the one that no one knows.
He's the boy they sent to Downing Street to do a woman's job.

DO YOU HAVE
WHAT IT TAKES?
YEP

If You Want a Better Life

I was brought up on union songs and the idea that unions are a good thing. I was appalled—and saddened—to discover in 1995 that eleven to fourteen percent of the U.S.A. workforce is unionised. In Britain it is in the mid twenty-percent range and in Australia in the low forty-percent range. On February 15, 1990, the *Independent* declared: "WORKERS FACE RETURN TO MASTER AND SERVANT LINK" and continued with, "Employees' rights have deteriorated to a point where conditions could be becoming ripe for resurgence of trade unionism." Idea for a song . . . ?

Where have all the unions gone?
Long time passing *(etc.)*
When will we ever learn?
When will we ever learn?

alternative title: "A Better Life"
words and music: Peggy Seeger
disc 26

vigorously
CHORUS
C F C G7 C
If you want a bet-ter life, you got to make a change,
F C G7 C
And if you want to make a change, you need a u - nion too;
F C G7 C
And if you want a u- nion, you got to learn to fight,
F C G7 (F7) C
'Cause when you got a u- nion, you got to make it fight for you.

Chorus: If you want a better life, you got to make a change,
And if you want to make a change, you need a union too;
And if you want a union, you got to learn to fight,
'Cause when you got a union, you got to make it fight for you.

Sitting in the barroom, head in your hands,
Got to talk to someone, yes, you need a friend;
Trouble at the factory, trouble on the line—
Tell it to the union, it's the best friend you can find. *(chorus)*

Sitting in the canteen, when your shift is done,
Trouble in your life now, yes, you need someone.
Change in regulations, trouble on the ward—
Take it to the union, it's what you got that union for. *(chorus)*

Do we stand united? Do we divide and fall?
Is it one for one now, or is it all for all?
So put the screws on that trouble spot
And use the union, the most useful tool we've got. *(chorus)*

Better wages and conditions—is that all we need?
What about the food we eat and the air we breathe?
If you want your union to make a better life,
You better make your union help to keep this world alive. *(chorus)*

Just beCause

December 20, 1989. No declaration of war—you just move into a smaller country with a massive invasion of troops, blanket bombing, and high-tech weaponry. It is becoming part of the American way of life. (It was once part of the British way of life, too, when we were a major imperialist country and our "borders"—even though they were halfway around the world—were being "threatened.") Panama's leader, General Manuel Noriega, was explicitly accused of drug-running and implicitly accused of being unenthusiastic about the U.S.A.'s plans for Nicaragua. Unfortunately, he also bore an uncanny resemblance to Kaddafi. He surrendered on the 3rd of January and was arraigned on drug-trafficking charges. President Bush was pleased with the campaign, which he dubbed "Just Cause." At least 325 people died for it.

words and music: Peggy Seeger
© 1992 Peggy Seeger (1)

insistently
JUST be- CAUSE he has an ar- my and a na- vy,
JUST be- CAUSE he wants to strut in front of Gor- by,
JUST be- CAUSE he wants to see the Ni-ca-ra-guan sce- ne- ry,
JUST be- CAUSE No- ri- e- ga looks just like Kad - da- fi.

JUST be-CAUSE he wants to prove that he's a big boy now.
JUST be- CAUSE he might be cra- zy.
JUST be- CAUSE... JUST 'CAUSE.

Just beCause he has an army and a navy,
Just beCause he wants to strut in front of Gorby,
Just beCause he wants to see the Nicaraguan scenery,
Just beCause Noriega looks just like Kaddafi.

Just beCause he wants to simulate ferocity,
Just beCause he's full of cunning perspicacity,
Just beCause he wants a private drug monopoly,
Δ Just beCause he wants to prove that he's a big boy now.

Just beCause he has a touch of insecurity,
Just beCause he has a leaning towards hypocrisy,
Just beCause he's casual about diplomacy,
† Just beCause he might be crazy.

« Just beCause . . .
Just 'Cause.

Guilty

March 1990. A call from the publisher. Pampers, who make disposable nappies, want to use "The First Time Ever I Saw Your Face" in an advert. I never used disposables for my children, even in the days when I had no one to help with their care and no washing machine. It just never occurred to me to buy, use once, and throw away something I could buy once and use again and again. "Guilty" is about disposable nappies and deforestation; it is about aerosol sprays and the ozone layer; it is about the local and the global. (For a detailed history of how this song was written, see "In Particular.")

alternative title: "I Accuse"
tune: Peggy Seeger
words: Peggy Seeger and Irene Scott
disc 15A, 20, 21
© 1992 Peggy Seeger (1)

urgent
Am
We been rip-ping up her bel-ly, we been sick-en-ing her blood,
A7
We been try-ing to con- trol her since we crawled out of the mud;
Dm
No, we did-n't kill for pas-sion, we did-n't steal for need,
15 16 Am
We ra- vaged her for pro-fit, we de- voured her for greed.

15
Am G Am Dm
pow-er that's tear-ing her a-part, She gave us pa-ra- dise,
E7 Am
But when the dev-il rules the an-gels pay the price.
16 Am
re - mem-ber... She gave us heav-en...

We been ripping up her belly, we been sickening her blood,
We been trying to control her since we crawled out of the mud;
No, we didn't kill for passion, we didn't steal for need,
We ravaged her for profit, we devoured her for greed.

We kill the other creatures, put poison on the breeze,
Blow bombs up in her desert and pour oil on her seas;
We put acid in her rainfall, cut down her precious trees,
Dissolved the ozone layer till we brought her to her knees . . .

Our numbers are too many, what are we breeding for?
Our numbers are too many, still we're breeding more;
She gave to us her beauty, the treasures of her heart,
She gave to us the Δ power that's tearing her apart,

She gave us paradise . . .
But when the devil rules the angels pay the price.

When you can't walk on the beaches, when all the birds are gone,
When cities turn the night to day, when darkness comes at dawn,
When you fear the summer sunshine, when you dread the morning dew,
When you're scared to eat and drink and breathe, † remember . . .

She gave us heaven . . .

P.S. Pampers had to use another song.

Dear Pampers,

Night Song

A particularly lovely evening in a glorious part of France. We were driving along a river at sunset, going home to our small rented farmhouse to cook a dinner, have a bottle of wine, sit by a log fire, and go to bed.

words and music: Peggy Seeger
disc 15A, 20, 21

High in the hills where the valley hides,
Where the moon gleams on the quiet pool;
Deep in the rock the salmon glides
Where water is clean and cool.

Deep in the earth where roots entwine,
Far below the night owl on the wing;
Down in the dark the field mouse lies
And listens to her babies sing.

In the dark and dead of night
A white cloud sails across the moon;
Deep in the warm and welcome bed
I'll lie and sleep with you.

Music note: *I wrote this tune for the radio ballad The Big Hewer. I feel that the best accompaniment is a texture of either sustained chords or a ripple of single notes. Such a background should have little rhythm of its own.*

Love Unbidden

Love is *wild.* A *bird* is hard to *hold.* Those four words appear in all three verses.

words and music: Peggy Seeger
disc 26

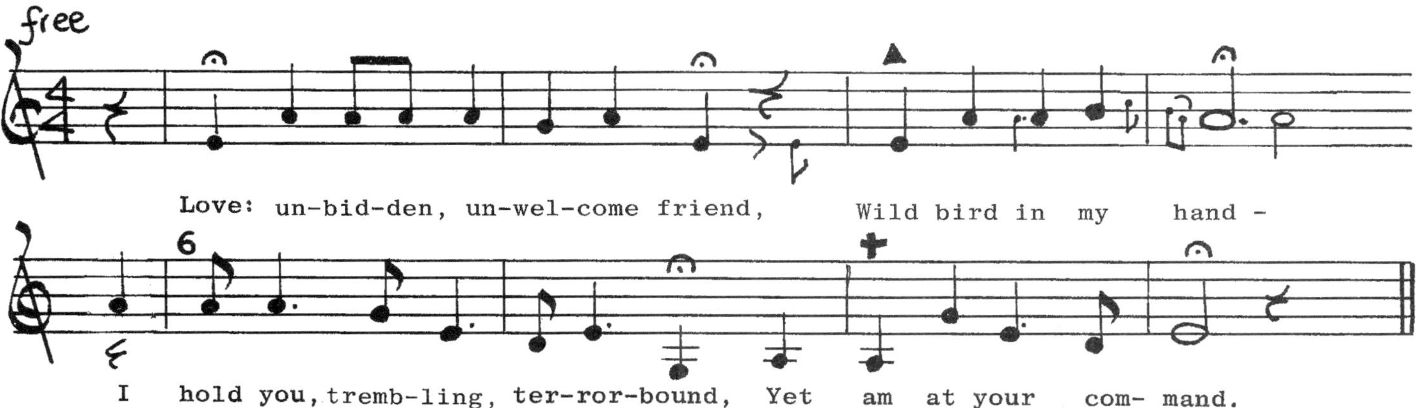

Love: unbidden, unwelcome friend,
Wild bird in my hand—
I hold you, trembling, terror-bound,
Yet am at your command.

Love: new-bidden, welcome foe,
Δ Bird forever wild—
Love: one moment loose your hold,
Let me rest awhile.

Love: though I be one of those
That dare not come to claim thee—
Hold me till my heartbeat slows,
† Wild bird, you have tamed me.

Irene, 1991

Da Dee Da Da

Appropriate for those times when you are in love and can't keep that inane smile off your face; when you want to say your lover's name over and over again; when you can't pass a telephone box without dialling the Magic Number; when all your senses are magnified with painful pleasure; when your heartbeat wakes you up (that is if you have been able to get to sleep) bang on the dot of 4:30 every morning; when you can't eat, which is probably why you feel light and airy and confused and dead sure of everything except your own worthiness; when you write a poem a day for The Beloved and in general spend one of the most serious times of your life enjoying feeling silly.

words and music: Peggy Seeger
disc 26

jaunty
C G F G 3 C G F G
Think of you, I'm slosh-y-slish-y, Think of you, I'm squash-y-squish-y,
C G F G Dm G7
Feel-ings go all wash-y- wish-y, Think of you, I'm bus-y, bus-y.
CHORUS
C F C F C D7 G7
Da dee da da, did-dle I dee! I love you, do you love me?
C F C F C G7 C
Da dee da da, did-dle I dee! I love you, do you love me?

C G F G to 3
Heart-strings go plink-y, plonk-y,

Think of you, I'm sloshy-slishy,
Think of you, I'm squashy-squishy.
Feelings go all washy-wishy,
Think of you, I'm busy, busy.

Chorus: Da dee da da, diddle I dee!
I love you, do you love me?
Da dee da da, diddle I dee!
I love you, do you love me?

Belly goes all chipsy-chopsy,
Flipsy-flopsy, turvy-topsy;
Toes are skipsy, feet are hopsy,
Heart thinks you're blue-ribbon noshy. *(chorus)*

Δ Heartstrings go plinky-plonky,
Fingers go all honky-tonky,
Eyes go winky, knees go wonky,
Everything is dory-hunky. *(chorus)*

Wanna go with you whither, whether,
Love you past the end of tether;
I will leave you never, never,
Love you ever, ever, ever. *(chorus)*

You Don't Know How Lucky You Are

Lie back and think of England . . . that was the advice given to many a Victorian lady about to embark upon the seas of matrimony. Sex was such a taboo subject that piano legs were rumoured to be covered with ruffles for fear of offending tender sensibilities. My grandmother was born in the 1860s. She was instructed by her mother on her wedding night to pretend to faint when conjugal operations began. Then when it was over, you "came to" with "Where am I?" (But how did you know it was over if you were in a faint?) In other words, you lay back and thought of England. My father told me that story. Over the years I have probably embroidered on it—as Victorian women often embroidered the strategically placed holes in their night-gowns—but you get my drift. Women were not supposed to be forward about sex. They were not supposed to enjoy sex. They were not supposed to know about sex. These same creatures who menstruated every month and who endured pregnancy and labour and motherhood, were not supposed to *know* about sex? I'm not sure I believe this. I think women were really attempting to keep men from knowing that they knew. Poor creatures, it would have been too much for them.

words and music: Peggy Seeger
disc 15A, 20, 21

Slow & casual
C
E7
Be- fore you pour the wine out and turn the lights down low,
Am
+5 A7
(Are you think-ing I don't no-tice that you're tak-ing it slow?)
Dm
7 G#7 G7
There's a lit-tle some-thing I want you to know:
F7
(Fm)
C
You don't know how luck- y you are ——.
▲(verses 3 & 6)
C
E7
I'm not the kind of wom-an who'd fol-low you a-round,
Am
A7
Who would-n't let you be your own man and al-ways kick-ing you a - round,

Before you pour the wine out and turn the lights down low,
(Are you thinking I don't notice that you're taking it slow?)
There's a little something I want you to know:
You don't know how lucky you are.

I'm not just any woman looking for any man
And I don't intend to change me to fit into your plan;
I'm a hell of an angel, and you'd better give a damn
You don't know how lucky you are.

Δ I'm not the kind of woman who'd follow you around,
Who wouldn't let you be your own man and always kicking you around;
Put you on a pedestal, then knock you down,
You don't know how lucky you are.

Now, I'm a woman knows how to use the door,
I'm writing you a love song and it's † one you can't ignore,
Lie back and think of England, 'cause I've been here before,
You don't know how lucky you are.

Are you the kind of man who won't share the dirt
Who can't clean out a toilet or sew a button on a shirt?
Before I start the race, boy, I'm checking out the turf,
You don't know how lucky you are.

Δ I'm not the kind of woman who cares to take a chance,
Who'd trade a lot of living for a little romance. . . .
Shall I go home now? Or do you want to dance
And find out how lucky you are? . . .
« 'Cause I know how lucky you are!

Morning Comes Too Soon

Nineteen ninety was a year for love songs in lots of different styles. This one, like "When Lovers Hide the Keys," is in the style of an Elizabethan song.

words and music: Peggy Seeger
disc 15A, 20, 21

▲ this should be a 4/4 bar on the Last Line of VERSE 2.

When I lie all night with you morning comes too soon;
The hour-hand too quickly joins midnight to afternoon.
Evening, come e'er day is done. Impatient lovers keep
But little time to work or dine; they love—then fall asleep.

When I lie all night with you morning comes too soon;
Let night begin whene'er we please, let day begin at noon.
Lovers work at lovers' play, lovers on each other dine;
Lovers turn the night to day Δ and make a fool of time.

When I lie all night with you morning comes too soon;
The hour-hand too quickly joins midnight to afternoon.
If time were mine to give and take, if time were mine to keep,
I'd give it all to lovers who make love—then fall asleep.

Swing Me High, Swing Me Low

If the child is small, you place it in a *very safe* swing, one in which it cannot wriggle and from which it cannot fall out. If it is an older child, it must be instructed to hold on no matter what. It is most effective if you stand in front of the child as you push the swing. When per (see "Glossary") works out what body part rhymes with the first **bold** word in line 3, per will attempt to keep you from reaching it. But the swing is inexorable and you pinch, pat, nip, kiss, and occasionally miss that part, singing its name as the swing brings the child towards you. The rhythm is set by the swing: push on the italicised word and let the swing come back to you on the underlined word. If you dramatise the key words and sing them with histrionic decibels, abrupt delivery, exaggerated humour, mock threats, wide staring eyes, *etc.*, while keeping the whole thing in the rhythm of the swing, the game can unfortunately go on and on and on—and on.

words and music: Peggy Seeger
© 1992 Peggy Seeger (1)

Swing me high, *swing* me low,
Swing me over the *o*-cean.
Be*fore* I **go**, I'll *pinch* your toe,
When*ever* I take the *no*-tion.

Ideas for line 3:

You'll *turn* to **jelly** when I *pat* your **belly**,
Won't *it* be **grand** when I *tickle* your **hand**,
I'll *stand* and **stare** and *pull* your **hair**,
It won't **harm** to *joggle* your **arm**,

And if you cannot think of a rhyme, nonsense is great:

Poodle and **clinger** will *foodle* your **finger**,

Or try and fool the child with a rhyme which could apply to several parts:

Be*fore* I **go**, I'll *grab* your el-**bow**,

A Good War

Seen in the light of ensuing events, the Gulf War (January 16 to February 28, 1991) almost seemed like the means to an end. On May 14, the British Construction Industry held a day's briefing for anyone who was interested in the reconstruction of Kuwait. Everyone was. There were firms of every size, involved in every aspect of building, from surveying, design, setting of standards, handling of legal and financial matters, to supplying materials and personnel. The speakers read like a *Who's Who* in international construction. The prospectus began, "Now that the initial hype has died down . . ." and went on to stress the fact that U.K. businesses were keen to help the unfortunate Kuwaitis. The little document abounds with terms like *extensive refurbishment,* and cool pronouncements about the *intended displacement of the Palestinians and other foreigners who held middle management and technical posts.* Britons are, presumably, not to be considered as "foreigners" because Britain helped to build modern Kuwait the first time. The inference is that we can tear down and build up Kuwait *ad infinitum.* And I thought the war (pardon, *hype)* was only about oil! . . .

words and music: Peggy Seeger
disc 15A 20, 21

with drive, a blues
F7 E7 3 Am
A good war is just what they need,
5 E7
Make sure that the sy- stem will be
Am C Dm Am
Free to ex- ploit, free to ex-pand,
Dm F7 E7 Am
Free to do an-y damn thing they can
10 F E7 Am
To make the re-ces-sion re-cede.

A good war is just what they need,
Make sure that the system will be
Free to exploit, free to expand,
Free to do any damn thing they can
To make the recession recede.

A good war's a war that'll last.
Make boredom a thing of the past;
Weep with the widow, cry for the kids,
Forget that your own life is on the skids,
While you're waiting for the crash.

A good war is just what they want,
Send the jobless off to the front.
When it's over, welcome your hero home,
Forget whose hands are in the honeycomb,
Could be an election stunt.

Cold war begins to get warm,
But we can't stop making the bombs,
The plagues, the poisons, the nuclear dreams,
Multinational plans and madmen's schemes,
Can't afford to disarm. (2)

A good war's a miracle which
Always makes somebody rich;
New contracts, reconstruction deals,
Relate Kuwait to British Steel;
Δ War is for fingers that itch.
War is for fingers that itch.
Too good for the few who're digging pay dirt,
Too bad for the many who really get hurt,
Targets are meant to be hit.
Targets are meant to be hit.

They're fighting for Esso and Shell,
For jobs for the boys as well;
And when they're done with Kuwait and Iraq
We'll still have the bastards on our back,
'Cause they're fighting for the system as well. (3)

Left-Wing Wife

Judy Small, the Australian feminist singer, and her partner Sue Dyson arranged our first Australian tour and were kind enough to accommodate us at their house in Melbourne. Their house is disastrous . . . it has a Jacuzzi and a backyard where you can sunbathe if you like to live dangerously. If you like to read but haven't much time, give up hope all ye who enter there. There are books, pamphlets, leaflets, tracts, documents, newspapers, magazines . . . and that was where I saw this wonderful cartoon. I took the situation, the detail and the punch-line and padded them out. I dedicate it to Toshi, my brother Pete's wife, who was in my mind while I was writing it. *Her* dedication; care; attention to detail; humour; and twenty-seven-hours-a-day, eight-days-a-week work schedule will have to be dealt with properly in another song.

words and music: Peggy Seeger
disc 26

she's in a hurry

When the phone be- gan to ring, her hands were in the dish-es,
Her feet were in her slip-pers and her head was full of wish-es;
She sighed and dried her hands and took the ba-by from its cot,
Lift- ed the re- ceiv- er but the caller'd giv-en up.

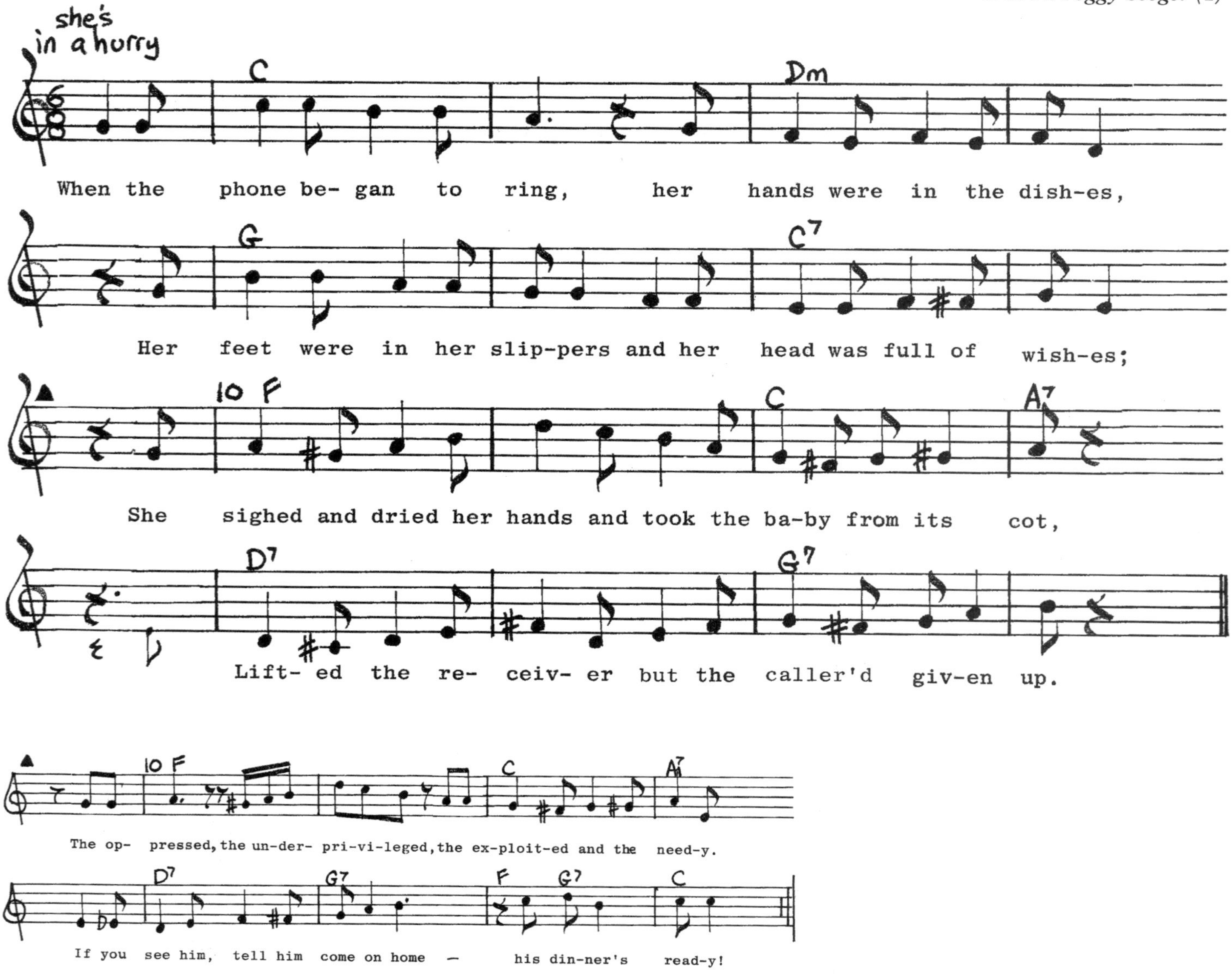

some day my prince will come

When the phone began to ring, her hands were in the dishes,
Her feet were in her slippers and her head was full of wishes;
She sighed and dried her hands and took the baby from its cot,
Lifted the receiver but the caller'd given up.

She changed the baby's nappy, put the dinner on and then
Put the garbage out, the laundry in when the phone began again.
She quickly ran to answer it and tripped over the toys
Scattered round the kitchen by her tribe of little boys.

some day my prince will come

She lay there in a daze upon the kitchen floor,
She thought about the fighters who get up and come back for more;
She thought about her sanity and the book that she was writing—
The phone continued ringing and the kids had started fighting.

She never reached the phone 'cause the baby started crying,
Dinner started burning, it was time to do the ironing,
But once again the phone began. "May I speak to Earl?"
My husband isn't home, he's gone out to save the world,
Δ The oppressed, the underprivileged, the exploited and the needy.
If you see him, tell him come on home—his dinner's ready!

Music note: I used the English soldier's song "Browned Off" as a jumping-off tune.

bog off

Primrose Hill

The Isabella Plantation in Richmond Park, London, is breathtaking in May. It has been laid out for colour and its sculptured vistas are both wide and intimate. The visitor is dwarfed by the enormous rhododendron bushes, whose blossoms are every shade of yellow, pink, orange, white, and purple. Ducks paddle on little meandering brooks that are spiked with lilies and curtained with monkey flower and cresses of every sort. Aristocratic trees salute the sky, their toes nibbled by small ground flowers. The eye moves up the trunk and down again, landing softly on a crew-cut carpet of grass and gliding to shrubby azaleas that have so many blooms on them that you cannot see any leaves. There are flowering bushes you have never seen before, anywhere. Just before you reach the open parkland again, you are given a pond filled with ducks, geese, moorhens, coots, and black swans. Try and be in love when you go there for the first time.

tune: Peggy Seeger
words: Peggy Seeger and Irene Scott
disc 15A, 20, 21

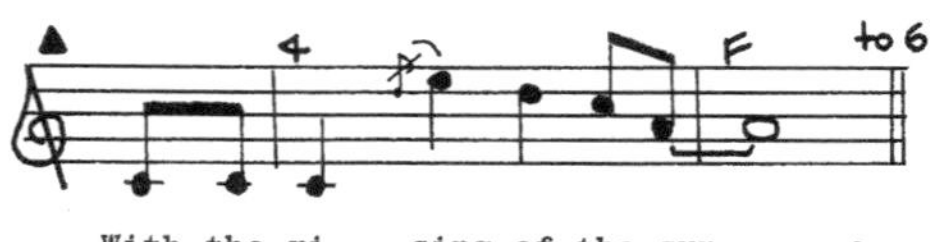

I used to think that love was blind,
But love can surely see—
Among the flowers of the field
I found one for me,
    I found one for me . . .

Chorus: Come and walk in Richmond Park,
Come and walk in town—
Come and sit on Primrose Hill
And watch the sun go down,
    Watch the sun go down.

The turtle dove longs for a mate,
Hear her mournful cry—
Long before I saw your face
I dreamed of you and I,
    Dreamed of you and I . . . *(chorus)*

Tomorrow's sky is overhead,
Moon and stars combine—
Will you come and share my bed
And join your life with mine,
    Join your life with mine? *(chorus)*

Every day begins anew
Δ With the rising of the sun;
Every time I look at you
Love has just begun,
    Love has just begun . . . *(chorus)*

Music note: We find that slowing down slightly at the end of lines 2 and 4—i.e., going out of rhythm slightly—keeps the song from sounding mechanical.

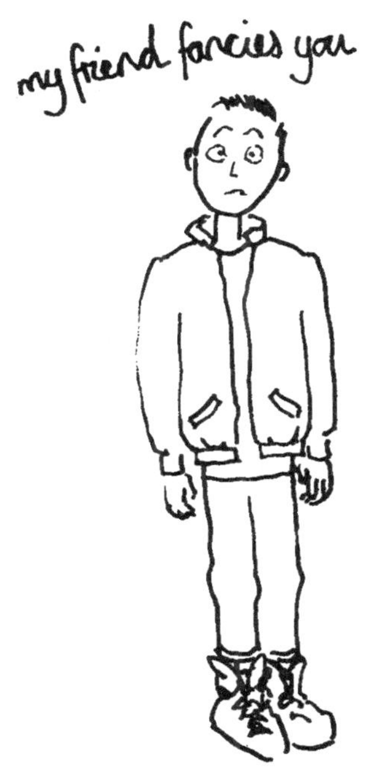

Getting It Right

After three months of rigorous dieting, aromatherapy, steambaths, and general misery, my size 16 jeans hung on me like a rhinoceros skin. Time for a new pair. I went to London via the Underground (my first mistake). The salesboy (in his mid teens) advised a size 15. No, I want size 12. O.K., but I couldn't get them on and had to resort to the time-honoured method. I lay on my back on the floor of the shop, along with several teenage girls who were trying to get into sizes 8 and 9 and allowed the boy to place his foot on my stomach. He trod and I breathed in, he trod and I breathed in (*etc.*), gradually enabling me to work the zip up to my waist. He then helped me to my feet, because the jeans kept me from bending my knees. To quote Oprah Winfrey, under similar circumstances, "That was the most unhealthy day of my life." Turning in front of the mirror like a chicken on a spit, I looked great. With an insouciant flip of the wrist, I tossed my rhino skin to the salesboy (my second mistake) and tottered out. John Wayne had just such a swagger—probably because *his* jeans were also too tight. Back to the Underground, where I found that it is well nigh impossible to go down steps when you cannot bend your knees. Hanging onto the rail, leaning backward then forward and flinging my straight legs out in a series of awkward kicks, I worked out a way of descending that was so grotesque that it cancelled any chic image I might project. My groans and grunts attracted the attention of a trim little old lady coming *up* the stairwell. She stopped, considered and approached me, her face full of concern. "May I help you, dear?" she said. I was thirty-eight years old.

If I sat down I had to unzip the jeans first. *And* I regained the weight within six months. It was the latest entry in a catalogue of punishments to which I had subjected my body in order to lose not the seventy-five pounds that weighed Oprah down but the ten pounds that have dogged my hips, my thighs, and my mind since my mid twenties. Starvation, pummelling, binding, steaming, running around the house in a Michelin-man suit . . . for ten pounds. These days I don't even own a set of scales. I swim, gym, practise yoga, walk a lot, and eat carefully. And as for the ten pounds . . . what ten pounds?

tune: Peggy Seeger
words: Peggy Seeger with Irene Scott
disc 15A, 20, 21

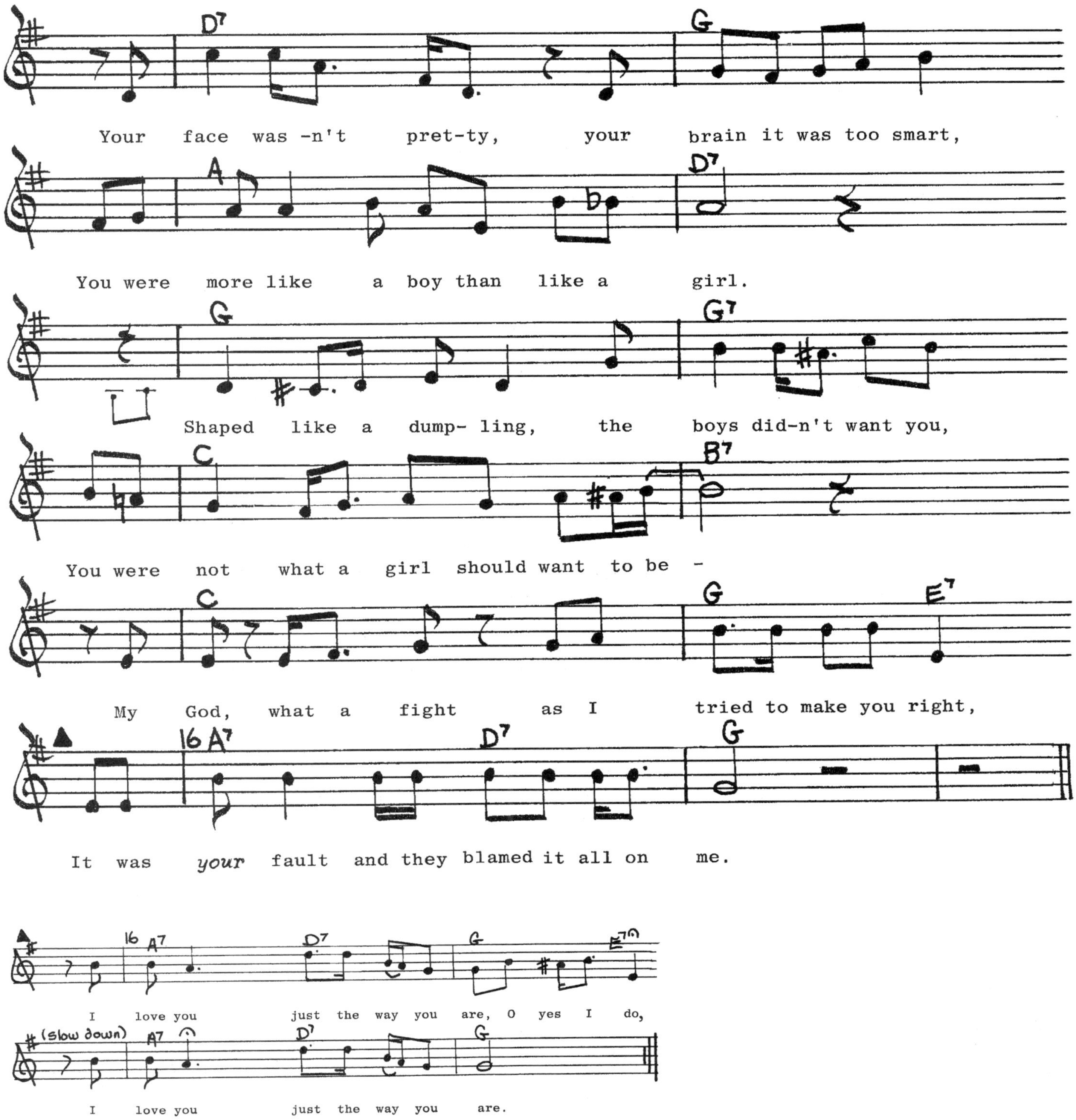

Your face was -n't pret-ty, your brain it was too smart,

You were more like a boy than like a girl.

Shaped like a dump- ling, the boys did-n't want you,

You were not what a girl should want to be -

My God, what a fight as I tried to make you right,

It was *your* fault and they blamed it all on me.

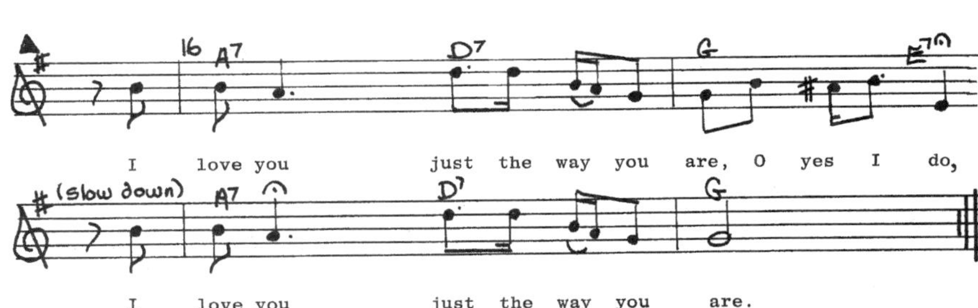
(slow down)
I love you just the way you are, O yes I do,
I love you just the way you are.

You were never what I wanted, they told me from the start,
Your hair was thin and straight, it wouldn't curl;
Your face wasn't pretty, your brain it was too smart,
You were more like a boy than like a girl.
Shaped like a dumpling, the boys didn't want you,
You were not what a girl should want to be—
My God, what a fight as I tried to make you right,
It was *your* fault and they blamed it all on me.

So I painted and I shaved you, tortured and depraved you,
Starved you till your bones were poking through;
I made you walk in high heels, made you run in tight skirts,
My God, the things I did to you!
I bought all the things they sold me, did all the things they told me,
They promised you'd be perfect in the end—
Although I always thought you might *someday* get it right,
You were my enemy, you never were my friend.

But when they started telling me that a surgeon (for a fee)
Could shift bits of you from here to there
By adding to your breasts and subtracting from your thighs
And by lifting your face up through your hair.
Then I began to see this game was not for me,
The goal-posts were moving every day—
So I gave up the fight, I didn't want to get it right
If winning meant giving you away.

So I stand here at the mirror and strip them of the power
To manipulate our beauty and our pride;
They have everything to gain from our discontent and shame
So they're the only ones who'll *always* get it right;
But you're looking mighty fine as you deal with Mother Time,
Though you're past the age when they think I should care—
My body, my friend, forgive me if you can,
Δ I love you just the way you are, O yes I do,
I love you just the way you are.

Panic not Dr Brown, a few expert
cuts, tucks, and transplants, and
you will wake up as the
little puppy I've always
wanted you to be

Vital Statistics

What else is there to say?

words and music: Peggy Seeger
disc 26

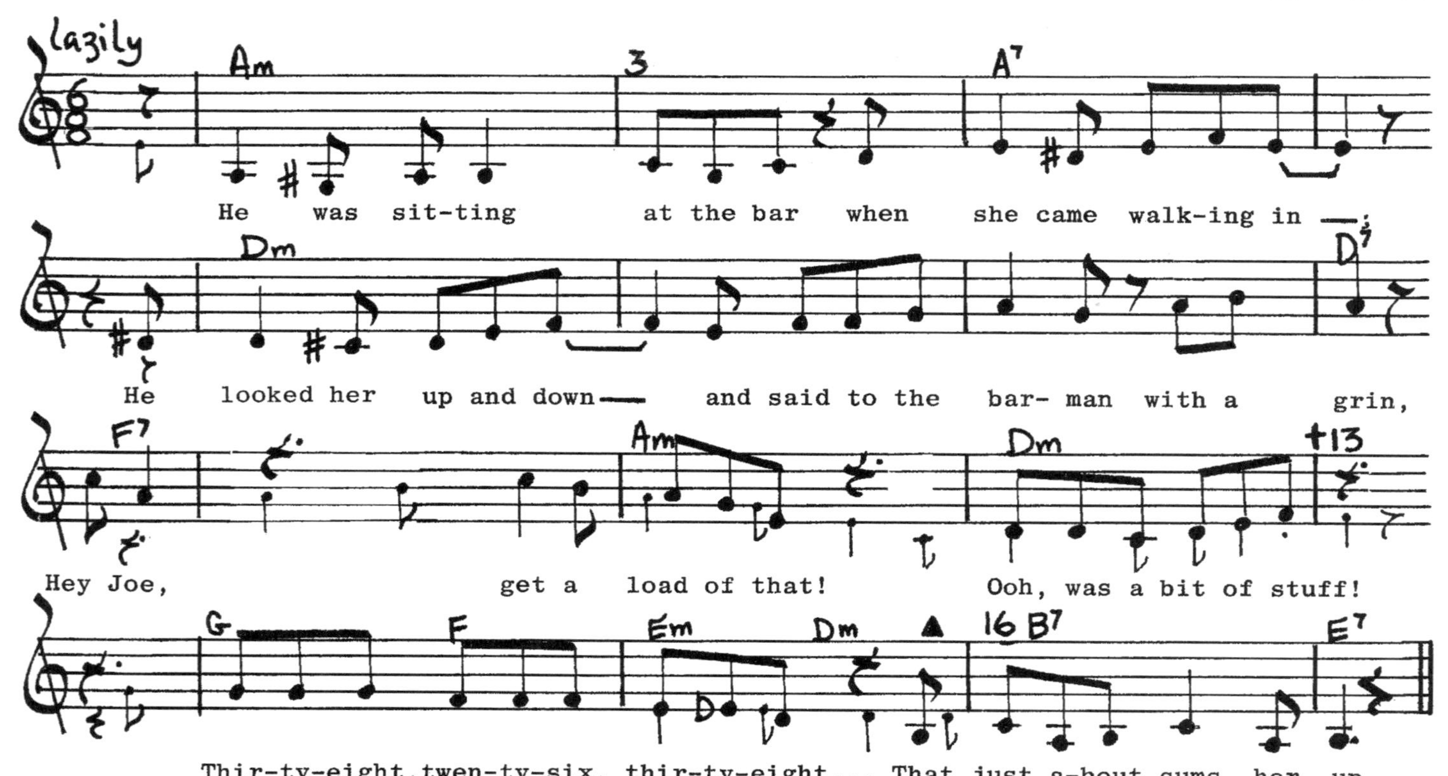
lazily
Am
3
A7
He was sit-ting at the bar when she came walk-ing in
Dm
D7
He looked her up and down and said to the bar- man with a grin,
F7
Am
Dm
+13
Hey Joe, get a load of that! Ooh, was a bit of stuff!
G
F
Em
Dm
16 B7
E7
Thir-ty-eight, twen-ty-six, thir-ty-eight... That just a-bout sums her up.

16Am
E7
I on- ly want-ed to chat.
G7
C
E7
I was on- ly be- ing friendly, Joe, and she went and took it wrong;
A
G
F
Em
Dm
B7
E7
But if she's gon-na get per- so- nal, I'll be mov-ing a- long.
Am
to 3
She says, Three ...is just what

+13
G
F (retard)
Em
Dm
Am B7
E7
he-ro: Three, for-ty-one, fif-ty-two, for-ty-two — ZE - RO.

He was sitting at the bar when she came walking in;
He looked her up and down and said to the barman with a grin,
"Hey Joe, get a load of that! Ooh, what a bit of stuff!
"38–26–38 . . . that just about sums her up."

He whistled and winked as she looked around and went to join her friend,
Stamped his feet and clapped his hands, the show was just for him;
"38-D, the size for me!" he called in a raucous voice.
"She's the sort who's there to sort the men out from the boys."

She came to the bar and called to her friend, "Hey Maggie, come and see!
"A prime example of 42–52–41 . . . 3."
Says he, "Now don't get *personal,* no need to talk like that.
"I thought you were a lady, Δ I only wanted to chat.
"I was only being friendly, Joe, and she went and took it wrong;
"But if she's gonna get *personal,* I'll be moving along."

She says, "Three . . . is just what Nature gave when she put you on the shelf.
"You've only got one *personal* thing, a thing you made yourself:
"From the bottom up, let's have a look and see what makes the † hero:
"3–41–52–42 . . . ZERO."

Music note: Make it funky.

For a Job

Southwest Tasmania: We heard that there was an anti-logging demonstration in East Picton and decided to join it. We travelled for several hours through the remains of a glorious rain forest. On the one side was desolation stretching up the hill: mud, deep ruts from the machinery, broken and twisted remnants of the kingdom that still existed on the *other* (downhill) side of the road: beautiful, ancient, enormous trees soaring upwards, identity intact. Birds blossomed in the upper branches and the leaves sang. The local logging town was literally up in arms about the protest. Loyal citizens had bombed out one of the demonstrators' cars and gangs of angry loggers were patrolling the roads. They weren't demonstrating against the increased mechanisation that was putting them out of work, or the fact that when the forest was all cut down they would not have jobs. Ahead of us on the road was a logging truck nearly hidden by its load of monster tree trunks. On the tailgate was a bumper-sticker reading GREENS COST JOBS.

tune: Peggy Seeger
words: Peggy Seeger and Irene Scott
disc 26

a blues, with melodic improvisations

(Am) F7 E7 Am F (Dm) 3 Am
He'd give the world for a job 'cause the job's his world.

D7 G7 C
The earth's his oyster, he's the pearl -

Dm E7 Am
Gives him some-thing to do, mon- ey in hand,

B7 9 E7
With - out a job a man's not a man.

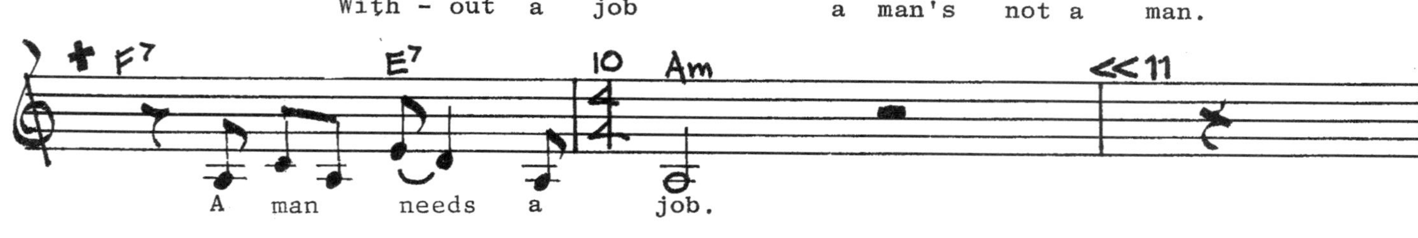

He'd give the world for a job 'cause the job's his world.
The earth's his oyster, he's the pearl—
Gives him something to do, money in hand,
Without a job a man's not a man.
A man needs a job.

Δ Man on a mountain, tearing that mountain down.
Man in a forest, building another town—
The world is his wherever he goes,
To do what he wants with, 'cause the world owes
Every man a job.

What would he give for a job? His heart and his lungs,
Mutilate his body, father mutant sons—
Silicon and lint, asbestos and coal,
The world wants life, man wants control,
But he'd give up life for a job.

Δ Ivory hunter, nuclear engineer,
Rain forest logger, arms trader, financier—
Creators of junk food, acid rain, CFCs
And all those things that bring death and disease;
† Made to waste, made without heed,
All those things that nobody needs.
So is a job just a job?

He'd give the world for a job, he's running wild;
Blindfold, brainwashed, self-centred, Pavlov's child—
Turn forest to desert, turn heaven to hell,
Turn home into nothing, will we live to tell
How we gave the world for a job?
« The whole world for a job.
We gave the world for a job.

Music note: This is best sung almost casually, with lots of melodic variations.

Bush Has Gone to Rio

The U.N. Conference on Environment and Development in Rio was held in June 1992. President Bush went grudgingly on June 12th and stayed for one day. He implied that saving the planet would not benefit the present American economy, which of course is true. It seemed fitting to deal with this matter in a style based on a children's song. It's the same idea as "My Old Man's a Dustman."

tune: traditional Anglo-American ("It Ain't Gonna Rain No More")
new words and trad. arr.: Peggy Seeger

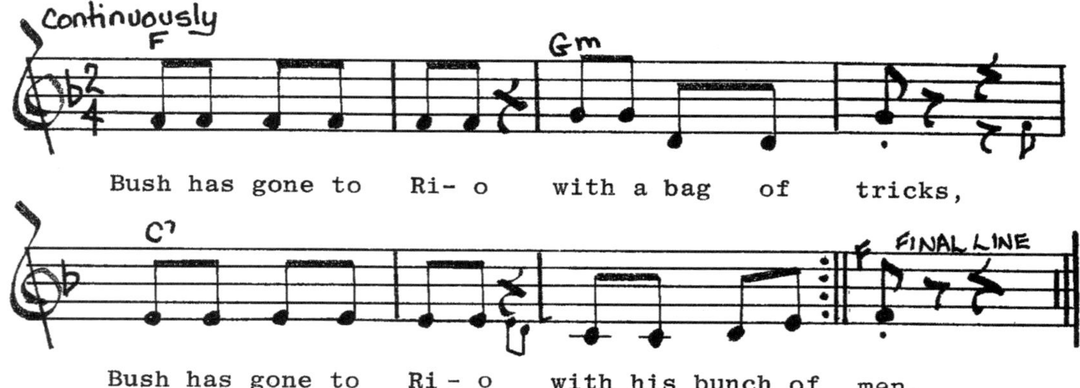

Bush has gone to Rio with a bag of tricks,
Bush has gone to Rio with his bunch of

PRIncipled diplomats who want to grab it all,
The thought of world democracy is just a lot of

BALderdash and nonsense, what Georgie doesn't want
Is sharing what we've got with a lot of other

COUNTries who are poor or black or just down on their luck,
So Bush is off to Rio to tell them all to

Find a way without him, 'cause he don't want to lose
The profits and the business, so he's prepared to

SCREW the people, SCREW the climate, SCREW the earth and then
Make the world a safer place for Yankee businessmen.

The Baby Song

Every two weeks we add fourteen million humans to our number. Is having children a human right? Is the world finite, with limited space and resources? Is the earth flat?

tune: traditional English ("London's Ordinary")
new words and trad. arr.: Peggy Seeger
© 1992 Peggy Seeger (1)

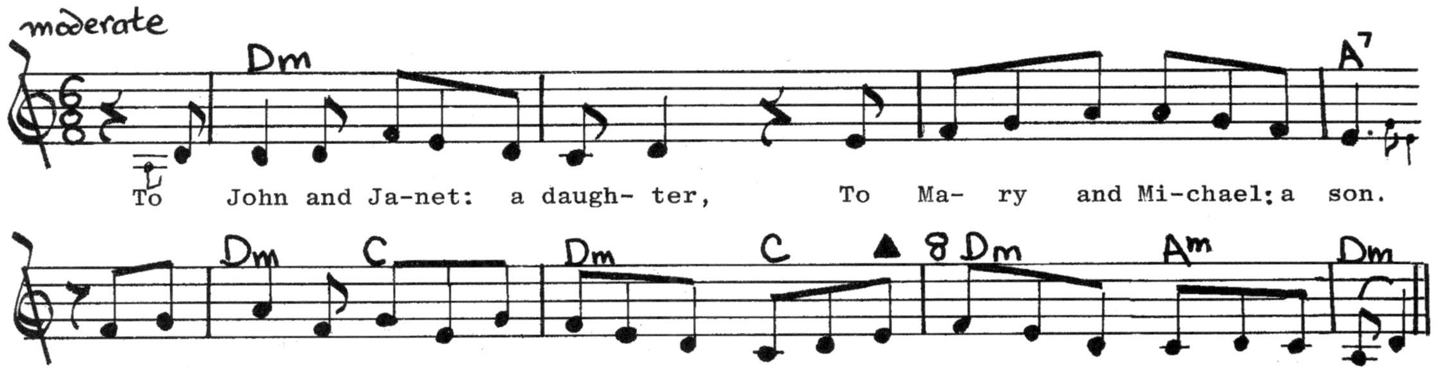

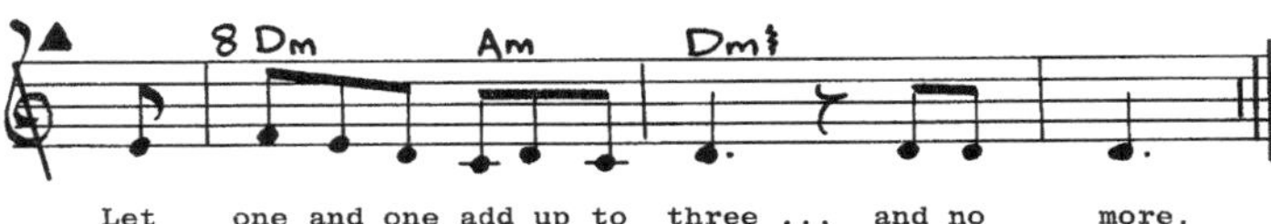

To John and Janet: a daughter,
To Mary and Michael: a son.
To the earth: a flood of consumers who feed
On her blood and her flesh and her bones.

A treasure is there for the taking,
And humans are clearing the coffers;
From the low to the high each parent will buy
Whatever the culture can offer.

Metal and plastic and rubber,
Leather and paper and wood;
Each baby we add must be fed, must be clad
From the market that once was the world.

Each baby will want running water,
A house and a job and a car,
Petrol and oil and places to park
When they don't want to stay where they are.

More roads, more buildings, more cities,
More sewage, pollution, and dirt;
And each baby will make more babies that take
And use up more and more of the world.

So from David and Annie: a forest,
From Penny and Peter: a river.
For most every baby that comes to the earth
Is a taker and rarely a giver.

So man and woman, consider
Before you go out on the spree;
John and Janet: remember the planet,
Δ Let one and one add up to three . . . and no more.
Let one and one add up to two.

Music note: Choose your own final phrase.

Use It Again

A cheerful little song about one of the most important things in the world.

words and music: Peggy Seeger

with bounce
F
Bb
F
When you peeled that po- ta- to, what did you think
G7
C7
As the peel piled up in the kit- chen sink?
F
Bb
F
You could- a made com-post or soup for the day
C7
F
But you did-n't use it, you threw it a-way.
F7
It could have made your gar- den grow,
Bb
C7
And po- ta- to-peel soup is the best, you know.
F
Bb
(F)
But that po- ta- to peel died in the gar-bage dump
F
C7
F
With the glass and the cans and the plas- tic junk.

When you peeled that potato, what did you think
As the peel piled up in the kitchen sink?
You could'a made compost or soup for the day
But you didn't use it, you threw it away.
It could have made your garden grow,
And potato-peel soup is the best, you know.
But that potato peel died in the garbage dump
With the glass and the cans and the plastic junk.

Chorus: You didn't even use it, you threw it away,
You didn't even use it, you threw it away;
You didn't even save it for a rainy day,
You didn't even use it, you threw it away.

Buy all the groceries, put 'em in a bag,
Haul 'em to the bike, the mini, or the Jag.
You could save that bag for a rainy day
But you used it once and you threw it away.
Fold it up and use it again,
Use it for your things when you go to the gym;
But that bag went along to the garbage dump
With the metal and the rubber and the plastic junk.

Chorus: You used it once and you threw it away, *(etc.)*

A box for paper and a box for tins,
Another for plastic and a garbage bin,
One for bottles and old jam jars
And when they're full, put 'em in the car.
Just think of the fun you'll have that day,
Recycling the rubbish on its way;
Everyone can learn a new game to play
Called "Use it, save it, and take it away."

Chorus: Use it, save it, and take it away,
Use it, save it, and take it away;
Don't look now but it's a rainy day,
Use it, save it, and take it away.

The world makes soil, the world makes air,
It's always here, it's always there;
The earth recycles our water and wind,
She'll use it and use it and use it again.
She gives us presents every day
And we use them once then throw them away;
We'll use up the world if we don't learn when
To use it and use it and use it again.

Chorus: Use it and use it and use it again,
Use it and use it and use it again,
Make potato-peel soup! then say Amen.
Use it and use it and use it again.

Joe and Mika's Wedding

One of the best weddings I've ever been to. My niece Mika married Joe Bossom in the summer of 1992. Two months later, on August 29, her parents (my brother Pete and his wife, Toshi) celebrated by throwing open their hillside home in upper New York State to several hundred guests. Napoleon would have balked at the preparations, but Toshi just rolled up her sleeves (and lots of other peoples' sleeves!) and waded in. The big central kitchen table was continually piled with meat, fish, fowl, vegetables, and condiments of all kinds and an army of scrubbers, peelers, choppers, and stirrers attacked it daily—for weeks. Every pot and pan came out, was put to use, its contents emptied into containers which then disappeared into freezers and fridges. Dishwashers, floor-sweepers, and go-fers came and went . . . and when they went, Toshi just carried on.

On THE DAY, there was a tent with food, food and more food . . . tables of breads, tables of meats, tables of fruit . . . the watermelon had a table to itself. A canoe had been cleaned, painted, and lined with aluminium foil and greenery before being filled with a dozen huge dishes of salad. Corn-on-the-cob and mussels boiled in two great vats. Chilled beer and soft drinks were buried in barrels of ice. The bride and her six-foot son sang a bawdy song as the wedding cake was brought in. Champagne was handed around in beautiful little cups that Mika, a potter by trade, had made specially—one for each guest to drink a toast from and then take home as a memento. The band played, Joe brought out his great highland bagpipes and everyone danced. This song was my contribution. My niece Sonya put it on this little songsheet and made copies for everyone. One of the best weddings I've ever been to.

tune: traditional Scots ("Mari's Wedding")
new words and trad. arr.: Peggy Seeger
© 1992 Peggy Seeger (1)

Joe and Mika's Wedding

CHORUS:
Up the hill we all must go
To eat and drink and do-si-do,
To talk and sing, 'cause don't you know
It's Joe and Mika's wedding.

Just about a year ago
Mika fell in love with Joe;
Bossom's face went all aglow,
"We're going to have a wedding."
Mika said, "There's got to be
A party on a Saturday,
Two-hundred friends and you and me,
Now THAT's a proper wedding!" (Chorus)

Glad you made it up the hill,
Happy that you're fit and well,
Hope you're going to eat your fill,
'Cause this here is a wedding.
All of this is just for show,
The knot was tied two months ago,
This is just to let you know
We want to share the wedding. (Chorus)

There's duck and chicken, goose and squid,
Good for ego, good for id,
And garlic tells the world you did
Join us at the wedding.
Chili with and without meat,
Pickles sour, puddings sweet,
Stuff yourselves from head to feet,
Don't leave us with leftovers. (Chorus)

There's mussels, salads, salsa, beer,
Spiked fruit punch and the water here
Is just like wine, it's sweet and clear,
Mountain dew for the wedding.
Down the hill you'll find a brook,
(But don't go down, there's poison oak,)
On a table there's a book,
Leave a message for the wedding. (Chorus)

Mika made the toasting cups,
Toshi filled your bellies up,
Pete repaired the road and cuts
For parking at the wedding.
Friends and family lent a hand,
Swept the house and cleared the land,
But Joe's the piper, he's the man
Who HAD to have a wedding. (Chorus)

So here's to beans and bread and beer,
Here's to peace - far and near;
To friends and family who came here
To celebrate the wedding.
Here's to lovers near and far,
Here's to Him, here's to Her
Just reach up and catch a star,
That's how you make a wedding. (Chorus)

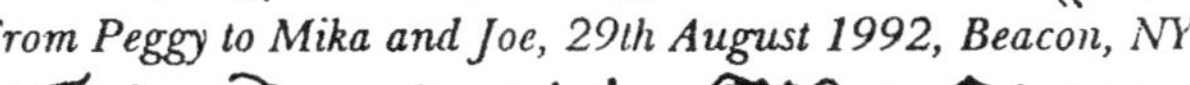
From Peggy to Mika and Joe, 29th August 1992, Beacon, NY

So Long Since I Been Home

Whatever the reasons for the travelling, two weeks away from home always seems to be my limit.

words and music: Peggy Seeger
disc 26

Lying here in the dark, wishing it was day,
Lying here in the dark, wishing it was day,
Lying here in the dark, wishing it was day,

Chorus: So long, so long since I been home,
O love, remember me.

In your arms, in your bed is where I want to be, *(3 times) (chorus)*

Open up your window and look towards the sea, *(3) (chorus)*

Winter s coming on and the wind is cold and keen, *(3) (chorus)*

The rabbit has a burrow, the little bird has a tree,
The rabbit has a burrow, the little bird has a tree,
Everyone has a home, there's no home for me, *(chorus)*

Lying here in the dark, living in my dreams, *(3) (chorus)*

It's a Free World

The place, the protagonists, the smoke are all real. From there on, this is a recurring fantasy of mine.

alternative title: "Free World"
words and music: Peggy Seeger
disc 26

with gusto
F
Bb
C7
I like Mis-sus Bridg-e's, I go to Mis-sus Bridg-e's,
I eat at Mis-sus Bridg-e's eve- ry Fri- day (for break-fast);
There are on- ly sev- en tab - les, And flow- ers on the ta- bles,
And smo - kers at the ta- bles on a Fri - day.

A7
Dm
G7
C7
F
to
'CAUSE IT'S A FREE WORLD, DE- MO - CRA- CY AND ALL THAT,
IT'S A FREE WORLD, LAISS-EZ-FAIRE AND ALL THAT,
AND IF IN-DUS-TRY CAN DO IT, SO CAN I——!

Gm
I thought of Moth-er Jones, I thought of Ro-sa Parkes,
18 C7
F7
So-journ-er Truth and Ro-sa Lux-em-burg, it's them I have to thank;
20 Bb
F
D7
Guer- ril-la folk have taught me if free-dom you are want-ing,
G7
C7
to
If head-on fights are daunt - ing use the flank. So...

18 C7
F7
to 20
Sweet corn is for den-si-ty and len- tils for du- ra- tion, The

Δ I like Mrs. Bridge's, I go to Mrs. Bridge's,
I eat at Mrs. Bridge's every Friday (for breakfast);
There are only seven tables, and flowers on the tables,
And smokers at the tables on a Friday.

Δ Now, you may think I'm joking, but some smokers when they're smoking
Don't notice if you're choking or you're dying.
There's this one fellow, Andy—a real chain-smoker—and he
Blows smoke right at me till I'm crying.

Δ I asked him quite politely, in fact I asked him nicely,
"Would you mind not smoking on a Friday?
"Don't like it when I'm eating, don't like it when I'm breathing,
"Don't like it anywhere or any day."

Δ He told me, "It's a habit. I choose to have it,
"And you choose to come here on a Friday.
"So *you're* the problem, not me, and if I choose to rot me,
"You've got no right to stop me 'cause it's my way.

† "'Cause it's a free world,
"Democracy and all that,
"It's a free world,
"Laissez-faire and all that,
"And if industry can do it, so can I!"

Δ The smokers cheered him loudly, he lit another proudly.
As for me, I looked around me for a friend.
I thought of world pollution, I thought of evolution,
I thought of revolution and I paid my bill and left.

« *I thought of Mother Jones, I thought of Rosa Parks,*
Sojourner Truth and Rosa Luxemburg, it's them I have to thank;
Guerrilla folk have taught me if freedom you are wanting,
If head-on fights are daunting use the flank. So . . .

Δ I ate corn on Sunday, I ate beans on Monday,
On Tuesday leeks and lentils made a high day.
I tell you I'm not joking, by Thursday I was floating
But I'm ready for the smoking on the Friday.

Δ I sat down next to Andy. I smiled at Andy.
He lit up. I let off a beauty.
I sat and read the paper and chatted with the waiter,
And let my compost maker do its duty.

« *Beans are for pitching, leeks are malediction,*
∞ *Sweet corn is for density and lentils for duration,*
The recipe's been tested, it hasn't yet been bested—
Add cabbage for perfume and concentration.

Δ Andy he turns yellow, the atmosphere is mellow,
The percussion section's way over the top.
It soon put Andy's fag out. Andy hung the flag out.
Andy swore and choked and muttered, "Stop!"

Δ I told him, "It's a habit. I choose to have it,
"And you choose to come here on a Friday.
"And if you don't like it I guess you'll have to hike it
"'Cause I'll fight for farters' rights until I die.

† "'CAUSE IT'S A FREE WORLD,
"LIBERTY AND ALL THAT,
"IT'S A FREE WORLD,
"SELFISHNESS AND ALL THAT.
"AND IF ANDY CAN DO IT, SO CAN I!"

Δ* He changed his day to Thursday. I changed my day to Thursday.
He changed his day to Wednesday, so did I.
The waitress she was cheering, her bronchitis it was clearing,
And she was volunteering for the Tuesday.

Δ I like Mrs. Bridge's, I eat at Mrs. Bridge's,
I breathe at Mrs. Bridge's every Friday (for breakfast);
There are only seven tables, and flowers on the tables,
And no smokers at the tables any day.

† 'CAUSE IT'S A FREE WORLD,
STRATEGY AND ALL THAT,
IT'S A FREE WORLD,
CRUDE COMEDY AND ALL THAT,
AND IF I CAN DO IT—*SO CAN ANYBODY.*

**Music note: I always move up to G for this verse then back down to F for the final two stanzas. I generally speak the last three words.*

Come on, Andy,
take it like a girl

Body Language

On July 19, the *Times* carried a fascinating picture of John Major preparing for a television interview. He is sitting and gazing down at his crotch, where his hands seem to be busy with something. The subtitle tells us he is arranging his tie. The heading is arresting: "GLUED TO OUR SEATS BY BODY LANGUAGE . . . See how the Prime Minister holds those rigid, karate-chop fingers bonded together as though from an accident with superglue . . . how he crosses those thick trunkish legs at times of stress. . . ." Oh well—he should be grateful that his philtrum wasn't mentioned.

tune: Peggy Seeger
words: Peggy Seeger and Irene Scott
© 1993 Peggy Seeger (1)

lazy
Am
A7
D
Am
Once there was a bat-tle on the box, Cam-era, ac-tion and lights;
Dm
E7
Am
B7
F7
1
E7
Ques -tion and an-swer, dodge and duck, John-ny's sit-ting down to fight.
A7
Dm
He smiles when you men-tion a de-fi-cit in trade,
G7
C
E7
He cross-es his legs when a ref-er-ence is made to the So-cial Chap-ter;
A7
Dm
He's ever so con-trolled, he's e- ter-nal-ly on hold,
Am
E7
Am B7
E7
2
Am
He's a slow, slow, slow ve-loc-i- rap- tor. time.

Once there was a battle on the box,
Camera, action and lights;
Question and answer, dodge and duck,
Johnny's sitting down to fight.

    He smiles when you mention a deficit in trade,
    He crosses his legs when a reference is made to the Social Chapter;
    He's ever so controlled, he's eternally on hold,
    He's a slow, slow, slow velociraptor.

Δ Watch the body language, read the lips,
The minister who never was prime.
Rigid torso, frozen hips,
Johnny's running out of time.

Isn't It Time to Go, John?

July. Probably the first of the big image-breaking crises suffered by John Major, Britain's Prime Moneystar at the time. Nadir, a Cypriot entry-pruner allegedly involved in picking peppers at Polly Peck, had made a timely exit (see "The Party"). The PM was embroiled at the time in EEC busy-mess in general and the Maastricht muddle in particular. He sought the support of the Northern Irish Onanists (a favour that might have to be repaid at any time) just before Christchurch was winched out of the Tory net by Paddy Pantsdown's Lateral Demi-craps. *And,* it was reported that our John used *swear* words! . . . Michael Mates (MP, who was into cars not condoms) was probably innocent of bribery but he confessed anyway. Norman Lamont (MP in charge of the Piggy Bank) and David Mellors (MP whose affairs still haven't been sorted out) kept us all entertained with their goings and . . . comings. John Major instigated his Back to Basics morals campaign which may follow him to the end of his pubic days. Michael Heseltine, Michael Portillo . . . it seems that there is always a Brutus waiting in the wings ever ready to take over the unenviable position of leading Britain. This song has been updated at least a dozen times since the *urtext.* This is the August 1994 version—Major went minor on May 1, 1997. (P.S.: This is a British song-note.)

tune: English music hall ("Are We to Part Like This, Bill?")
new words: Peggy Seeger and Irene Scott
trad. arr.: Peggy Seeger
© 1993 Peggy Seeger (1)

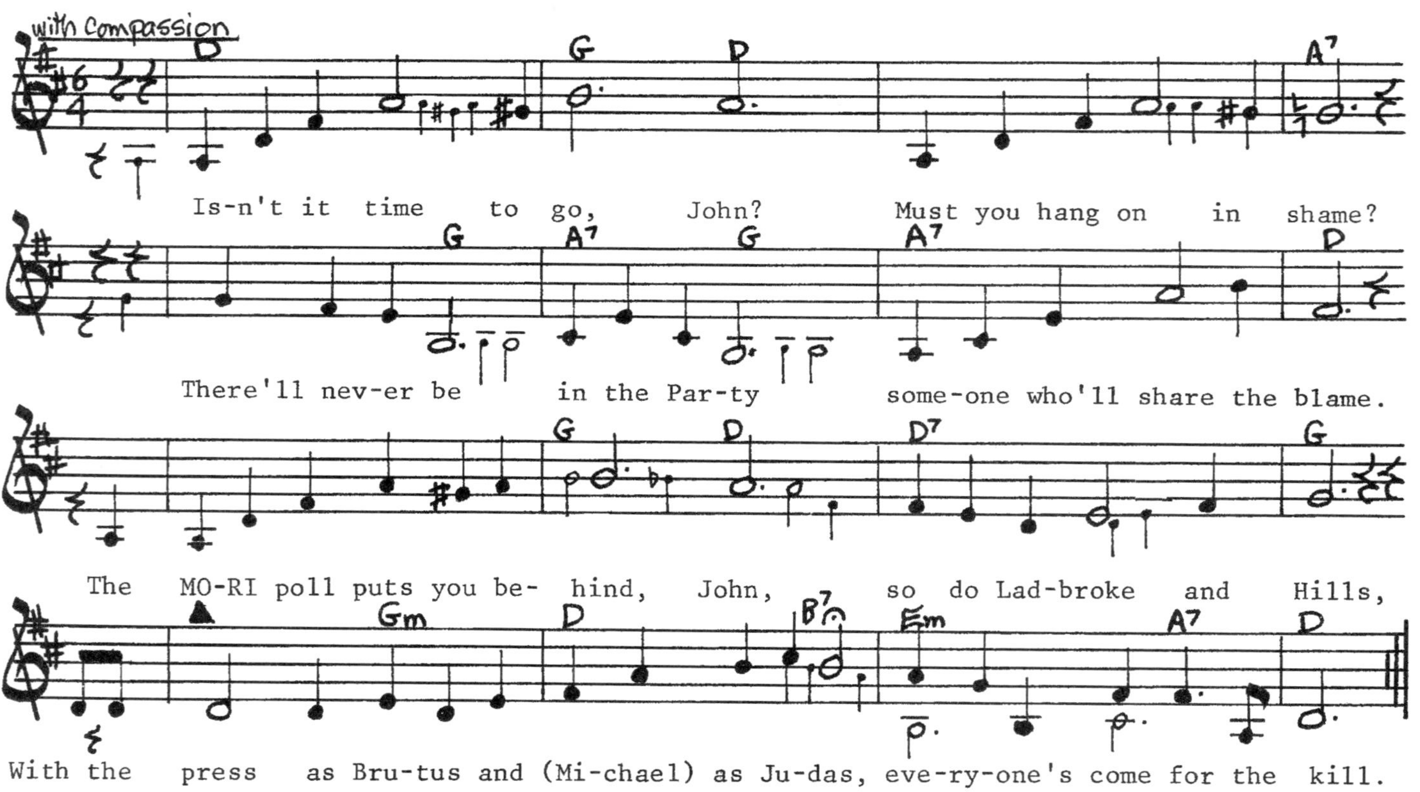
with Compassion
Is-n't it time to go, John? Must you hang on in shame?
There'll nev-er be in the Par-ty some-one who'll share the blame.
The MO-RI poll puts you be- hind, John, so do Lad-broke and Hills,
With the press as Bru-tus and (Mi-chael) as Ju-das, eve-ry-one's come for the kill.

last verse
Nix-on had Wat-er-gate, Bush had Dan Quayle, The (etc.)

Isn't it time to go, John? Must you hang on in shame?
There'll never be in the Party someone who'll share the blame.
The MORI poll puts you behind, John, so do Ladbroke and Hills,
With the press as Brutus and (Michael) as Judas, everyone's come for the kill.

The way to go forward is back, John, Back to the Basics of life;
Back to the days when no one was gay and Prince Charles was in love with his wife.
When single mums kept out of sight, John, and Europe was far, far away,
When the Irish were Paddies and playwrights and navvies—those golden days.

(to be spoken intimately while accompaniment continues):

Norma is waiting at home, John, patiently cooking your peas,
Norma is there, always there, and whatever you do, she's pleased.
Home is where you belong, John, and even you *have to admit*
That home is the only place, John, where you won't land in

The issues are bigger than you, John, chapters of blunder and crime,
A country that's headless, homeless and jobless, slipping backward in time.
Everyone has a cross to bear: Napoleon had Waterloo,
Δ Nixon had Watergate, Bush had Dan Quayle, the Tory Party has you.

• *For your interest, here is the original 1993 text:*

Are we to part like this, John? Must you hang on in shame?
Surely there'll be in the Party someone who will share the blame.
The MORI poll puts you behind, John, so do Ladbroke and Hills,
There's Mates and Lamont, and Mellor and now . . . Paddy is poised for the kill.

The issues are bigger than you, John, chapters of blunder and crime,
A country that's headless, homeless, and jobless, slipping backward in time.
You've papered some cracks in the House, John, and borrowed the Lambeg drum,
But your new friends at Stormont won't be so conformant when pay day comes.

Norma is waiting at home, John, patiently cooking your peas,
Norma is there, always there, and whatever you do, she's pleased.
Home is where you belong, John, and even you have to admit
That home is the only place, John, where you won't land in Maastricht.

Christchurch has given a warning, Brussels is playing it cool,
Nadir could squall, more heads would fall, and swearing won't change the rules.
Everyone has a cross to bear, Napoleon had Waterloo,
Nixon had Watergate, Bush had Dan Quayle, the Tory Party has you.

The Party

Like "Affair of State," this song is about the *dramatis personae* of an intriguing political imbroglio. It had the same classic ingredients—sex, money, and crime. The size of the cast was monumental, for the press was playing Perry Mason, instigating searches and following every innuendo until even Princess Diana herself was implicated, albeit from a distance. This song was commissioned in the morning and written in the afternoon . . . but evening came too soon and trying to keep pace with events proved impossible. We updated it hourly for two weeks before we gave up (at the stage printed below) and went on to chronicle John Major's inability to control John Major. (see "Body Language" and "Isn't It Time to Go, John?")

tune: Peggy Seeger
words: Peggy Seeger and Irene Scott
© 1993 Peggy Seeger (1)

wry, conversational
Dm
C
4 Dm
This song is a- bout a big Par-ty That man -y rich peo - ple at- tend,
Gm
Dm
8 E7
A7
Where the mu - sic is quite à la car-tie, And peo-ple give wat-ches to friends.

8 E7
retard
A7 to 1
While Na- dir has his thumb in a hole in the --- jam.

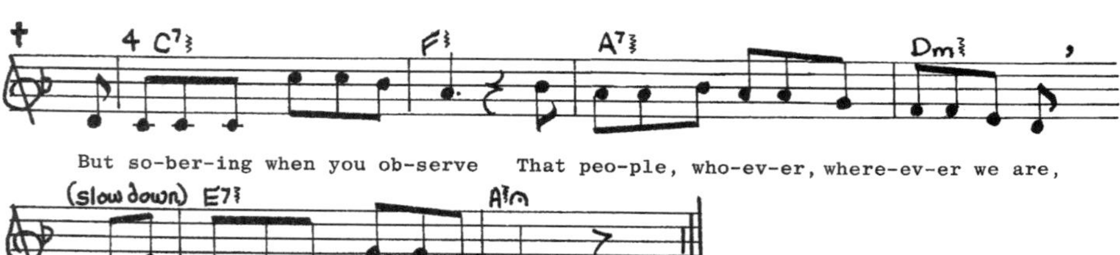
4 C7
F
A7
Dm
But so-ber-ing when you ob-serve That peo-ple, who-ev-er, where-ev-er we are,
(slow down) E7
Am
Get the gov-ern-ment that we de-serve.

This song is about a big Party
That many rich people attend,
Where the music is quite *à la cartie,*
And people give watches to friends.

It's a party where business is pleasure
And the principle purpose of life;
There's old-boy connections and Honours
And strangers lend cars to your wife.

It's a good old Party tradition
(Thatcher and Ryder could swing it a treat).
But why wasn't the car a Nissan?
'Twould have made the occasion complete.

Files weren't opened, like Crippen's,
The Party just banked a big cheque.
And the guests would have not started strippin'
If Polly'd not gone and got Pecked.

The press busted in on the caper,
Eager to follow the Hunt;
The Queen will be getting the vapours,
For Di's fallen into the punch.

In gallops the galloping Major,
His eyes are beginning to glaze;
He's a cross between Judas and Nero:
He fiddles while pipers get paid.

Two light-footed dastardly villains
Skipped to hold on to their scalps.
The one jumped his bail for three million
The other's in bed (in the Alps).

Maggie dressed up as Orlando,
Then Mates got up and sang;
Clinton attended as Rambo,
Saddam was let off with a bang.

The plot gets thicker and thicker
As Parkie and Teb lend a hand;
The beat gets quicker and quicker
Δ While Nadir has his thumb in a hole in the—jam.

The Party's exciting, intriguing, bizarre,
† But sobering when you observe
That people, whoever, wherever we are,
Get the government that we deserve.

Yankee Doodle 1993

June 26: President Clinton orders a missile attack on the Baghdad headquarters of Iraqi military intelligence in retaliation for an alleged plot to assassinate President Bush a year earlier. If you can look east you can look south. And if the passage of time is no object . . .

tune: traditional U.S.A. ("Yankee Doodle")
new words and trad. arr.: Peggy Seeger

Yankee Doodle's marching south
Led by Mister Clinton,
The time has come to take revenge
For the death of Mister Lincoln.

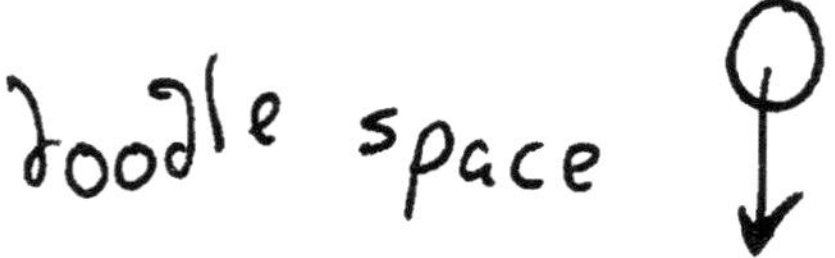

On This Very Day

Kerry has a daughter and twin sons. My son Calum has a son from an earlier relationship. Together they made Ella blossom. They set the day for their wedding: March 25, the very day of the year that I first met Ewan in 1956. Although I have occasionally been tempted to sing "Talking Matrimonial Blues" at certain weddings I have attended, I have enjoyed the recent family nuptials hugely and have made songs for them (see "Joe and Mika's Wedding" and "Autumn Wedding"). For this song, I bought one of those little books that tell you what happened in the past on your birthday. The book gives the religious festivals and mentions the saint associated with the day. It also commemorates historical events (some of them quite bizarre) and, most significant, lists the names of people whose birthdays are the same as yours. As you are kind of born again on your wedding day and your hopes and passions often resemble religious ecstasy, I figured that many of these sentiments, facts, and myths would be appropriate.

words and music: Peggy Seeger
disc 26

cheerfully
G C G
On this ver - y day some folks passed a- way;
C G A7 D7
Some got born, some had kids, some gave up and ran a-way;
G D7 G7 C G
Some went off to war, some went back to bed;
C G (A7) D7 G
Some got di-vorced, and of course, oth-ers they got wed.
CHORUS D7 G G7
On this ver- y day, on this ver- y day,
C G A7 D7 G
The world has been a bus-y place on this ver- y day.

On this very day some folks passed away;
Some got born, some had kids, some gave up and ran away;
Some went off to war, some went back to bed;
Some got divorced, and of course, others they got wed.

Chorus: On this very day, on this very day,
The world has been a busy place on this very day.

On this very morn, Elton John was born,
Mrs. Bartók dropped her load, Aretha Franklin hit the road;
Henry the Second's mum lost inches off her tum
Thus Rosamund Clifford's fate was sealed on this very day. *(chorus)*

On this day it befell that the Angel Gabriel
Told Mary she'd receive (by post) a baby from the Holy Ghost;
And would you believe there's a patron saint for thieves?
St. Dismas pardons all your sins on this very day. *(chorus)*

On March the twenty-fifth in eighteen-ninety-six,
The Olympic Games were launched in France; a poor young Greek hitched up his pants
And ran the marathon. Do you wanna know what he won?
A year's free grub and free shoeshines until his life was done. *(chorus)*

Thirty-eight years ago, I want you all to know
I met his dad, his dad met me, we got our kids and they got we . . .
And this big handsome man, the thought of him began
In a basement room in Kensington on this very day. *(chorus)*

As the years go by, you may look back and sigh
And say, "Do you remember when . . . ?" and want to live it all again.
May the years be kind, may you keep this in your mind:
Make each day a special one like this very day.

Final chorus: Like this very day, like this very day,
Make each day a special one, like this very day.
* 'Cause Kerry and Calum tied the knot on this very day.

**This line is sung to the same tune as the last line of the chorus.*

'...and they lived happily ever after
until the birth of their first child when
he went to pieces and she went off sex entirely.'

- *Any good public library has books that tell you what happened on any day of the year, so the song may be remade over and over. Here's a version for New Year's Eve.*

On this very day, some folks go astray
Some get drunk and fall asleep,
Some make vows they'll never keep,
Some prefer to clown and turn things upside down,
But now I'll tell you what took place on this very day.

Chorus: On this very day, on this very day,
The world has been a busy place on this very day.

In the year of 313, the Emperor Constantine
Permitted those who worship Christ to share this worldly paradise.
Sylvester was the Pope, kept the infant church afloat.
So now it's called Sylvester Day on this very day. *(chorus)*

On this very morn, John Thompson he was born.
In case you don't know what he done, he invented the tommy gun.
Light bulbs beat the dark in the town of Menlo Park
And Ellis Island depot opened on this very day. *(chorus)*

Prokofiev first was seen in the pit at seventeen,
Frank Sinatra on this day began to do it all his way,
And on this very night, John Denver saw the light,
Matisse, Odetta—both were born on this very day.

A jockey rode to fame, Willie Shoemaker by name.
Around the racecourse Willie steered 400 winners in one year.
In 1923 we broadcast overseas,
And overseas answered us—on this very day. *(chorus)*

There may be many here for whom the brand new year
Opens on a different date—but we can all still celebrate
Each other's New Year's eve; we can, I do believe,
Make each day a hopeful one, like this very day.

Final chorus: Like this very day, like this very day
Make each day a hopeful one, like this very day.

Everyone Knows

In 1994 there were an extraordinary number of sex scandals in the ranks of Tory MPs. Any other leading political party or government would have placed these in the Boys-Will-Be-Boys folder and filed them away under Business as Usual. Even the Victorians didn't threaten, as John Major did on February 27, that anyone in his little army who strayed would put his job at risk. Up until then, it was tacitly assumed that romps on the sideline were acceptable (1) if you did your job well and (2) if you weren't found out. It is said that a standing prick has no conscience. Parliament at that time was ninety percent male. Just how conscientious is the ship of state when a large proportion of its members are, at any given time, rampant?

music: Pegger Seeger
words: Peggy Seeger with Irene Scott
disc 26
© 1994 Peggy Seeger (1)

Lazy
G A7
Eve-ry-one knows you can't trust a wo-man when-ev-er that time rolls a-round;
D7 G G7
Eve-ry-one knows she can go cra-zy when her main-spring gets un-wound;
C Cm G B7
At that cer-tain time, a wom-an is prone To in-dis-po-si-tion and it's not un-known
E7 A7 retard D7
For her to be touch-y, a lit-tle bit slow, So we can't entrust her with run-ning the show.
back into rhythm
G A7
Eve-ry-one knows you can't trust a wo-man, she might slip out of gear-
D7 G G7
She bays at the moon, she's a walk-ing womb a doz-en times a year.

C Cm G E7
Low on e-go, high on id, Vic-tim of her hormones, her mind's like a sieve,
A7 D7 C7 D7 G
You can't trust a per-son who might flip her lid Eve-ry twen-ty-eight days.

Everyone knows you can't trust a woman whenever that time rolls around;
Everyone knows she can go crazy when her mainspring gets unwound;
At that certain time, a woman is prone
To indisposition and it's not unknown
For her to be touchy, a little bit slow,
So we can't entrust her with running the show.
Everyone knows you can't trust a woman, she might slip out of gear—
She bays at the moon, she's a walking womb a dozen times a year.
Low on ego, high on id,
Victim of her hormones, her mind's like a sieve,
You can't trust a person who might flip her lid
Every twenty-eight days.

Everyone knows you can't trust a man whenever that time rolls around;
Everyone knows he can go crazy when his mainspring's overwound;
The needle points north, south, east, and west,
He's never at peace, never at rest,
Victim of his hormones, running too fast,
Steering the ship with his mind on the mast.
Everyone knows you can't trust a man, things can slip out of gear—
He's a walking, talking divining rod ten-thousand times a year.
And the power and the glory, the whole damn show,
Everything except that old status quo
Can all go to hell when the signal says *GO* . . .
Any time of day.

REAL chic is always ahead of its time

Turncoat

1994

As far back as the 1920s, women have been actively agitating for the right to officiate at the altars of the Church of England. As of March 12, 1994, women may now *man* those pulpits—as priests, not as priestesses. The issue has been accepted by the majority of the church but the dissenters are vociferous and many of them have voted with their feet. At first the attention was on clergymen (from the highest bishops to the lowest servants such as Reverend Flatman) who were leaving because they felt that the administration of religion was men's work. Members of the ordinary public, Members of Parliament, the Duchess of Kent—the media made much of their desertions to other denominations. There are several agitational groups (with names like Forward in Faith and Ecclesia) who represent the warlike sector of a male clergy who, let's face it, inserted themselves into a matriarchal system several thousand years ago, usurped practically all of the positions of power, and brought forth the churches as we know them today. The situation has its funny moments but it's tragic as it reveals so clearly the how wide and deep the chasm between the sexes really is.

P.S.: March 13, 1994, Mother's Day. I watched the first female service at Bristol on television this morning. Reverend Valerie Woods was officiating and I must admit that the dignity of the ritual was beautifully combined with an informality of approach that I have never experienced in a Church of England service. The interviewer addressed her as Val. Would the Reverend Flatman have been thus addressed by his first name? Would we even *know* his first name? Reminiscent of office protocol? . . .

tune: extrapolated from "A-Begging I Will Go" (trad. English)
new words and trad. arr.: Peggy Seeger, disc 26A
© 1993 Peggy Seeger (1)

The men of God have come ashore,
Pursued by macho thinking;
Because the women have come on board
They think the ship is sinking.

The Reverend Flatman told his flock
That women would be very
Welcome at his altar—
To be wed or to be buried.

But women priests are devil's work
And the Reverend cannot tarry;
He's off to join the Catholic Church—
To worship Virgin Δ Mary.

When Lovers Hide the Keys

words and music: Peggy Seeger

My arms went round her waist and hip,
She never said me nay;
But when I sought her cheek and lip,
She turned her face away.

My love has gone I know not where,
O, let me follow you!
And if I am not welcome there
I know not what to do.

Nor bar nor bolt nor cruel clock
Δ Can so destroy a lover's ease
As minds that close and hearts that lock
When lovers hide the keys.

Music note: Bar 4: to play a D7 chord while singing in D minor enhances the aura of sadness and discomfort that should permeate this song. If it's too much for you, go for the Dm.

Old Friend

I first met Ralph Rinzler in the spring of 1954. I was going to college in Massachusetts at the time and a bunch of us decided to go to the Swarthmore Folk Festival. Somehow we got hold of an old hearse and about a dozen of us piled into it and slid south on the icy highways. I was standing, shivering, on the steps of the registration hall when the tall boy ahead of me turned around and smiled. Instant summer sunshine. "Are you cold?" I nodded the obvious and he said, "Save my place," and vanished in a red-haired, long-legged lope, returning minutes later with a huge baggy sweater which he put at my command, along with himself, for the whole weekend. We became fast friends. We corresponded, we travelled hither and yon by scooter in and around New England and, whenever our paths crossed, yon and hither in England, France, Germany, Switzerland, and Italy. The instruments went with us and the music triangulated our comradeship. Our lives and our work settled us in different countries and decades passed during which I took to singing, songwriting, and raising children in England. He became a seminal mover-and-shaker in (to put it possibly too succinctly) the legitimising and popularising of folk music through his work at the Smithsonian in Washington, D.C. We re-established good contact in the early 1990s. Ralph was my special friend—he died on July 2, 1994.

words and music: Peggy Seeger
disc 26

Smoothly
G G7 C G 9
Old friend, com-rade of mine, once a- gain you're on my mind.
D7 G G7 Am D7
There's al-ways a place and there's al-ways a time to think of days gone by;
G C G
We spent too long a- part and there's so much in my heart I want to say
D7 G
Be-fore we say good-bye.

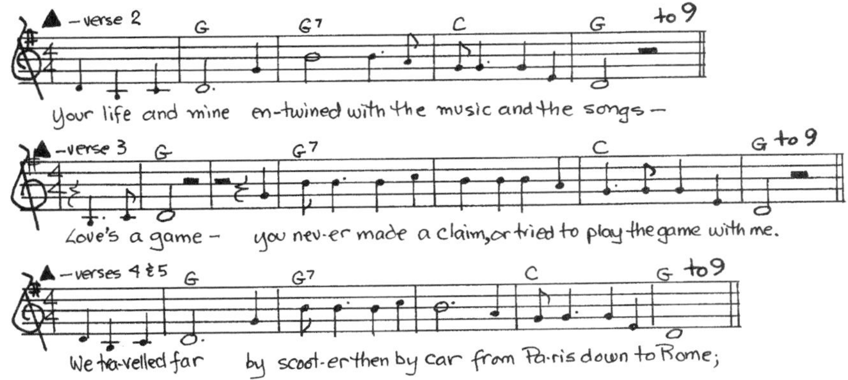

Old friend, comrade of mine, once again you're on my mind.
There's always a place, and there's always a time to think of days gone by;
We spent too long apart and there's so much in my heart I want to say
Before we say goodbye.

∆ Your life and mine entwined with the music and the songs—
Our future was set from the moment that we met we were old, old friends;
The work that was our play carried us away then brought us home,
Brought us home again.

∆ Love's a game—you never made a claim, or tried to play the game with me.
That set you apart with your own place in my heart where you will always be;
As a woman among men, it was hard to find a friend—then you were there,
And with you I was free.

∆ We travelled far by scooter then by car from Paris down to Rome;
In Germany we clowned, in Switzerland broke down, we were so young then;
We parted and we aged but our rainbow didn't fade—we remained,
We remained old friends.

(repeat first verse)

∆ Now you are gone and like the music and the songs you come into my mind.
If the good we have done ensures that we live on, you will never die;
Your friends hold you dear and we'll keep you with us here, so never say
Never say goodbye.

Music note: Compare this tune with that of "Hello Friend."

1956

1990

You Men Out There

On February 17, 1995, there was a splendid celebration of seventy-five years of women's suffrage, held in Knoxville, Tennessee. There were speeches, singers, and a play written specially for the event by Candace Anderson. This piece was our contribution to the event. It's not a song: It's a poem, a rap, a monologue, a rhymed speech. I've put it into an irregular verse form because that seems to make it less formidable to learn.

words: Peggy Seeger and Irene Scott
disc 26

You men out there: you've shown real strength,
Listening to me go on at length
About women this and women that
Almost as if the other half
(Well . . . forty-eight percent) of the human race
Wasn't worth the time and space
They occupy.

Stop surreptitiously checking your watches,
Hands instinctively covering crotches,
Inspecting your nails, rearranging your shoes.
It's understandable: you're confused.
And your father's father and his dad's dad
And his pop's papa and all the lads
And their uncles, sons, and brothers, too,
Probably felt the same as you—
Confused.

But from where *we're* at, here's how it looks:
Long before the time of books,
Women were magic, women were mystery.
Way before the start of history
Before space travel and megacities
Females were heading planning committees.
Women searched the fields and hedges,
Hunting flowers, herbs, and sedges;
Roots for soups, leaves for healing,
Plants to enhance loving feelings.
Wise women (now called witches)
And powerful women (now called bitches)
Managed life and death and birth,
Cared and shared with Planet Earth.

When the Golden Age came to a stop,
There were the men, up on top.
I guess it starts with lust and love
Where a man spends a lot of time up above.
But somehow women got redefined
And got accustomed to tagging behind,
Got used to living by manners and graces
And being judged by our figures and faces.

Before long you were peeling our bananas,
Opening doors for us, moving our pianos.
Then you got busy—you had a ball,
Making, breaking, rearranging it all.
The Taj Mahal, the game of chess,

Safety pins, the printing press,
Chemotherapy, burglar alarms,
Money, ice cream, nuclear arms,
X-rays, battery farms,
Wired bras, designer cars
Opera houses, disco bars,
Income tax, revolving doors,
Glass ceilings, wars . . . and wars.
Mozart, Lenin, Picasso, Descartes—
Charting the stars, transplanting hearts . . .

We all admit that you've done wonders,
And if at times they seem like blunders
Or look like a recipe for global death
Women everywhere will have to accept
That we didn't stop you or slap your hand
As we travelled the road to No-Man's Land.

Still—you're up there in the driver's seat
And we're down here with the balance sheet.
We're answering a question you didn't ask:
We want to go forward into a past
Where humans were part of a natural whole,
Where we didn't hunt, exploit, or control
Every plant and animal species,
Where we didn't cover the world with faeces
Of one sort or another.

* As for the vote:
It's not the answer to a woman's prayer
But it's a start and it's kind of fair,
And as women living in the world of man,
We have to use every tool we can.

So: Forward to the past—with attitude;
And backward to the future—with gratitude
For the battles our foremothers fought and won,
For the battles we're winning, one by one.
Informative action—and I do believe
In what we women are going to receive
In what we women, if we want, can take:
Fifty-two percent of the cake.
Fifty-two percent of control;
And in terms of democracy's rigmarole
That's only—one person one vote.

You men out there: it's a time of change,
Of redirection—and it *does* feel strange.
It'll get less so hour by hour,
But remember—it isn't easy relinquishing power.
We know.

**Alternative line: Yes, we have the vote.*

Autumn Wedding

This song could well be sung at the nuptials of any seasoned couple but it was made for my brother Mike and his wife, Alexia Smith. Irene and I were on a three-month summer pilgrimage around the United States, ending up at Lexington, Virginia, for the August wedding. We knew we were going to write a song—but how to get just the right tone for these two wonderful lovers? Having seen them dancing together, we wanted it to be a stately waltz. We talked about it as June passed by, and then most of July—but no song emerged. So I jumped in by myself and produced a starting text to a Scots tune in 3/4. When Irene heard it, she jumped in with both feet and boots on. *The tune is gloomy—no one would dance to that or be happy on hearing it!* Peggy put *her* boots on. She liked the tune *(it is in waltz-time!)* and now the text and its concept were both tied to it in her mind. Irene put heavier boots on, dropped the *sotto voce* (which hadn't really been *sotto)* and the argument escalated. *It may be in waltz-time but you can't waltz to it!* We were in an RV camp at the time, in a redwood forest in northern California and the other campers were more than just interested. Irene asked me to waltz, there by the fire, in the RV camp, to *that* tune. Boots off now, we were barefoot. Our fellow campers watched with fascination as we alternated between arguing and dancing while we sang the song. She was right—you couldn't dance to it (but then, I reminded her, I am lousy at waltzing anyhow). She then hummed a music-hall tune while we danced and within five minutes I had a new tune in my head. We travelled all the way across the country altering prepositions, shifting lines, exchanging this word for that one, making sure that all corners were rounded and all rough surfaces subjected to a lightning folk-process. I still can't waltz—but Mike and Alexia danced to "Autumn Wedding" on August 27, 1995.

tune: Peggy Seeger
words: Peggy Seeger and Irene Scott

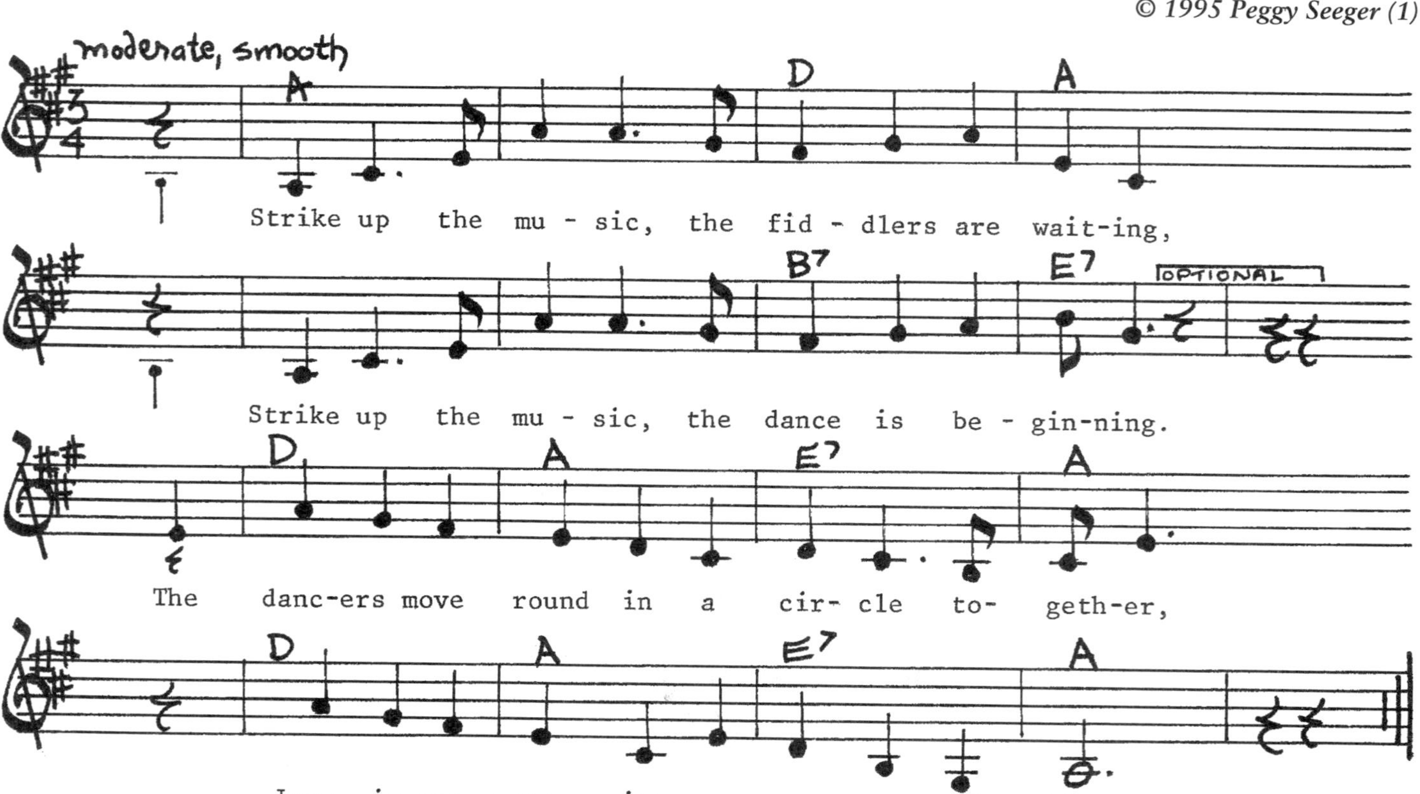
moderate, smooth
A D A
Strike up the mu - sic, the fid - dlers are wait-ing,
B7 E7 OPTIONAL
Strike up the mu - sic, the dance is be - gin-ning.
D A E7 A
The danc-ers move round in a cir- cle to- geth-er,
D A E7 A
Love is pre - par - ing an au - tumn wed - ding.

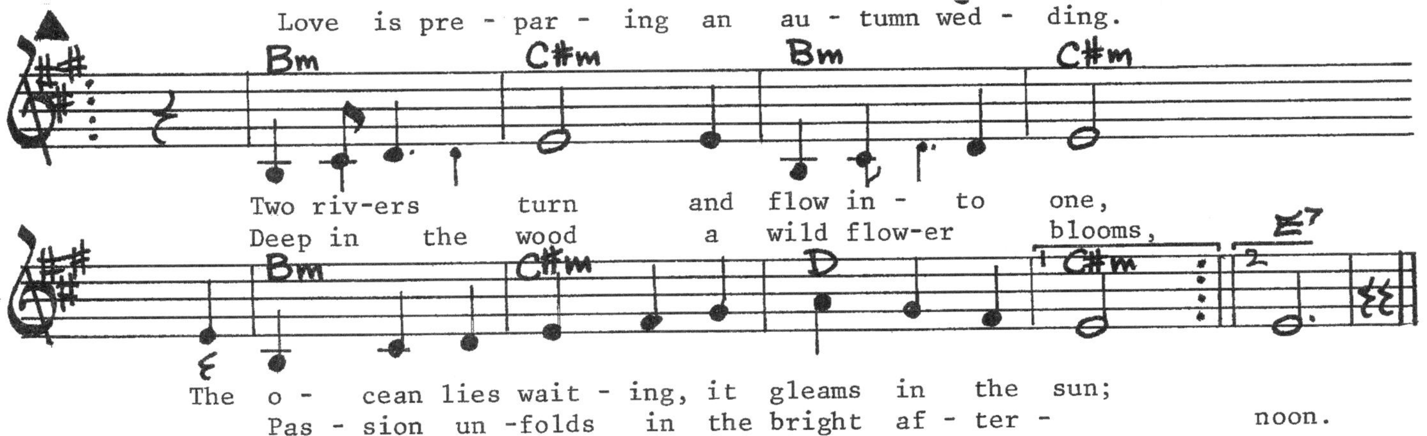

Strike up the music, the fiddlers are waiting,
Strike up the music, the dance is beginning.
The dancers move round in a circle together,
Love is preparing an autumn wedding.

Two circles form and partners are changing,
As they move round, two strangers are facing;
They smile and touch hands and part without knowing that
Love is preparing an autumn wedding.

Walking and talking and dancing together,
No mention of love, no word of forever;
Two birds on the wing, wheeling and turning,
Love is preparing an autumn wedding.

A full life has taught him the price of tomorrow,
A full life has taught her to lead as she follows;
Both of them seasoned yet supple and bending
Love is preparing an autumn wedding.

Δ Two rivers turn and flow into one,
The ocean lies waiting, it gleams in the sun;
Deep in the wood a wild flower blooms,
Passion unfolds in the bright afternoon.

It's never too late, it's never too early
To sing and make music, to dance and make merry;
The circle of life is wheeling and turning,
Love is preparing an autumn wedding,
Love is preparing an autumn wedding.

Δ *Music note: I find it quite effective here to slide an Am chord (on the second, third, and fourth strings) up two frets to make the Bm, then two more frets to make the C♯m while playing deep A and E on the fifth and sixth strings.*

A Wonderful World

A grave new world.

words and music: Peggy Seeger
disc 26

cheerfully
F C7 F Bb F
A - dam and Eve were giv - en two leaves and kicked out of the gar-den;
Bb F G7 C7
Their on - ly crime when it came to the crunch was fail-ure to say 'beg your par-don';
F C7 F Bb F
Off they went with-out pay-ing the rent and in-vent-ed a ci-vi-li-sa- tion
Bb F G7 C7 F
That ripped off more than an ap-ple or two as the years rolled on.

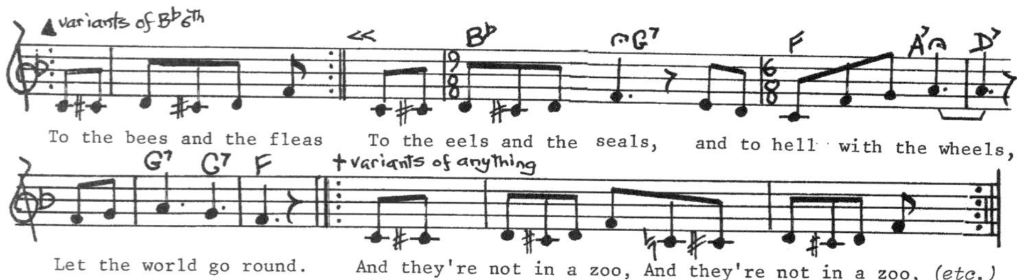
variants of Bb6th
To the bees and the fleas To the eels and the seals, and to hell with the wheels,
Bb G7 F A D7
G7 G7 F
Let the world go round.
+variants of anything
And they're not in a zoo, And they're not in a zoo, (etc.)

Adam and Eve were given two leaves and kicked out of the garden;
Their only crime when it came to the crunch was failure to say "beg your pardon";
Off they went without paying the rent and invented a civilisation
That ripped off more than an apple or two as the years rolled on.

God looked down and said with a frown, "What are you doing to heaven?"
We're only making a home for the kids and Adam has got to earn a living,
Felling the trees, pulling the weeds, building the town of Gomorrah,
Won't it be nice when it's under control, when the wheels go round?

Chorus: Then, won't we have a wonderful world, won't we be in clover
When all of the ground is covered with towns and the countryside cemented over,
All of the land belonging to man and no snakes in the garden,
And one big mall to service it all as the wheels go round.

Our garden will have no spiders or bugs, no animals but the pet ones,
Or ones that you skin and ones that you eat, that *moo* and *oink* and *cluck* and *bleat*,
No need to wail about saving the whale, the elephant or the tiger,
'Cause they'll be gone, but we will go on as the wheels go round.

We can beget as much as we like, the world is made of elastic,
And when the water and food give out, we'll manufacture more from plastic,
Paradise lost? We don't give a toss! We can live under bubbles
And sing about the sea and the sky as the wheels go round. *(chorus)*

When the land is filled, we'll certainly build cities out in the Atlantic.
The moon will shine on the factory ships—nothing could be more romantic,
And when the sea is as thick as a soup, we'll all walk on the water.
No, it's better to drive, 'cause you know you're alive when the wheels go round.

Judgement Day is well on the way but our race will go on running,
We're so busy doing we don't know what and we don't know why but it's lots of fun,
So how can there be a finishing line when we don't know where we're going—
But aren't we having a heavenly time as the wheels go round?

When we've drained the marshes, cleared the trees, levelled the hills and mountains,
Choked the rivers and killed the seas, put frames around the falls and fountains,
Then we'll add the finishing touch: a rocket aimed at heaven,
And we'll head for the moon while humming this tune as the wheels go round.

Chorus: Then won't we have a marvellous moon, once we've done it over?
The craters and deserts all covered with homes and all the rest cemented over,
You can believe that Adam and Eve are great at renovation.
It's a pity the stars are a little too far as the wheels go round.

God gave a yell, angry as hell, he says, "I was mistaken.
"Man believes the world is his, he's un-creating my creation,
"Now I retract, I'm taking it back, I'll give it to flora and fauna,
Δ "To the bees and the fleas,
"To the bears and the hares,
"To the trees and the seas,
"To the germs and worms,
"To the bugs and slugs,
"The fox and rocks,
"The dogs and hogs,
"The cats and bats,
"The goose and moose,
"The louse and mouse,
"The flamingo and dingo,
"(Of course the horse)
« "To the eels and seals
"And to hell with the wheels,
"Let the world go round.

(You can put a small instrumental break here.)

"To the loach, the roach,
"The tiger, the spider,
"The albino rhino,
"The loon, the baboon,
"The mosquito, the cheetah,
"And Uncle Anteater,
"The kangaroo,
"The cockatoo,
"The shrew, the g-nu . . ."

† And they're not in a zoo,
And they're not in a zoo,
And they're not in a zoo,
And they're not in a zoo,
And they're not in a zoo,
(etc., *to fade out)*

Music note: The chorus is sung to the same tune as the verse.

Call On Your Name

Written in an RV camp in Cape Cod. Can't decide whether it's "Call Out Your Name" or "Call On Your Name." Singing it for a while will decide.

words and tune: Peggy Seeger

smooth
A
A7
D
There once was a time when your heart and mine
I would soon-er have died than be ta-ken from your side,
1
E7
2
Told the sto - ry that has no end;
I was
wel-come: your lover & your friend.
CHORUS
Now I call out your name, Call out your name,
Call out your name and I hear no re-ply.
The dark, roll-ing sea lies be- tween you and me,
How I long for the days gone by.

There once was a time when your heart and mine
Told the story that has no end;
I would sooner have died than be taken from your side,
I was welcome: your lover and your friend.

Chorus: Now I call on your name, call on your name,
Call on your name and I hear no reply.
The dark rolling sea lies between you and me,
How I long for the days gone by.

I remember the day you turned your face away
And your heart took its leave of mine.
Since you've altered in your mind it's as if the hand of time
Points forever to the days gone by. *(chorus)*

When love is bright and new, there's little you can do
To cast shadow where the sun shines strong.
When love begins to cool it turns lovers into fools
Who but weep and sing love's old song.

Final chorus: You're far far away, so far away
Too far away to hear your lover cry.
The dark rolling sea lies between you and me,
How I long for the days gone by.

Vote for Leni Sitnick!

Leni's been on the Asheville (North Carolina) political scene since the early 1980s. She's a mover-and-shaker, a Maker of Good Things Happening, a St. Georgina with a Ph.D in dragons. She's been known to storm unannounced onto the site of a projected parking lot to save a large, old tree. She's mustard at diplomacy and public relations, her style being one of warmth and sharing. She's been (among other things) an author, lecturer, small-business owner, designer, consultant, a sitter-on-boards, a holder of senior posts, a city councilwoman. She has three children and two grandchildren who all live near her and with all of whom she is on excellent terms. No mean feat. She has time for friends. She answers her own phone. If you drop in unannounced she will sit down at the drop of a hat to talk or listen. After years of considering to run for mayor, she finally took the leap in 1997. I made two songs as my contribution to this campaign for a real people's representative. The other one was a radio squib designed to last exactly one minute. (By the way—she won.)

words and music: Peggy Seeger

At last she's made the final leap, now it's definite-nick:
She's heading for the mayor's seat, her name is Leni Sitnick.
She'll bring the public back into all matters politic-nick;
She has your future on her mind: Vote for Leni Sitnick!

Chorus : Who's the one who knows the ropes, shares your worries and your hopes?
Who's the one deserves your vote? WHO BUT LENI SITNICK!

Life's a puzzle full of pieces that don't seem to fit-nick;
She can put them all together: Vote for Leni Sitnick!
Life has pitched a lousy ball, it's landed in your mitt-nick:
It's time to start the game again along with Leni Sitnick. *(chorus)*

You're fighting for a better deal, you're not about to quit-nick;
She's right there in the ring with you, her name is Leni Sitnick.
She sticks to all her promises right through thin and thick-nick;
For politicians, that's a record: Vote for Leni Sitnick! *(chorus)*

She didn't come here yesterday and she's not about to flit-nick;
She's earned the right to be our mayor: Vote for Leni Sitnick!
She's sat on boards and councils and committees infinite-nick;
If you can name it, she's been there, her name is Leni Sitnick. *(chorus)*

England's old prime minister, his name was William Pitt-nick,
Couldn't hold a candle to the one called Leni Sitnick.
Like Samson, Leni's got long hair, like Samson, she'll admit-nick
That long hair gives you extra strength: Vote for Leni Sitnick! *(chorus)*

Don't refrain, don't abstain, just be definite-nick.
If you want the best for Asheville: Vote for Leni Sitnick!
There's one thing I forgot to say, I almost did omit-nick—
Now I'll say it loud and clear: VOTE FOR LENI SITNICK! *(chorus)*

Love Will Linger On

And on and on . . .

alternative title: "Dawn Will Follow Dawn"
words and music: Peggy Seeger

somewhat freely
D A7 D G A7
Now now when the moon is high in the sky,
D G or Em D A7
Now now when the moon is low;
D A7 D G
A song sung by the small bird deep in the dark wood rings:
chorus
D A7 Dmaj 7th G
Dawn will fol-low dawn, Love will lin-ger on
Em7 A7 D
And on till the end, Till the end.

alternative final chorus line:
Em7 A7 D
And on and on till the end.

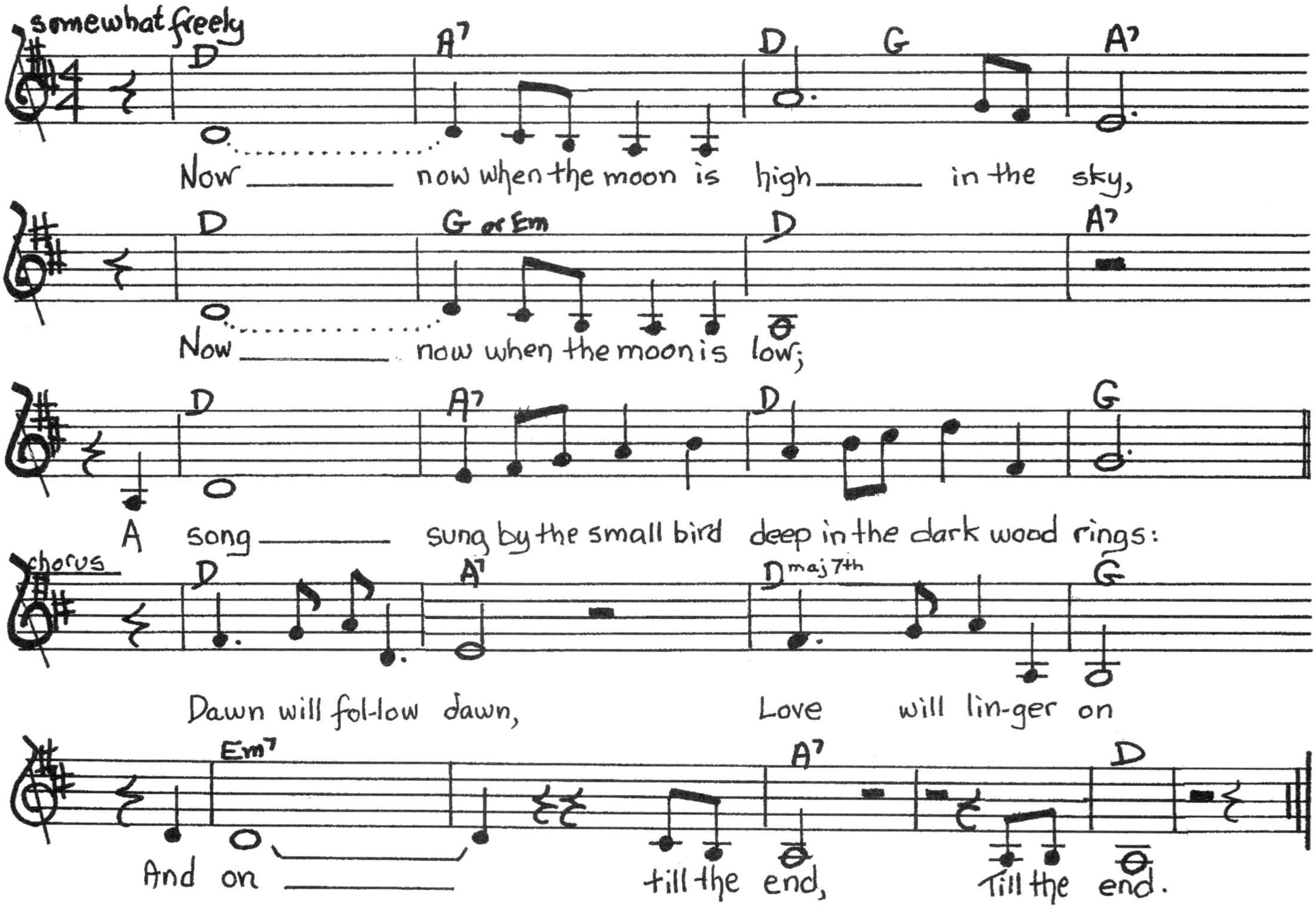

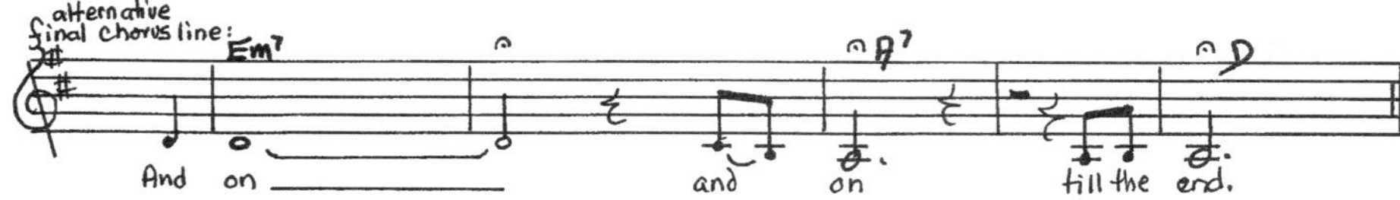

Now—now when the moon is high in the sky,
Now—now when the moon is low;
A song sung by the small bird deep in the dark wood rings:

Chorus: Dawn will follow dawn,
Love will linger on
And on till the end,
Till the end.

Now—now as a flower turns to the sun,
So—now I turn to you;
The song sung by the living soon to be dead and gone. *(chorus)*

Now——our tide of love runs high,
Now——the tide is low;
The song sung by a flood whose tide will forever roll. *(chorus)*

Music note: This is best sung slightly out of rhythm.

Peggy and Irene, 1998

What a Life!

A fitting ender.

word and music: Peggy Seeger

jaunty
C
F
I've been a- round a long time, they say I'm well pre-served,
C
(D7)
G7
Some say I'm o-ver the hill but I'm just round the curve;
C
F
I loved one man for thir-ty years, loved him till he died -
C
D7
G
Now oth-er guys are af-ter me - there's nine, to be pre-cise.
CHORUS
F
C
O, what a life! What a life!
G7
All these fel-las fuss-ing o-ver me;
C
F
I want to live a-lone and man-age on my own
C
G7
C
But there's all these fel-las fuss - ing o- ver me.

I been around a long time, they say I'm well preserved,
Some say I'm over the hill but I'm just round the curve;
I loved one man for thirty years, loved him till he died—
Now other guys are after me—there's nine, to be precise.

Chorus: O, what a life! What a life!
All these fellas fussing over me;
I want to live alone and manage on my own
But there's all these fellas fussing over me.

WILL POWER gets me out of bed and tries to make me smile,
Then I go and visit JOHN and sit on him awhile;
I have a drink with EARL GREY, he's always hot for me,
And crafty ARTHUR RITIS keeps me constant company. *(chorus)*

JIM NASIUM is boring but he keeps me fit and trim,
AL ZYMER phones me up but I won't talk to him;
JACK DANIELS keeps my spirits up (but only now and then)
A little goes a long way—it's the same with all the men. *(chorus)*

I'm a slave to Mister MACINTOSH, I'm practically his wife;
Hand-in-hand with MIKE ROSOFT, we're writing up my life.
As long as I'm in charge I don't care who's in on the deal,
But you can bet that I won't let MACDONALD make my meals. *(chorus)*

Music note: Verses 2 and 3 are a musical version of a joky paragraph that I found in a magazine.

Subject Index

This section will help you if you are interested in a particular issue and want to find all the songs in the book dealing with that subject. The small songs, the squibs, are starred (*). Those that were composed using the radio-ballad technique are marked (†).

It's a Natural Thing
Londonderry Down
Maggie Went Green
Manner of the World Nowadays
A Matter of Degree
* One Step, Two Step
The Party
* They Sent a Boy to Downing Street
Villains' Chorus
Where Have All the Felons Gone?

U.S.A.:

Big Man
A Good War
* A Lovely Little Island
Items of News
* JUST beCAUSE
L.B.J., What Do You Say?
* N is for Nobody
Please, Mr. Reagan
* The Presidential Bodyguard
Uncle Sam
Votecatcher in the Rye
Watergate
* Yankee Doodle 1993

Other:

Che Guevara
The Children
Sentimental Journey
Song of Choice
We Are the Young Ones
We Remember
When I Was Young

Unions and Industry

Dustmen's Strike 1969
If You Want a Better Life
My Old Man's a Dustman
† R.S.I.
† Union Woman II
Women's Union

Economic Issues

Poll Tax:

Can't Pay, Won't Pay
Fifteen Ways to Beat the Poll Tax
Just the Tax for Me

Rent Strike:

Hey Ho, Cook and Rowe!

Inflation:

Out of My Pocket

Money:

The Pay-Up Song

Political Campaign:

Vote for Leni Sitnick!

Racism, Fascism

Racism:

The Ballad of Jimmy Wilson (U.S.A.)
Hello Friend (Britain)
I Support the Boycott (South Africa)
No More (South Africa)
Prisons (South Africa)

Fascism:

Crooked Cross (Britain)

Personal—me, my family and friends

Family:

Autumn Wedding
Little Girl Child
Lost
Lullabye for a Very New Baby
My Son
Once Again
On This Very Day
Song for Calum
Song of Myself
Thoughts of Time

Friends:

Fitzroy Coleman
Harry's Eats
Old Friend
Song for Charles Parker
Vote for Leni Sitnick!

Love—serious and otherwise

Autumn Wedding
Call On Your Name
Da Dee Da Da
Darling Annie
Garden of Flowers
I'll Never Go Back to London Again
Jimmy Gray
Joe and Mika's Wedding
Love Unbidden
Love Will Linger On
Morning Comes Too Soon
My Love and I Are One
New Spring Morning
Nightshift
Night Song
Old Friend
On This Very Day
Primrose Hill
So Long Since I Been Home
That's How the World Goes On
When Lovers Hide the Keys

Accidents and Disasters

The Ballad of Springhill
† Buffalo Holler
Cambrian Colliery Disaster
Lifeboat *Mona*

Miscellaneous

Abbey Wood Roads
Billy and George and Me
Come Fill Up Your Glasses
Swing Me High, Swing Me Low

Glossary

This section contains notes on terms, ideas, acronyms, people and places that, had I included them in the body of the book, would have made for complicated reading and many footnotes. Being both Yank and Limey, I am not too sure which terms are fully understood on each side of the Atlantic so I may have unwittingly included some words that everyone knows. Nevermind - people who don't have English as their first language will find this motley collection invaluable. If you don't find the word you want, it may be in a phrase - for instance, *lorry* appears in the phrase *fell out of a lorry* and may be found under the words *lorry* and *fell.* I have favoured English, not American, spellings (colour, labour, tyre, favoured, etc). Some of the words (for instance *crack, boot)* have meanings other than those given here - my definitions apply only to usage in my songs.

A.A. Automobile Association (Britain)

Afghanistan Invaded by Russia on December 27, 1979

Agent Orange A toxic herbicide and defoliant used in the Vietnam War. Its use is now restricted.

aggro Short for aggravation (Britain)

a.k.a. Also known as

America Shorthand for North America, unless otherwise specified

audience All the definitions in the O.E.D. suggest the act of hearing or listening. Its contemporary usage suggests, to me, the presence of a large number of consumers who have assembled to passively absorb a cultural product. Any ideas for a word that doesn't mean just *listening*?

Backing Britain In January 1968, a group of five women in Surbiton decided to work harder and "Buy British," thus launching the Backing Britain Campaign. They worked so hard that their firm decided it did not need so many workers. The innovative five were among those fired.

bag Handbag, purse; as carried by females (Britain)

bang Beckenham Anti-Nuclear Group (Beckenham, Kent, being a suburb of London)

bang-up job A really good job (Britain)

barmy Crazy, flighty, silly (Britain)

battery farming A system for raising, fattening, and handling domestic stock. The animals and birds are caged tightly and allowed little or no exercise. Humans do this to one another as well. Humans go mad. So do animals.

BBC British Broadcasting Corporation: government sponsored radio and television

bob A shilling (in old English currency)

Bogside The Catholic area of Derry, Northern Ireland

bonds A British government-run lottery, drawn once a week

box television set (Britain)

boot The trunk, as in a car (Britain)

Britain A term disliked by all people in the U.K. except the English, many of whom still prefix it with the adjective "Great." One really should not use it but there is no substitute. Like "America" (see above) it is a shorthand term and it represents the sometimes uneasy coalition of England, Scotland, Wales, Northern Ireland, the Isle of Man, the Channel Islands, the Isle of Dogs, *etc.* I believe Scotland has recently opted out with a referendum.

broo The (un)Employment Exchange (Britain)

bwana Master, boss (South Africa)

Canary Wharf The name by which the monstrous skyscraper (Canada House) is known, probably because it was built (in the late 1980s) at Canary Wharf in East London.

cap the rates See rate-capping

Castle, Barbara Minister of Transport in Harold Wilson's Government (see "Follow Harold round the Bend")

CFCs Chlorofluorocarbons, the gases (produced by fridges, aerosols, the manufacture of polystyrene, etc.) that are contributing heavily to the destruction of the ozone layer

C.I.D. Central Intelligence Department, London

Clifford, Rosamund One of Henry II's mistresses. She was allegedly poisoned by Queen Eleanor of Aquitaine in 1176.

clobber Clothes (Britain)

collier, colliery miner, mine (Britain)

Connolly, James One of Eire's best-known patriots, he organised the Irish Socialist Republican Party. He took a leading part in the Easter Rebellion in 1916 and was executed by firing squad that same year. We remember.

couch potato Inactive, compulsive consumer of television

Coventry To send or put someone to Coventry: to refuse to associate with them

crack (both verb and noun) Talk, gossip, social intercourse (chiefly Ireland)

Critics Group A self-help group organised and run by Ewan MacColl and Peggy Seeger. The purpose of the group was to help folk revival singers to sing folksongs more "authentically," to write new songs, and to better understand the folk revival. It ran from 1964 to 1971.

Daily Mirror One of the British tabloid newspapers

Dalkon Shield A dangerous brand of I.U.D. (see below)

Dallas A 1980s TV soap-opera about a rich Texas oil family

DC-10 Douglas Company plane that was responsible for several tragic crashes. It is no longer in production.

Debrette's Debrette's *Peerage* is *the* listing of titled, landed, privileged (*etc.*) persons in Britain.

De Danaan An Irish musical group

digs Living accommodation (Britain)

Dr. Martens (pronounced Doc Martens) A heavy boot or shoe with the unique Dr. Martens sole

do-si-do (pronounced doe-see-doe) A figure in U.S.A. square-dancing and contra-dancing; from the French *dos à dos*: back to back

dustman Britain's word for garbageperson

EEC European Economic Community

Enquirer The *National Enquirer*, probably North America's best-known disreputable weekly tabloid

fags Cigarettes (Britain)

Falls Road The major Catholic area of Belfast, Northern Ireland

fell out of a lorry A description applied to stolen goods (see lorry) (Britain)

Festival of Fools A yearly political/theatrical documentary put on in the New Merlin's Cave in London by the Critics Group, from 1965 to 1971. The research was done by the members of the group and the songs and script were written almost entirely by Ewan MacColl.

first floor In England, the first floor is equivalent to the U.S.A.'s second floor; the British equivalent to the U.S.A.'s first floor is the ground floor.

flutter on the Pools A try at the Pools, a weekly lottery based on the football scores. The prizes can run into seven figures.

forbye Besides, in addition

Four Freedoms Described in Franklin Roosevelt's State of the Union Speech, January 6, 1941: freedom of speech, freedom of worship, freedom from want, and freedom from fear

Four-Minute Warning See note for "Four-Minute Warning."

F.P.A. Family Planning Association (Britain)

gaffer Boss. The term is generally used on construction sites and in factories in Britain.

Gilwell Brand name for a small compact set of cooking pots and pans carried by serious campers

GP Family doctor (general practitioner) (Britain)

Golden Reed Makers of business machines are prone to giving them nostalgic or quasi-magical names.

Greenham Common See notes for "Carry Greenham Home" and "Woman on Wheels."

grub Food

Guardian One of Britain's more respectable daily newspapers

he, him Third-person-singular masculine pronouns used when referring to objects whose gender has not been designated (such as babies, members of higher professions, artists, government personnel, *etc.*), the assumption being that the world is male unless otherwise specified. Not used when referring to the earth or to forms of transport.

High Holborn A street and an area of central London

Hill, Joe Swedish-born songwriter and industrial organiser (U.S.A.). He was framed on a trumped-up murder charge and executed by firing squad in 1915. We remember.

Holloway Road A London road on which England's most (in)famous women's prison is located

Hoover A brand of vacuum cleaner. To hoover (Britain) = to vacuum (U.S.A.).

I.B.M. International Business Machines

I.C.I. Imperial Chemical Industries

Independent One of Britain's more respectable daily newspapers

I.R.S. Internal Revenue Service (U.S.A.)

I.U.D. Intra-uterine device for contraception; a.k.a the "coil"

Jara, Victor Chilean left-wing singer who was murdered in the Santiago stadium massacre in September 1973. We remember.

Jesse Jesse Helms, a conservative senator from North Carolina. Enough said.

Karl and Rosa Karl Liebknecht and Rosa Luxemburg, founders of the German Communist Party, were murdered in 1919. They became a symbol of the heroism and the dedication of communists everywhere. We remember.

kirby grips Bobby pins (Britain)

kiri A stick with a round bulbous end, used for keeping "order" in South Africa

Kobayashi, Takiji Radical Japanese poet, believed to have died during torture at the hands of the Japanese in 1933. We remember.

kudzu An eastern Asian creeping vine with large, compound leaves and purple-red flowers. It was introduced to the U.S.A. as ground cover and cattle fodder. It is virtually taking over whole sections of the Southeast U.S.A. When unchecked, it climbs trees and telephone poles, covers deserted houses, drapes over electric cables. It is apparently edible and medicinally useful. Goats love it.

Ladbroke and Hill Two large firms of British turf accountants (bookies)

Lambeg drum The drum that is associated with the Protestants in Northern Ireland. It is huge—2 feet 6 inches deep and 5 feet in diameter. It is beaten with thin whiplike sticks and is virtually a war-drum whose distinctive rhythms and ritual usage are handed down from father to son. The drum is used on the Apprentice Boys' March on July 12 when the Protestants march en masse through Catholic areas of Belfast to celebrate the outcome of the Battle of the Boyne (1690).

lifted Stolen (Britain); can also mean 'arrested'

like a shot Immediately (Britain)

Limey British person (especially a sailor) from the time when limes were introduced on British ships to combat scurvy

loo Toilet; from the French *l'eau*: water

lorry Truck (Britain)

Lumumba, Patrice Leader of the Congolese national movement, then first premier of the independent republic of Congo (now called Zaire). He was deposed in 1960, captured and paraded ignominiously through the streets and assassinated in 1961. We remember.

man(kind) General term often used when referring to boys, women, girls, babies, *etc.*

MacLean, John (1879–1923) Considered the greatest of the Clydeside (Scotland) socialists, jailed three times for sedition due to his opposition to World War I. We remember.

Major, John Britain's prime moneystar between Margaret Thatcher and Tony Blair

Marriage Guidance A British organisation, formed to help troubled marriages. Now called Relate.

Mondlaine, Eduardo Dynamic leader of FRELIMO, the Mozambique freedom fighters' organisation. He was assassinated by Portuguese colonialists in February 1969. We remember.

Mooney, Tom U.S.A. union organiser who was framed on a murder charge and, despite mass protests, jailed from 1916 to 1939. We remember.

MORI poll Market and Opinion Research International, one of Britain's major opinion polls

MP Member of Parliament (Britain)

Nader, Ralph The founder/captain of Nader's Raiders, a team of consumer-affairs lobbying researchers who from the mid sixties onward exposed irregularities in consumer protection, pollution, freedom of information, *etc.*

nappy Diaper (Britain)

National Front Britain's main fascist party

never-never The instalment plan (Britain)

Newt (Gingrich) Candace Gingrich's brother. A clever fellow.

Newton, Huey One of the founders of the U.S.A. Black Panther Party

NHS Britain's National Health Service

noshy Familiar form of nosh: food (Britain)

Number Ten 10 Downing Street, the official London abode of the British Prime Minister

O.E.D. *Oxford English Dictionary*

off-putting Daunting (Britain)

on the make Ready and willing to promote or take part in activities that are of dubious legal nature. (Britain) In the United States, the term has quite a different meaning.

Owld Sod Ireland (usually referring to Eire)

Oxfam Oxford Committee for Famine Relief, one of Britain's largest charity organisations

pad Bed, home, place to stay

Paisley, Ian Northern Irish MP and politician; representative and spokesperson for the loyal royal right; a Presbyterian minister and leader of the militant Protestant party, the Democratic Unionists

Parks, Rosa Born 1913, the African-American woman who refused to "move to the back of the bus" on December 1, 1955. One of the major sparks that led to the fire of the American civil rights movement.

per Short for person—an experiment (not original) at introducing a non-gender-specific personal pronoun into the English language. The idea was stolen from (I think) Marge Piercy.

pers Possessive of per

perks Perquisites, a casual profit additional to normal revenue

petermen People who open safes without the key, combination, or permission of the owner. It should probably be peterpersons but it would seem to be more of a male occupation.

philtrum The furrow between the upper lip and the nose

P.I.B. Prices and Incomes Board (Britain)

Pools, the A British national lottery based on the outcome of football games

Porton Down A biological and chemical defence establishment in Wiltshire, England

post They watch your post (Britain) = they check out your mail (U.S.A.)

pram Short for perambulator, or baby carriage

PR Public relations

quid A pound sterling in English currency

radio ballads See "In Particular"

rate-capping Until the mid 1980s, local councils in Britain were able to decide for themselves what they would spend. Thatcher's government put an end to this, setting an upper limit, or cap, on the rates collected from property holders (see notes for "Can't Pay, Won't Pay" and "Fifteen Ways to Beat the Poll Tax").

Reagan, Ronald A former sports reporter whose autobiography *Where's the Rest of Me?* was published in 1965.

round the bend Crazy, mad (Britain)

R.S.I. Repetitive Strain (or Stress) Injury

RUC (Northern Ireland) the Royal Ulster Constabulary: an official Protestant order-keeping force into whose ranks the outlawed B-Specials went after their dissolution in 1970

RV recreational vehicle (motorhome, camper, *etc.*)

Sandino, Augusto Nicaraguan national hero. He led the 1926 uprising and other insurrections until, under orders from the U.S.A., he was murdered in 1934. We remember.

Sands, Bobby Went on hunger-strike at Long Kesh prison (Northern Ireland) in 1981 in protest against the authorities' refusal to treat him and his fellow IRA internees as political prisoners. He died on May 5 after sixty-six days, the first of ten such hunger-strikers. We remember.

Sani-Flush A brand of toilet cleaner (U.S.A.)

Saracen A type of tank used to police Northern Ireland

sari A length of cotton or silk draped around the body, worn as a main garment by Hindu women

scarper To escape, get away (Britain)

Scholl Siblings Hans and Sophie Scholl, two Munich University students, members of the Weisse Rose (White Rose) Catholic resistance organisation in Nazi Germany. They were publicly beheaded in February 1943 after taking part in the enormous student uprising, the first that had occurred in the Third Reich. We remember.

Schehr, John One of the leaders of the German Communist Party Politburo. Arrested in 1933, he was publicly beheaded in 1934. We remember.

Schwartz, Johann A German activist in the 1930s. He was publicly beheaded. We remember.

screws Prison warders (Britain)

Separatists A section of the population that wishes to separate from the main body politic

shadow British political term. The party that is not in power has a shadow prime minister and a shadow cabinet.

Shankill (Road) The major Protestant area of Belfast, Northern Ireland

silent majority The dead . . . an ancient folk-term used (unwittingly?) by Richard Nixon in one of his most famous speeches

sitcom Situation comedy

Sizewell One of England's nuclear power installations

sjambok A rhinoceros-hide whip (South Africa)

Skelton, John English poet (c. 1460–1529), court poet to Henry VII; known for his caustic satirical style

skiffle music Often called "poor man's jazz." It has all the elements of rhythm, melodic improvisation, and the "beat" necessary to true jazz, but it substitutes the human voice for the jazz band's front line (trumpet, trombone, clarinet, *etc.*). The 1950s were the heyday of skiffle in Britain.

snuff it To die (Britain)

Social Chapter A section of the Maastricht Treaty that pertains to the social dimension of the EEC

Spaghetti Junction The tangle of motorways just north of Birmingham, where the M6, the A38M, the A38, and the A5127 all meet

spidermen The building workers whose name comes from the ease with which they negotiate the webs of scaffolding, however high, on a construction site

S.P.U.C. Society for the Protection of the Unborn Child (Britain)

SS-20 A type of Russian long-range nuclear missile

Stormont The seat of the Northern Ireland government in Belfast

Survivalists One of the various factions that wish to declare independence from the U.S.A.'s federal government

Taelmann, Ernst Leader of the German Communist Party in the 1920s. He was jailed by the Nazis in 1933 and died in a concentration camp in 1944. We remember.

Tebbit, Norman (a.k.a. "the Chingford Skinhead") Margaret Thatcher's Employment Secretary, who told the unemployed to get on their bikes, like his old dad, and go and find work

Telecom One of Britain's telephone companies

Thatcher, Margaret British Prime Minister from 1979 to 1990 (although future generations would probably be forgiven for thinking it was 1879 to 1890 due to the results her reign had on Britain). Also known variously as "the Iron Lady," "the Lady with the Blowlamp," "the Plutonium Blonde," "the Enid Blyton of Economics," "Pétain in Petticoats," and innumerable others, many of them patently sexist. We try to forget.

THORP Thermal Oxide Reprocessing Plant in the Sellafield complex (see note for "The Invader"). Incorporated into its original charter is its intention to accept nuclear waste from all over the world.

Times One of Britain's more acceptable daily newspapers

Trident First-strike nuclear weapon, capable of unleashing 224 warheads, each of which is twenty times as powerful as the Hiroshima bomb and accurate to within ninety metres

trolley Trolley (Britain) = gurney (U.S.A.)

U.K. United Kingdom, to be regarded in the same light as Britain (see above)

VAT Value Added Tax, an indirect tax on goods and services that replaces purchase (sales) tax. A percentage of VAT helps to pay the running costs of the EEC.

VDU Visual display unit (screen and keyboard)

Velcro Brand name for a type of fastener consisting of male and female barbs that link together

velociraptor A voracious fictitious prehistoric species created by Spielberg in *Jurassic Park*. Its acting abilities (and those of its extinct contemporaries) far outshone those of the human cast in the film.

VIP Very Important Person

Wallace, William Scots patriot (1274–1305) who drove the English out of Scotland after the Battle of Stirling (1297). Betrayed by informers, he was hanged and then drawn and quartered in London. Sections of his body were sent to the four quarters of Scotland as a warning. The film *Braveheart* has been made about his life. We remember.

War on Poverty The programme was launched on January 8, 1964, when President Johnson, who had just taken over after the death of Kennedy, vowed to wage a "war on poverty."

Webster, David Webster was conducting research into secret South African military organisations when he was assassinated in 1988. We remember.

Wilson, Harold See note for "Follow Harold round the Bend"

winkle A small edible shellfish found on the coasts of Britain

winkle out To prise out, as a winkle out of its shell (Britain)

Young, Jimmy BBC radio presenter who has boasted a morning crap show ever since I can remember

zigzags The markings on either side of zebra (pedestrian) crossings on British roads. It is illegal to stop a vehicle on the zigzags. (Zebra rhymes with Debra in Britain, by the way.)

Discography

This is not a complete discography for Peggy Seeger, only a discography of the songs included in this book. We have tried to be comprehensive, but there may be post-1997 reissues and new compilation albums of which we are unaware.

Argo Records (England)

1. *The World of Ewan MacColl and Peggy Seeger, Vol. 1*—SPA-A 102/ 12″ disc with Ewan MacColl/1969/no longer available.

Blackthorne Records (England)

2. *Penelope Isn't Waiting Any More*—BR 1050/ 12″ disc with a chorus of women/1976/ no longer available but issued by Rounder Records with a slightly different track list (see **Rounder,** below).
3. *Cold Snap*—BR 1057/ 12″ disc with Ewan MacColl/1977/available only on Folkways issue (FW 8765).
4. *Hot Blast*—BR 1059/ 12″ disc with Ewan MacColl/1978/available only on Folkways issue (FW 8710).
5. *Different Therefore Equal*—BR 1061/ 12″ disc with a chorus of women/ 1979/available only on Folkways issue (FW 8561).
6. *Kilroy Was Here*—BR 1063/ 12″ disc with Ewan MacColl/ 1980/available only on Folkways issue (FW 8562).
7. *Freeborn Man*—BR 1065/ 12″ disc (mostly Ewan MacColl)/1983/available only on Rounder Records (disc and cassette) (Rounder 3080).
8. *Items of News*—BR 1067/ 12″ disc with Ewan MacColl/1986/no longer available but copies may be obtained from Roots Music (see "Recording Companies" section).
9. *Familiar Faces*—BR 1069/ 12″ disc/1988/no longer available but copies may be obtained from Roots Music (see "Recording Companies" section).
10. *Housewife's Alphabet*—BR 20525/ an untitled 45rpm single/1977/no longer available.
11. *Parliamentary Polka*—BR 20535/ an untitled 45rpm single/1977/no longer available.
12. *Daddy, What Did You Do in the Strike?*—BSC 1/ limited edition cassette with Ewan MacColl/1984/songs written for the 1984–85 Miners' Strike/no longer available.

13. *White Wind, Black Tide*—BSC 2/ cassette with Ewan MacColl/1986/limited edition issue, commissioned by the Anti-Apartheid Movement, London/no longer available.

Cooking Vinyl (England)

14. *Naming of Names*—COOK C 036 *and* COOK CD 036/ cassette and CD with Ewan MacColl/1989.

14A. *Folk on 2*—MASH CD 002/ CD with Ewan MacColl/1996 (issued by the BBC).

E.M.I.

15. *No Tyme Like the Present*—EMI 2556/ 12″ disc with Ewan MacColl/issued in conjunction with Larrikin Records (Australia) 1976.

Fellside

15A. *Almost Commercially Viable*—FECD 130/ CD (same as #21). Due out in spring 1998.

Folkways (U.S.A.)—see also above items 3, 4, 5, and 6

16. *From Where I Stand*—FW 8563/ 12″ disc, solo album/1982.

17. *The New Briton Gazette, Vol. 1*—FW 8732/ 12″ disc with Ewan MacColl/1960.

18. *The New Briton Gazette, Vol. 2*—FW 8734/ 12″ disc with Ewan MacColl/1963.

19. *Folkways Record of Contemporary Songs*—FW 8736/ 12″ disc with Ewan MacColl/1973.

19A. *The Folkways Years*—C-SF 40048 and CD-SF 40048/ cassette and CD, a solo album/1992/ produced in conjunction with Smithsonian Folkways, a definitive compilation of traditional and original material.

Golden Egg Productions (England)

20. *Almost Commercially Viable*—GRADE 1/ cassette with Irene Scott as No Spring Chickens/ 1992.

21. *Almost Commercially Viable*—GRADE 2/ CD with Irene Scott as No Spring Chickens/ 1993/virtually the same as No. 20 but with two more tracks.

Nectar Masters (England)

21A. *The Legend of Ewan MacColl*—NTMC/CD502/ Ewan MacColl compiler/1995.

Oneworld (England)

22. *We Have a Dream*—1WPS/ 12″ disc/a compilation of artists/ 1984/no longer available.

Prestige International

23. *A Lover's Garland*—INT 13061/ 12″ disc with Ewan MacColl/1959–62/no longer available.

Redwood (U.S.A.—now defunct)

Issued a cassette of No. 9 above. Many of its items will be reissued on 26A.

Rounder Records

24. *At the Present Moment*—ROUN 4003/ 12″ disc/cassette with Ewan MacColl/1973.

25. *Penelope Isn't Waiting Any More*—ROUN 4011/ 12″ disc of women's songs with a chorus of women/1977.

26. *An Odd Collection*—ROUN CS/CD4031/ cassette and CD of songs composed by Peggy solo and with Irene Scott/1996.

Rykodisc

26A. *Period Pieces*—Tradition TCD 1076/ CD of women's songs, all of them written by Peggy 1963–1994. Some are reissues, some are re-recorded. Due out in spring 1998.

Topic (England)

27. *Chorus from the Gallows*—12T16/ 12″ disc/mostly Ewan MacColl, songs of crime and criminals/1960.

Vanguard (U.S.A.)

28. *Newport Folk Festival, Vol. 2*—VRS 9084/ 12″ disc, a compilation of artists/1960/no longer available.

Miscellaneous issues

29. *We Are the Engineers*—a single with no prefix, put out by the Amalgamated Engineers Union, England, in the early 1970s/no longer available.

30. *Living Folk*—VPA 8093/ 12″ disc/recording of a live concert given by the Critics Group in Milan, 1969/Albatros (Italy) 1970/no longer available.

31. *Songs of Struggle*—AMSWU 91/ a double-cassette set of political songs, with Ewan MacColl/Australian Metal and Shipwrights Union, Sydney, Australia/1977/no longer available.

31A. *The Legend of Ewan MacColl*—NTMCD/ CD, a Ewan MacColl compilation/Dino Entertainment, Ltd, London, England/1995.

32. *Parsley, Sage and Politics*/a boxed set of three cassettes (three hours)/interviews, radio-ballad style, about the lives of Peggy Seeger and Ewan MacColl. Skilfully and imaginatively put together by Mary Orr and Michael O'Rourke, 2737 NE 25 Street, Portland, OR 97212, U.S.A./Available!

Bibliography

Essential Ewan MacColl Songbook. Peggy Seeger (Oak Publications, New York, *forthcoming*).

Ewan MacColl–Peggy Seeger Songbook. Contemporary songs. In collaboration with Ewan MacColl (Oak Publications, New York, 1963).

Freeborn Man. Contemporary songs. In collaboration with Ewan MacColl (Oak Publications, New York, 1968).

New City Songster. Edited by Peggy Seeger. A magazine of contemporary songs which appeared in twenty volumes from 1965 to 1985. *No longer available,* but some odd volumes are available from Roots Music (see "Recording Companies"). Full set contains over 500 songs. Now available on microfiche. Information from: University Publications of America, 4520 East-West Highway, Suite 800, Bethesda, Maryland 20814.

- ***Recommended Reading:***

Complete Rhyming Dictionary. Clement Wood (Dell Publishing, New York 1992).

The Mother Tongue. Bill Bryson (Penguin Books, London, 1991).

The Necessity of Art. Ernst Fischer (Penguin Books, London, 1978).

Ruth Crawford Seeger: A Composer's Search for American Music. Judith Tick (Oxford University Press, New York, 1997).

Copyright Information

(1) © Peggy Seeger, administered by

Harmony Music, Ltd.
Onward House
11 Uxbridge Street
London W8 7TQ
England
telephone: +44 [0]171 221 4275
facsimile: +44 [0]171 229 6893
e.mail: 100557.2772@compuserve.com

(2) © Stormking Music, administered by Harmony Music, Ltd.

Stormking Music
250 West 57th Street
Suite 1218
New York, NY 10107
U.S.A.
telephone: 212/586-6553
facsimile: 212/459-9035

Recording Companies

1. **Blackthorne Records, Ltd.,**(now defunct). Information from Penny Smith, 26 Cromwell Road, Beckenham, Kent BR3 4LW, England (tel: + 44 [0] 181 650 1337). Stock available from Roots Music, 9 Derwent Street, Sunderland, Co. Durham SR1 3NT, England (tel: +44 [0] 191 567 0196)

2. **Cooking Vinyl,** 10 Allied Way, London W3 ORQ, England (tel: + 44 [0] 181 960 9000)

3. **Nectar Masters** (England), Dino House, 10 Allied Way, off Warple Way, London W3 ORQ , England (tel: +44 [0]181 743 6165)

4. **Fellside Records,** 15 Banklands, Workington, Cumbria CA14 3EW, England (tel: +44 [0] 1900 61556)

5. **Folkways Records,** c/o Smithsonian/Folkways, 414 Hungerford Drive, Suite 444, MD 20850, USA (tel: 301/443-2314)

6. **Rounder Records,** 1 Camp Street, Cambridge, MA 02140, USA (tel: 617/354-0700)

7. **Rykodisc** (England), 78 Stanley Gardens, London W3 7SZ, England (tel: +44 [0] 181 746 1234)

8. **Rykodisc** (USA), Shetland Park, 27 Congress Street, Salem, MA 01970, USA (tel: 978/744-7678; fax: 978/741-4506; e.mail: info@rykodisc.com)

9. **Topic Records,** 50 Stroud Green Road, London N4 3EF, England (tel: +44 [0]171 263 1260)

Index of Titles and Alternative Titles

Alternative titles are shown in *italics.*

Index of First Lines